Making Italian America

CRITICAL STUDIES IN ITALIAN AMERICA

series editors: *Nancy C. Carnevale and Laura E. Ruberto*

This series publishes works on the history and culture of Italian Americans by emerging as well as established scholars in fields such as anthropology, cultural studies, folklore, history, and media studies. While focusing on the United States, it will also include comparative studies with other areas of the Italian diaspora. The books in this series engage with broader questions of identity pertinent to the fields of ethnic studies, gender studies, and migration studies, among others.

Making Italian America

CONSUMER CULTURE AND THE PRODUCTION OF ETHNIC IDENTITIES

Edited by Simone Cinotto

FORDHAM UNIVERSITY PRESS   NEW YORK   2014

Library of Congress Control Number: 2014931627.

Printed in the United States of America
16 15 14   5 4 3 2 1
First edition

Contents

Part II   The Politics and Style of Italian American Consumerism, 1930–1980

**Part III   Consuming Italian American Identities in the Multicultural Age,
1980 to the Present**

Acknowledgments

I've gotten a lot of help in completing this book. The series editors, Nancy Carnevale and Laura Ruberto, agreed with me about the potential of the Italian American case to illuminate the dynamics of consumer culture in twentieth-century America (and beyond) and supported the project from beginning to end. The director of Fordham University Press, Fred Nachbaur, also embraced and promoted the idea of the book from the very start, being the ideal editor ever since. Will Cerbone was a dedicated and most helpful assistant editor. The readers the Press lined up offered valuable comments. Yiorgos Anagnostou was especially insightful in his highly useful critiques. Bob Oppedisano provided editorial advice and many astute commentaries on the issues the book addresses. Gerald J. Meyer and Mark Naison commented on an early draft of my own chapter, even bringing into the discussion personal recollections about the early rock 'n' roll scene in New York City and the social environment that was its hotbed. Joe Sciorra provided a wealth of information, contacts, and ideas. My master's student Maria Zizka skillfully polished the English prose of a few chapters, including mine.

The idea of this book first originated from the graduate course "Italian Signs, Italian Values: Producing and Consuming Italian American Identities" that I taught as a Tiro a Segno Visiting Professor at New York University in the academic year 2008–2009. For that I thank the chair of the Department of Italian Studies, Ruth Ben-Ghiat; the director of Casa Italiana Zerilli-Marimò, Stefano Albertini; and the exceptionally bright and participative students who took the course, offering great feedback. Some early results found their way into a special issue of *VIA: Voices in Italian Americana* dedicated to "Consumer Culture in Italian American History." I am so grateful to *VIA*'s Editor Chiara Mazzucchelli and founding editors Fred Gardaphé, Paolo Giordano, and Anthony J. Tamburri for their interest in and support of the project.

Very special thanks are due to the wonderful contributors to the volume, who believed in the value of the collection, handed me their intellectual work, and trusted me in being able to bring the endeavor to a successful end. Thanks to you, putting together this book has been nothing but pleasurable, instructive, and rewarding teamwork.

Finally, throughout the time I was editing *Making Italian America*, my children Ferdinando and Cristina provided me with a million great moments of fun, intimacy, and companionship—I really love you guys!

Making Italian America

All Things Italian

ITALIAN AMERICAN CONSUMERS, THE TRANSNATIONAL
FORMATION OF TASTE, AND THE COMMODIFICATION
OF DIFFERENCE

Simone Cinotto

My long European trousers had been replaced by the short knickers of the time, and I wore black ribbed stockings and new American shoes. To all outward appearances I was an American, except that I did not speak a word of English.
—LEONARD COVELLO ON HIS FIRST DAYS IN NEW YORK, 1896 (*THE HEART IS THE TEACHER*, 1956)

I was born and raised a Guido. It's just a lifestyle. It's being Italian, it's representing, family, friends, tanning, gel, everything.
—PAULY D FROM MTV'S REALITY SHOW *JERSEY SHORE* (2009)

This volume brings together new scholarship on the cultural history of consumption, immigration, and ethnic marketing, focusing on the case of an ethnic group whose material culture and lifestyles has profoundly fascinated, disturbed, and influenced American culture: Italian Americans.

The purpose of this introduction and the fourteen essays in the volume is to reread Italian American history in the light of consumer culture, in the process producing an analytical framework to reflect on the ways ethnic and racial groups have shaped their collective identities and negotiated their place in the consumers' emporium and marketplace of difference that is the global United States. Taken as a whole, the fourteen chapters of the book illuminate the crucial role that consumption has had in shaping the diasporic identities of Italians in America and illustrate why and how those same identities— once incorporated in commodities, commercial leisure, and electronically reproduced images—have become the object of desire for millions of American consumers.

The attraction of consumers for Italian American signs and values may well be considered a reflection of the paradigmatic nature of the Italian American saga for the overall cultural experience of modernity. At the outset of the twentieth century, nearly three million migrants from rural Italy provided the unprecedented expansion of the

U.S. economy with an inexpensive labor force, as part of a massive global human movement out of the recently unified country (29 million people between 1876 and 1976). In the United States, turn-of-the-twentieth-century immigrants, their descendants, and further new arrivals from Italy became members of a culturally diverse society, developing complex ethnic and racial identities, while maintaining a sense of affiliation—and often actual transnational relationships—with the diasporic home across the Atlantic.

Both the construction of Italian American ethnicity via consumption and the consumption of commodified Italian American identities have been in fact intensely transnational processes; shaped as part of intense movement of people, goods, money, ideas, and images over more than a century between Italy and the United States that has significantly transformed both nations. Yet, the recent scholarship on the transatlantic history of consumer culture has ignored the Italian American case. Important works like Victoria De Grazia's *Irresistible Empire* and Mary Nolan's *The Transatlantic Century* have privileged the eastbound direction and traced the *exportation* to Europe of American marketing cultures and consumer dynamics.[1] Fewer and more marginal are the studies that explore how U.S. consumer culture has in turn been shaped by European products, sensibilities, and ideas.[2] Even the histories of European immigration in the United States have not contributed to developing a genuine two-sided analysis of the circulation of consumer cultures between the continents, privileging a vision of American consumerism as an assimilating force and failing to acknowledge the role of immigrants in shaping it.[3]

Indeed, Italian immigrants to the United States have been much more often studied as producers than consumers. A rich and often exciting historical scholarship has insisted on their role as labor migrants at the most advanced edge of the capitalist world system and participants in the American and international working class, unions, and radical movements in the years from 1890 to 1940.[4] Explorations of their relationship with the marketplace, the political reflections of their participation to consumerism, and the saturation of their diasporic experience with mass media and consumer products have been minimal.

Virtually unbeknown to academic literature, however, consumer culture has had a tremendous importance in the Italian experience in America, from the formation of the decision to emigrate, to the redefinition of identities involved in migration and settlement projects, to the development of long-term translocal flows of consumer products, capital, ideas, and images that have accompanied those of mobile Italians. The simple idea of belonging to the diasporic nation of "Italians," bonded not only by common origins and heritage, but most conspicuously and meaningfully by a common *taste*, importantly emerged in the United States in the dimensions of consumption and the marketplace. In the process, diasporic Italians changed the U.S. landscape of consumption and popular culture dramatically and permanently.

The first proposition of this book is that looking at the ways Italian Americans have navigated the world of commodities, commercial leisure, and consumption of domestic and public spaces allows acknowledging the *creative agency* of the different generations of immigrants in inventing meaningful and culturally successful ethnic identities, and ultimately defining and claiming their place in both American society and the modern

Italian diaspora. By "culturally successful ethnic identities," I mean a visible and coherent array of values and styles widely shared in the group and defining the group as an active and empowered collective entity in the society at large. The emergence of these "culturally successful ethnic identities," very significantly rooted in a working-class immigrant culture, benefited the purveyors of things Italian in the United States, reverberated in the creation of an ethnic middle class, and reinforced transnational links with the diasporic home.

The making of these recognizable identities, to be sure, was achieved at the cost of the marginalization of alternative identities, and occasionally of the exclusion and even victimization of subjects inside and outside the group. They have often been deployed to construct ethnic and racial hierarchies and some of them have been heavily patriarchal in nature. Nevertheless, this volume argues, the subaltern origins of these identities, embedded in a culture of resistance to assimilation, group solidarities, and assertiveness, have made them meaningful for and usable by other working-class people, including African Americans and other people of color (as I and John Gennari argue in my own chapter on the Italian American hegemony in early vocal rock 'n' roll and his chapter on Italian American coaches in college basketball respectively). Even more evidently, women, gays, and lesbians within the group have rearticulated and reclaimed some of the Italian American identities shaped in ethnic consumer culture and lifestyle for their own liberation and subjectivization purposes. A number of chapters in this book (Vittoria Caratozzolo's, Maddalena Tirabassi's, Elizabeth Zanoni's, and Marcella Bencivenni's) address evidences of Italian American women's empowerment through the embracement and celebration of Italian American identities emerging from the navigation of the world of goods, discriminating taste, and distinctive ethnic lifestyle. Lesbian and gay Italian Americans have confronted their discrimination within the group while reclaiming ethnic expressions of solidarity, bonds of affection, storytelling, humor, material culture, and taste to produce original Italian American lesbian and gay identities.[5]

As a number of classic thinkers on consumer culture have emphasized, consumption is just another form of *production*—a production of meanings and values. Consuming subjects use and construe the commoditized objects, images, and experiences they acquire in the marketplace (or merely desire and fantasize about) in ways that are contextual and situational—depending on the class, race, and gender identity of the subject—and often unpredictably subvert the uses and meanings originally intended by the purveyor or manufacturer.[6] Goods, actually, can turn into or cease to be commodities and have different meanings for different people at different points of their "lives." The exchange value of things and experiences is influenced by the culturally determined desire of consumers to possess them or live them and the meaning they inflate into them, thus configuring consumption as cultural production of value.[7]

Making Italian America, then, highlights in the first place the symbolic and material *work* of Italian immigrants and their descendants in inventing distinctive styles of everyday life by selectively spending their budgets; juxtaposing in a consequential syntax objects that had belonged to different contexts of material culture; serving as economic as well as cultural mediators in representing things and values as "Italian"; and, by doing all that, articulating their individual and collective ethnic selves. By way of distinct consumer culture, immigrants creatively shaped a transnational Italian American taste and meaningful Italian American identities.

The second contention of *Making Italian America* links the remarkably private act of consuming with public expressions of Italian American cultural diversity—and their commodification. The essays in the book identify in the consumer practices of Italian immigrants the very source of Italian American cultures and *styles* that have been variously branded as "ethnic" and conspicuously become objects of "consumption of the other" in the American/global market for difference. In other words, the two levels of the immigrant production of Italian American identities via consumption and of the cross-cultural consumption of Italian American identities embedded in commodities and experiences have been inextricably interrelated. Articulating their individual and collective identities as styles by means of their consumer choices and behaviors, Italian immigrants to America—and their children and grandchildren—have framed public self-representations that, in an economy increasingly revolving around symbolic production, have been marketed and incorporated in everything from the most celebrated "three Fs"—food, fashion, and film—to popular music, spectator sports, tourism, politics, public memory, and higher education.

Looked at in this way, Italian American consumer culture is both a central feature of the ethnicization of Italian immigrants to the United States—that is, the production of their own brand of American cultural citizenship—and very much part of the process of United States nation-building as a multiethnic state since the late nineteenth century. Italian ethnicity in America has been consistently consumed as an inherently working-class subculture and an expression of racial liminality (as the racial status of southern Italian immigrants was especially suspect and disputed)—so to serve as a mirror play of opposites for other Americans to define their own racial, cultural, and social identities.[8] At the same time, as changing cultural and political climate disempowered the criticality of Italian American otherness, Italian ethnicity has been gradually integrated in the mystique of the "Nation of Immigrants"—the grand narrative of the incorporation of Ellis Island immigrants into the mainstream flow of American life—and consumed as such.[9]

The third and final chief argument of the book is that the production of Italian American identities via consumer culture spanned the entire twentieth century—and beyond. Looking at Italian American history through the lens of consumer culture helps to overcome both the common interpretation of the Italian American experience as discontinuously broken into two discrete parts by the disappearance (ca. 1945–65) of predominantly Italian urban working-class enclaves ("Little Italy") and the tendency of most histories of modern consumer culture to grant only to the middle class and affluent individuals the creativity and agency to use marketable goods and symbols for conscious self-making and self-expressive projects.

In this sense, *Making Italian America* especially confutes the widely accepted notion of *symbolic ethnicity*, which the noted sociologist Herbert Gans used in the late 1970s (at the time of the "white ethnic revival") to define the consumer experience of affluent white ethnics in late-capitalist, multicultural America. According to Gans, while early twentieth-century first- and second-generation European immigrants had their ethnicity inscribed into their bodies and had to live with it twenty-four hours a day in their urban ghettos, late twentieth-century suburban consumers of ethnic origin could jump on and off of it as they pleased and use ethnicity situationally and intermittently, much as with any other activity on which they liked to spend their leisure time. Gans dismissed the undertakings with which new ethnics could imaginatively create and recreate their malleable *self* (e.g., subscribing to Italian American newsletters, supporting scholarships for the study of Italian, or rooting for the Italian national soccer team) as "symbolic," or recreational, unimportant because they did not bear connections with real, measurable determinants of social life—income, marriage patterns, residence, and education, which by the 1980s practically equalized American Italians with Jews, Irish, Poles, Swedes, and Greeks.[10]

To this book's perspective, the "symbolic ethnicity" statement is problematic on two counts. First, it denies turn-of-the-twentieth-century rural Italian immigrants and their working-class offspring any agency in their relationship with the material and symbolic value of the commodities and services they liked, disliked, purchased, or fantasized about. Because of their lack of resources and racial status—Gans suggests—they simply had to bear such relationship, with no conscious project or determination detectable on their part. Anchoring ethnicity to class and other determinants that he sees as strictly dependent on class, Gans makes "real" ethnicity disappear into nothing the moment the individual moves up the social ladder (a Polish American teamster and an Italian American plumber make for a Polack and an Eye-talian, but if they go to college, become lawyers or dentists, and relocate to the suburbs, they become two undistinguishable white middle-class Americans, and their expressions of ethnicity become "symbolic," that is irrelevant). Gans's position not only pairs and fits in with the way many histories of U.S. immigration in general, and Italian immigration in particular, have been written, but it also mirrors the understanding of *lifestyle* as a sociological concept connoting "individuality, self-expression, and a stylistic self-consciousness" in exclusive relation to the consumer culture borne out of the transition from a Fordist society based on mass production and consumption to a consumer-oriented postindustrial society in the 1970s. This insistence on lifestyle as a specific privilege of the postmodern middle-class consumer, common in consumer studies, not only subscribes to the idea that consumerism obliterates class—the materialist drive functioning as an alternative to class-based identities and politics—but also implies that only people with money can develop a discerning taste for goods, so to *consciously* express status and create distinctive identities.[11]

Making Italian America consistently challenges Gans's contentions. The concept of lifestyle (*genre de vie*) was in fact originally coined by French sociologist Maurice Halbwachs in 1912. Studying comparatively the consumption patterns of French and American workers, Halbwachs identified their preference for "forms of consumption that gave a sense of collective life, such as large midday meals, clothing and public entertainment," so that "consumption reinforced working-class subcultures."[12] Notwithstanding the high constraints on their purchases (rent, fuel, food, and clothing absorbed most of the budget, so actual discretionary money was virtually nil), working-class people like Italian immigrants to industrial American cities consciously assigned meaning to what they purchased and consumed, and, most important, *how* they consumed it.

It is especially the work of Pierre Bourdieu, though, that releases lifestyle from the monopoly of the late-capitalist middle-class consumer. For Bourdieu, all classes, including the subaltern, determine their own distinctive tastes and preferences, which they recognized as legitimate and meaningful in the framework of the antagonistic relationships they develop with one another. In Bourdieu's view, economic capital is just one of different forms of capital (social and cultural capital being the others) that in different degrees classes possess, accumulate, and articulate in their lifestyles. It is through an active work of distinction that class differences, such defined, are eventually embodied in what Bourdieu calls the *habitus*—ways of walking, gesturing, talking, and behaving that are inscribed in the body during early socialization and remain with the individual regardless of the social mobility he or she may experience in life. Ethnicity finds a place in Bourdieu's model as his notions of social capital (the capacity to build social relations based on one's own specific social identity and embeddedness in a group) and cultural capital (exclusive knowledge effectively usable in social relations) actually account together for the performative dimension of ethnicity. The bountiful Sunday dinners of Italian immigrants could seem wasteful, indigestible, and vulgar to middle-class observers, but for immigrants they were crucial occasions of solidarity building and fun, in which familiar, nutritious food intended to regenerate and sustain hard-working bodies would be exchanged and consumed. They defined the practice as "Italian," at the same time as they tended to see "American" food habits as pretentious, bland, and unwholesome.[13] In other words, even poor early-twentieth-century immigrants had to *selectively* exercise their consumer choice in order to define their lifestyle as both working-class *and* Italian—separate and discrete from other working-class subcultures. The resulting taste, generated by their practices of ethnic and class distinction was passed down to subsequent generations and translated into their Italian American bodies.

Making Italian America contradicts symbolic ethnicity on another count. Gans's contention that when no significant socioeconomic data distinguishes any longer Italian Americans from other European American groups, Italian ethnicity becomes disposable and shallow—an empty superstructure to what really counts, class and institutional politics—simply misses the fact that symbolic consumption has always been, and is more and more with the receding relevance of class in the definition of social identities, the code by which people and groups make sense of themselves and their place in society, tell who they are, where they think they come from, and what they want to become.[14] Ethnicities in modern and postmodern America are better understood as adaptive, flexible, and evolving strategies to specific socioeconomic, political, and cultural contexts, rather than as a pure biological and cultural heritage, eventually destined to linear, progressive exhaustion over the generations and through social mobility.[15] Italian American ethnicity, throughout its evolution, is better understood as a *style* than tradition; it can only be disclosed with attention to the textual and social practices of identity invention, continual change, and consent; and consequently needs acknowledging and historicizing of the crucial role of the choice and use of things, images, and experiences available on the market.[16]

Looking at the ways Italian Americans navigated the world of goods and other Americans consumed the culture they produced thereby is to disclose a long historical process and to address the existence and cultural, social, and economic meaning of an Italian diaspora. Indeed, the affiliation to a distinctive diasporic consumer culture is what most closely connects the experience of turn-of-the-twentieth-century migrant workers to that of contemporary cosmopolitan inhabitants of a global Italian *confederation of taste*, regardless of the quantity of "Italian blood" running in their veins.

Immigrant Geographies of Consumption:
Body, Home, and Community

Upon arriving in the United States in numbers at the turn of the twentieth century, Italian migrants were massively confronted with otherness—that is, with differences in language, appearance, habits, beliefs, and memory that set them apart from the rest of the population. The first section of the book, "Immigrants Encounter and Remake U.S. Consumer Society," shows how, as they proceeded to construct their *self as alien*,[17] consumer culture functioned as an immediate and convenient terrain of mediation, understanding, and representation of difference.

In the peak years of migration, 1890–1915, the cameras of pioneering social photographers Jacob Riis and Lewis Hine immortalized the distinctive lifestyles and identities that Italian immigrants to New York City articulated around the way they dressed, decorated their apartments, celebrated religious and life-cycle events, and spent their leisure time, as well as the shopping institutions (pushcart markets, grocery stores, cafes, restaurants, barber shops, and Italian-language theaters) that represented ubiquitous features of the urban communities where many of them lived.[18] In other words, Riis and Hine vividly illustrated the existence of a distinct Italian immigrant consumer culture; one that was formed in dialogue with the emergent urban commercial culture of the era—"the developing infrastructure of bourgeois consumption; the sanitized 'dream worlds' of the movie palace, department and chain stores"[19]—yet was far from representing its lower-class mimicry or being intended as a fast pathway to Americanization. When novelist Pietro di Donato described Italian immigrants in terms of consumer preferences, he did so by opposing them to those of "Americans": "To my people, the Americans were colorless, unsalted, baloney munchers and 'gasoline' drinkers without culture, who . . . listened to caterwauling, imbecilic music, and all looked more or less alike."[20]

Social workers of the time similarly described the ways in which Italian women in the American city made sense of new material environments and capitalist market conditions to address unique needs and preferences in the matters of nutrition, clothing, and health, as well as maintaining reliable family and community relationships.[21] In the meantime, these observers reported, Italian girls cautiously but steadily worked to conquer spaces of autonomy from patriarchal authority by joining urban working-class consumer culture. They constructed much of their identities as second-generation Italian Americans through the class-mediated access to readymade fashion, cosmetics, and commercial leisure.[22]

The body was in fact the most accessible canvas into which immigrants could inscribe their new identities and social relations through consumer culture, a first example being the relationship with food and diet. The relative abundance of food provided by the American marketplace—representing one of the most conspicuous expectations in poorer Italians' migration projects—paved the way for a full anthropological transmutation of Italian American bodies. As soon as 1909, Franz Boas demonstrated the inconsistency of the postulates of scientific racism by measuring the bodies of a sample of Italian immigrants to New York and highlighting the changes those underwent because of a richer diet and healthier environment. "From rickety, dwarf-like parents, a spawn of giants is born," noted a middle-class Italian traveler to New York in the early 1930s. "When you enter some Italian homes, and mother and father introduce you to their children, you are immediately prompted to ask: 'are they really *your* children?' "[23] Italian American bodies' growing occupation of space signaled the important rupture of an immemorial experience of scarcity and long-standing class-bounded barriers grounded in consumption. In fact, returning migrants to southern Italian villages, embodying the change, posed an immediate threat to the local elites, which reacted by denouncing such "loss of modesty and respect" on the part of mobile peasants as the most vicious consequence of migration.[24]

Italian immigrants articulated their work of self-reinvention and civilization through varied techniques of the body. In fact, while reflexive investment in the presentation of the self and body maintenance has been described as a typical expression of middle-class postmodern consumer culture,[25] Italian immigrants excelled in the creation of plastic lifestyles via the consuming body. As the quotation from Leonard Covello's autobiography suggests, many immigrants to New York quickly abandoned their old-world clothes to dress in "American fashion," taking advantage of the cheap, mass-produced, readymade clothing themselves assembled in the city's sweatshops (a striking example of Marx's commodity fetishism!)

Vittoria Caratozzolo's opening chapter in this volume discusses from a fashion studies perspective Italian immigrant women's "change of clothes" and the gendered and cultural dialectics it entailed. The "change of clothes" terrain was heavily contested, sparking class, gender, and generation struggles within families and communities, locally and transnationally, but the change itself was largely understood as a necessary prerequisite to participate in the host society's competitive labor market and larger public culture, without necessarily relinquishing or masking one's own ethno-racial affiliation.

Similarly, the new requests for health and efficiency, dictated by the transformation of the immigrant subject into the Fordist proletarian body regulated by industrial time and the rhythm of the city, were increasingly met with the help of professional medicine and commercial drugs, in place of folk medicine and traditional remedies. Yet, the transition had to be articulated in a familiar "language." In the 1910s and 1920s, the interior pages of the most popular Italian newspapers in the United States, *Il Progresso Italo-Americano*, were packed with ads for pills, tonics, and innovative therapies promising to cure unnamed or uncertain diseases that, by weakening the body and morale of Italian immigrants, challenged their capacity to survive the hard daily struggle with "America." The same adagio was played by the ads of mixtures against constipation, which assured relief from the unprecedented problem of coping with abundance.

A particular kind of body maintenance and discipline concerned the control or modification of phenotypic features like skin color, eye shape, and body form as evidences of race. Broadly identified as "swarthy"—a color connotation that matched their suspended racial identity and functioned as an ultimate judgment on the place they belonged to in the American social hierarchy—Italian immigrants activated strategies of bleaching and passing, typically making use of the tools made available to them by the American marketplace. However, since even in southern Italy dark skin had signified a lower-class status, efforts at whitening had to be cautiously performed in order not to be perceived as threatening manifestations of social mobility and challenge community sensibilities. Among Sicilian immigrants from the town of Cinisi to the East Side of Manhattan in the early years of the twentieth century, for example, women's striving for a whiter body was met with harsh, jealous reproach. "Gee! Look at the daughter of so and so. In Cinisi she worked in the field and sun burnt her black. Here she dares to carry a parasol." Or, "Look at the *villana* [serf]! In the old country she used to carry baskets of tomatoes on her head and now she carries a hat on it."[26] However complicatedly, first- and especially second-generation immigrant women were enthusiastic consumers of beauty powders, lipsticks, perfumes, and hair dyes—as advertising in *Il Progresso* also suggest—which allowed them to modify their appearance and racial persona. By the 1920s, their significant presence in the market for beauty products, and white powder in particular, resonated in ads such as those for Pompeian Beauty Powder, which claimed that, overcoming the misconception according to which "we are white women and therefore we must use white powder," the product was designed for those with "olive skin, the clear dark skin we frequently see on beautiful Spanish or Italian women."[27] Italian American women's problematic racial in-betweenness had become a cosmetic industry's marketing target.

The effort of immigrant consumers at making sense of the world through commodities can be further appreciated by looking at a second site of migrant consumption—the home.

The determination to attain homeownership, either in America or in Italy, was a key social goal and a pivotal element of the consumer behavior of Italian immigrants. Their culture—rooted in the rural background shared by most of them—viewed owning property as a fundamental source of autonomy, empowerment, and security in times of unemployment, sickness, and old age. The prospect to accumulate enough money to return to their home village and buy a house was thus one of the most important motives for the activation of migration projects. The massive flow of remittance money that migrants sent back to the country of origin was in fact largely meant for purchasing living properties.[28] For turn-of-the-twentieth century Italian migrants, acquiring property in the first areas of arrival, like the Mulberry District and East Harlem in New York, proved to be largely impossible. But when economic conditions—namely, the availability of jobs for women and children—indicated that they could achieve homeownership in areas of secondary migration, often recently reached by public transportation, Italian immigrants pursued that goal with fierce willpower. They did not hesitate to mobilize all family resources, moving hastily from one rented apartment to another in order to save on rent, doubling up or opening the door of their homes to boarders, sacrificing their children's hopes for social mobility through education, and encouraging girls to work outside the home. As part of the process, they made a huge investment in gender as the productive force of a new family culture.[29] As soon as the end of the 1920s, many had fulfilled their Italian American Dream. In New York, for example, a full third of the households with an Italian-born head of family owned their homes by 1930 (nearly all of them in Brooklyn and the other outer boroughs).[30]

Maddalena Tirabassi's chapter shows that Italian immigrants consistently constructed their homes, owned or rented, as a private space of ethnic/diasporic domesticity, leisure, and consumption, typically mingling commercial culture and traditional handcrafts and taste. Even under conditions of poverty, Italian immigrant women used mass-produced furniture and wallpapers as well as handmade embroidery and religious art to decorate their modest kitchens and bedrooms, pursuing notions of domesticity that, while dramatically novel if compared to the circumstances of their rural past (for most of them, running water was a particularly welcome innovation), also widely departed from those of middle-class Americans. The kitchen, differently from the seclusion and specialization that characterized it in the middle-class home, functioned as an open space of multitask production and consumption, which assembled the purpose of a dining room, a parlor, and a workplace.[31] When budgets allowed it, Italian immigrants showed no timidity in investing in appliances that would enrich the scope of their ethnic brand of domesticity. In Chicago in the 1920s and 1930s, Sicilian immigrants used their state-of-the-art, installment-purchased Victrola gramophones to play and dance to Italian records and tuned in their new radios to listen to Italian-language programs sponsored by Italian American food producers and caterers.[32]

Overall, modern consumer culture provided Italians in America with materials and codes for the restructuring of domestic rituals. Much often, the psychological stress posed by the circumstances of migration reflected on increasing worries of immigrant males, parents, or religious/political authorities about the behaviors, mores, and sexuality of women, the continuing loyalty of the second generation, and the solidity of the diasporic family as an institution. The response was frequently the ritualization of domestic life and private consumption, that is, the transformation of the immigrant family festive and everyday events in ritualized sites of consumption, within which expression of group solidarity and symbolic representations of gender and generational relations of power were performed. The religious and secular festivities of the year and life cycle produced the home as an *ethnic haven*, which contrasted with a worldly and alienating public world. It was in this context of celebration of family communion, memory, and cultural difference that the production, preparation, and consumption of ethnic food gained much of their symbolic power, and skills in food preparation came to embody ideals of womanhood. Original food patterns were revisited and reinvented as a result of market conditions, the availability of ingredients, exchange between cooks, and so on, but the resulting Italian American cuisines were held and felt as authentic on the account of their cohesive social relevance. Even resistance to the pattern was articulated through "tradition": young women refusing the fleshy body that immigrants thought revealed a good predisposition to maternity and thus enhanced their daughters' chances in the marriage market relied on Lent for fasting and attaining the slim figure that was requested by contemporary consumer culture models.[33]

Middle-class reformers took full notice of this most defining trait of Italian American consumer culture: they were shocked by the amount of money that poor and working-class Italian families spent on baptisms, confirmations, wedding parties, and funerals, instead of using it for far more "urgent" or "useful" purposes.[34] From the immigrants' point of view, however, this behavior made a lot of sense—they were doing an investment in family and community ties, to maintain group solidarity and delay the embrace of middle-class values by its members, even when they entered skilled and office jobs or independent businesses and their income rose. This ethnicity- and class-determined project of pathway to social mobility also matched their much-discussed disinclination to invest in their children's education, especially as far as girls were concerned.[35]

A third place of consumption that was object of intense material and emotional investment on the part of Italian immigrants was the community. In all the urban enclaves where they came to represent a significant share of the population, Italian immigrants surrounded themselves with ethnic stores, markets, restaurants, and professional services (the notion of "ethnic" being signified by the cultural character of the goods and wares those sold, the green, white, and red colors or the Italian language of the shop signs, the language spoken by and the ethnicity of the owner and personnel). Notwithstanding the fragility of these businesses, weakened by the competition caused by their number and the poverty of their customer base, until World War II modern consumer institutions such as the chain stores or the supermarkets made characteristically very little inroads into Italian neighborhoods. Italian immigrants' attachment to ethnic businesses can be explained with the high amount of social capital and cultural capital of the ethnic entrepreneurs, who were typically deeply embedded in networks of family and community relations and possessed the exclusive capacity of understanding and meeting the special needs of fellow Italians. But immigrant loyalty was also a consequence of the fact that "Italian" barber shops, pool rooms, restaurants, and so on marked the urban landscape with specific signifiers of identity and provided the community with a sense of self-sufficiency in terms of the material needed to nurture its cultural specificity.

At the neighborhood level, consumer institutions and practices practically *made* the Italian immigrant communities. Much earlier than many of them turned into homeowners—thus developing a direct financial interest in the state of their community—Italian immigrants heavily invested, emotionally as well as monetarily, in neighborhoods that in the eyes of most other city dwellers looked like unattractive, crime- and poverty-ridden slums. Historian Robert Orsi has recounted the story of the early Italian immigrants to East Harlem in the late 1880s: bricklayers and hod carriers who, after their backbreaking workdays, returned home to donate their labor and skills to the construction of a new Italian church dedicated to the Madonna of Mount Carmel. By piecemeal building the church, they planted deep roots in the original swampland on the bank of the East River, roots they watered with their own sweat. The church was supposed not only to be a place for local Italian Catholics to worship and to host a very popular replica of the annual feast of the Madonna that was held in the small southern Italian town from which many of the immigrants came, but also to stand, as it does, long after they were gone. The consumer behavior of Italian immigrants embodied their significant investment in their neighborhood. In Italian Harlem, the annual *festa* of the Madonna was the occasion for consuming and filling the public space of the neighborhood of Italian smells, flavors, colors, and sounds, thus reclaiming for the Italians those streets, tenements, parks, and empty lots.[36] The settings in which the many events centered on commensality were held in Harlem—the local churches, funeral homes, restaurants, apartments, streets, and backyards—created a geography of consumption and belonging that became inscribed in immigrants' bodies and created *locals* out of residents.[37]

The concentric sites of consumption of the body, home, and community were traversed and encompassed by nation—an idea of "community" expressed in imagined, diasporic terms that complicated and completed the local meaning of neighborhood.[38]

In her chapter, Elizabeth Zanoni details how Italian immigrants' conspicuous fondness of imported goods, from cigars to laces to olive oil, witnessed their attempt at articulating their diasporic nostalgia, identity, and taste through shopping, as well as the centrality of consumption in the project of diasporic nationalism—regularly encouraged as it was by the local/transnational immigrant mercantile elites and their supporters in the Italian government abroad. Film studies scholar Giorgio Bertellini's chapter follows in the same transnational vein, illustrating how Italian-produced films likewise found a vast audience in New York City theaters, encompassing motives of emotional longing and diasporic nationalism among immigrant spectators well into the decades of the maturation of a modern urban consumer culture, the 1920s and 1930s.[39]

The idea that an Italian nation was consistently made through consumption, taste, lifestyle—the product of immigrant community's complex negotiations and identity remaking—was quietly appropriated and popularized from the outside, by many non-Italian cultural mediators. Early twentieth-century social workers, doctors, teachers, and settlement house activists applied to this idea negatively—striving to use consumption to "Americanize," that is, modernize Italian immigrants. They taught Italian women to use mass-produced brand soap and cloth diapers, to rely on professional midwives, to avoid "irrationally anti-economic" ethnic stores, and do away with the dirty foods and merchandise they sold.[40] Prohibition (1920–1933) was just the extreme manifestation of wide-ranging progressive consumer reform efforts aimed at facilitating the transformation of immigrant peasants into citizens, immigrant women into dependable mothers and housewives, and immigrant men into disciplined and efficient workers: the resistance to such articulation of power/knowledge and the negotiation of an ethnic identity in the interstices of old and new, "Italian" and "American," discourses are integral part of the creative work of the Italian immigrant consumer that needs to be brought to light here.[41]

But popular novelists, illustrated magazine reporters, ashcan painters, early travel guide writers, and filmmakers took a different path from that of the reformers. Expanding on social photographers and social workers' early representations, they discursively created a diasporic Italian nation in consumer culture through the transformation of Italian American "types" into *spectacle*.[42] These operators of a nascent cultural industry imagined the poor, Catholic, dark-haired and olive-skinned southern Italian women and men who populated the quarters of the great American cities as the latest offspring of an ancient Mediterranean civilization redolent of magic, sensuality, honor, and vendetta—a treasure trove of cultural difference against which other American consumers could dialogically construct *their* identity.[43] Theodore Dreiser, for example, recounted at length of his expeditions to Italian Harlem—"Here, regardless of the presence of the modern tenement building and the New York policeman, you may see such a picture of Italian life and manners as only a visit to Naples and the vine-clad hills of southern Italy would otherwise afford." Dreiser would travel uptown to catch a glimpse of "a moody-faced, somber-eyed, love-brooding Romeo" stabbing the young, black-eyed object of his unfortunate love in a burst of rage and jealousy. The blood that would be spilled, Dreiser anticipated in lust ("Girls have been stabbed here, been followed and shot—I have seen it myself"), would have provided him with the thrilling experience of a primitive, unmediated authenticity. "[Italians] love and hate," proclaimed Dreiser, "and death is the solution of their difficulties—death and the silence of the grave. 'She will not love me! Then she must die!' The wonder of the colony is the *frankness and freedom* with which its members take to this solution."[44]

In the gaze of the American flâneur,[45] Little Italies thus became "sites of cultural disorders ... the source of fascination, longing, and nostalgia for those people, especially in the middle class, who were developing bodily and emotional controls as part of the civilizing process."[46] At a time, with the passage of the racist 1924 immigration law that reduced new arrivals from Italy to a trickle, when the preoccupation for the racial dangerousness of Italian immigrants for American biological wholeness and democratic polity gradually faded into their fungibility for the rising mass entertainment and ethnic tourism industries, Italian Americans emerged as the quintessentially exotic European American ethnic group, ready to be commoditized in a variety of products and experiences.[47] In the 1920s, when New York's Greenwich Village was constructed as a proto-tourist destination for slumming, a post-Victorian urban theme park promising easy sexuality and escape from restraint, Italian immigrants, their bodies, and their consumer behavior were a consistent element of the package. The black apron and shawl of the Italian woman swiftly stepping into an Italian bakery and the white undershirt of the whistling Italian teenager in front of a candy store turned them into the "locals" who imbued the place with meaning and identity, a sense of primal sensual authenticity, rootedness, and safety. The consumption of Italian American subjects was instrumental to the consumption of Italian American places. The bohemian writers, actresses, radicals, gays and lesbians, as well as middle-class Midwestern visitors to New York who patronized the Village's Italian restaurants and speakeasies were attracted by their Mediterranean flavor, racial liminality, and exciting cultural difference.[48] In sum, narratives of Italian American otherness were from the very beginning both largely based on the public identities that immigrants shaped and displayed by means of their selective acquisition and use of goods and the seductiveness of those same identities for a wide and diverse American consuming public.

In her chapter, Dominique Padurano explores much of this same territory, as she takes on the story of pioneering body-builder Charles Atlas (né Angelo Siciliano) to illuminate the paths of the commodification of the Italian American male body against the backdrop of the consumer culture of the 1920s and 1930s, its insistence on body presentation, and the graphic power in the "representation of the other" of mail-order catalogs and photo magazines.

Can a general statement on the wider moral and political significance of Italian immigrant consumer culture and its cross-cultural consumption be drawn? In the closing chapter of the first section of the collection, Marcella Bencivenni begins to answer the question by identifying the arguments Italian socialists and anarchists elaborated about the challenges and opportunities the labor movement was presented with in the face of capitalist material abundance and shortcomings in its egalitarian distribution.

Bencivenni discusses in particular the original ways in which Italian radicals tried to accommodate their critique of American consumerism with their efforts at offering organized moments of leisure and material enjoyment for militants and sympathizers.

Overall, Bencivenni's findings corroborate the argument that, not identifying with and rather expressing outright skepticism for the very premises of consumer capitalism, the Italian immigrant consumer culture elaborated between the 1900s and the 1930s was an original working-class project of survival and self-representation vis-à-vis American life. As such, it was not necessarily, or not necessarily felt as, an alternative to the radical movements of social reform to which many Italian American women and men participated in those years. Left-wing Italian American artists such as the painter Ralph Fasanella and the novelist Pietro di Donato used the sharing of food, wine, and other material joys of ethnic domestic life among immigrant construction workers and their families as a recurrent expression of class solidarity, sociability, and community.[49]

The Politics of Italian American Consumer Culture: Class, Gender, and Race

The second section of the volume ("The Politics and Style of Italian American Consumerism, 1930–1980") continues to explore the political meaning of the Italian American participation in consumerism, expanding the analysis to New Deal and postwar America. It was only in the 1930s and 1940s that the chance to participate in the high levels of consumption that up to that point had been the prerogative of the middle class was open to a number of working-class Americans, which included the vast majority of Italian immigrants and their children.[50] At first sight it certainly seems that most Italian Americans used their novel purchasing power in a politically conservative way, privileging private consumption over public involvement. Italian immigrant consumerism definitely revealed an appreciation of the tangible material rewards, especially in terms of a rich family life, that the American capitalist system could provide. This appreciation was the carrot that, combined with the stick of their victimization as racial inferiors, Mafiosi, violent radicals, and "enemy aliens," advised many Italian Americans to retreat collectively from the public arena by the time the United States entered World War II, and, later, often assume a social and political conservative stance.[51] Italian immigrants are also conspicuously absent from all major historical accounts of working-class consumer activism.[52]

Still, as Stefano Luconi argues in the chapter that opens the section, this impression is to a certain extent a consequence of the fact that although Italian Americans were a critical electoral component of the New Deal coalition, very little has been written about their participation in support of the Roosevelt administration's programs of national welfare. Luconi takes on the issue from the perspective of the recognition of the "consumer interest" that was a central feature of the New Deal's political economy, arguing that Italian Americans vocally reclaimed an "American standard of living" for working-class consumers and especially participated in and benefited from the New Deal's social policies on housing (a crossroads which, giving the virtual racial segregation that these policies would eventually entail, dramatically accelerated the Italian American endorsement of a "white" identity along with an "Italian" one.)[53]

By the outset of the Cold War, Italian Americans were among the obvious beneficiaries of the postwar politics of mass private consumption based on the state-supervised, Keynesian contract among capitalists, producers, and consumers. Thanks to the GI Bill and other concurrent pieces of legislation, second-generation Italian Americans could go to college, participate in material affluence as they never had before, and even join the white flow out of inner cities and into the suburbs.

In her chapter, Danielle Battisti shows that the appreciation of so many Italian Americans for the material rewards that American liberalism had delivered to them was used as a transnational Cold War weapon—a means to convince Italians in Italy to choose the promise of American consumerism over communism in a crucial political moment in which the "homeland" was at the forefront of the clash between the two worlds. Battisti emphasizes how public campaigns like the mass letters that Italian Americans sent to their relatives in Italy to convince them to vote for anticommunist parties in the watershed elections of 1948 had in fact a double purpose: one international, influencing the self-determination of Italians in Italy and keeping the country in the U.S. sphere of influence; and one domestic, proving to other Americans that (despite indications or fears to the contrary) the levels of material consumption Italians had achieved in America had decisively won them to the cause of capitalism and Americanism.

Indeed, after the war, second-generation Italian Americans identified in consumerism and the conspicuous dismissal of the consumer tastes of their parents the pathway to social mobility and full American citizenship. Yet, many clues suggest that at that point they had internalized this set of values and meanings to such an extent that they continued, consciously or unconsciously, to make sense of an all-changing world through it. The continuing, selective incorporation of marketplace materials to shape ethnically defined lifestyles, was especially apparent among those who in the 1950s and 1960s still occupied the ranks of the urban working class, and at that point interpreted their being "Italian" as an synonym for not being "Black," "Puerto Rican," "Jewish," or "Irish," more than in relation with some shared historical ancestry. The underlying survival of the principles of the consumer culture that the immigrants had shaped a few decades earlier was certainly helped by the fact that those principles were still in high demand in postwar America as a supply of appealing diversity: as such, they continued to be incorporated in American culture at large via cross-cultural consumption.

Every major ethnographic account of Italian American life in the 1950s and early 1960s—supposedly the age of consent, mass consumerism, and timidity toward the public manifestation of ethnic diversity by the children and grandchildren of Ellis Island immigrants—would in fact draw attention to the persistence of a distinctive Italian American consumer culture. Nathan Glazer and Daniel P. Moynihan largely understood Italian American ethnicity in New York as a culture coalesced around the interests, agendas, and styles of consumption of "homeowners in Staten Island, the North Bronx, Brooklyn, and Queens."[54] New York Italian Americans, as represented in *Beyond the Melting Pot*, emerged as "defenders of neighborhood," dedicated lovers of and investors in their home, turf, consumer institutions, and working-class lifestyles, ready to guard them and preserve them by any means necessary from the threats of urban change—a mindset that by the mid-1960s would result on occasion in overt grass-roots antiliberalism.[55]

Gerald Suttles concurrently compared the preference of Italian Americans in Chicago's Addams area for shopping in neighborhood stores and ordinary clothing (print cotton dresses and low-heel shoes for women; work shoes, black denim pants, and sleeveless undershirts for men) to blacks' much more enthusiastic attitude for fashion in self-presentation and lower dedication to shopping places operated by in-group members. Similarly to Glazer and Moynihan, Suttles concluded that by way of their consumer practices, Chicago's Italians "declare either a commitment to their own ethnic section or an *indifference to wider social rulings.*"[56]

The "urban villagers" of Boston's West End, as described by Herbert Gans, likewise demonstrated a "selective acceptance of the outside world" through their use of consumer goods and the mass media.[57] According to Gans, Boston's working-class Italians identified closely with the neighborhood, and worked, worshipped, and socialized locally. The consumption of television quintessentially reflected Italian Americans' skepticism and even cynicism toward larger society's values and discourses. It was taken as a given, for example, that quiz shows were prearranged. "Television commercials," accordingly, "are sometimes watched raptly, and then bombarded with satirical comments which question exaggerated or dishonest claims and meaningless statements." In general, the West Enders interpreted "the media content so as to protect themselves from the outside world and to isolate themselves from its messages unless they wish to believe them."[58] Their penchant for big refrigerators, Gans insisted, witnessed once more the importance they gave to food as a medium for reinforcing family and community bonds against centrifugal dreams/nightmares of social and physical mobility. Cautious about buying on installment, though, Boston's Italian Americans showed extravagance in little else, such as new outfits with which to celebrate major holidays and make a good appearance with their peers. Just like their Chicago counterparts, West Enders did not care about the latest fashion—something they felt was representative of the distant, unnecessarily affected, or unauthentic ways of middle-class life. Rather, young Italian men preferred to display their idea of style, taste, and masculinity through care for their cars, a fact that reinforced their popular designation as "greasers," a racially charged stereotypization that hinted at the dangerousness of Italian urban working-class youth as potential delinquents.[59]

Indeed, as second- and third-generation working-class Italians mostly articulated their whiteness out of fear of identification with the blacks and Puerto Ricans with whom by the 1950s and 1960s they increasingly shared the same urban space, racial liminality continued to be part of Italian American public identities. The ethnic youth subcultures the two concluding chapters in this section of the book deal with, Italian doo-wop and Guido, were elaborations originating from the "greaser" image and its race and class contents.

My own chapter on Italian doo-wop situates the hegemony of young working-class Italian singers in a black musical genre in its constructed embeddedness in the life of the Little Italies of New York and its being part of the cultural strategies of "defense of the neighborhood." At the same time, the emerging, "deterritorialized," mass market for rock and roll provided Italian doo-wop the opportunity to break away with the parochialism and territoriality of late 1950s and early 1960s Little Italies and reach out to a multiethnic audience of young non-Italian (including black) consumers. Paradoxically, the most appealing features of Italian doo-wop among cross-cultural consumers were exactly the authenticity, urban rootedness, and "tough" uncompromising attitude that the young Italian performers of the music conveyed.

With his chapter, Donald Tricarico extends further in time the analysis of the pattern, by discussing the formation of the Guido youth subculture in the late 1970s, through its developments in the 1990s and 2000s. Also deeply influenced by black music (disco, and later rap), Guido appears like a strategy of ethnic identification—responding to a specific geographical, social, and cultural context—that derives its material and meanings from consumer culture and articulates them in the form of style. Just as it happened to Italian doo-wop, Guido's roots in consumerism brought in turn about its commodification and transformation into spectacle for the consumption of wider cross-cultural markets. The popularity of MTV's reality show *Jersey Shore* (2009–12), which exposes the adventures of a group of Guidos and Guidettes, is the last and most notable evidence of the continuing marketability of the (working-class and racialized) Italian American body, uncontrolled expression of emotions, "tribal" sense of family and community, and full capacity of sensual enjoyment.

The aestheticization and commodification of working-class and racially in-between Italian American identities has now a long history, just as the equally historical consumer needs they are made to satisfy. Late 1950s doo-wop and late 1970s Guido subcultures were at base expressions of the "selective acceptance of the outside world" among the urban working-class Italian Americans whom Glazer and Moynihan, Suttles, and Gans discussed—an ethos of *controlled alienation via consumer culture* that accounts for a key Italian American discourse soon to be transformed into a widely marketable identity. Both Italian doo-wop and Guido have not been challenges to the established capitalist system and racial order, but strong statements of ethnic identities and style vis-à-vis "the system," as well as loud manifestations of working-class leisure, pleasure, and appreciation of the material prizes "the system" made available in exchange of work. Similarly, the Italian American singers, actors, and comedians that dominated American popular entertainment in the 1950s and early 1960s all possessed (to different degrees) a defiant, uncompromisingly blasé approach, a charming outcast identity, a characteristically plebeian cunning, and a certain dose of clannishness, which coalesced in their attitude about *working the system*—that is, getting the most from the dominant economic/cultural complex in terms of material rewards and recognition, while resisting being absorbed by its foreign values and codes of behavior. Dean Martin, Connie Francis, Louis Prima, Frankie Valli, and especially the immensely popular Frank Sinatra demonstrated the dramatic fungibility of such cultural traits as embodied into distinctive Italian American style.[60]

In the American popular culture lexicon, in fact, the crooner, the doo-wopper, and the Guido, have functioned much like another quintessential Italian American type—the cinematic gangster. As Robert Warshow famously argued in his 1948 article, "The Gangster as Tragic Hero," the (Italian) protagonist of the gangster film "speaks for" a middle-class audience in that he "is what we want to be and what we are afraid we may become."[61] The immigrant gangster's—and the crooner's, the doo-wopper's, and the Guido's—appeal to such an audience derived from the challenge they brought to the largely middle-class myth of work ethic, which demands self-control, self-discipline, conformity, and obedience to superiors in order to achieve upward social mobility in modern America. Especially in moments of social and economic turmoil like the 1930s and the 1970s, Italian gangsters on film and TV—from *Little Caesar* (1931) to *The God-father* (1972) and *The Sopranos* (1999–2007)—have scorned and demystified the American Dream of hard work and upward mobility not only by hinting at the fact that the Dream may not deliver what it promises, but showing that success can be achieved instead by manipulating the rules, enjoying adventure, glamour, and sex, and retaining one's own individual identity and awareness of being different in the face of depersonalization, massification, and bureaucratization. Italian American masculinity, indeed, has prevalently been represented as intractable to discipline, as part of the violently "artistic cum proletarian" temperament of Italian male subjects—examples spanning from Rudolph Valentino to Benito Mussolini, Enrico Caruso, and Charles Atlas.[62] As Warshow argues, the gangster's life and appeal to spectators are defined by his desire to "assert himself as an individual, to draw himself out of the crowd."[63] Even the gangster's fall and brutal death—just like Sinatra's misadventures with women, the law, or the entertainment industry, which seemed at various points to mark "the end" of his career—are consumed as the final chapter of a dramatic struggle between the individual and the moral and social order. The fall and demise of the "hero" signal the need that the moral and social order he transgresses is finally restored and reinforced, witnessing how such an Italian American identity have of course been meant to be consumed with a touristic approach, as a temporary escape from self-discipline and restraint, rather than adopted in everyday life.

Like any other marketable Italian American identity, the "working-the-system" narrative and its commodification have regularly been heavily racialized, gendered, and transnational. While every discourse about Italian American styles has multiculturally made explicit or implicit reference to the immigrants' heritage rooted in the Old World, as an indelible mark of difference that even generation passages could not dilute,[64] the American career of Sophia Loren exemplifies the continuous *circulation* of discursive meanings and representations between Italy and the United States, which has also constantly taken place. Loren—herself an avid consumer of Hollywood movies as a young girl in Naples—began to receive offers from major Hollywood studios after she had starred in Italian films such as *The Gold of Naples* (L'oro di Napoli, 1954), in which she played the character of a voluptuous and foxy lower-class woman. In the late 1950s, the actress finally immigrated to the United States to sweep box offices and film magazines. On the American screen, "she became the embodiment of a highly subversive idea of unabashed female sensuality that was both attractive and seen as typical of the spontaneous popular world. . . . Defiant and flirtatious, she was a woman who retained control of her sexuality and administered herself as she best thought fit."[65] Transcending and complicating the Madonna/whore dichotomy entrenched in the Mediterranean "honor and shame" complex, Loren offered American audiences a womanly counterpart to the stylish insubordination of Italian American male gangsters, crooners, and doo-woppers, and fresh evidence of the ingrained *Italian* character of the working-the-system narrative.[66]

Overall, in the face of their own social mobility as a group, in the 1950 and 1960s Italian Americans catered to the imaginary needs of the rest of America as the perfect representatives of an otherwise receding white working-class ethnicity. In the "real world," second- and third-generation Italian Americans were moving to better neighborhoods and Little Italies were fading away, with all their nastiness and glamour. Yet, being among the poorest of the immigrant groups that had arrived to America at the turn of the century, and at the same time being more often homeowners than renters, a number of them remained in the ranks of the working class and in the inner cities, where they were supposed to be preserving white ethnic neighborhoods from racial integration and decay. Even for suburbanized Italians, those who had stayed back in "darkening" and "browning" ex–Little Italies were the heroes that provided them with a place to return to, if only for the annual procession of the saint or weekend shopping. Postwar Italian Americans were intelligible yet different, not as distant in space and time as their cousins abroad, yet racially distinct and not completely assimilated.

A convenient reservoir of otherness for midcentury and pre–civil rights American nation-building projects, they seemed to have just the right amount of cultural capital to be credible endorsers of a variety of ethnic-branded products. Italian American food, for example—a mass-reproducible, canned, and packaged version of which was being made available to American tables by the national food industry—conveyed the values of authenticity, solidarity, and commensality contextualized in sites such as home, family and community, to which postwar white middle-class America looked with longing and nostalgia. Those values and places were very much part of the culture of the era, and yet sensed as paradises lost.[67] The consumer values and meanings Gans talked about in his discussion of refrigerators were graphically represented, with no need for translation, in a popular 1969 commercial for Prince Spaghetti. In the commercial, twelve-year boy Anthony Martignetti (real name) ran past the open-air market, bocce courts, and rows of tenement houses in the Italian North End of Boston to come home to his mother and be embraced in a warm, nurturing, heavily matriarchal atmosphere of good food and family. "Prince Spaghetti—Share It With Your Family," the closing caption read.

These class, race, and gender-inflected identities, established in the 1950s and 1960s in the Fordist market for cross-cultural consumption, have adaptively survived as part of the trend of continuity within change that has been happening on the terrain of the "consumption of the Italian American other" since the 1970s. Although the latter is most specifically the subject of the third and next section of this book, these continuities need to be pinpointed here. Italian American–branded goods and images fared very well in the new postindustrial market for commodified diversity of the 1980s and beyond, but—notwithstanding the emergence of a new consumer regime and new consumer subjects—commercialized Italian American identities have continued to be desired and pursued mostly because of their heavily racialized, urban working-class style contents. Italian American public identity, as represented in consumer culture, has continued to be the repository of a sort of "safe danger" for American consumers of different races, genders, and classes—as it had previously been for the thrill-seeking visitors of the Italian Greenwich Village in the 1920s and the record buyers of Italian doo-wop in the late 1950s.

On one hand, *Italianità* has been sold and purchased as a reassuring anchoring to memory and tradition, as embodied by a family-, community-, and place-oriented people, in the face of intense social and cultural change. On the other, it has represented an exotic reminder of a past racially inflected primitivism and working-class vociferous ethos that non-Italians can now more than ever consume with a touristic, or even condescending, approach without any of the implications that the actual experience of the lifestyle would imply.

Since the 1970s, film and television in particular have been frantic producers and purveyors of this dual Italian American image, enormously contributing to crystallize meanings that have in been in turn incorporated in a multitude of commodities and commercial leisure experiences. Hollywood, especially, reflected and fostered the interest for the working-class subculture and racial liminality that past generations of Italian Americans had constructed through their consumer culture and lifestyle by electing the Italian American as its typical white ethnic character.

In the 1970s, three very popular, award-winning, films emerged as exemplary representations of a type of Italian American life that effectively met the needs, desires, and fantasies of many American viewers of the post–civil rights era. The momentous *The Godfather*, besides offering spectators a truculent but engaging noir story and diasporic postcard images of Sicily, addressed the problem of the fate of the American family after Women's Lib and the Moynihan Report—the 1965 study that made a case for the social underperforming of blacks being a consequence of the high number of single-parent households in the community. The traditional patriarchal family that was under attack on many fronts, *The Godfather* suggested, was a haven of solidarity and counter-individualization in which everyone counted as a member of the group, and as such was never left alone. The ethnic rituals of the Italian American family helped to romanticize and dramatize such nostalgic and reassuring—if painful—tale.

Whiteness, an issue that ran underneath *The Godfather*—except for the Moynihan Report–reeking scene of the general meeting of Mafia families, in which the bosses agree that blacks are not human because they lacked respect for the family—emerged more vividly in *Rocky* (1976) and *Rocky II* (1979). In the movies, Rocky Balboa is a gentle, simpleminded, uneducated, and unarticulated working-class Italian American man who lives in a deindustrializing, decaying, and unemployment-ridden inner-city neighborhood (South Philadelphia). The plot opposes him on the boxing ring to a talented black rival who is just his opposite: Apollo Creed is the world heavyweight champion; lives a life of luxury, sports jewelry and fancy clothes; and has a flamboyant personality, especially in the presence of the media. However, Rocky, the underdog proudly representing his own people under the nom de guerre "Italian Stallion," fights unexpectedly well, leading his opponent to the last round, where—as the opening of the second movie makes clear—a fraudulent split decision of the jury denies him the victory he would have deserved. Much of the second chapter of the saga follows Rocky as he unsuccessfully tries to find a job in order to perform his prescribed role of male breadwinner, since his fiancée is expecting a child. In the process, Rocky is laid off (because of cutbacks) by a black supervisor from the meat packing plant where his soon-to-be brother-in-law has landed him a job. As historian Matthew Jacobson has noted, seen against the backdrop of the liberal social policies of the era, *Rocky* consistently hinted at a mounting "black privilege" that was holding white ethnics down despite their hardworking, law-abiding, and family-centered ethics (Rocky is not depicted as a racist, so if minorities actually deserved compensation, he was paying for somebody else's faults). The "fixed" decision of the jury in the first Rocky's fight accordingly reminded spectators of the controversial Supreme Court decisions on affirmative action policy they heard about on the TV news.[68] *Rocky* and *Rocky II*, in short, were ostensibly consumed as part of what Jacobson has called "white grievance cinema," and the fact that an Italian American working-class male was selected to serve most powerfully such discourse revealed what kind of Italian American identities were in highest demand by the cultural industry of the time.

Gender and race are also key factors in *Saturday Night Fever* (1977), the tale of a young Italian American man (Tony Manero) who through his skills as a disco dancer tries to escape his dead-end job in a white, but significantly browning, working-class neighborhood (Bay Ridge, Brooklyn). *Saturday Night Fever* raises again the point that when Italian working-class males want and manage to achieve social mobility, they do so through their idiosyncratic artistic attitude and impatience for the rules (a concept that also strongly resonates in the almost contemporary Martin Scorsese's *Raging Bull* [1980]). However, this narrative, which the viewer is asked to identify with, is not an option open to "consumable" Italian women (much like in *The Godfather*, *Rocky*, and *Raging Bull*). In *Saturday Night Fever*, the only woman who appears to have agency by second-wave-feminism-era standards is the blonde, blue-eyed, white woman who had already achieved an independent life in Manhattan, and may or may not, according to her autonomous judgment, accept Tony Manero as her dancing partner. The only Italian girl, who attempts to break out from the future of submission that awaits her as a "good Italian woman," is punished by being raped by two of Tony's closest friends. In the wake of ethnic revival, the Italian American ethnicity that was intended for the consumption of a vast American and global audience emphasized, rather than revise, time-blessed representations of all-compassing family life, strong gender roles, working-class ethos, and racial in-betweenness, consistently responding to the touchy dilemmas and interrogations about the future opened up in American society by the political and cultural legacy of the 1960s.

The ambivalence of this Italian American image, largely conceived to be consumed through a white middle-class eye (even if the actual audience was much larger than that) becomes even clearer when the representations of Italian Americans as consumers in post-1970s film and TV are taken into account. Consistently with the basic factor in the process of commodification—the emphasis on deeply entrenched race- and class-determined characteristics that confirmed Italian American identities as clearly different and hence easily consumable—representations of Italian American consumers were built upon a well-known discourse of middle-class cultural hegemony: the reproach and disdain for the nouveau riches, the lower-class people who lack the cultural capital and taste to deal with economic resources and material abundance they are not used to possess, and act out of the rules of behavior the middle class itself has prescribed as appropriate.[69]

Here, too, a long-term process has been at work. On October 24, 1906, the popular humor magazine *Puck* published a two-vignette cartoon under the caption "It Is Happening Every Day." In the first vignette, two well-dressed "Native Americans" comment on an Italian immigrant couple just off the boat in New York: "More Italians coming here! Gee whiz, how do they expect to make a living, anyway?" "Well, in the first place, you know they don't live as *we* do, old man." In the second vignette, captioned "In Just About A Year or Two," the two Americans are flabbergasted to see the same Italian couple cruise in a luxury car, the man sporting a comical general's uniform and the woman wrapped in an exaggerated bulk of furs and feathers. A quarter-century later, in the classic gangster movie *Little Caesar*, Rico Bandello is ridiculed because he lacks the consumer cultural tools to properly use and enjoy his newly acquired possessions. When he appears in the mansion where the corrupt tycoon he is trying to overthrow lives, he makes countless gaffes because of his inability to evaluate the value of goods. He thinks that it is the golden frame that makes a painting expensive. When he accepts a cigar, he spits out its tip and flicks the ash on the carpet. And when his associates present him with a golden watch, he juggles with it since he does not know how it works. All the luxury the Italian gangster is surrounded with at the top of his trajectory from rags to riches through violence only serves to emphasize that he is out of his natural environment, to make him artificial and pathetic, and to foreshadow his upcoming disastrous fall.

Four decades later, it still is lower-class spending ignorance and lack of taste that put Rocky in trouble, as he squanders in one day all the money he earned with his fight of a lifetime against the black champion—on a black leather jacket with a tiger on the back, a fur coat for his unpretentious girlfriend, and some watches (*Rocky II*). The Jewish American woman protagonist of *Goodfellas* (1990) extends the same criticism to the habit of Italian American women in the community the movie is about of overusing cosmetics, wearing too much eyeliner, and overstyling their hair.

By the end of the century, *The Sopranos* offered the most complex and nuanced representation of Italian American life to be consumed by millions of American and worldwide viewers. The TV series presented an unprecedented parade of professional Italian Americans (psychologists, lawyers, doctors, BMW car dealers, restaurateurs, and so on) busy enjoying an articulated and cultured transnational Italian American lifestyle. Characters in *The Sopranos* know how to use, and they mark their (ethnic) distinction through Versace dresses, sophisticated *haute* Italian cuisine, and even membership in Italian American organizations. However, many of the characters viewers are prompted to identify with—most notably Tony Soprano—are actually working-class people who have experienced significant social mobility, but cannot escape living by their embodied habitus. What is markedly consumed with *The Sopranos*, thus, is the feeling of cultural and emotional inadequacy of prosperous people of humble origins (and racialized as not completely white) in a very complex, fast-changing, antidepressant- and Viagra-powered affluent society, in which an unparalleled variety of opportunities, choices, and identities are open to everyone to embrace, so no one really knows what he or she wants or who he or she is anymore.[70]

Tony Soprano is definitely the complex type of Italian American consumer this book details has historically existed in reality, as he shapes his lifestyle through the consumption of SUVs, capocollo, Prozac, Italian suits, boats, and emotionally touching trips to the Italian church in New Jersey his turn-of-the-twentieth-century immigrant grandfather contributed with his hands to build. Notwithstanding his wealth and his status as feared Mafia boss, he is quite openly mocked and derided by middle-class fellow golf players for his lack of taste and cultural capital. In this respect, Tony Soprano is just the last victim in a long tradition of Italian American consumers who had to bear this sort of angered criticism and scorn.

It comes as no surprise, then, that the latest very popular representation of Italian Americans on TV, MTV's reality show *Jersey Shore* (first aired in 2009), is about a youth subculture that translates into ethnicity a "flashy" consumer style. Through the display of gold chains, gym-built abs and biceps, mini-dresses, tight shirts, and thongs, the Guidos of *Jersey Shore* loudly reclaim an inherently working-class right to nonmediated fun and pleasure, to which ethnicity adds the meaning of group cultural identity. Commodified practices of self-presentation and body maintenance that include heavy tanning and surgical breast enhancement in fact make up for a mimicry of the racial characteristics—swarthiness and excessive maternal fecundity—that original *contadini* immigrants embodied as perpetual marks of subalternity in America.[71] The cultural industry's fascination with Italian American identities once again resides in what those can provide in terms of class, gender, and race difference, as in a distorted mirror that projects onto Italian American subjects, places, and cultural artifacts the desires and fantasies of film, television, and lifestyle magazines consumers. *Jersey Shore*'s Guidos—just like Tony Soprano, when he has sex with a one-legged Russian immigrant or beats an arrogant lawyer to a pulp—let viewers vicariously experience the true, genuine, and transparent enjoyment of life and pleasure that middle-class self-discipline prevents them to experience, as least in everyday real life—and that may resonate "authentic" and true to other working-class people, white, black, and Hispanic. They show no inclination or patience for the delayed gratification the middle-class ethics of success prescribes.[72]

Continuity and Change in the Transnational Formation of Taste

The third and final section of the book, "Consuming Italian American Identities in the Multicultural Age," illustrates how the consumer styles, patterns, and meanings elaborated by early-twentieth-century immigrants and further developed by the American-born generations in or out receding urban enclaves, resurfaced, to be transformed and redirected, in the wake of the new consumer economy which dawned in the early 1970s.

Historians and theorists of consumer society agree that the counterculture, civil rights movement, and resuming immigration of the 1960s constituted a turning point which revolutionized American consumer culture, ironically paving the way for the triumph of late-capitalist consumerism in the Reaganite 1980s and after. The new fragmented identities that had emerged from the antiestablishment cultural movements of American society of the 1960s soon consolidated into many different "consumer clusters"—women, the young, blacks, Latinos and Latinas, Asians, and all their subsegments. On their part, faced with market saturation, falling prices, and rising labor and raw material costs, American corporations not only began a massive program of deindustrialization—by automating, subcontracting, and delocalizing production where labor was cheapest and nonunionized—but virtually abandoned mass marketing, focalizing on small-batch and rapid-turnover product lines aimed at distinct consumer segments. The empty space left by fading work was filled by a swelling cultural industry whose most enduring role was to inflate commodities with symbolic value, so that the new postmodern consumers, liberated from the constrictions of modern social order, could go ahead and fashion their individual selves through selective consumption of a multifarious variety of goods and experiences. In this context, cultural difference and ethnicity became themselves commodities, as they added significant value to products. A dramatically expanding class of cultural mediators and marketers of any kind and status oversaw the entire process, while new institutions and sites of consumption, like the mall and themed environments, radically changed American public space and ways of everyday life.[73]

Italian Americans, arguably more than any other European ethnic group, were main actors in the different stages of this process. The political turmoil and ensuing struggle for cultural identity of the 1960s suggested even to many middle-class Italian Americans that the simple white American identity for which they had been striving for, reaping material rewards in the process, was not desirable anymore. Through ethnic associations, ethnic festivals, ethnic literature, ethnic film and TV, ethnic food, heritage tourism, and study abroad programs, they increasingly reclaimed a different kind of whiteness—a hyphenated American identity that paid homage to their unique heritage and experience in the United States. Largely articulated through ethno-directed consumption, the Italian American "ethnic revival" had political, as well as social and cultural purposes. Italian American ethnic revivalists borrowed their language of protest and political identity from black nationalism and emerging multiculturalism—as witnessed by the infamous Italian-American Civil Rights League—reclaiming their own past of discrimination and marginalization at the hand of the dominant Anglo-Protestant elite.[74] This discourse often turned into a conservative statement of unaccountability, if not hostility, toward the requests of blacks and other minorities of color for reparation—in the form of civil and social rights—for the racism they have suffered. "If our ancestors were not perpetrators, but victims of American racism," some Italian Americans have reasoned, "if they managed to make it in America with no help from the State, but working hard and limiting consumption, why should African Americans, Latinos, and recent immigrants deserve a better treatment, one that has to be supported by we taxpayers?"[75]

On the sociocultural side, as sociologist Marcus Lee Hansen famously stated in his "law," psychological and emotional dynamics played some part in the wish to rediscover the lost legacy of the immigrant grandparents: the third generation reclaims what the second generation struggled to forget.[76] But the longing for and the excavation of the immigrant past and memory related to larger changes linked to the transition toward a postmodern/multicultural U.S. society. The exhaustion of modernity as the overall framework of the present and the future left Italian Americans with a sense of loss and confusion (so central, to use a popular culture example, in Tony Soprano's ruminations about his father's generation and the disappearance of the "real men" and real relations that populated the Italian community he grew up in). The "end of work," with its corollary of a shrinking working class, vanishing social conflict as it had been known and articulated since the nineteenth century, and culturalization of the entire society,[77] turned the Italian immigrant past into something that was neither threatening nor shameful anymore, but a heritage to cherish and be proud of, an authentic lifestyle that had gone forever but could be experienced vicariously through images, sounds, and memories, visited as a tourist attraction in ghettos turned into Disneylands.[78]

Genealogical research, self-made family history, and community oral history exploded as a mass phenomenon among Italian Americans one or more generations remote from poor, illiterate Ellis Island grandmothers and grandfathers who had been conveniently kept in the closet of memory. The worth of the investment was legitimated by history departments in the best American universities—whose faculties now included many third-generation immigrants—which concurrently began to celebrate the immigrant saga, and within it particularly the resistance of first-generation protagonists to be melted in the assimilation pot (now seen as the Golem of immigration history).[79] With the ethnic revival—a quintessentially postmodern social movement—new ways and meanings of consumption and sociability opened up to the vast public of Italian Americans with the necessary disposable money, time, and culture. If the Italian Americans of Glazer and Moynihan, Suttles, and Gans thought, acted, and consumed Italian as an attribute of class, for Italian American ethnic revivalists class was an attribute of ethnicity; and for marketers of Italian Americana a further factor of cultural differentiation in the ethnic package that was increasingly produced, sold, and consumed in the marketplace.[80]

The interest of corporate America in the Italian American market demonstrated, in fact, that the association of ethnicity with the lifestyle of the lower classes in enclosed communities had ultimately broken down. On one hand, "ethnic" product lines could appeal to vast cross-cultural markets; the hard work of establishing the marketability of the products having often already been made by independent ethnic businesses. Corporations like Pillsbury, which in 1975 acquired Minneapolis Totino's Pizza from Rose Totino for $20 million with the intention of keeping the original brand, know-how, and network of distributors alive, knowingly invested in a consumer sector (frozen pizza) with high potential growth.[81] On the other hand, Italian ethnics had at this point an unprecedented buying power to go with their ethnic-oriented needs and preferences: by the 1980s, Italian Americans as a group had reached income levels that set them well above the national average, and many among the most enthusiastic ethnic revivalists were upwardly mobile people, who felt that their ethnicity was not only compatible with a successful economic and social life, but augmented their social and cultural capital.[82] Major national brands advertised their high-end products (cars, clothes, shoes, cruises, and so on) in the magazine *Attenzione*, launched in 1979, with messages specifically tailored to its upscale Italian American readers.[83]

The chapters in this section of the book investigate the post-1970s encoding of "Italian Americanness" in the branding of products, images, and experiences (fashion, spectator sports, urban tourism, and food respectively), the marketing strategies of Italian American memory, and the uses and meanings constructed through both self- and cross-cultural consumption of Italian American identities.

Courtney Ritter's chapter opens the section by suggesting that Italian American "identity shopping" has been complicated and enriched since the 1980s by the arrival of new appealing, high-scale "made in Italy" goods and images, which are expressions of a globally popular "Italian Way of Life." Ritter focuses on the fortunes of Italian men's fashion in the U.S. market, effectively connecting the production side, based in "Third Italy" (the industrial districts made of networks of small firms and workshops in northern and central Italy), and the consumer side—notably, the embodiment of a "reconfigured" Italian American identity into designer men's suits.

John Gennari discusses the Italian presence in a popular, widely televised sport—NCAA college basketball—noting that that (differently from baseball and boxing) has been much more conspicuous among coaches than players. From Gennari's study, Italian American basketball coaches of the 1980s and later appear as the most credible interpreters and mediators of an inherently black culture—the best basketball playing—for the wider interracial markets of fans. Just like in the case of Italian doo-wop a few decades earlier, what black and white spectators alike really "buy" with Italian basketball coaching is "authenticity," an heritage of racially and class-inflected identities, and the entire universe of memory and cultural references that has been built in consumer culture around the urban experience of Italian Americans.

In the third chapter in the section, Ervin Kosta compares two New York's Little Italies—the best known around Mulberry Street in Manhattan, and the Belmont/Arthur Avenue section in the Bronx. Kosta frames the historical trajectories of the neighborhoods—from immigrant enclaves to popular ethnic theme parks for international tourists—within postindustrial urban change and the turn of cultural production into most profitable investment for financial capital.

Finally, by deconstructing advertisements from Italian-themed chain restaurants, such as Maggiano's Little Italy, Bertucci's, and Olive Garden, Fabio Parasecoli's chapter proposes that "eating the Italian other" today in these Italian-themed environments accounts for the consumption of a hyperreal simulacrum of Italian American life. Even more than in Gennari's basketball coaching, authenticity in the chain restaurants Parasecoli analyzes is a "product"—a company strategy carefully crafted with the methodology of postmodern pastiche, including the irony.

By the early 1980s, the ways of life that immigrants created in face-to-face communities had clearly been submerged by social change, suburbanization, and intermarriage. Nonetheless, taken together, the four chapters in this section offer the evidence that an Italian American ethic and aesthetic had by then entered the consciousness of many Americans through consumer culture, and that such a moral affiliation was, and still is, felt as significant and important for many people in everyday interactions. How can be otherwise explained that, in the year 2000, the number of Americans reporting Italian ancestry increased by one million since the previous 1990 census—the equivalent of a new mass migration? Commentators agreed on attributing in large part such an impromptu rise exactly to a popular culture event, namely the immense popularity of HBOS's TV series *The Sopranos*, which, by unveiling and superbly dramatizing fascinating aspects of Italian family life, community culture, and consumer styles, pressured many Americans to endorse an Italian American identity and check the "Italian American" box on the census form.[84]

Conclusion: Consumer Culture as Transnational Circuit

A lesson to be drawn from the cross-reading of Ritter's, Gennari's, Kosta's, and Parasecoli's chapters against the backdrop of the essays in the first section of the book is that the difference in the consumer cultures of late twentieth-century Italian Americans and early twentieth-century immigrants has been more one of intensity than of the nature of the forces at work. Multicultural-age "new ethnics" obviously have a different access to time and space, much more purchasing power, and a greater variety of goods and experiences available than early twentieth-century immigrants ever had, but the consumer cultures of both the former and the latter have been consciously articulated by their makers in response to and in the context of specific social needs, both have borne a strong and explicit relationship with ethnicity, and both have followed similar dynamics—notably, (1) the original combination of high-brow and low-brow elements in diasporic Italian culture and (2) the transnational breadth of the elaboration of consumer styles and tastes.

Common strategies of ethnic consumerism include the harmonic juxtaposition of elements from high and low Italian/Italian American culture. For turn-of-the-twenty-first-century Italian Americans, the peasant culture of the forbearers is definitely less an heritage to actively endorse than to excavate and celebrate through conferences, books, DVDs, food, and travels back to the ancestral "home." The relics of the immigrant past are necessarily transfigured in the effort to revive them for present use; extracted from memory and separated from their contextual use-value, they are consumed as simulacra filled with symbolic and emotional value—as in the case the horns that immigrants used to wear on necklaces or at the belt loops of their pants to chase away the evil eye, now turned into fancy jewelry. Yet, now that it has been transformed into an icon of stability and rootedness, reminding us of a heroic "immigrant era" when social relations were genuine and authentic, the peasant past of the immigrants has the authority to sit alongside and be consumed as a worthy complement of the high Italian culture that Italian Americans also reclaim as their own patrimony. The long legacy of the Italian taste for beauty, running across Roman and Renaissance art, literature and poetry, futurism and neorealist film, and recent accomplishments in design, fashion, and cuisine, is reclaimed and consumed in museums, film festivals, car dealer salons, and restaurants, as well as by enrolling in graduate programs abroad, and including stays in Florence, Rome, and Venice on trips primarily intended for visiting Italian relatives and the native villages of immigrant ancestors.[85]

Immigrants of the turn of the twentieth century went to just the same great lengths to coalesce apparently irreconcilable cultures into a diasporic consumer culture. They generally lacked the power and the venues to articulate self-representations of their place in America, but the marketplace provided them with a site for negotiating their social identities at the intersection of the spheres of culture, economy, and politics. On one hand, immigrant consumer choices were aimed at the celebration of the heritage of southern Italy, a lost world they had abandoned as one has to abandon childhood innocence to enter adulthood disenchantment. That heritage—southern Italy, or *black Italy*—was what made them racially different and refractory to complete assimilation in America; it was their stigma and their problem. Still, they indulged in the consumption of objects, like popular religion paraphernalia, that hinted at the darkest of rebellions: a reclamation of their own primitivism, exactly the cultural feature that worried and fascinated so much modern Americans.[86] However, their consumer culture at the same time reinterpreted and appropriated *white Italy*; the classical world of Roman greatness, cradle of the Western civilization and its racial superiority, the Renaissance, and the masters of opera. Italian American elites have celebrated high Italian culture well before the ethnic revival of the 1970s; diasporic institutions like the Casa Italiana at Columbia

University operated for that purpose since the age of mass migration, trying to draw boundaries between the refined sphere of the cultured few and the embarrassing expressions of the lower immigrant masses. Yet, immigrant workers continuously trespassed those boundaries. While topping nearly all other immigrant groups in terms of illiteracy rates, immigrants could recite Dante's *Inferno* by heart, could sing the arias of the most famous Puccini, Rossini, and Verdi operas, and rejoiced when they heard the names of Michelangelo, Leonardo, or Raphael, as if they could actually partake of the fame of those great artists. Italian American food producers knew only too well about the immigrants' fondness for Italian cultural celebrities: they used their names and effigies for their brands and packages as a way for donning American-made Italian-style foodstuffs with authenticity and authoritativeness.[87] It was in the creation of an Italian American consumer style that the two clusters (subaltern, dark southern Italy and hegemonic, white man's Italy) were first reintegrated.

The second, related, area of contact between late and early twentieth-century Italian American consumers has been their similar capacity to assemble transnational material cultures and ideas about the good and the bad, the beautiful and the ugly, the pleasurable and the gross, so coherently to shape a *diasporic Italian taste*. If the approach employed by Paul Gilroy to delineate the many reincarnations, and yet the interrelatedness, of black culture on every sides of the Atlantic is taken as model, this diasporic Italian taste appears what has most effectively bonded together people everywhere on the planet—and whose biological heritage not necessarily can be tracked down to Italy—who recognize and affiliate themselves in a set of sensibilities that are discursively narrated and lived as "Italian."[88] Again, it is clear that the resources and technologies available to late twentieth-century Italian American ethnics have broadened immensely the possibilities for the consumption of transnational goods, culture, and identities. Since the 1960s, the appeal of Italian film, fashion, and food among the American and global upper-mobile middle class, which repositioned Italy at a high rank in the international market for the cultural difference, offered Italian Americans exciting opportunities of investment and pleasure in ethnicity-making.[89] A booming cultural industry, and in particular lifestyle media (magazines, film, TV, the Internet), provided ethnic consumers with a variety of models to choose from.

In these arenas, a new group of cultural mediators started disseminating knowledge about Italian identities and how to consume them from an Italian American angle. These tastemakers increasingly were "new transnational Italians," professional people who were born in Italy but spent part of their life in the United States as freelance workers or employees of Italian companies or government; or multicultural Italian Americans who did part of their professional training in Italy.[90] In the realm of food, for example, a new wave of Italian cookbook authors and hosts of popular cooking TV shows emerged by the 1970s and 1980s. Marcella Hazan, Giuliano Bugialli, and Lidia Bastianich were a particular diasporic group of middle-class Italians who relocated to New York, and, albeit with little or no culinary experience, found themselves in a privileged position to spread the word about "authentic" Italian cuisine, helping to establish it as the highly valued cultural commodity it is today, and, in the process, recruiting a vast group of Italian American followers.[91]

Since the turn of the millennium, the liberalization of markets and technological change in transport and information, resulting in a dramatic experience of time-space compression, seemed to have changed the very nature of diasporic consumer practices. Italian American consumers can not only fly to their diasporic home in a few hours and at cheap rates, but also buy Italian products on eBay in a matter of seconds; watch live Italian TV on the RAI web site; graphically explore any angle of past and present Italian culture on YouTube; find and chat with Italian friends or relatives on Facebook; and "walk" the streets of their grandmother's Calabrian town with the "street view" function of Google Maps. What are, then, the points of contact with the experience of the immigrants of one century earlier?

The first, I maintain, regards the consuming transnational social fields that early-twentieth-century migrants also inhabited, albeit with a much more dilated experience of time and space. Elizabeth Zanoni's chapter in the first section of the book highlights the magnitude of Italian imports in the United States before World War II and the role that immigrants played in fostering the commercial flows. But the observation of the other end of the field—that is, the communities where migrants came from, very often returned to, and their nonmobile relatives lived—illustrates the scope of the links that the connections between migration and consumption established between Italy and the United States (and numerous places elsewhere). Anticipations of enhanced consumption, visions of better material existences, and fantasies about alternative lifestyles in America were a formidable factor in setting in motion new human mobility from Italy. Ocean-liner company agents and recruiters of cheap labor skillfully created those images, spurred by the bulk of earlier migrants' enthusiastic letters and suggestive photographs and stirred up by the evidence inscribed onto the bodies of returnees. The acculturation of Italian migrants as American consumers, therefore, actually began in Italy, and was a central factor in their transnational migration projects. In his account of life in a remote small village in Basilicata in the 1930s, Carlo Levi related that "the mail faithfully brought remembrances from overseas [New York], gifts to their families from those blessed by fortune. . . . They sent a stream of scissors, knives, razors, farm tools, scythes, hammers, pincers—in short, all the gadgets of everyday use. Life at Gagliano was entirely American in regard to mechanical equipment as well as weights and measures, for the peasants spoke of pounds and inches rather than of kilograms and centimeters. The women wove on ancient looms, but they cut thread with shiny scissors from Pittsburgh; the barber's razor was the best I ever saw anywhere in Italy, and the blue steel blades of the peasants' axes were American. The peasants had no prejudice against these modern instruments, nor did they see any contradiction between them and their ancient customs."[92] It was not only production, but also consumption, to shape the transnational lives of both migrant and nonmobile Italians in the age of mass migrations. And it was not only production but also principally consumption that shaped the notion that Italy was their diasporic home.

The formation of a diasporic Italian consumer universe, most importantly occurring in the corridor linking Italy and the United States, has continued to develop. Since the turn of the twentieth century and to this day, merchants and migrants, and the products they have sold and purchased have created a thick network of financial, technological, commercial, and imaginary bonds between Italy and the United States. Italian American consumer identities and consumer practices have evolved within this increasingly thick and now more than one century old network. Significantly, as a result of the *layers and layers* of circulating images and meanings between Italy and the United States, post-Fordist Italian American consumers did find an unmistakable "family air" in the high-end products that the new Italian economy offered on the American marketplace since the 1980s. The elegant and exclusive "made in Italy" men suits of Armani, Versace, and Dolce e Gabbana often revealed the inspiration of the flashy suit of the Hollywood gangster, as Courtney Ritter shows, and were advertised through images of Scorsesian Italian American types of urban men, sensually thick-lipped, olive-skinned, defiant, and confrontational.[93]

Another example of the historical formation of a transnational Italian American taste, and the role of a transnational marketplace in shaping it, is provided by espresso coffee, a very poignant definer of Italian American identity. In an early episode of *The Sopranos*, two of Tony's middle-aged wiseguys, Paulie "Walnuts" Gualtieri and Salvatore "Pussy" Bonpensiero, find themselves in a fancy coffee shop where everyone orders lattes, caramel macchiatos, and decaf cappuccinos. Perplexed by the scene around him, Paulie, a memory-keeper of old-school Italian America, begins a tirade against "the rape of the culture" by white Americans. He rants that these Americans ate "pootsie" before Italians gave them the gift of their cuisine, and now reap the benefits of the immense popularity of Italian food—"pizza, calzone, *buffalo moozarell*, olive oil." "But this, this espresso shit, this is the worst," Paulie concludes, defiantly stealing an Italian coffee maker on the way out as his protest against cultural colonialism. Still, when Paulie says, "*we* invented this shit," he is appropriating a history whose origin cannot be correctly referred to an Italian American *we* (in the sense Paulie himself would understand the pronoun—the turn-of-the-twentieth-century southern Italian immigrants and their American-born children), but to a diasporic Italian *we* with its center in northern Italy.

To be sure, coffee has occupied a significant material as well as symbolic space in the Italian American experience from the very beginning. As a high-status commodity, only accessible on the market for cash, coffee—along with white wheat bread, beef, and sugar—was among the most dreamt-about goods for turn-of-the-twentieth-century rural Italians. Immigrants to America interpreted the possibility to consume such foods on an everyday basis as one of the most tangible, revolutionary, results of their migration project. Accordingly, they transformed coffee in their all-occasion and all-purpose drink. Social workers noted that a cup of strong black coffee was always offered to them when they visited Italian households and lamented that Italian parents always gave coffee to their children (sometimes with a sip of liquor in it) for breakfast.[94]

However—differently from Italian American staples like spaghetti and meatballs or veal parmigiana—espresso and cappuccino were not invented by anonymous cooks, such as Paulie's grandmothers, in Little Italy's modest tenement house apartments. Espresso originated in a Northern Italian, urban, public middle-class milieu and was premised on the development of a specific industrial technology. It was invented as late as 1905, when the Pavoni firm began manufacturing an Ideale coffee machine in Milan. The name of the coffee derived from its being prepared "expressly" for the individual customer by using steam to "express" hot water through the coffee. The espresso machine soon traveled to the United States, and by the 1920s it had become a ubiquitous feature of Italian restaurants in New York, conveying an effective idea of *modernity* with its chromium-plated appearance. After the war, espresso was further transformed by the introduction in 1948 of the Gaggia Classica machine, which used a hand-operated piston to drive the water through the coffee producing a shorter beverage topped by a cream of essential oils, and later by the appearance of the Faema E61 in 1960—a semi-automatic machine incorporating an electric pump operated by a simple switch.[95]

All these technologies and identities have further circulated transnationally between Italy and the United States, being *integrated* into Italian American culture, in a continuing series of diasporic borrowings, which transformed espresso in the distinctive, global Italian-style of coffee drinking that it is today. The history of espresso, and the loss of memory that associates it mistakenly to turn-of-the-twentieth-century immigrant origins, convey paradigmatically the transnational and multidimensional nature of the construction of Italian American identities in the marketplace. The unending transnational construction and reconfiguring of Italian American taste is what most effectively bridges the modern and postmodern experience of Italian American consumerism.

Making Italian America shows that for more than one century, Italian Americans of all walks of life have consistently shaped and publicly proclaimed their diasporic ethnic identity through consumption. They have thus constructed their collective identity less as an institutional political affiliation than as a community of taste united by a system of values embedded in things and shared consumer practices—with political valence. They have not done so in a vacuum, of course, but in a dialogic relationship with multiple others, and these multiple others have in turn consumed Italian American identities variously inscribed in commodified things, images, and experiences. In this society of the simultaneity, in which the past and the future are flattened and presentified, Italian Americans have a history, or better, many usable pasts of migration, transnationalism, and material and symbolic cultural production that very likely will continue to fulfill multicultural consumers' needs for time to come.

PART ONE

Immigrants Encounter and Remake
U.S. Consumer Society

The Shaping of Italian American Identities Through
Commodities and Commercial Leisure, 1900–1930

1

Visibly Fashionable

THE CHANGING ROLE OF CLOTHES IN THE EVERYDAY LIFE OF ITALIAN AMERICAN IMMIGRANT WOMEN

Vittoria Caterina Caratozzolo

There is more within me.
—GEORG SIMMEL, "FASHION" (1895)

Come all you foreigners and jump into this magic kettle. Your clothes, ugly and ill-fitting . . . will be exchanged for the last Fifth Avenue clothes. The magic process is certain.
—SIMON LUBIN AND CHRISTINA KEYSTO, "CRACKS IN THE MELTING POT" (1920)

In fashion, of course, part of the medium is always the live person experiencing its life.
—ANNE HOLLANDER, *SEX AND SUITS* (1994)

Dress is conventionally considered to be a second skin, bound up with the physical dimension of the body. However, such interpretation might imply naturalization disregarding that dress is also a historically determined cultural construction. This article will investigate the impact of dress-code changes upon early Southern Italian immigrant women in New York City at the turn of the twentieth century. The aim is to point out the twists and turns that marked the lives of these women during their passage from an artisanal mode of production, revolving around the family unit, into an industrial consumerist environment set in an urban culture. Sources range from movies, including Emanuele Crialese's *Nuovomondo* (*Golden Door*, 2006), photographs from Augustus Frederick Sherman's and Lewis W. Hine's archives as well as from my personal collection, and excerpts from texts by sociologists, fashion scholars, theorists of photography, writers, and immigrants' memoirs. The main subject of this chapter questions the stereotypical dichotomy between tradition and fashion and proposes, instead, an interpretation that blurs the boundary between these two semantic poles of clothing and offers a deeper understanding of migration phenomena as a theoretical issue, also relevant to the contemporary debate on these topics.

In the effort to study how early Italian immigrant women reconfigured their clothed identity upon their arrival in New York City, this chapter takes into account Alain Corbin's idea of "mechanisms driving emotions."[1] From his perspective, there are no means to unveil the possible feelings and behaviors of someone who lived in the past other than attempting to see through their eyes. Accordingly, photographs help fulfill the effort to retrieve the emotions of many ordinary people. Moreover, this chapter embraces Crialese's narrative, to which it is indebted throughout the following prologue, for the capacity to animate the gaze of migrants, and to highlight the theme of clothing before their crucial crossing of the ocean. In Crialese's *Nuovomondo*, clothing appears to be essential gear for entry into the New World, particularly as an element of empowerment associated with male characters. This lopsided approach in terms of gender stimulated my curiosity about why women, on their part, have put on their body the anxiety of leaving their homeland.

Prologue

"How'll you get to America? In rags? We have to arrive looking like princes!" exclaims *Golden Door*'s main male character, Salvatore Macaluso, while pulling apart his two scuffling young sons, Pietro and Angelo. Before embarking on the ship that will take them to the New World, they just received the few secondhand garments to present themselves at their best from the priest of their rural Sicilian village, Petralia Sottana. Shoes, cloaks, and hats were selected among several garments that once belonged to princes and brigands, considered the most influential people in the community at the time. In this cultural context, dress codes are meant to guarantee readability of the established social order inscribed into a patriarchal ideology. Any shift in clothing, therefore, would distort social function in that transparent regime.

For Salvatore Macaluso, secondhand garments appear endowed with the animistic power of affecting the wearer's spirit. Clothes maintain the formidable presence of their past owners, who are now conjured up to protect him and his family setting off for America. His two sons, however, cannot fully endorse this reassuring feeling. In fact, Pietro and Angelo regard this improvised wardrobe with a mix of repulsion and attraction. Their emotional response triggers an unexpected scuffle and results in a scattering of all their new clothing. How could their shabby, coarse, and fleece rags, responsive to both their everyday drudgery and daydream attitudes, be substituted with hats, trousers, and shoes already misshapen by different silhouettes and postures, human and social qualities, all narrating other bodies and different lifestyles? In the end, despite their sense of uneasiness, they cannot help but acquiesce and accept their turbulent, vestimentary experience as a mark of the unbalanced relationship between their feelings and the emergence of an appearance renegotiation. We can predict Pietro and Angelo's rite of passage to adulthood as well as to the New World will soon entail a significant change in their approach to clothing, both literally and figuratively. They undergo a transmutation that filters through a sartorial concern—the need for a new dress code able to fulfill their expectations free from any hierarchical connotation.

While the Macalusos' initial approach to immigrating soon precipitates into the palpable as well as the spiritual substance of clothing, their fellow female travelers Rita D'Agostino and Rosa Napolitano, two young villagers betrothed to Italian American bachelors, react differently to their impending existential turn. While the doctored photo-postcards representing the New World as a land of wonders with giant vegetables and golden *piccioli*-laden boughs beguile Rosa, the glittering propaganda sends dark reverberations across Rita's mind and body. Her decision to leave her homeland proves to be a curse; she cannot talk, sleep, or eat anymore, and she feels a snake twisting in her belly. A folk magic healer attempts to untie her from this *fascination* in order to help her recover.[2] Folk magic as a socially constructed practice, which was widespread throughout the rural Italian population, functions as a strategy for protecting people from the precariousness of life and the lack of rational alternatives to face human vicissitudes. Indeed, in their cultural role, magic rituals and their therapeutic influence provide Rita with a framework for the dramatization of her vulnerability and, at the same time, the preservation of her personal integrity. Unlike the Macaluso men—who unleash their emotional energy through clothing and elect them as a momentous step in their approach to America—Rita's main concern revolves around her own body and both the real and imaginary practices that her community reserves to it. In her experience, the body still maintains its cultural supremacy over the representative role of dress.

The movie ends before letting spectators know whether, once in the United States and far from the cultural latitude of magic folk rituals, Rita will be given the opportunity to go through a deeper and more self-conscious experience of clothing. Nonetheless ironically, in the fresh perspective offered by the New World, the fascinating role of clothes will soon represent a secular and commodified version of the old magic practice. The knack for dramatization of Italian immigrant women revives an enactment of their own performative selfhood in a different social and cultural context.

A Passage to Merica

The response of both male and female Italian migrants to their own departure from the homeland revolves mainly around the crosscutting narration of body and clothes as sensitive apparatuses of their visible and palpable presence at the intersection between the self and external reality. Yet, the art of appearance is not a paramount concern of their everyday life. Immigrant community is, in fact, far from considering the question of what to wear as a crucial aspect in the fashioning of their own self-image. At the time of the turn-of-century-mass migration wave, the culture of appearance in Italy was still a privilege of aristocratic and bourgeois elites interested in preserving their visible monopoly of social and financial prestige. By contrast, the bulk of the population—craftsmen, peasants, and destitute laborers—arranged its own aesthetic self-presentation within a repertoire of social and economic constraints, as well as a culturally defined suite of goods. They had access to a few garments apart from everyday basic items of clothing, those functional to their work routines, to the adorned regional costumes donned on ceremonies or festive occasions. Within this confined vestimentary regime, ritualized by the alternating rhythm of working days and holidays, the choice of a few details such as the color of ribbons or petticoats, as well as the design and pattern of embroidery, reflected the wearer's taste and mood. The limited possibility did not undermine the traditional dress structure—generally imbued with local inflections—or its main social and symbolic meanings. It existed, nonetheless, and played the significant role of signaling the wearer's own taste within the "common self-awareness and common memory" of the whole community.[3] Not only did individual choice concern some aspects of the dress design, but it also encompassed the realm of practical use. As a fluid practice in different social circumstances, the vibrant art of wearing demoted traditional dress to the order of fixed entities and uncontaminated authenticity, making it, over time, porous to inspirations and incorporations coming from different cultural styles and representations.

Along this trajectory, clothes may be perceived as extensions of the people who wear them, as Marshall McLuhan put it, and, as such, they make a special contribution to concurrent processes of identification and differentiation of individuals in their social interaction. However, any interpretation that would dehistoricize and naturalize the early attitude of Italian immigrants to clothing is misleading. Rather, it is in the wake of the reflection suggested by Elizabeth Wilson in her influential work *Adorned in Dreams* that the long cultural debate surrounding the close proximity between people and clothes requires further investigation. "A part of this strangeness of dress is that it links the biological body to the social being, and public to private. This makes it uneasy territory, since it forces us to recognize that human body is more than a biological entity. It is an organism in culture, a cultural artifact even, and its own boundaries are unclear. . . . Dress is the frontier between the self and the not-self. In all societies the body is 'dressed.'"[4]

As key requisite for any symbolic treatment and humanization of the living body, the antinaturalistic origin of clothing—in considering the differences which substantiate the dress codes of immigrants in their transition to a new clothing system—paves the way for an interpretive approach that would avoid the stereotyped simplification of situating them on both sides of the great divide between the semantic poles of traditional dress and fashion.[5] Under the umbrella of the Western-fashion hegemonic discourse, the stiff dichotomy of tradition and fashion styles produced mystifications about those who, not sharing a fully fashion-determined clothing system, appear to be doomed to the still immemorial pose of a purportedly immovable folklore, as people that "allegedly have no individuality, progress and . . . are 'exiled' from modernity."[6] By contrast, this chapter suggests that the reformulated clothing of immigrants, particularly of women, may be viewed as a manifestation of their dynamic and sometimes contradictory social practices and tactics, in the constant search to produce and negotiate their own shifting cultural subjectivity in a rapidly changing world.

In his groundbreaking essay "Fashion," first published in 1895 and reprinted in 1905, Georg Simmel clearly demonstrates how the active or passive presence outside the dominant fashion realm asserts a concurrent inhabitance of a different worldly space.[7] Since then, the history of cultural industry proves how this presence represented a source of inspiration for the latest fashion trends.[8] For instance, in 1987, about one hundred years after the turn-of-the-century early migration wave, the Dolce & Gabbana spring–summer collection revived, remodeled, and self-exoticized Sicilian garb worn by immigrant women, while Ferdinando Scianna's suggestive photos set in the sun-drenched streets of his native Sicily immortalized the trend. This kind of revival provides insight into how, over the past fifty years, fashion ransacked and cannibalized the past in search of usable images and styles, which are then, as Valerie Steele remarks, "ripped out of context . . . ruthlessly stripped of most of their original meaning."[9] Performing a patronizing "colonization" of past fashion styles and of visual elements drawn from different vestimentary traditions, the continuous rewriting on clothing made a decisive contribution to soften the perceived boundaries between fashion and costume. By contrast, more than one century ago, early Italian immigrant women's clothes were perceived and represented in America as visual and material signs of otherness, set against the backdrop of emergent forms of the mainstream mass-produced fashion.

Upon their arrival under the impressive shade cast by the Statue of Liberty, all immigrants' first direct contact with the United States happened at Ellis Island, the mandatory admission station since 1892, located a mile off the tip of Manhattan. Immediately, immigrants faced scrutiny directed toward their bodies and dresses. Passengers also submitted to medical inspections and mental tests that, according to medicalized inclusion/exclusion criteria whose biopolitical valence is not here accounted for, determined which immigrants were deemed worthy to go through "The Golden Door." From this study perspective, the deprivation of their clothing, as a symbolic treatment of the self and exposure to the anatomical determinateness, forced immigrants out of their "second skin" into a helpless status. Being precipitated into the perception of their body as an inexorable entity, they were not only prompted to feel how intimate the relationship between body and dress was, but also to become self-aware about such interaction. Shortly thereafter, their next steps into "La Merica" would make them conscious of how dress, now fully perceived as situated on the boundary between self and other, could in its ephemeral nature engage the body into a dynamic relationship. They would in addition become conscious of the fact that, differently from what they experienced about their received corporeity, the image of one's own dressed body could be revamped and even reinvented.

Arguably, this process of undressing and redressing can be also interpreted as a reenactment of "the endless quest for identity that enables our 'I' to engage in its work of self-construction, its search for an ideal image and for a legible identity that can actually be recognized by the Other."[10] In short, immigrants' severe experience of displacement and estrangement at Ellis Island paved the way for the process of their self-construction and future encounter with fashion—being indeed the ceaseless search for a satisfactory image of the self aligned in with the endless renewing of garments and thus with the fueling of fashion trends.[11]

Significant and dialogic relationships with others contextualized and marked the manner in which immigrants presented and posited themselves. Given this interlocutory scene, the complexities of varying layered relations between the self and the multitude of others straddled between two continents constitute a continuous narration and negotiation of dressed identities. Consequently, uses and meanings of clothes do not depend exclusively on their substantial structure and style, but also establish an ongoing cultural and social interaction. Along this trajectory of abstraction, the syncretism between person and dress has become more and more rootless, contingent, and inscribed on the surfaces of things and bodies. In this light, it is no coincidence that the elective and more significant vehicle of promotion became the photographic plate, written with light and emotionally responsive to ambience.

At Ellis Island, Italian immigrants experienced the impact of their clothed identities on the American public visual scene for the first time. Augustus F. Sherman, Chief Clerk at Ellis Island and amateur photographer, asked some immigrants, especially women, to wear their best native garb for his photographic sessions:

> As they wait, a little drowsy, a little nervous, a man approaches and introduces himself as Augustus Sherman. He tells them that he would like to take their picture, to photograph them—a concept they are not sure they understand. They follow him anyway. Perhaps if they refuse, it would not be a good idea. Perhaps it is yet another part of the entry process. He brings them into a room with a screen positioned in front of the window blocking the light. . . . "Do you have a special shawl that you would like to wear?" he asks. The woman's eyes brighten as she says, "Yes." Her most prized possession is a shawl given to her by her mother. She unfolds it and drapes it around her shoulders. The man then sets up a strange-looking box on legs, with a cloth draped over the back. In his right hand is an even stranger-looking device that he holds aloft. "Look at the camera," he intones, and it is rapidly translated into their native tongue. A flash, a blink of the eyes—something has happened for which the stranger is eternally grateful and the family, more than just a little puzzled, returns to the bench to wait for entry into a new life.[12]

At the threshold of the New World, Augustus F. Sherman celebrated Italian women, among many others immigrants, in their best holiday finery through his portraits. Even before these folk garments and accessories absorbed into New York's standard clothing and lifestyle, he knew the most traveled route by Italian immigrants, from Battery Park to the district of Mulberry below Fourteenth Street in Lower Manhattan, looked like a "sea of clothing."[13] The impressive image testified to the fact that, upon their arrival, relatives of immigrants invited them to drop, like empty cocoons, most of their old clothes along the walk. This ebb of native rags, however, ran parallel to the flood of new, readymade American clothes just released by the nearby Garment District huddle of blooming factories. Once included in the social texture of New York City, clothed identities underwent a further crucial transmutation. As one can appreciate from Sherman's photo collection, which accounts for the phantasmagoric first stage of these identities in transition, the Ellis Island platform offered a true spectacular gallery of characters. It was a unique time and space, a compressed presence of people from all over the world, captured in the flavor and the flagrancy of their differences through the language of clothes.

Sherman very likely perceived the impact of the vibrant and precious variety of styles that characterized immigrants by distinctively structuring their presence in the world. His urge to record those irreducible modes of identity stemmed from his consciousness that they would quickly fade into the homogenizing streams of Americanization and, in particular, under the conforming dictates of fashion. From this point of view, his photographic drive seems neither to fulfill a cataloguing task nor to represent an exotic visit to the lives of others. His gaze, rather, highlighted how, at the gate of New York City, humankind revealed itself as a multitude whose appearance was plural, varied, and lively. As Susan Sontag remarked about American photographers in general, Sherman's stance seems characterized by the fact that he, like many of his coeval and renowned colleagues—notably, Jacob Riis and Lewis W. Hine—did not rely on "the permanence of any basic social arrangements," and was an expert "on the 'reality' and inevitability of change."[14] From this perspective, the newly popularized photographic technology played a significant role in the reconfiguration of immigrants' appearance. Sherman's photographs preserve the memory of traditionally clothed identities while processing the dematerialization of those very identities and introducing immigrants to a representational regime. In other words, the experience of immigration encompasses the capability to conceive and familiarize with your own self as "other." Immigrants explored a deeper form of self-dramatization as a necessary step to perform a "radicant" subjectivity—which meant they would set their roots in motion and jeopardize traditional figures and signs, according to Nicolas Bourriaud's definition.[15] The phantom side of the self and its history converged in a fictionalized projection, which materialized in a new clothed identity. This conceptual passage marked the opportunity to enter a new vestimentary regime, one hinged on the preliminary imaginative dimension of consumption.[16]

Sherman's interest in both representational registers of dress and image provides a different view of Italian immigrants, particularly female immigrants. The fanciful scarf used as a headwear emphasized their traditional dress, while the aura emanating from their style ritualized the photo session. Posing in their best apparel—a white pagoda-sleeve shirt blooming from a bodice over a dark gathered skirt with a colorful woven silk sash—Italian women bore witness to their survival after crossing the "big ocean" and celebrated their admission to the New World. In the urban scenario of New York City, however, their best Italian garb, rich in tactile and visual substance, expressed a remote craftsmanship deeply ingrained in social customs that clashed with the emergent mass-manufactured styles of the new social and cultural context. So, it comes as no surprise that a coeval portrait by Lewis Hine of an Italian woman in her regional attire at Ellis Island was titled "Madonna," reflecting the traditional Italian iconography of both religious and noble figures.

Transfixed into a romanticized past, Italian women's most representative apparel conveyed its untranslatable alterity. The shot consigned its luminous trace to the entropy of the individual and collective memory and doomed it to a future reclassification as a costume in an ethnic museum display case.

Encountering American Clothing

In rural Italy, photography was mainly a posthumous act, which registered a physical image at a passing moment, while in America immigrants began to appreciate photographs for their own use. Photographs marked a key passage toward a new citizenship, a change of approach, which worked synchronically to their change of clothes. During

Figure 1.1. Augustus Frederick Sherman, *Italian Woman*. Courtesy of Aperture Foundation and Statue of Liberty National Monument/Ellis Island Immigration Museum.

the early years of mass Italian immigration, the act of posing for an individual or group portrait in one of the many photography studios on The Bowery was a vital sign of adaptation to the uses of the recently adopted country. By wearing fresh, fashionable clothes, immigrants relied on the photographer, whose work included the arrangement of the scene to demonstrate immigrants' first public representation as "American-looking" people. Like a contemporary stylist, the photographer set up a picturesque backdrop and kept "a stock supply of jewelry and watches that the client could borrow as props if he or she had yet to acquire these emblems of prosperity."[17] The photos were then sent, as postcards, to relatives and friends back home as a personal statement of self-improvement and respectability. It is no coincidence that photography as a medium of mass presentation and communication, as Susan Sontag pointed out, always plays a central role in social interactions: "Photographs taken in the nineteenth and early twentieth centuries rarely fail to make visible markers of status. We associate this with posing. . . . With posing, whether in a studio or in pictures of people taken on the sites of work and recreation, there can be a conscious construction of what is seemly, appropriate, attractive."[18]

The visually communicative languages of dress and photography provided immigrants with easy and affordable technologies crucial to revamping their appearances.

Figure 1.2. Portrait of Catherine Ciccone, mid-1920s. Personal collection of the author.

Most of the photos sent to Italy in those years indeed represented how immigrants participated in a modern networked reality. Not only did these media prove of paramount importance in the process of consent and alignment to the American mainstream culture and values undertaken by immigrants, but they also offered, according to Marshall McLuhan, a significant contribution to "a new codification of experience collectively achieved by new habits and inclusive collective awareness."[19] From this vantage point, both fields of clothing and photography expose the ambivalent quality of being "dispositifs," in Michel Foucault's phrase, of independent self-making as well as of adherence to mainstream models and standards. The American promise of emancipation from both poverty and the configuration of elites in Europe were now caught between these two confronting poles of experience. The articulated process of Italian immigrant women's social and cultural integration contemplated acts of compliance as well as acts of resistance that, through an array of intergenerational positions, accounted for their extensive empowerment in both private and public life. Hybrid attitudes punctuated their transition into a new clothing regime. Driven by social reformism and mirrored by "the urge to appropriate an alien reality," Lewis Hine and Jacob Riis contributed to a detailed representation of the Italian colony's life since the late nineteenth century while documenting their relocated endeavors.[20] Even though their social documentation paved the way for discriminatory and "policing narratives," their account of female immigrants' everyday practices still works as a useful source of information for greater participative and "ethnopathic" interpretations.[21]

A 1912 photo by Lewis Hine testifies to the way Italian immigrant women began to modify their life and self-display. It depicts a woman advancing at a brisk pace along the streets of the Lower East Side of Manhattan to deliver her homework, a bundle of just finished garments carried on her shoulders. She is wrapped in her tartan worn-out shawl over a full striped skirt with a checkered apron. Her clothing is similar to the drudgery uniform she used to wear in the Old World, except for the unusual presence of a pocketbook she firmly holds in her left hand. Although it is just a simple accessory of her outfit, this little object succeeds in revamping her traditional appearance by attracting the viewer's gaze. Her energetic gesture, which challenges and balances the exhaustion etched on her face, is too resolute to be confined to the simple reasons of usefulness or vanity represented by the pocketbook. Escaping any definite interpretation, the driving force of that gesture moves her as well as the viewer into a "blind field," where each reciprocally "animates" the other.[22] One wonders whether the use of the pocketbook might be her tactical device against drudgery and exploitation, a projection of her fantasy-self into quite a different lifestyle, or, instead, her response to the emergent marketing ploys and strategies of enticement, which home in on desire, as a pivotal factor in producing a new consumer consciousness. What is truly surprising about her performance is that she is no longer part of the faceless, interchangeable multitude of foreign bodies at work, captured by Hine and Riis. In fact, she gains visibility by carving out an interstitial personal style for herself, which highlights her quotidian creative way of knitting together material objects, behaviors, and circumstances conventionally separated in the stereotypical representation of Italian immigrant working women.

Fresh and imaginative forms of self-fashioning connected the experiences and the contingencies of earning a living in the attempt to afford a better quality of life—one of the main reasons Italian women migrated to the United States. At the turn of the twentieth century, they flocked in droves to work in the flourishing Lower East Side sweatshops and factories, especially in the garment industry. In her autobiography, Edna Woolman Chase, the authoritative editor-in-chief of *Vogue* from 1914 to 1952, highlighted the development of fashion in the United States, a process generated mostly by the synergetic action of both the growth of the garment industry and the essential contribution of immigrants:

> The element primarily responsible for fashion's change of pace in America was . . . the enormous expansion of the women's garment industry, the ready-to-wear, that giant growth with branches all over the country but with the roots deep in New York, deep as the foundations of the Seventh Avenue skyscrapers. . . . The great factor in the building of the garment industry, besides the sewing-machine, the cutting-knife, and other purely mechanical advances, was the waves of immigrants who poured into the country. . . . In 1900 the Italian needleworkers arrived, but for the last two decades of the century most of those who came were from Central and Eastern Europe.[23]

Interestingly, in 1905 according to Miriam Cohen findings in a sample from the state census,

Figure 1.3. Lewis W. Hine, *Woman Bearing Home Work on Her Head*, ca. 1912. Courtesy Library of Congress.

46 percent of all single Italian-born women over the age of sixteen were wage earners, twice the percentage for all single American women over the age of sixteen. Moreover, nearly the 62 percent of women between the ages of sixteen and twenty-one, the largest group of single women living at home, reported occupations to the New York State census takers. In 1925 matters had changed little: 43 percent of all single first-generation women worked outside the home, and the younger women again reported higher rates of gainful employment. Among the second-generation women, nearly 61 percent listed occupations. Italian families in New York did not insist that wage–earning daughters stay home to work rather than go to a factory. Homework was reserved for young children and mothers. . . . The U.S. Bureau of labor reported that half of the female shop force in the men's garment industry was Italian, and for the clothing industry as a whole (both men's and women's clothing), one-quarter to one-third of the female employees were Italian, the largest single ethnic group. The overall work patterns for Italians show just how well the women responded to employment opportunities. The fashion industry—garments, millinery, and artificial flowers—accounted for 80 percent of Italian female workers in 1905. In 1925, 64 percent of all Italian women (averaged for first and second generation) worked in the fashion industry, while another 21 percent in other factories.[24]

As a formidable working-class presence, Italian women experimented with the factory site as the most cogent path to "Americanization": "Perhaps the chief evidence of Americanization . . . appears when the daughter of the family begins wage-earning. For this she goes directly to the factory."[25] It represented the cutting-edge system of a confrontation; on one hand, it was a powerful structure to "fit" immigrants into the American life and make them active participants in the building of the nation, while on the other hand, the factory provided immigrants with the opportunity to manipulate the dominant apparatuses, adapting them to their personal process of cultural translation and material appropriation. The factory acted as both a disciplining dispositif and "a primary means for internalizing habits and practices."[26] The undertaking challenged Americanization in those years because, as Elizabeth Ewen pointed out, it meant "also the initiation of people into an emerging industrial and consumer society." That process extended beyond the immigrants themselves and concerned "the lives of most of the people who might be called Americans," producing sweeping changes in the nature and the quality of their daily life.[27] From this perspective, Italian immigrant women, and especially the younger ones, pursued the construction of their self-expressive identity by both enacting mutable, creative, and tactical *uses* of the dominant-order dispositifs, and, concurrently, by contrasting their family patriarchal-oriented conception of women as male-dependent and yet pivot of the whole domestic economy.[28] Thus, their early years of immigration were characterized by many conflicting phases in the attempt to conquer agency and to produce new meanings of accepting or refusing representations and rituals performed within a shared social space.

In her *Workshop to Office*, Miriam Cohen argues that the entrance to the factory workforce was a direct way of approaching peer culture and making new friends for young Italian immigrant women: "For Italians, as for other employed women, working in a group of women allowed many the first opportunity to speak freely with peers outside the presence of their elders. Within this female world they discussed current boyfriends or the latest romantic novels and magazines."[29] While conversations with workmates provided them new images and roles to present themselves on the public sphere, the apprehension of "patterns of speech, manners, level of schooling, attitudes"[30] offered them ways of appropriating the cultural forms and the recreational activities now available—from clothing to movies, from social clubs to dance halls. The fashioning power of socialization had a deep impact on their path to self-improvement as the social reformer Josephine Roche testified in her touching "The Italian Girl" (1914), although she also remarked that the daily toil, household chores, and cultural family constraints allowed average Italian girls to experiment and enjoy only limited forms of autonomy and leisure:

> Against this strictness of another land are constantly beating all the news, free customs of America. The conflict begins as soon as Carlotta gets her working papers and takes her place in the factory. Inevitably the influences of the new life in which she spends nine hours of the day begin to tell on her. Each morning and each evening, as she covers her head with an old crocheted shawl and works through and from the factory, she passes the daughters of her Irish and American neighbors in their smart hats, their cheap waists in the latest and smartest style, their tinsel ornaments, their gay hair-bows.

A part of the contents of their pay envelops goes into the personal expenses of those girls. Nor do they hurry through the streets to their homes after working-hours, but linger with a boy companion making "dates," for a "movie" or an "affair." Slowly but surely their example is beginning to have its effect on the docile little Italian whose life has hitherto swung like a pendulum back and forth between her labors at the factory and the duties and restraints of home. She begins to long for the same freedom that the other girls enjoy. But freedom does not mean for her, what it means for the American girl, trained in a different school from the beginning. She has not the same hard little powers of resistance, nor can she make the same truculent boast of being able to "take care of herself."[31]

Yet, Josephine Roche's comments did not fail to record that even though economic necessity opened the factory's doors to the Italian girl, it did not "make her otherwise more independent of her family" and that "the economic as well as the emotional basis" of her kin represented "a valiant front to the forces of personal independence that me[e]t her American life, at school, in industry, and in recreation." As social reformer, Roche advocated a social endeavor to reduce the gap between the Italian girl and the lifestyles of "her American sisters": "the community to which she has come, bringing her all—her health, her strength, her industry, and her children—owes it at least to her to safeguard the innocent joys of her youth."[32] Roche's benevolent drive was to be soon crosscut by the tough, empirical action of the garment industry.

Social worker Louise C. Odencrantz's study *Italian Women in Industry* (1919) helps explore some of the ambivalences that characterized the relationship between Italian immigrant women and the Lower East Side garment factories in the early twentieth century. She points out, for instance, how the minute subdivision of work that informed the mass-production model of the garment industry did not allow a full valorization of those skilled dressmakers trained in Italy, in public or convent schools: "Few of the Italian women who had learned to do fine hand embroidery in Italy were employed on a process where this knowledge was of value to them. Although a number were employed in the needle trade, the majority was doing unskilled finishing. . . . A finisher of dresses complained that she had to learn the trade all over again when she came here because in Italy there was more handsewing, and no subdivision of processes. If one worked fast there, people would say that the work was badly done and everyone was thought to do as beautiful sewing as possible."[33] This organization of labor, as stigmatized by Odencrantz, established the model of the assembly-line manufacturing process, which is not only the emblematic representation of the capitalistic production, but also "the aesthetic reflex of the rationality to which the prevailing economic system aspires," as Siegfried Kracauer put it.[34] If the affirmation of a mechanized and fragmented work conception contributed to enhance the values of speed, repetition, and quantity, the American way of production marked, from a different perspective, a decisive step toward the democratization of fashion. This phenomenon consisted of a concoction of economic, aesthetic and conceptual elements, which affected the life and taste of Italian immigrant women. Initially, many of them, frustrated by the assembly-line procedures that determined a minute subdivision and specialization of labor tasks, disregarded their Italian sartorial tradition as well as their ambition to learn how to make a whole garment:

"Coats go through forty-odd processes in the making. There is no such thing as a tailor in the ready-made business now."[35] Later, however, the loss of the holistic conception about the making of the garment as well as the dissociation of commodity from the idea of labor made a substantial contribution to the shift of their involvement from production to consumption. The more they became skilled bushelers, operators, drapers, and pressers, and thus confined to the same tedious and fragmented work—Odencrantz pointed out that "these words were 'Italianized' on the Italian newspapers' advertisements because they had no equivalent terms referring to specialized occupations which did not exist in Italy"—the more they were attracted by the fashion display apparatuses, from advertising to shop-windows, which initiated them to the imaginative pleasure of consumption as a central aspect of the increasing capitalism economy.[36] In her inspiring work *Immigrant Women in the Land of Dollars*, Elizabeth Ewen reported the daydream activity that punctuated Adriana Valenti's repetitive work gestures, allowing her to imaginatively refashion the meaning and the pleasure of the production/consumption nexus: "I'd make up stories in my mind while I'm working. I'd say, 'What kind of person's going to wear this dress. Is she a good person? Where is she going to go?' . . . you are creating something and someone is going to enjoy."[37]

This experiential discontinuity, however, did not make Italian immigrant women swing from everyday life toils to the fascination with the commodity form. On their path to full citizenship, the amelioration of their working-class status became indeed more and more one of their major concerns. As mentioned, for young women in their teens and twenties, garment factories were not only the venue of their first forms of socialization and conviviality outside the domestic space of tenement buildings, but also an arena for playing out their social role as actively engaged in the conflicts connected to the public sphere of labor. While, on one hand, being factory workers marked their cultural distance from "the homebound history of their mothers,"—introducing those girls to new habits and consumer values; on the other, it meant "an education in exploitation . . . and in excesses of discipline"—as witnessed by Grace Grimaldi in her description of the work condition in a blouse-making factory: "You couldn't open your mouth. God forbid you came five minutes late or they'd actually throw you out of the place. . . . You couldn't even go to the bathroom. We were treated like slaves. I worked for Scher Brothers—a place people of my generation never forgot. He was a real slavedriver. He used to pick people from the boat and use them for slavery. But people had to earn. So when you want to earn your own, you take anything."[38] These complaints, far from being the solely emotive response of a young woman suffering everyday toil, were some decades later confirmed by her contemporary Edna Woolman Chase. In her 1954 autobiography, she passionately expressed her the predatory vein of fashion productive system in its emerging phases: "The early history of garment industry is not pretty. The exploitation of workers went on with a ruthless disregard of human rights, a ruthless exhaustion of human energy, akin to the rape of the land, when in savage pursuit of wealth the railways and the oil and the mining interests cut down the forests and destroyed the earth. Still the business grew."[39] Woolman Chase's criticism—still resonating as a severe warning about the impact of our present globalized fashion industry on our human and environmental vulnerability—was reformulated and detailed in Elizabeth Ewen's analysis of the average intolerable conditions in early garment factories: "A twelve to fourteen-hours day was common. Workers were often cheated out of their full wages—clocks were slowed down during working hours and sped up at lunchtime. Works were charged for needles, thread, mistakes, and even electrical power (if there was any). . . . The sanitary conditions were deplorable, the working conditions unsafe; floors collapsed in small lofts incapable of carrying the weight of machines and people, the doors were locked when work began, and shop fires were common."[40] In a later study, however, Nancy C. Carnevale highlights how, comparatively speaking, new factories' conditions were certainly better than what, from the late nineteenth to the early twentieth centuries, afflicted married Italian women and their children at home. At war with misery, they labored over garments in their squalid tenement apartments striving night and day to save money, cent by cent, crouched over buttonholes and skirts to hem. In those years, they represented about 98 percent of all home finishers in New York City. Or, also, better than women engaged in finishing garments in sweatshops still located in tenement living quarters "under the watchful eye of their often exploitative compatriot, the contractor."[41]

In the early 1900s, new garment factories began supplanting tenement sweatshops that declined progressively under the effects of the 1892 law forbidding the manufacture of garments in tenements by nonfamily members.[42] Interestingly, however, though homework system was often under attack by reformers, unions and regulatory agencies, it resisted any opposition:

> Nothing was able to eradicate the practice completely in this period. This speaks to the economic importance of homework at that time, both to the garment industry and to the homeworkers themselves. Contrary to common understanding, homework was not "a residual form of production" left over from preindustrial times; rather, it was integral to the industrial revolution in the core of capitalist economies. It also reflects the weakness of unions—which, together with the New Deal government of the 1930s, were finally able to bring homework at an end, at least for some time. Italian homeworking women remained largely invisible to New York State legislation, who in essence refused to recognize the women as workers and legislate accordingly. Just as in the case of sweatshops, most legislation around homeworkers in the garment industry was aimed at protecting consumers rather than workers.[43]

According to this narrative about the impact of work conditions on Italian-American women workers, the garment world—production and consumption strategies included—was broad enough to contain contradictions and complications. The novelty with Italian young women who began their work life in factories, and particularly in shirtwaist factories, consisted in their being consciously involved in this complexity: their continuous attempt to find solutions and to negotiate their new social and cultural position, as well as their aspirations. Wearing the neat and svelte shirtwaists they themselves produced after the drawings of Charles Dana Gibson, as an icon of the new emancipated and active woman, they pursued new models of agency aiming at the visibility denied to their mothers. As a true product of the American ingenuity in clothing design—a basic and versatile model that combined blouse and skirt, adaptable to every life circumstance and affordable to everyone—the shirtwaist revealed to be the suited uniform when they audaciously took part in struggles against exploitative and demeaning conditions. In her innovative work on Italian female activists in New York City Garment Trades from 1890s to 1940s, Jennifer Gugliemo discusses the historiographical sources that portray Italian women as passive and nonmilitant because of their scarce participation in the 1909 "Uprising of 20,000." The strike orchestrated by the Jewish women workers who "responded to the reluctance of the ILGWU' s [International Ladies Garment Workers' Union] male leaders to support them by aligning themselves with middle-class progressive and feminist activists in the Women's Trade Union League (WTUL)."[44] Guglielmo, revising scholars' conclusion that Italian garment workers did not join the strike en masse because they were "unorganized and unsympathetic to the union movement," contends that such scarce participation was in part due to the fact "they were not convinced that either the ILGWU or the WTUL were committed to their particular struggles."[45] Italian women played instead a pivotal role in workplace actions and "their ability to organize co-workers and neighbors often proved crucial in winning labor struggles, especially in clothing and textile industries, where they outnumbered men in the rank and file."[46] And indeed, one year later, they became visible participants in the 'Great Revolt' of 50,000 cloak–makers. Moreover, Guglielmo counters also historians' assumption that Italian women "could only be organized after and with the support of Italian men." Indeed, she highlighted how after the 1910 strike, Italian women not only consolidated their activism, but also "formed the majority in the newly formed Organizational Committee of the Italian Branch of the ILGWU, which became the Italian Branch, or Local 25, after the 1913 strike."[47] Their organization and tasks revealed to be impressive: "Organizers met with workers in community meetings, and found work in garment shops that were non-union. They visited women and listened to their grievances, brought them into the union, and encouraged them to shape and direct the movement— all at the risk of arrest and beatings from employers and police. They planned workplace committees, distributed leaflets, and ran educational and publicity programs, cultural activities, demonstrations, strikes, picket lines, soup kitchens, and theatre troupes. Organizers used key newspapers, such as the popular socialist Italian-language weekly *L'Operaia* (to which thousands of women garment workers were subscribers by 1914), to create a community of *lavoratrici coscienti* (politically informed or 'conscious' women workers)."[48] Could one imagine a more vigorous treatment for the shock caused by the Triangle Shirtwaist Company fire that in 1911 claimed the lives of 145 young immigrant seamstresses?

Positioned at the crucial intersection of reproduction, production and consumption, Italian women workers not only did embody and cope with the conflicts engendered by the emerging fashion system's power, but they also participated in the "American ideals of democratic action."[49] In so doing, they went beyond the mere struggle for survival as their incisive motto: "Bread and Roses" revealed.

Migrating into Mainstream Fashion

Because of a varied conception of clothing, fashion became the seductive place to experiment with opportunities about self-appearance. For Italian immigrant women, a more articulated interaction between body and dress represented a way to emancipate themselves from a costume designed to mark and enhance patriarchal ideals of modesty and fertility. Through their work at the assembly line, immigrant women perceived that their bodies were no longer unique shapes to be measured with the scale of strict domestic ideology but, rather, members of size groups that sounded paradoxically liberating.

With the advent of standardized sizing, body configuration underwent a process of geometrical abstraction, which questioned the strict dependence of dress to body. New clothing lines emancipated subjection to the bodylines and proportions of the past. The real structure of the garment coincided with its technological construction and acted cognate to the streamlined trait of the modernist aesthetic. This cultural shift proved to be an essential premise to the development and the democratized expansion of fashion. This shift, in fact, designed individuality out of sameness and out of participation in common styles of clothing. As Georg Simmel puts it, "It is peculiarly characteristic of fashion that it renders possible a social obedience, which at the same time is a form of individual differentiation."[50] The phenomenon of fashion is indeed marked by the basic irony of being supposedly about singularity, while it pursues more effectively social uniformity. In 1962, Roland Barthes reformulated this contradiction in his influential essay "Le dandysme et la mode," specifying that fashion intervenes in the social arena as "an intermediary power between the absolute individual and the total mass of society . . . modern democratic society has made fashion into a sort of cross-subsidizing organism, destined to establish an automatic equilibrium between the demand for singularity and the right for all to have it."[51] Interestingly, Italian immigrant women inhabited a particular position in which they experienced, across a short span of time, the dramatic passage from the constraints of costume to the excitement of the standardized dress, consumed into the new collective arena of identities in transition. They lived a novel experience that later normalized the conventional rules and dysfunctions of a consolidated fashion consumerism.

In the 1920s, designers such as Madeleine Vionnet, Coco Chanel, and Jean Patou launched styles that, scorning restrictive and redundant ornamental styles, emphasized clothes' functional features and stressed the fabrics' performance. Thus, they paved the way for simpler silhouettes, whose more comfortable and free-fitting lines granted women greater freedom of movement and the necessary degree of practicality and easy elegance.

Interestingly, in 1911, some years before the full affirmation of the modernist aesthetic in fashion, Matilde Serao wrote a surprising editorial dedicated to sequins, on *Il Progresso Italo-Americano* front page. It was a very curious topic even for a sartorial concern. The article was titled "È stata vinta?" and focused on the presumed disappearance of sequins, which had functioned as a precious decorative element for evening gowns throughout the previous decade.[52] Her theme hinged upon the question of whether sequins would be substituted by *voilage*—bias-cut layers of lightweight material—as the avant-garde sartorial invention to create bewitching effects of impalpable volume without the use of superfluous decorative motifs. In questioning, she announced and promoted the coming fashion lines. Had she also already envisioned, one may wonder, that, only a few years later, the modernist fashion was to deeply influence American women and Italian immigrant women alike? Indeed, thanks to the new styles, all became aware that dresses, now supple as a second skin, could cling gently to their body and therefore engage it in a vast array of mutable imaginative performances, as illustrated in personal photo collections.

Again, photography works as a medium to transfix a moment of pivotal changes. A wedding photo from the mid-1920s belonging to my personal collection depicts a family party of three generations of Italian Americans. Among them are the bride, two women, and a little girl. They exemplify how they have incorporated American standard lifestyles. The bridal dress line, inspired by the fashion trends of the time, is in pure flapper style with a shapeless bodice, dropped waist and short skirt. The headdress, richly beaded, reflects the trendy close-fitting-cloche model with a veil of silk illusion flowing into a royal train. The bride's sister wears an audacious sleeveless dress in the same 1920s style perfectly mirrored by her crimped hair. Differently, their mother's silk *charmeuse* dress, with its lacy V-shaped collar, adheres to a more conservative style in tune with her too severe expression for that joyful moment. At her feet, her granddaughter, in a nonchalant legs-crossed pose, resembles a flapper in miniature. Their distinct attitudes tell us of a different engagement with the material world of fashion. All of them seem to have accepted the idea that looking like an American means to put on style. Yet, the grandmother's body language partially disavows this general consideration. While her daughters' attitudes reveal that they have conspicuously appropriated mainstream fashion lines, conveying their renegotiated personal and social identity through the nonverbal communication of dress and body, she resists wearing fashionable clothes as an expression of her own identity. Assuming a stiff, assertive posture—stressed by her reluctant expression, and her gray hair parted in the middle and pulled back—she conveys through visual signs her emotional belonging to her past representative register. Her attitude brings to mind the archetypical great-grandmother, Umbertina, the founder of four generations of Italian American women, and eponymous character of Helen Barolini's paradigmatic novel. Like most first generation immigrant women brought up in a modest register of dress and appearance, she refuses to indulge in excessive self-adornment except for family events or religious festivities. Interestingly, the following passage from *Umbertina* describes the significant encounter between the protagonist and Mrs. Brown, who is, in Umbertina's opinion, the epitome of the American woman. Mrs. Brown apparel, considered a mere frivolous attribute of the body, does not attract Umbertina's eyes. The true target of her severe gaze is, instead, Mrs. Brown's body. The excerpt offers a cultural confrontation of bodies, those regarded as "dressed" entities, in key with Umbertina's conceptualization of her own body as a piece of garment:

> Umbertina would nod and smile and say, "yessa, yessa" to Mrs. Brown when they met, but she would be thinking to herself how ugly American women were—so sharp and angular with thin little faces and pinched noses and lips; she wondered how they gave birth from such bony frames. She herself had girth; she rounded and billowed beneath her full skirt despite the hard work. She wore no corsets as the other Italian women did, but let herself flow in generous waves of flesh.[53]

The clash of cultural clothing codes was a main cause of contention between mothers who continued to preserve the old patriarchal way of life and daughters who raced

Figure 1.4. Wedding portrait, mid-1920s. Personal collection of the author.

toward new Americanized forms of fashion. Maria Franzetti complained about the tension that eroded her own conception of the Italian family: "My children misunderstand me when I advise them what style of clothes they should wear. I blame styles and clothes on some of the stuff in magazines and the movies of this country. If I had my way I would like my children to follow some of the old disciplinary laws of the old country."[54] Josephine Roche provided another example of transgressive response to the family's cultural restraints in her "The Italian Girl": "Filamina Moresco, whose calm investment of $25 in a pink party dress, a beaver hat, and a willow plume was reported as a little less than act of a brigand."[55]

Yet, this generational conflict did not prevent the gradual growing engagement with fashion that paralleled immigrant women's constant upward social and economic mobility. In spite of any claimed devotion to patriarchal values, mothers themselves blurred the boundaries among gendered roles within the context of families' economic conditions. Susan Porter Benson concurs:

> The evidence suggests that gender figured in both breadwinning and consumption in ways that defied as well as confirmed conventional gender expectations. The male breadwinning ethic was far from universal among these families. . . . Many women felt

an obligation to earn some or all of the family support, even when husbands and/or fathers were present and earning. . . . Virtually every Women's Bureau study and every collection of family case studies provide examples of gender-boundary crossing . . . in families linked to every industry studied, and in families of all origins. . . . Working-class partnership marriages involved definite, if subtle and partial, breaching of the boundaries between gender roles. These breaches came about not because of a belief in some abstract notion of gender equality but because the material conditions of life in the American working class reinforced some people's willingness to improvise and to put order goals above the maintenance of dominant-culture gender constructions. Working-class people made adjustments in one area of their lives in order to relieve pressures and lighten burdens originating in other areas of their lives.[56]

The shift from being a mere contributor to the family economic improvement, by working indoor as well as outdoor, to the self-consciousness of being a wage-earner was a decisive step in the direction of immigrant women's economic independence. It, there-fore, had an immediate effect on their consumption practices: "For these women, bread-winning was not just a way to have more money, but also a way to have 'different' money. . . . Many women earned wages in order to move from a plane of bare existence to a level where small extras and humble luxuries enhanced their lives."[57] Interestingly, Miriam Cohen gave further account of the family's negotiating strategies and tactics over working daughters' wages:

> Like working-class women from other ethnic groups, Italian women spent more money on clothes than did other members of the family. Italian families spent only about 15 percent of the family income in clothing, but, according to one study, female wage earners spent from 20 to 25 percent of their earnings on clothing. Daughters usually turned over their pay to their mothers, but this did not mean that they lost control of their income. Where family permitted, working daughters openly set aside a portion of their income for personal clothing expenses because they knew that daughters could and would secretly withhold wages if conflicts arose. In this way Italian parents made concessions to the realities of wage labor and to the fact that their daughters had the desire for and ready access to the artefacts of popular culture.[58]

In the early twentieth century, New York City rivaled Paris and London as the new world city of fashion and became a vivacious center of commercial culture destined not only to elite fashion consumption but also, admittedly, conceived to conquer mass mar-ket customers to fashion clothing and imagery. It was no surprise that women from an immigrant milieu could afford the latest styles from Paris. William Leach pointed out how American urban retailers sent fashion buyers overseas to get the rights to repro-duce the models from Paris couturiers "for a broader, less affluent clientele at exactly one-third the cost. The upper class French trade, in other words, became an American mass market."[59] Moreover, this commercial expansion made New York City the site of an unprecedented democratization of fashion through the extension of Simmel's trickle-down social theory. It was an enlarged spatial dimension where displayed glamorous goods could *fascinate* new consumers. Georg Simmel defined a new emphasis placed on the art of commodity presentation in his review of the Berlin Trade Fair in 1896 as "the shop-window quality of things." The production of goods thus yielded to the production of customers and the emergence of shopping as a leisure activity: "Shopping was no longer about satisfying basic needs, but about creating new needs."[60] Immediately upon arrival in the New World, Italian immigrant women perceived how a new set of clothes could magically liberate them from their greenhorn status. They became more and more encouraged in their primary insight and were soon involved in consumption practices. Female immigrants bargained for fashion items with peddlers, who, well versed in the latest display strategies, transformed public thoroughfares into semiprivate changing rooms with mannequins, mirrors, folding chairs and carpets. As their taste and desire for the best readymade clothing became mature, they would spend hours enjoying the powerful entertainment of the dazzling department stores where they would buy ready-made clothes and accessories, paying cash or utilizing an installment plan. Another passage from *Umbertina* helps to visualize a scene of conspicuous consumption in the swirl of urban rhythms of the period: "Before she was married, had two fur coats and several Paris gowns from Marvin Miller. . . . She and Sara spent every Saturday afternoon going downtown shopping, and on their way they would stop for a minute at the shrine of St. Rita to pray for good fortune in courtship."[61]

Like the fictional characters of Umbertina and her two daughters, many early Italian immigrant women experienced, through conflicts as well as through progressive phases of education and acculturation, the multifaceted world of fashion not only as a medium for their integration but also as a performative device invested with the emotional charge that accompanied their relocation into the new cultural context. The transformative power of fashion fueled their participation into both challenges and opportunities offered by the urban commodity culture of modernity. Fashion revealed indeed to be a pliant social medium to recast their subjectivity as a practice rather than a given condition—a dynamo of processes of distinction and self-cultivation indoor as well as outdoor. As a collective phenomenon, fashion affected the social fabric and offered to the whole citizenship a common language imbued with the burning sense of the present—a spatial-temporal conflation determined by the collective fascination with the dictate of the latest clothing styles. Embracing the industrial formula of the culture of appearance and beauty—included the seduction of the new cosmetics—meant therefore to be engaged in a "gluing" social experience "by which we are read and come to read others, however unstable and ambivalent these readings may be."[62]

At this intersection of private and public life, fashion consumption represented for Italian American immigrant men and women the ready medium not only to experience modern subjectivity, but also to explore how agency in consumption was at the core of the complex and controversial relationship between democratic citizenship and market strategies. From this standpoint, it is worth touching upon the fashion panorama immediately after the decades that marked the blooming of garment industry. Since the 1930s, a group of insightful, independent designers, mostly women, addressed their perception of apparel to reinventing it as a pragmatic and democratic art, independent from Paris designers' style. In the 1998 exhibition *American Ingenuity. Sportswear 1930s–1970s*, the fashion theorist Richard Martin, curator of the Costume Institute of The Metropolitan Museum of Art from 1993 to 1999, advanced the idea that these insightful designers "were the pioneers of gender equity, in their useful, adaptable clothing, which was both made for the masses and capable of self-expression."[63] It comes as no surprise that this American reformulation of clothing culture paralleled the Great Depression years: "This period saw the transition to consumer-oriented policies in response to public demands grounded in the recognition that to be a fully enfranchised citizen meant being a consumer and participating fully in the consumer economy."[64]

Visibly fashionable, at the turn-of the century, Italian American immigrants invested in commodities which, reconstructing the subject-object relation, represented the material counterpart of their imaginary activity. Starting from the first photographs they took as signs of their personal success in the New World, they were not only involved in common practices of consumption but also of self-consumption. Multiplying their own portraits through mechanically reproduced images on portable surfaces such as postcards, buttons, or pocket mirrors, Italian American immigrant women let the representation of their appearance, until then mostly ascribed to the order of the "essence" and "symbolic," be absorbed into the multivalent dynamics of the imaginary.

Conclusion

This study has taken its cue from Crialese's *Nuovomondo*, in which characters do not fully accommodate the complex nexus between dress and body but enact it in two gendered discursive instances. I assume that the traumatic experiences marking early Italian immigrant women's passage to the New World might have been lived as occasions to develop a dress awareness integral to their conscious self-representation. A punctual interaction of gazes, whose communication centered on self-display apparatuses, mediated every advance in their "navigation" toward a new different social position. Dress, filtered through the essential contribute of photography, thus refocused on a central situated bodily practice. At the intersection of the structuring influences of a new social context and the immigrant woman's subjectivity, the clothed body functioned as a dialectical arena for the performance and the articulation of her own self-fashioning identity.

With regard to immigrants' controversial passage from traditional dress to fashion styles, my outlook aims at overcoming the received notion of a stiff dichotomy between the two, in the attempt to interpret it along with the process of abstraction Italian immigrant women underwent to achieve a more complex awareness of their agential subjectivity.

In this respect, my goal is also to highlight a theoretical issue that still exists in our time. Fashion, which relies on a more arbitrary, unstable, and ambivalent relation between signs and referents, was the readymade staging ground that allowed Southern Italian immigrant women to achieve and perform their multilayered existential positions. Today, costume and fashion are entangled in a more elaborate interaction, one that persists in the latitude of clothing globalization; still, one of the most privileged sites to experience the practice of an ongoing multicultural translation. All of us, as agents of this practice, pay homage to migrants for their incessant process of self-fashioning and participate in a creative short circuit between these two semantic poles.

2

Making Space for Domesticity

HOUSEHOLD GOODS IN WORKING-CLASS
ITALIAN AMERICAN HOMES, 1900–1940

Maddalena Tirabassi

The dictum of the late Cardinal Manning, "Domestic life creates a nation," is absolutely sound. The corollary is additionally true: the lack of domestic life will unmake a nation.
—E. R. L. GOULD, "THE HOUSING PROBLEM IN GREAT CITIES," 1899–1900

At the turn of the twentieth century, Italian immigrants to the United States experienced a shift from the preindustrial culture of subsistence to one of mass consumption.[1] The home was one of the key places where this change was most visible and tangible. Initially a site of consumption that drew much attention from reformers, social scientists, and photographers working among Italians, the urban immigrant home was forgotten when mass immigration ended. In 1974, anthropologist Carla Bianco noted that sixty years after the Italian Ethnographical Society held its first congress in 1911, "specialized studies on Italian immigrant folklore are still lacking."[2] Even today, serious study of Italian vernacular culture in the United States remains unfinished, although promising research begins to appear in specialized books and journals.[3] As folklorist Joseph Sciorra has noted, "Sunday dinners, basement kitchens, and backyard gardens are everyday cultural entities long associated with Italian Americans, yet the general perception of them remains superficial and stereotypical at best.... Folklore provides ... new ways of understanding how individuals and groups reproduce and contest identities and ideologies through expressive means."[4]

This essay may be also read as an attempt to deconstruct American culture from the bottom up by analyzing through immigrants' adjustment to U.S. consumer society the interplay of Old World culture and traditions with a modern environment and showing how transnational relationships with Italy brought to the development of "glocal" identities still at work.[5] In so doing, it follows the recent transnational research, carried on both in Italy and in the United States, by exploring the beginnings of Italian American consumerism in the domestic realm.[6] Leaving behind them a world of scarcity with few available objects, Italian immigrant women developed a distinctive domesticity in urban America. Drawing from notions, values, and aesthetic standards embedded in their traditions and religion, they slowly embraced contemporary consumer culture. While doing so, many immigrant women resisted middle-class social reformers' attempts to "sanitize" their homes and to "protect" them from the perils of industrial society. Younger immigrant women, on the other hand, welcomed the opportunity to improve social status by participating in the many initiatives offered by the settlement house movement. In the most progressive settlements, some young immigrants even got better acquainted with "Italy's" highbrow culture and language. These notions were largely foreign to them, as many maintained exclusive feelings of affiliation to their *paese* (hometowns). The development of an Italian American ethnic identity was, in fact, a crucial step in the process of achieving full citizenship in the host country. By transforming their material culture into an Italian American lifestyle, immigrants created a unique, coherent identity. Exemplified in the vernacular environment of Little Italies and complemented by the images of *Italia Grande* with its classic Roman and Renaissance heritage, Italian American identity became widely represented in urban American culture and in architectural landscape. By analyzing both the interplay and the cultural dissemination between Italy and the United States, this chapter illustrates the first stages in the formation of multicultural Italian identities that would circulate on a global scale.

The "Old Country"

Most Italian migrants to the United States came from very poor rural agricultural towns in Southern Italy.[7] According to the 1877–1882 Italian Parliament Commission (better known as Inchiesta Jacini, from the name of its director, Stefano Jacini), the rural population living conditions were sparse. *Contadini* (peasant) houses were typically a 270-square-foot room, with no floor, unplastered walls, and only a single opening that served simultaneously as door, window, and chimney.[8] In Abruzzi, the Inchiesta Jacini reported that one room accommodated the whole family, and often animals as well, with a pile of straw used for a bed. An investigator found a single-room stone house for the whole family together with their pigs and chickens. A heap of straw served as a bed for many children. The situation was similar in other regions of rural Southern Italy. In the province of Salerno, poor farmers lived in haystacks.[9] In certain areas of Calabria, parents and children shared the same bed—a straw mattress—and the one or two rooms of their house with the pig and the donkey.[10] In Abruzzi and in Puglia, houses were generally dirty, and, as one observer reported, "the pig was almost always in the same room where the family lived."[11]

Across Sicily and rural Southern Italy, hygiene and privacy were unknown concepts in most destitute households. The notion of "home," as we understand it today, was hardly meaningful since houses served merely as sleeping places while the vast major-ity of quotidian activities were performed outside. Among better-off farmers, however, "the bed was the most important piece of furniture." Sometimes women even fastened a piece of embroidered linen in a deep frill around the legs of the bed's framework to beautify its appearance. In Southern Italy, "peasants' beds were much larger than the modern American double-bed standard [because] they often had to accommodate not only the parents but their more or less numerous offspring; sometimes [they] were so high that a stool was needed to climb into them." The wife took care of the mattress, or the whole bed where there was one. She often hung a crucifix or a figurine of a saint over the bed.[12]

While taking responsibility for the sleeping place, women from *contadino* families also worked in the fields like men. No easy line could be drawn to separate agricultural labor from housework; women faced domestic chores no man undertook. An *Inchiesta* investigator noted that, while men remained idle during long winter months, women turned to wintertime chores like spinning wool, making canvas, and weaving. In fact, women toiled yearlong to make cloth and clothing. With the help of their children, they also tended animals and gardens. Additionally, women alone were responsible for laun-dry, mending, and food preparation.[13] Even though the *contadino* diet was simple and monotonous, cooking was a time-consuming chore repeated daily.[14] In other words, rural women worked full-time, but housekeeping and childrearing were not their main occupations, or even their second priorities. Never would they define themselves as *casalinga* (housewife). Descriptions of peasant dwellings indicate how modern concepts such as "housework" or "housewife" fit poorly to the lives of rural Italian women in both the North and the South.[15]

Emigration was the only way for rural Italians to improve their housing, opening opportunities for women to experiment with American middle-class notions of domes-ticity.[16] The effects of early twentieth century emigration rippled across agricultural communities in Italy. For example, an observer in Puglia noted that, "the conditions of *contadino* houses vary according to the destination of migrants. . . . Peasant dwellings tend to be better in the villages where emigration is largest and has occurred for the longest time."[17] Investigators described the houses of the *Americani* (those who returned from sojourns in the Americas) as white and clean, with brick or tile floors, separate kitchens, and a clear separation between the living areas and the stables.[18] The *Ameri-cani* houses had plastered walls, proper windows, internal staircases, and upstairs rooms. Some even had balconies and shutters, sturdy wooden doors, and tiled roofs.[19] In other villages, American returnees introduced acetylene lighting or applied to the municipality to get electricity in towns that still lacked piped water and sewage. The contrast between the homes of migrants and the "old black houses, piled on top of each other and separated only by torturous, dark little streets" impressed middle-class observers.[20]

Early Italian ethnographers faced the additional challenge of studying the would-be migrant material culture because, as the aforementioned descriptions demonstrate, the rural Italian communities stored very few material possessions in their homes. Even with this challenge, a small group of intellectuals from the Florentine school of Lam-berto Loria and Ferdinando Martini attempted to tackle the research. They introduced the discipline in Italy with the purpose of exploring the kaleidoscopic Italian local folk traditions as well as investigating the material culture of Italian emigration.[21] They originally hoped to create a section dedicated to Italians abroad in the Mostra di Etnografia (Ethnography Exhibit) to be held in Rome to celebrate the fiftieth anniversary of Italian unification. As the research unfolded incompletely, the organizers decided to develop the ideas further by holding a panel on the topic of migration during the First Italian Congress of Ethnography in the fall of that same year.[22] Amy Bernardy, the most prominent Italian migration expert of the time, was selected to present a paper along with ethnographer Francesco Baldasseroni. Bernardy focused on the United States, and in particular on the "Ethnography of Little Italies," a subject she explored previously in her research.[23] Bernardy explained the choice of limiting her analysis to North America: "As our colonies to the United States have a higher quota of emigration from the south— i.e., from the regions rich of the most tenacious traditions and superstitions—it is best to begin our work from there, picking up the many elements of ethnographic practice that they offer us."[24]

Bernardy, however, felt from the first moment that ethnography was not the most suitable framework for the study of Italians abroad because of the lack in Italian folklore scholarship and the scarce number of possessions transported by migrants across the Atlantic. She noted that the belongings of migrant women usually included a dowry chest full of bridal blankets, embroidered sheets, pillows and pillowcases, towels, cooking tools, and a range of religious items. While examining the dowries of Sicilian women during her study of the agricultural towns of Milocca at the end of the 1920s, Charlotte Gower Chapman listed similar objects: cooking utensils, a stable and chest, chairs, a broom, linens, and a mattress cover.[25] When migrant women entered the United States at Ellis Island, they typically carried these dowry items in their luggage.[26] In *An Italian American Odyssey*, B. Amore detailed the belongings of an immigrant woman: a few dresses, a bridal bed cover with yellow silk fringes, a hand-woven bed cover crochet square (a part of her dowry), bed sheets with red embroidered initials, crochet lace sheets, mattresses, pillows, medications, photographs, music sheets, letters, passports, a cross of St. Lawrence Lapio, prayer books, holy cards, rosaries, reliquaries with Santa Filomena, a knife and cup with initials, jewelry (coral earrings, specifically), porcelain and stuffed dolls, cooking utensils, mortar, handmade copper pots, a ravioli cutting-wheel, and the books *Andrea da Barberino*, *The French Royal Family*, and *Lives of the Saints*.[27]

In America

Domestic life in the tenement apartment houses, often the first residences for Italians in the large industrial cities on the East Coast, contrasted inherently with middle-class American moral and aesthetic standards. In the eyes of middle-class Americans, tenements were overcrowded illegal hotbeds full of the worst social consequences—school truancy, child labor, epidemic diseases, and promiscuity.[28] "The recent Tenement House Exhibition in New York marks a noteworthy event in metropolitan sociological history," a reformer noted on 1900. "Some were amazed, some saddened, and probably all were impressed with the unanswerable demonstrations, by means of models, photographs, and charts, of the close relations between bad housing, bad health, bad morals, and bad citizenship."[29] Both American and traveling Italian middle-class reformers insisted on the same images of dangerous overcrowding when describing Italian immigrants' housing conditions. In New York City, Boston, and Philadelphia, many Italian immigrants lived in three-room apartments composed of a sitting room/parlor/working room that at night became a bedroom for children, a kitchen, and a dark bedroom. The only source of heating was generally the kitchen stove, as immigrants often used kerosene for lighting and coal for cooking. Three of four families shared one toilet located in the hallway.[30] Bernardy also noted similar housing conditions on the West Coast, where Italians lived "in single property houses, but also they keep boarders here." Italian immigrants paved the yards in front of their houses with bricks or gravel instead of following the predominant American lawn culture. Backyard vegetable gardens were ubiquitous from the very first days of Italian immigration to California.[31]

Reformers believed the inconsistent separation of home and work to be the primary reason for Italian immigrants' substandard living: "Macaroni is made in every block of the Italian neighborhoods of New York," one reformer reported. "In many streets you will find three or four little shops in one block of houses, with the macaroni drying in the doorways and windows. The front room is the shop, the family living in the middle and rear rooms, and these are invariably overcrowded. The Italians not only have large families, but keep lodgers, and the front shop then becomes a sleeping and living apartment as well as the other rooms. The paste is mixed and pressed by a machine into long strings, which are hung on racks to dry. . . . A child lay sick of diphtheria in the back room where the physician visited her. The father manufactured macaroni in the front adjoining room, and would go directly from holding the child in his arms to the macaroni machine, pulling the macaroni with his hands and hanging it over racks to dry. This macaroni was then sold up and down Elizabeth street. Within the fortnight the Board of Health disinfected a house on East Twenty-ninth street where there was a case of scarlet fever. Macaroni was drying in the yard and in the windows of the house during all the time of the child's sickness."[32]

U.S. and Italian officials who visited Italian immigrant homes criticized the boarding system, a popular institution from the turn of the twentieth century through World War I, when most Italian migrants were single men looking to work temporarily in the United States and then return to Italy. Social reformers generally condemned boarding as promiscuous and thus immoral. But from the migrants' perspective, the boarding system was an efficient and inexpensive purveyor of the most important cultural signposts in their diasporic life in America: language and food. The *bordo* or *pensione* (boardinghouse), usually run by a woman from the same village or region of the boarders, not only enabled Italian women to work within the house, but also offered single men familiar food at a cheap price and the opportunity to speak their native dialect. In her reports to the Italian General Commissariat for Emigration, Bernardy denounced the boarding system as a corrupted form of serfdom that not only jeopardized immigrant women's sexual morality but, additionally, contributed to the numerous cases of incest and venereal diseases found in Italian immigrant families.[33]

Italian and American reformers understood taking in boarders to be a practice consistent with Italian migrants' extreme thriftiness, a tendency reformers also denounced as a cause for immigrants' bad housing circumstances: "One of the chief objectives of the Italians in this country is to own his home," Phyllis Williams wrote. "He lives under the most crimpled and sordid conditions to save the money necessary for the down payment."[34] Bernardy noted accordingly that "because of pauperism, discouragement, and to save money, our [fellow citizens] in America do not make any distinction between a good and a bad house."[35]

In New York's Little Italy, the kitchen was the best-lit room in the apartment because it often faced the street or the backyard and it was also the best heated because of the stove. In most two- and three-room apartments the kitchen thus became the *soggiorno* (living and dining area); it served as a multifunctional workroom and parlor by day and children's bedroom by night. These tenement "best rooms" were decorated "just as in Sicily." Small curtains wrapped around the sink and laundry tubs and cupboards displayed china upon lace cloths. A variety of saints' pictures, holy items, palms, and ribbons decorated bedrooms.[36] In Chicago, Bernardy reported seeing monumental high beds with clean linen and big pillows in Italian homes.[37]

Many sympathetic reformers encouraged this search for beauty but found its limits in the poverty experienced by many immigrant families. A social worker noted, "It is futile to begin with discussions of the interior decoration of a girl's room when working with girls who live in overcrowded tenements and do not have rooms of their own."[38] Numerous laws aimed at improving immigrant living conditions passed in the first decade of the twentieth century, as did laws concerning women and child labor. City health departments held immigrants' health under strict scrutiny. Nevertheless, social workers admitted that the survival of immigrant families often depended on eluding these same laws.

Italian American homes changed with time as immigrants assimilated American commodities into traditional concepts of furnishing and interior decoration. The ethnographer Carla Bianco, who conducted field research during the 1960s, studied an immigrant community originally from Roseto, Puglia, that established a village with the same name in Pennsylvania. She found in the town's older houses: "narrow back gardens intensely cultivated by the oldest members of the families and still very reminiscent of Southern Italian gardening. Here grapevines, tomatoes, fig trees, zucchini and broccoli, garlic and onions are the most recurrent items while all of the traditional Italian herbs and spices, such as parsley, mint, oregano, basil and the precious chamomile, are given the greatest care." These two-story houses followed "a general Pennsylvania style and what distinguishes them as Italian is more a matter of details and use than of architectural style. Kitchens are very large and are used as family rooms, while living rooms are reserved for guest and special occasions." On the other hand, Bianco also found strong signs of Americanization in the homes of second-generation Rosetani: "The picture changes in the outskirts, where young couples or wealthy families recently moved. Here the houses tend to be surrounded by large green lawns with trees and ornamental gardens, with evident pretense of elegance and very similar on the whole to the patterns proposed by such popular magazines as *Better Homes and Gardens*."[39] Although overdecoration could potentially be read as an indicator of ethnicity, these interiors reflected an aspiration to middle-class values: large living rooms, small but very well equipped kitchens, abundance of curtains, carpets, vases, statuettes. The dreamlike

Figure 2.1. Ralph Fasanella, *Family Supper*, 1972.

representation of *Italianità* in Ralph Fasanella's painting, *Family Supper* (1972), shows a small room *full* of people and *objects*: a cupboard, a crucifix, a sewing machine, and many shelves covered with embroidered fabrics.[40]

Middle-Class Aesthetics vs. Immigrants' Aesthetics

The late nineteenth century transition from a rural to an industrial society transformed the relationship between housing and consumption in the United States. The home became both the site of technological innovation convergence and refuge.[41] By the end of the century, the Victorian home, with its heavy furniture and redundant decorations, gave way to modern styles inspired by Colonial Revival and the Arts and Crafts Movement.[42] Responding to colonial-era aesthetics and combining the use of natural material, craftsmanship, and technological innovations, these styles shunned European-inspired and mass-produced commodities and instead tried to translate Modernism into simplicity. Social reformers embraced these new aesthetic standards, seeing in them a means to modernize and Americanize immigrants. As a 1910 *Home Economics* article declared, "Every article in a room . . . should have a reason for being there."[43] Similar notions, combined with the reformers' other motto, "safety, sanitation and morality," dictated the rules that immigrants needed to follow in the decoration of their homes as well as their domesticity.[44]

Figure 2.2. "A Parlor View in a New York Dwelling House," 1854. Courtesy Victorian Vignettes.

Mabel Kittredge, a leading expert in home economics of the time, set precise rules for working-class homes. She advised immigrants to adopt yellow paint, discard wallpaper, and hang shelves everywhere (in the dining room for china, in the living room for books, and in the kitchen for utensils).[45] In order to keep their homes clean, she suggested covering the beloved pictures (often magazine clippings) hung on walls with easily washable shellac.[46] Kittredge advocated predictably for room differentiation (the functions and spaces of the kitchen, dining room, bedroom, and living room had to be separated), and also recommended avoiding unnecessary furniture.[47] For Kittredge, decorations had to emphasize simplicity; lace curtains, "riotous upholstery" chair and couches, valances, feather bedding, and fancy linens were dust collectors and therefore unsanitary. Instead, she proposed iron beds as an alternative to vermin-infested bed frames and stained oak floors.[48]

Italian women, who came from a bare existence in rural settings comparable to Colonial America, were attracted to the opulence that characterized Victorian homes and, as soon they could afford it, took advantage of mass-produced items to embellish their homes with Victorian-style engraved furniture and fabrics.[49] A Boston settlement worker reported the case of a soon-to-be-married young woman who, after attending a home furnishing course inspired by post-Victorian standards, invited the social worker to her new house, where "her small living room was overfilled by the inevitable 'parlor set' while plush curtains hang at the windows and on either side of the door." The immigrant woman told the astonished worker, "You must remember you have had your plush days."[50]

In Victorian-style carpets and curtains, working-class immigrant women saw symbols of taste and status. In the comfort of new, richly furnished houses, they felt at home in America. As historian Elizabeth Cohen remarks, theirs "was not a simple emulation of middle-class Victorian standards with a time lag due to delayed prosperity, but rather a creative compromise forged in making the transition between two very different social and economic worlds."[51] As Jean-Christophe Agnew concurs, "immigrant workers and their families entered hesitantly, if at all, into the developing infrastructure of bourgeois consumption—the sanitized 'dream worlds' of the movie palace, department and chain stores. And when new goods and services were purchased, they were often incorporated into imported, inherited, or in other ways alternative systems of meaning."[52] Such stylistic incorporations (Elizabeth Cohen's "compromise") involved more than Victorian-style furnishing. By examining Lewis Hine's photograph "Mauro Family Assembling Feathers"—an image frequently examined from a sociological perspective to illustrate the dynamics of home work in the tenements—from a material culture

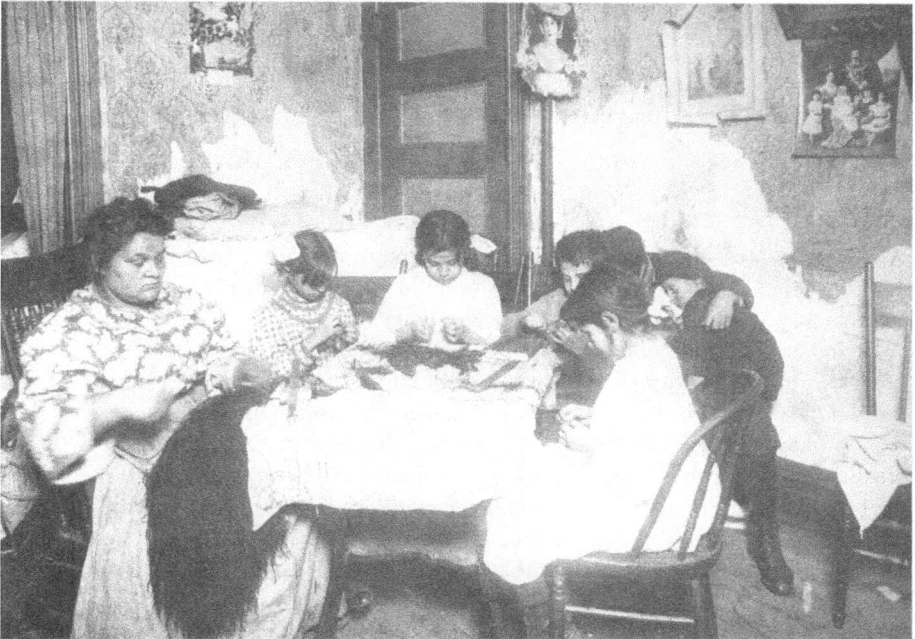

Figure 2.3. Lewis Hine, *Mauro Family Assembling Feather Goods, 309 E. 110th St., New York City,* 1911. Courtesy Library of Congress.

perspective, one notes the immigrant concept of "American" style home decoration in the wallpaper (albeit torn), the furniture (tables and chairs), the picture frames, the curtain behind the mother, and the fashion poster. Hanging on the walls are crumpled pictures of Crucifixion and the Italian royal family, representing the vestige of the past even though these items were most likely made in America.

At the beginning of the twentieth century, programs aimed at the assimilation of immigrants into U.S. society were mostly the work of progressive social reformers who instructed gradual social and economic improvement. But after World War I, as immigrant naturalization and citizenship became pressing political issues, the inclusion of immigrants into U.S. polity was achieved through more structured strategies. The International Institutes, founded by the Young Women's Christian Association in 1912, responded efficiently to this purpose. Very active in the interwar years, International Institutes insisted on the study and the knowledge of immigrants' culture upon the assumption that cultural diversity, if properly framed within United States laws and founding principles, could provide the context for successful integration of immigrants into the host society.[53] To this goal, "nationality workers"—first- or second-generation immigrant women who belonged to the same group they worked with—brought change from within the immigrant community.[54] Institute workers operated through a close-knit network of local clubs and introduced immigrant women to middle-class American domesticity. Their home economics courses taught "migrant women [who] don't know how to manage a house in America, being unfamiliar with the washtub, the sink, the range stove, and all the paraphernalia of American housekeeping," how to shop, cook with gas, and prepare proper food for babies.[55]

Immigrants' Religious Aesthetics

Since the church was the place where Italian migrants almost invariably came in contact with beauty and the arts in their native villages, religious aesthetics deeply shaped Italian migrants' taste. Church paintings, statues, carved sculptures, laces, and altar ornaments represented a fundamental part of migrants' early aesthetic training every time they attended Mass or Confession. Decorations in their American homes, therefore, tended to relate to religious items and inspirations.

Religion was, of course, a crucial element in the diasporic formation of Italian American ethnic identity, even though, as immigrant scholar and public leader Leonard Covello has observed, "Religious sentiments were not, in any great measure, a product of the Roman Catholic Church, but were independent development of primitive Roman practices or survivals of the alien customs of successive conquerors."[56] In their faith, migrants to America reproduced popular *contadino* religiosity mixed with Southern Italian superstitions.[57] Vernacular religious and superstition objects became the main adornment in many immigrant homes. Bernardy, in her search for immigrant folklore, reported amulets against the evil eye, images of saints, glass bells with holy figures hung on walls and from ceilings, together with remains of garlic, onions, and tomatoes. She also found "Countless scapulars, amulets, crucifix of gold, silver and coral against the evil eye . . . circles of gold to be applied to the ears of men to treat eye diseases, medicated wrists angina, erysipelas attached on the images of saints."[58]

Joseph Sciorra has recounted the story of Natale Rotondi (1924–2009) of Benson-hurst, Brooklyn, who painted an *ex voto* after surviving cancer and hung it "in the inner sanctum of the master bedroom."[59] Alice Sickels, a social worker of the Inter-national Institutes of St. Paul, Minnesota, in the mid-1930s wrote, "The investigator looked for distinguished marks of heritage in the Upper Levee households. None was found. The folk costumes of Abruzzi, reproduced for the St. Paul folk festival, are bar-ren of needle work. . . . Houses are neat, few have real charms. . . . The item of decora-tion most frequently found is a large photograph of an elaborate Italian American wedding party or of Confirmation. . . . Inexpensive holy pictures were seen in nearly every house and in fact in nearly every room. . . . They were not copies of old masters, nor were they especially Italian. Only few Italians have a *presepio* (miniature repro-duction of Nativity scenes). Social workers' tastes might differ."[60] At around the same time, another "nationality worker," Sicilian American Clara Corica Grillo, wrote about a *presepio* in Boston: "The other instance in which religion played a small yet pictur-esque part was in the habit of an old [Italian] woman who in the midst of squalor clung to the Old World custom of setting up at home a crude, gaudy nativity scene at Xmastime. This custom is dying out and as also Roman Catholic might be considered as the poor woman's only way of expressing her hunger for pretty things."[61] In second-generation Italian immigrant homes in Pennsylvania, Bianco also noted various reli-gious or magical objects: horseshoes hanged on the wall or door, horns, *santini* (holy picture cards), plastic statues of all sizes, metal or clay candles, scapulars, blessed palms, votive beads, bottles of miraculous water, several statuettes of saints and Madonnas for home worship, and medals. In the house of a woman from Ciociaria (a region close to Rome) she found the Statue of Liberty (that she called "Santa Liberata") next to the Madonna di Montevergine, placed on a bureau with a perennial lamp and artificial flowers.[62]

Early in the twentieth century, a Boston settlement worker recalled her neighbors' response to a circulating collection of photographs depicting famous paintings that were to be hung temporarily on the settlement walls: "The 'Holy pictures,' as all of the Madonnas were called, were always welcomed, but the lack of color made them un-attractive, all the other pictures were 'tucked away' waiting to be returned."[63] Another Boston social worker, Gladys Fraser, cited the typical example of Italian women crafts to be religious objects, such as chalice veils. Immigrant handcrafts exhibits, very popular activities in settlement houses and International Institutes, were intended "as a practical working outline for those believing that the most effectual social approach to any na-tionality is made through appealing to its distinctive racial heritage of beauty, color and design." Very often, social workers' expectations experienced frustration because the Americanization of tastes proceeded swiftly. Gladys Fraser complained: "Again and again foreign women have shown me their 'American' needlecraft—the pillow top with its American beauty rose and cotton Woolworth edgings, the peek-a-boo crocheted yoke and the flimsy colored silk underwear—imagining that I should appreciate these productions far more than their native embroideries. It is not a pathetic parody of a machine-made American taste, that foreign women, capable of doing the most exqui-site needlework, of belling native yarns into color combination of rare strength and beauty . . . should so easily renounce their traditional old world artistic standards?"[64]

When Alice Sickels planned a "Mythical International Village" in 1935, she summarized aptly the middle-class American attitude toward immigrant culture: "At the far end of the Market Square, the visitor stops in front of a Florentine house, where delicious spaghetti and Italian cheese are served in strange contrast to the dignified architecture."[65] Renaissance art and food established ostensibly the "best" Italians could contribute to American culture.

Most of the efforts social workers made to direct Italian women toward what they thought were traditional female activities, such as crochet and embroidery, utterly failed. In Italy, these activities were typical of lower middle-class women and, therefore, foreign to most peasant migrant women. In her reports, Bernardy dedicated only a few lines to domestic handwork, noting that immigrant women had "almost completely abandoned" crochet and embroidery. Furthermore, during the mass migration from Italy, it was nearly impossible for women to develop their own businesses. At the first Congresso Nazionale delle Donne Italiane (Italian Women's Congress) held in Rome in 1908, a proposal was put forward to create "ancillary industries" (small businesses in weaving and manufacturing of straw braid, lace, and embroidery) with hopes of curtailing the mounting women's migration. The project, however, faced immediate failure as young women preferred to emigrate and seek employment in factories abroad.[66] George Pozzetta studied a similar effort to revive and to preserve the artisanal industry of lace work and embroidery among Italian women in America. These efforts hoped "to rescue women from at least some of the economic and social evils commonly associated with the factory system."[67] Unfortunately, this initiative was also unsuccessful. At the International Institute of St. Paul, Minnesota, "The older women sit idle hands, until (it) is time for the evening spaghetti. No flowering plants, no patterns of gay needlework to bright the long winter day," Sickels observed.[68] In many settlement houses, "Italian handicraft" group work returned the smallest attendances. In the 1920s, at Boston's International Institute, the Italian "Business and Industrial Club" showed greater interest in table etiquette lectures, as well as interior decoration, and color scheme, all subjects young women deemed useful for their prospect of upward mobility in America.[69] Second-generation Italian girls also preferred courses on Italian arts and language.[70]

Overall, with the material resources available in America, Italian immigrants shaped the kind of domesticity they idealized but could not attain in Italy. In the United States an Italian man could very rarely be a breadwinner, supporting his family with his wage alone: strong social pressures were made on women to provide free domestic labor and simultaneously contribute supplementary money into the family economy. Women's wage earning in sweatshops and canneries mimicked the close links that existed in subsistence-economy rural Italy among domesticity, production for self-consumption, informal family group work, and the most rare salaried work. Female Italian immigrants insisted that work—even wage-earning—belonged in the domestic arena. This notion remained an important challenge to American middle-class notions of domesticity that unmistakably demanded the separation of home and work. As a result, immigrant female domesticity remained a controversial topic, one strongly marked by "ethnic" difference. Similar to adaptations in housing and diet,

Italian American domesticity fulfilled mostly "Italian," rather than "American," social ideals and values.

Italian Signs in America

American consumerism deeply influenced Italian American working-class taste and material culture but this process was not solely unilateral. Thousands of Italian construction workers, those employed in the unprecedented transformation of U.S. cities at the turn of the twentieth century, contributed by shaping the urban American landscape. The Italians left deep marks in American environment and architecture because of the continuous interweaving of professional and unskilled migrants in the construction work trade—architects, engineers, artists, craftsmen, artisans, masons, plasterers, and carvers. Migrant workers who found occupation participated in major construction projects, including urban infrastructure development of railroads, subways, bridges, and dams. Additionally, many migrants, regardless of their occupation, built their own homes, both in rural and urban areas. Chicago-born Italian American writer Fred Gardaphé recalled his grandfather bringing home "stolen" bricks from the shipyard every evening and using them to build his house.[71] The values of *contadino* thriftiness and loyalty to traditional dietary habits meant the transformation of unused land adjacent to Italian American houses, either in backyards or vacant lots, into truck gardens. "Italian" churches, cemeteries, and shrines dotted Italian immigrant neighborhoods. Migrant settlements in areas they transformed into "ethnic" neighborhoods altered U.S. urban landscape. With the arrival of Italians, street intersections became nodes resembling the squares of European cities. The same streets along which "Italian" banks, restaurants, and grocery stores sprouted, often staged religious processions and diasporic national celebrations. It was the lifestyle of the residents, even more than the particular buildings or the landscape, which made the areas where migrants lived distinctive, and shaped them into "Little Italies." As demonstrated, the reasons for Italian immigrants' strong attachment to place were rooted in traditional Italian culture; homeownership was the defining social goal of their migration experience. The building of one's own home was the greatest symbol of success and a tangible way to make sense of an otherwise foreign environment. As sociologist Jerry Krase noted, the lasting imprint Italians left in American cities was embodied in the material they used most often to write out their presence: stones and bricks.[72] Italian homes better withstood the fires that often devastated the American cities built chiefly of wood. High rates of Italian homeownership and a strong sense of place lent stability to Italian enclaves in the United States; Italians tended to stay longer than any other ethnic group both in areas of first and second settlement, sometimes even for more than two generations.

Italians did not shape urban American landscape only through the direct influence of migrant labor and the work of skilled professionals in the architecture and construction trades, but also via the import of Italian architectural models. New York City offers many visible and interesting examples. Highly skilled Italian workers dramatically decorated buildings and subway stations with stuccoes and mosaics. Italian immigrants also contributed widely to the Arts and Crafts Movement.[73] Some of the major works that transformed the face of the city at the turn of the twentieth century were based on Italian architectural models.[74]

Conclusion

Further studies are needed concerning Italian migrant folklore and domesticity in transnational perspective. The experience of Italian immigrants at the turn of the twentieth century in the United States, however, demonstrates a material culture shaped by the scarcity of available objects due to poverty and balanced by the strength of traditions and models brought with them to America. Aesthetics rooted in religious experience as well as the differentiation of space within and outside the home persisted through difficult beginnings in overcrowded tenements and perpetuated through generations, as exemplified by backyard vegetable gardens and "ethnic" neighborhoods. The Italian cultural construct of *la bella figura* (making a "good showing," as a way to accumulate social capital, preserve honor, and avoid shame), so deeply embedded in Italian American identity, best typifies the experience of migration and ethnicization. Ethnographer Gloria Nardini defined this construct as the key to "Italian American social interaction." The centrality of *la bella figura* complex made first- and second-generation immigrant *salotti* (living rooms/parlors) utterly unutilized, waiting for special guests to show up, and introduced the distinctive model of the two kitchens (the best one on the main floor meant to be used only on special occasions, and the other, in the basement, for everyday use).[75]

During the shift from a rural society and culture to an urban environment at the edge of the world's industrialism and capitalism, Italian migrants realized their domesticity and home ideals in a relatively short period of time, thanks in part to the abundant commodities made available to them by mass production. They remained, however, bearers and producers of strong culture that passed down through generations, leaving many unmistakable signs in American landscape and urban environment and conveying a distinctive Italian lifestyle. From the very beginning, Italians thus played an important role in the construction of American society and created an environment favorable to the millions of countrymen that were to follow. Considering the vernacular culture of Italian Americans is vital in understanding their successful incorporation in American society; they felt at home in America because, through their work, taste, and lifestyle, they participated in its construction.

The analysis of the construction of Italian American consumer culture though the developing of *glocalism* helps also to understand the process of United States nation-building as a multiethnic state since the late nineteenth century.

3

In Italy Everyone Enjoys It—Why Not in America?

ITALIAN AMERICANS AND CONSUMPTION IN
TRANSNATIONAL PERSPECTIVE DURING THE
EARLY TWENTIETH CENTURY

Elizabeth Zanoni

In 1939, Martini & Rossi ran an advertisement in New York's widely distributed Italian-language daily *Il Progresso Italo-Americano* (hereafter *Il Progresso*) that linked Italian American consumer desires and decisions to those of their *connazionali* back home.[1] After lauding the world-famous Piedmont liquor Fernet, the ad posed a question to its readers: "In Italy everyone enjoys it. Why not enjoy it also in America?"[2] Martini & Rossi was one of many Italian companies during the 1920s and 1930s that recognized and exploited connections between Italians in the United States and Italy to sell export products to an immigrant market. Such advertisements, while benefiting Italian companies and the merchants who traded in their goods, also presented immigrants in the United States an imaginary medium for identifying with and contributing to the land they left. This chapter explores how transnational communities of consumption were created through real and constructed networks of ethnic producers, sellers, and consumers by considering imagination as a critical site in the formation and perpetuation of social practices.

While buyers of Italian exports in the United States may not have physically traversed the Atlantic, advertisements for Italian products suggested that consumers abroad could experience Italy by buying Italian goods. As key actors participating in transnational commodity chains, immigrant buyers and sellers—even while situated in the United States—served as economic and cultural intermediaries shaping meanings of migration, consumerism, and nationality. Assuming the role of imagination as central in the formation of consumer practices reveals how the experience of mass migration influenced the way people interacted with commodities and the ethnic, gender, and class meanings merchants and immigrants affixed to them.

In his examination of contemporary global cultural flows, anthropologist Arjun Appadurai treats imagination as a form of social practice integral to understanding the complexities of the global economy.[3] From this view, imagination factors into the ways migrants organize and manage their lives and identities as individuals and as members of multiple, and sometimes competing, communities. Even when people do not move, they may consider their lives and actions as transnational. Historians of migration, however, have been reluctant to consider imagination in the study of migration across national borders. Because the powers of imagination are intangible, and therefore difficult to measure or quantify, scholars must think creatively, raise new questions about old sources, and use new sources to expand on existing work. Historians have begun to use autobiographies and letters to examine how people invented transnational identities, but further research is needed on migrants' imaginative spaces.[4]

Many advertisements for Italian products appeared in mainstream commercial Italian American newspapers such as *Il Progresso* or Chicago's *L'Italia*, published by *prominenti*, elite Italian immigrants. To the Italian American community, the ethnic press, including promotional material, served as a source of information and as a site where writers and readers produced cultural and consumer identities as ethnic Americans.[5] As source material, advertisements transport us into the imaginary realm and provide us entry, albeit indirect, into the fantasy worlds of people who do not leave behind many written sources. Theorists of visual and print culture have shown how advertising consists of a language of codes and symbols that viewers read, manipulate, and often contest.[6] U.S. consumer culture presented immigrants with a new and shared language for negotiating their interactions with American society, often in ways that reflected their transatlantic familial and economic lives.[7] A focus on advertising material for export goods allows scholars to consider how immigrant consumers were swept up in what anthropologist Denise Brenan calls, "transnational social fields."[8] Here, return migration was not only embodied, as *golondrini* migrant consumers physically moved back and forth across the Atlantic, but it was also imagined, as consumers in the United States returned in the imaginary by buying and consuming products from Italy. Advertisements for Italian exports are evidence of such tangible and cognitive links between producers and consumers in the United States and Italy, and the ways these links stretched across transatlantic spaces. Furthermore, after World War I and the onset of the global Depression, ads became a way for migrants to fantasize about Italy during a time when fewer Italians were actually able to cross the Atlantic.

While merchants, Italian companies, and Italian politicians recognized Italians' purchasing power, historians of the mass labor migrations of the late nineteenth and early twentieth centuries have largely overlooked Italians' consuming experiences, focusing instead on the role of immigrants as workers. Only a small body of literature discusses immigrants' complicated relationship with U.S. consumer culture.[9] Even fewer studies focus extensively on how immigrants interacted with consumer items from their sending countries, and how these exchanges altered immigrants' relationship to their homeland.[10] By exploring Italians' consumer identities and habits from a transnational perspective, this chapter expands on scholarship by historians such as Lizabeth Cohen and Meg Jacobs who describe consumption's role as a complex but ultimately successful tool of U.S. nation and citizenship building.[11] Instead, by buying and consuming items from Italy, immigrants acted as transnational consumers who formed their national identities around goods from their homeland, as well as around those in their host countries. It was not only Italians' participation in U.S. consumer culture that turned migrants toward consumption; rather, it was also migrants' transnational familial, community, and national sentiments that made consumption increasingly acceptable among a people more used to saving than spending. The consumption of Italian exports abroad in some cases strengthened migrants' ties to their homeland, while fostering a more distinct ethnic and Italian identity in the United States.

From Regional to National in Advertisements for Italian Goods

Advertisements for Italian exports during the late 1920s and 1930s presented Italian Americans with an image of an Italian nation and populace that was both regionally diverse and culturally homogenous. This seemingly contradictory representation reflected the prolonged and complicated process of national identity formation in the Italian American diaspora during the first half of the twentieth century. *Prominenti* elites had attempted to promote a sense of national belonging among Italian immigrants since the late nineteenth century, but until at least World War I, for the majority of Italian-speaking people either within or outside the country "home" signified a small town or *paesi*, rather than a uniform idea of an Italian nation.[12] Advertisements in the Italian American press suggest that merchants used lingering regional identities to sell and publicize both Italian products and a sense of belonging to a standardized consuming diaspora.

Many advertisements for exported goods promoted products as Italian regional specialties. The secret to Marsala Florio's popularity and excellence, a 1935 advertisement in *Il Progresso* declared, was the unique lushness of the Sicilian soil. Speaking of the House of Florio's Sicilian winery, the ad stated: "No other House has the vast vineyards, where the grapes are rich of iron, phosphorus and vitamins sucked from the abundant minerals of Sicily."[13] Pitching their product as a "symbol of the eternal living power of the glorious and volcanic Sicily," the advertisement appealed to Italian American's regional sympathies in Italy. Similarly, an advertisement for Pastene brand olive oil accentuated its product's Ligurian origins, assuring viewers that "Pastene's pure olive oil is a product from the Ligurian Riviera."[14] Such advertisements spoke to immigrant consumers in the United States whose identities were rooted in the particular regions and *paesi* of their sending country.

Advertising for Italian products highlighted the local origin of Italian goods, but at the same time carefully crafted a standardized image of the Italian consumer outside of Italy. Pastene concluded its advertisement for Ligurian olive oil noting: "The grand majority of Italian families in America have bought and preferred it for more than a half century."[15] In the United States, "Italian families" rather than Ligurian families bought

Figure 3.1. Publicity announcement. *Il Progresso Italo-Americano* (October 31, 1926): 7-S.

and used Ligurian olive oil. In another publicity announcement for *Il Progresso* from 1926, a crowned, statuesque woman representing Italy sits regally on a thrown; behind her are the coats of arms of major Italian cities including Rome, Palermo, Turin, and Venice. The ad read: "Italy needs to produce, to export, to expand. We want the good products of Italy everywhere no matter what it takes"[16] (see figure 3.1). In such ads, regionalism usually remained within the confines of the Italian peninsula; outside Italy's national borders, advertisements in the immigrant press more often represented its consumers as united "Italians" rather than as Ligurians or Sicilians.

The image of a standardized Italian American consumer projected in advertisements for Italian exports matched the aspirations of Italian politicians in the late nineteenth and early twentieth century who worried that Italians' cultural and linguistic divisions hampered Italy's efforts to gain colonial territory and prestige as an imperial power. Italian political elites hoped to harness the commercial markets opened by migrants and the financial remittances they sent home as tools of empire building.[17] To add this effort, Italy's Ministry of Foreign Affairs established and supported Italian Chambers of Commerce abroad in the late nineteenth century to encourage trade, promote Italian culture, and unify Italians worldwide through the consumption of Italian goods.[18] By the mid-1920s, forging a cohesive immigrant market around notions of *Itali-*

anità or Italianness became especially important for Benito Mussolini, who used the promotion of Italian products abroad as a diplomatic instrument to increase Italy's economic and political power.[19] At the same time, Italian academics, including ethnographers and folklorists, defined, studied, and "preserved" local cultural and food customs that fascists then incorporated into their nation-building discourse and used to inspire pride in a unified, imperialist Italy.[20]

Furthermore, by the early 1930s the rising popularity of Mussolini among both Italians and the U.S. public and Italians' shared experience of prejudice in U.S. society sparked new nationalist sentiments and a more cohesive identity as ethnics among some immigrants, while at the same time inspiring antifascist movements in immigrant communities.[21] Most scholars of fascism agree that while Mussolini's "New Italy" did generate new feelings of *Italianità* and pride for the immigrants' homeland, the majority of Italians in the United States remained largely uninterested in fascism as a political movement.[22] In the late 1920s, fascists began to acknowledge, extol, and commodify the very regional traditions and economies that Italian politicians had scorned among Italians in Italy and communities abroad just a decade before. Now, in their effort to promote commerce in Italian goods and a sense of national pride among Italians worldwide, fascists interacted with a flourishing immigrant cultural economy in which regionalism as an experience, language, and marketing strategy was already well established.

Advertisements in the Italian American press reveal an enduring dialectic between the local and the national, and between immigrants' everyday cultural and consumer identities and the diplomatic objectives of Italian political elites. This dynamic began at the turn of the twentieth century, as evidenced by publicity for exports in the Italian American press that advertised the regional origins of Italian products.[23] During the late 1920s and 1930s, a transnational convergence occurred between Italian fascists, who crafted and exploited regional customs to advance a collective national identity within Italy, and immigrants in the United States who, while informed by the regional traditions of their local *paesi*, increasingly conceived of themselves as sharing a common nationality. Promotional material for exports shows how tensions and alliances between the regional and the national manifested in both transnational market exchanges and in the quotidian experiences of buying, selling, and consuming in ethnic enclaves.

Italian companies hoped that as immigrant consumers returned home in the imaginary by buying and consuming Italian goods, the money from their purchases would materially traverse the ocean back to Italy. Immigrant entrepreneurs also sought to capitalize on the idea of Italy, but they did so in ways that retained profits in the United States In the early twentieth century, an increasing number of first- and second-generation immigrants began manufacturing and selling goods in the United States for a domestic market of ethnic and nonethnic consumers.[24] Italian exports competed with these U.S.-produced *"tipo italiano"* or "Italian style" goods, especially food products such as canned tomatoes and packaged pasta, as well as wines, cheeses, and cured meats. Already in the early twentieth century *Il Progresso* advertised a number of *tipo italiano* goods, including cigars, wines, and a variety of *paste domestiche*, or domestic pastas.[25] This competition intensified after World War I, when wartime needs in Italy, an attenuation of transnational migration, and new tariff duties after the Great Depression worked against foreign companies and instead provided opportunities for Italian American businesses to capture the immigrant market.[26] The growth of the *tipo italiano* industry reveals that while Italian companies and politicians attempted to control immigrants' transnational consumer habits, the very global nature of migration and trade created opportunities for immigrant sellers, producers, and consumers to produce habits and identities independent of nation-state and corporate designs. The Italian American press chronicled this market rivalry, publishing advertisements for both domestically produced *tipo italiano* items and Italian export commodities.[27] The money spent on goods produced by Italian American entrepreneurs and their descendants remained in the United States rather than traversing the Atlantic, making consumers' imagined returns less profitable for Italian companies.

By the 1920s and 1930s, Italian American immigrant entrepreneurs, like Italian export companies, used the emphasis on regional diversity to sell their domestically produced *tipo italiano* goods to an immigrant, and increasingly non-Italian clientele. In 1927, San Francisco's Italian Chamber of Commerce published a tourist food guide to San Francisco's North Beach that played up the "variety of types" in the city's "Latin Quarter." Visitors could expect to see people from all parts of Italy in the streets where "the ruddy, strong Piedmontese and the robust Ligurian, the fair Tuscan and Sicilian, mixed with French and Normal blood, present a colorful contrast." The guide, published in English and organized by cities within Italy, described gastronomic specialties from Rome, Bologna, Milan, and Florence, and provided regional recipes and basic information about Italian cooking geared specifically toward American housewives. The guide asserted: "Italy had many glorious traditions also in the field of gastronomic art, and every city has some culinary specialties which individualize every province. As each district has a different dialect so it has a different way of preparing food."[28] Italian immigrants in San Francisco hoping to lure nonethnic consumers into the city's "Little Italy" marketed regionalism as something that American tourists could experience by visiting North Beach, by buying Italian products, and by preparing Italian food in their own homes.

Just as advertisements for exports and *tipo italiano* goods in the Italian-language press offered immigrants an imaginary vehicle for returning home, San Francisco's immigrant entrepreneurial community implied that Americans too could visit or experience Italy without leaving the country. The guide stated: "The merchandise in the windows of the shops recalls to the cosmopolitan wanderer the sunny cities of Italy. In fact, a good many people find something of a resemblance between San Francisco and Genoa, or even some quarters of Naples." While Italian companies advertising in the ethnic press tended to homogenize Italian immigrant consumers, to a mainstream American audience, Italian Americans often presented themselves as regionally eclectic. Both Italian exporters and Italian American businesses used understandings about and images of Italy's regional diversity to sell olive oils, liqueurs, and other products and in the process used consumption to redefine meanings of, and connections between, nationhood and migration. Furthermore, evidence of the importance of regional identities in the promotion and selling of Italian exports, combined with the development of local *tipo italiano* goods, suggests that Italians in the United States neither relinquished their regional identities in the marketplace nor consumed only with the Italian nation-state in mind, as Italian companies and politicians had hoped.

Constructing Transnational Commodity Chains in Italian Products

Advertisements for Italian products in the Italian American press often conceptualized immigrants not only as a coherent consumer community, but also as vital economic actors whose purchases of Italian products made Italy's economic autonomy possible. Elvea, an Italian manufacturer of canned tomatoes, addressed its 1935 advertising to "Italians of America—Immigrants and Descendants." After arguing for the unsurpassed quality and superiority of Italian products and reminding immigrants of their patriotic duty to buy Italian goods, the ad noted Italy's need to acquire select U.S. merchandise through trade. Positioning immigrants as the pivot upon which transnational exchange turned, the ad contended that immigrants' purchases of Italian goods made it possible for Italy to then purchase valuable trade items from the United States. "In this," the ad spoke to immigrants, "you assume the important role of genuine and authentic international bankers." The advertisement positioned immigrant consumers as contributors to the vitality of both Italian and U.S. export markets. With immigrants' cooperation, the ad concluded, "Italy prepares to take her seat among the grand nations also in the economic realm."[29]

Elvea was one of many Italian export companies that drew attention to immigrants' roles in creating and sustaining transatlantic commodity paths in Italian goods. How global commodity chains have interacted historically with migrant communities is little known. Most research on commodity networks by sociologists, economists, and geographers center almost exclusively on contemporary political-economic operations of chain construction and pay little attention to the impact of mass migration on market operations.[30] New interdisciplinary work on global commodity chains, however, has considered how cultural assumptions guide and manage the various economic processes entrenched in commodity circuits.[31] Export publicity like that for Elvea discloses that Italians abroad did not interact with transnational and domestic markets merely as economic actors, but as cultural mediators who produced new spaces and meanings about migration, trade, and nationhood in the Atlantic political economy.

While advertisements represented consumers abroad as holding the power to bolster Italy's prestige on an international level in the diplomatic realm, they also connected immigrants' purchases to the wellbeing of individual Italian workers. A series of advertisements for Florio Marsala wine from 1937, for example, showed how promotional material constructed ethnic commodity chains between Italian laborers back home and immigrant consumers in the United States Such ads often featured photographs of the Florio plant in Sicily, where workers attached Florio labels to bottles of Marsala, alongside illustrations of attractive, handkerchief-clad young women harvesting grapes in vineyards. The advertisement reminded buyers that their purchases of Florio Marsala during the Christmas season aided the plants' workers, while offering a way for immigrants in the United States to send holiday wishes to Italians at home.[32] Advertisements displayed transactions between ethnic producers and consumers on a person-to-person level, while emphasizing how purchases of Italian goods abroad supported individual

Italian workers in Italy. The readers of these advertisements in the United States entered into Italian workspaces to see contented laborers profiting from their personal consumer choices abroad.

Conversely, a low demand for Italian products in the United States increased the hardships and sufferings of both producers and consumers in Italy. A 1926 advertisement for Italian American merchant L. Gandolfi & Company called on immigrants to resolve Italy's negative balance of trade by buying Italian products. Italy's trade deficit, the ad suggested, produced economic adversity among Italian workers: "Life in Italy today costs more than in every other part of the world; Italian workers—craftsmen of our future potential—are paid much less than workers in France, England, America and Germany," the ad reminded readers.[33] As trade with the United States languished, advertisements argued that workers' salaries decreased, keeping Italian workers in servile economic positions. Purchasing Italian commodities abroad raised living standards among Italians, allowing relatives at home the opportunity to participate in Italy's economy as consumers. Such publicity connected diasporic economies to Italy's economic health as a nation in competition with other European and global powers, and to the local well-being of individual workers in Italy, who produced the goods Italian Americans bought. Furthermore, the ad implied that immigrants' consumption of exports in the United States allowed Italian workers to consume back home as their purchasing power increased. Although markets for consumer goods often conceal expenses in commodity chains, such advertisements for Italian exports made a point of divulging these costs, particularly in the form of labor.

By entreating migrants to sustain Italian workers through their purchases in the United States, these ads constructed ethnic trade networks between producers and consumers. Simultaneously, advertisements created imagined ties between laborers on both side of the Atlantic. The 1935 Elvea ad stated that less trade between Italy and the United States was detrimental to both Italian workers and immigrant workers in America. "Without your collaboration," the ad read, "the U.S. could not export in Italy, and this would mean less work for some of you and an increase in unemployment in America."[34] The Elvea ad implied that consumption bound Italian workers together across the Atlantic in a way very different from Italian socialist and anarchist groups, which often rejected consumer culture as a capitalist entrapment and an impediment to promoting international class struggle.[35] Elvea portrayed the consumption of Italian exports in the United States as an expression of transatlantic solidarity between the Italian and Italian American working class.

A series of 1937 advertisements in *Il Progresso* for Motta brand *panettone* demonstrates how immigrants' imagined returns sometimes has the opportunity to wield real power over Italian commodity paths in both the diaspora and in Italy. The advertisements publicized Motta's special Christmas service for Italian immigrants to send the holiday sweet bread from the Motta factory in Milan directly to their friends and families in Italy.[36] The Motta holiday service allowed Italian immigrants, without leaving the United States, to exert an influence on their Italian relatives' laboring and consuming lives. By purchasing Motta brand *panettone* in the United States or by sending Motta bread to family members in Italy, migrants linked the transatlantic and domestic movement of goods, U.S. and Italian economies, and Italian consumers and producers on both sides of the Atlantic. Promotional material in the Italian-language press, therefore, depicted immigrants as active participants in transnational commodity chains as both producers and consumers.

Female Migrant Consumers as Guardians of Families and Commerce

Beginning in the 1920s, advertisements for Italian exports increasingly portrayed women as the principal buyers and consumers of Italian products, particularly food goods. This shift after World War I coincided with broader cultural and social changes that increasingly associated women with consumption, especially in industrialized countries, where middle-class notions of gendered divisions of space and labor involved women in a variety of market exchanges.[37] This shift in gendered messages in advertising material also coincided with demographic trends that created more gender balanced Italian communities in the United States During the late 1920s gender ratios within the Italian immigrant population began to equalize; while the total number of both Italian men and women migrants to the United States decreased during the World War I, increasingly restrictive migration laws, the global depression, provisions for family unification, and a growing second generation of Italians in the United States, increased the proportion of women to men in Italian communities.[38] U.S. census data show that females among Italians born in the United States rose from 31 percent in 1880 to 35 percent in 1910 and to 42 percent in 1930.[39] The more gender balanced Italian communities after World War I made women an increasingly lucrative target market for Italian companies and merchants.

While many ads connected immigrants' consumer choices to the livelihood of Italian laborers, advertisements featuring women more frequently tied such purchases to the maintenance of transnational kin ties and family roles. Anthropologists Sarah Mahler and Patricia Pessar have articulated a conceptual model for examining the ways in which gender operates through transnational processes, networks, and spaces. The "gendered geographies of power" model they have developed encourages scholars to investigate how gender functions simultaneously on many levels, including through imaginary forms of agency.[40] By presenting Italian exports as connecting Italian families across space and time, and by positioning women as guardians of Italian commerce, advertisements offered specifically female ways of returning home and contributing to family across the Atlantic. Italian American women's consumerist and migratory activities blended in ways that connected the private domestic realm to a transnational public sphere of commerce and trade.

Advertisements for Italian goods depicted Italian American women using exports to maintain culinary traditions, consumer practices, and familial commitments to their homeland. As historians of gender and consumption have articulated, the new consumer ethic and ready-made goods characterizing U.S. society changed immigrant women's relationship to the larger marketplace, in part by transporting them into the public arena as consumers with purchasing power, and sometimes even as political activists.[41] Less research has been done on how ethnic women interacted with products from their homeland, and on how such interactions redefined the roles of women and positioned them as links between domestic and global economies. Advertisements implied that purchasing Italian exports transported immigrant women generationally back in time and geographically across space to the households of their mothers and grandmothers in Italy.

The Italian American press portrayed women's purchases of Italian exports, particularly food goods, as strengthening transatlantic bonds against the danger of eroding links between Italian families in Italy and the United States. Ads for Bertolli brand olive oil, for example, implied that while women situated in the United States could not physically participate in the creation and continuation of kin contacts across the Atlantic, they made imagined exchanges with extended family in Italy by consuming the same Italian products. A 1932 advertisement in Chicago's *L'Italia* featured an illustration of a woman buying oil from a grocer proclaiming, "Olive oil used by Italians for four generations."[42] In another, an Italian woman professed to always ask for Bertolli, "the purest, unsurpassed, made-in-Italy olive oil that my grandmother and mother used before me."[43] Similarly, in a 1930 advertisement for Caffé Pastene, a wife chided her husband: "Tell me, are you not fortunate to have a spouse that cooks so excellently?" He responds: "Why yes! This coffee is as good as that made by my mother!"[44] Advertisements showed Italian immigrant female consumers actively engaged in transnational kin work; their purchases not only represented connections across Italian households in the United States, but revealed generational links to households in Italy, where the same products and methods of food preparation were used. Advertisements pictured women in the "modern" realm of the marketplace using money to make consumer choices on behalf of families that extended across the Atlantic. By referring to female consumers in Italy, such advertisements also portrayed Italian women as actively engaged in a consumer culture, even though most women in rural southern Italy, while experiencing new economic opportunities as buyers and entrepreneurs, remained largely on the periphery of an active consumerist marketplace.[45]

Promotional material also portrayed women using such transnational exchange with kin in Italy not only to solidify family and commercial bonds but also to perpetuate Italian familial structures that revolved around women's domestic roles as wives and mothers. While advertisements showed immigrant women using exports to maintain a distinctly Italian or ethnic consumer and national identity, these ads often resembled those for food products in English-language mainstream literature, which frequently presented women using their consumerist expertise to keep their families happy and healthy.[46] A large, half-page advertisement for Florio's Italian eggnog, "the sun of Sicily in a bottle," was marketed specifically to mothers concerned about the wellbeing of their children. The ad entreated women, "Protect your children in the struggles of life nourishing them with Zabajone Italiano (Italian eggnog)."[47] A 1935 advertisement for Locatelli brand imported cheeses urged consumers to buy authentic pecorino romano cheese, "so that the new generation of Italian Americans is able to perpetuate the tradition of taste, health, and nutrients."[48] Advertisements reinforced middle-class understandings of gender roles for immigrants around Italian products, while revealing merchants' desire to reach the growing number of second-generation Italian Americans who were less culturally and gastronomically linked to their homeland.

Advertisements often pictured women choosing authentic Italian exports over substitute, inferior-quality brands. Such ads connected women's everyday consumer responsibilities and choices to the preservation of both ethnic households and Italian trade networks. A 1932 advertisement for Bertolli brand olive oil in Chicago's *L'Italia* used a discussion between two *massaie* or housewives, one knowledgeable and one inexperienced, to portray women consumers as judicious custodians of Italian commerce. The expert housewife scolded her friend, and pointed to the English writing on the can indicating that the product contained only a minimal amount of real olive oil. She asked her friend: "You didn't realize that the grocer played a joke on you, in that he sold you sesame seed oil flavored with the addition of the smallest amount of olive oil?"[49] Like the expert housewives who purchased only Bertolli brand olive oil imported from Italy, women often represented the key and final link on an ethnic commodity chain in which mainly male Italian laborers in Italy produced goods purchased by consumption-savvy Italian American mothers and wives abroad. By describing women's consumer habits as linked to the household, the nation, and the transatlantic, advertisements disclosed the way gender functioned concurrently on many spatial and social levels that traversed transnational landscapes.

These images of the female consumer parallel research done by scholars who demonstrate the ways in which women come to embody the nation, and how ethnic communities and immigrants themselves viewed women immigrants as generators and maintainers of ethnic identity.[50] While the press employed a modernizing discourse to show women with money and the power of consumer choice, Italian companies used and continue to use traditional female figures in the packaging of their export products. Olive oil and canned tomatoes in particular utilized images of young peasant women in traditional costume contentedly harvesting fruit in rural settings—illustrations that connoted ideas of patriotism, purity, abundance, and a precapitalist rural past. Italian commercial iconography, therefore, portrayed Italian women both as consumers and as gendered representations of the nation to be consumed. Such varied images of women consumers in Italian American commercial newspapers reveal export advertisements as an important source for exploring ethnic conceptualizations of gender and their transnational consequences.

Conclusion

Historians of migration and economy have demonstrated that Italian export earnings and immigrants' financial remittances provided critical capital to the Italian economy.[51] Large financial returns facilitated Italy's industrial boom of the late nineteenth and early twentieth century by contributing to Italy's positive balance of payments. With one of the highest rates of return among international migrants during the age of mass migration, imagined returns were often realized, as Italian temporary laborers moved back and forth between, Italy, the United States, and other receiving locations.[52] Less attention, however, has been paid to the consuming diaspora itself, and how Italian exports sold, purchased, and consumed abroad affected immigrants' understanding of the country they left behind and of themselves as ethnic Americans. Advertising material in the Italian American press demonstrate that Italian companies, merchants trading in Italian goods, Italian politicians, and Italian American entrepreneurs all tried to create and then capitalize on immigrants' transnational lives by crafting specific ideas about what consuming Italian products could do for consumers abroad, and for the home country.

Advertisements presented products from Italy as more than consumer goods. Ads also represented monetary and psychological investments in Italy, as well as foundations upon which immigrants maintained imaginary and real ties with their home country. Merchants and political elites on both sides of the Atlantic attempted to unify Italians abroad through the consumption of Italian goods and to contain regional distinctions within the commercial and cultural confines of the Italian nation, even while immigrant entrepreneurs themselves often emphasized regionalism to sell goods. Advertisements also crafted ethnic commodity chains through representations and discussions of transnational connections between consumers and producers. Furthermore, ads provided gendered ways of returning home; publicity for exports showed a difference in the way men and women invented and enacted transnational consumer identities and bonds to Italy. These advertisements reveal gendered kin work as a central part of real and imagined transnational commodity chains that affected both sending and receiving nations. The globally dispersed Italian communities abroad, therefore, served as a resource for affecting social practices and meanings of both commodity and migration paths. Advertisements for Italian exports demonstrate how the cultural dimensions of migration organized and defined transnational markets and consumer identities. Advertisements reformulated the relationship between immigrants and their homeland to meet the market needs of Italian companies and the consuming desires and practices of Italians in migrant diasporas.

4

Sovereign Consumption

ITALIAN AMERICANS' TRANSNATIONAL FILM
CULTURE IN 1920S NEW YORK CITY

Giorgio Bertellini

On August 22, 1923, the leading Italian American newspaper, *Il Progresso Italo-Americano*, published an announcement authorized and signed by Benito Mussolini (figure 4.1).[1] While prominently displaying the words "Cavo Italiano" (Italian Cable), the advertisement invited Italian Americans to purchase shares of the Italian company Italcable (short for Italcable—Servizi cablografici, radiotelegrafici e radioelettrici SpA), to finance the laying of submerged transatlantic telegraph cables connecting Italy to the United States (figure 4.2).[2] Several New York banks were ready to welcome Italians immigrants' contributions. The announcement included the facsimile reproduction of the final section of a handwritten message that Mussolini had sent earlier that year to Italians living in America, on the occasion of his signing the contract between Italcable and the government. The message read: "The cable . . . is like a giant arm that the Mother country stretches toward her distant sons to attract them and make them partake of her pain, joy, work, and glory. Viva l'Italia!"[3]

While Mussolini's appeal may seem to rely on the backward-looking and nostalgia-filled rhetoric of a motherly embrace, the cable connection and its coverage highlighted the challenges of national sovereignty both in America—Italian immigrants' host country—and in the modern landscape of transatlantic news wiring and international communications.[4] Specifically, by defining the cable connection as an arm or a bridge between Italians and Italians in America, the advertisement identified a new egalitarian platform of shared technological progress and dialogue between Italy and the United States. In early 1920s America, in the context of a largely sympathetic recognition of Fascism as a regime based on industriousness, discipline, and work, the promotion

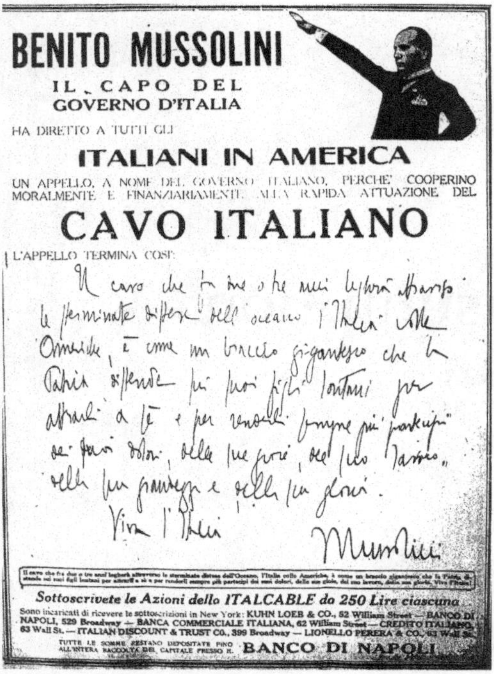

Figure 4.1. *Il Progresso Italo-Americano*
(August 22, 1923): 14.

of the cable resonated with Mussolini's and, more broadly, Italy's acceptance as *primus inter pares* in American media life.[5] As such, the Italcable episode seemingly revealed a new feature of Italian Americans' 1920s public discourse: one that both sought and vaunted Italy's national equivalence and cultural exchange with America on the basis of new communications media. With the new cable, the regime's public rhetoric vented Italy's continuous contribution to the development of new communication technology, following the turn-of-the-century century fame of Guglielmo Marconi, inventor of long-distance radio transmission, or wireless telegraphy. In the process, alongside the emphasis on production, the regime also began emphasizing Italians' access to, and consumption of, modern technology. The telegraph, just like films, record players, and, later, radio broadcastings, was meant to enable once destitute and marginalized immigrants to engage actively with their identity as Italians living in the United States through modern media. If this ideological stance should not strike us as utterly original—moviegoing has been a public consumption practice since the turn of the twentieth century—the circumstances of its expression were new.

In this essay I investigate whether and how 1920s Italian American film culture resonated with such assertive transnational connection. In particular, I look at how the largest Italian American newspaper, *Il Progresso Italo Americano*, articulated self-assured ideas of cultural dialogue and exchange through film reviews, reports about film reception and stars, and advertisements for new films or talent agencies. Although

Rete delle comunicazioni dell' Italcable.

Figure 4.2. "Network of Italcable," from La "Italcable" ed i suoi cavi per le Americhe: nell'inaugurazione del cavo Anzio–Buenos Aires XII Ottobre 1925 (Milan: Modiano, 1925), 4.

Il Progresso had its convenient commercial and political agenda with regard to cultural patriotism, the evidence it provides reveals a dense circuit of newsmaking and popular response, indeed a culture of film consumption, that positioned Italy and America not as opposed, but in dialogue with one another. For an emigrant community long accustomed to endure racial and cultural prejudice and perceived to be strenuously attached to European customs and lifestyles, the 1920s saw the emergence of a geocultural confidence that impacted ideas and practices of film consumption turning manifest and inescapable affiliation into choice. Ultimately the narrative of transatlantic underwater cables participated in a dynamic of proactive adaptation and conversation with America that turn-of-the-century immigrants' culture had dared to approach mainly through comedy and satire, most glaringly with immigrant vaudeville entertainer Farfariello's (the stage name of Eduardo Migliaccio) metalinguistic and self-deprecating humor.[6] Both in conjunction with Mussolini's rise to cultural and political fame in America and somewhat independent of it, what emerged in the 1920s were novel ways to consume "things Italian" and "things American." When reporting on the American circulation of new and reissued Italian films, the release of American films set in Italy, and the way Hollywood personalities publicly opined about 1920s Italy, Il Progresso stressed the emergence of a new, egalitarian channel of consumeristic discourse along the real and symbolic telegraphic Italy-America axis. It was a discourse, *Il Progresso* maintained, evident in a new awareness within the Italian American community of the importance of such effective technologies of communication as commercial advertisements, political advocacy, public relations, and stardom.

Transnational Film Spectatorship

In order to examine *Il Progresso*'s 1920s discourse on Italian Americans' film consumption, a methodological recasting is in order. Film historiography has long assumed that by the 1920s Hollywood's standardization of production and exhibition practices flattened immigrant audiences' culturally specific and often dissonant responses. Film historians' enduring preference for class difference as the main analytical vector to gauge moving pictures' mode of address and cultural impact, together with a perpetual reluctance (or inability) to consider the foreign press as a significant evidentiary source, have seriously constricted the research on silent film spectatorship.[7] Immigrants' cultures have remained marginal. Further, silent film scholarship has displayed a troublesome disregard for how historians of whiteness and racial difference have enriched our understanding of the racial and cultural diversity of America's working class before and after World War I and how their studies have challenged the narrative of immigrants' fast Americanization in the roaring 1920s. Exceptions have been rare.[8] Over the decades, scholarly assessments about film spectatorship in the 1920s have often sanctioned the industry's loud efforts to downplay earlier concerns about the behavioral dissonance and cultural insulation of foreigners and the lower classes in general. A resulting interpretative tradition has stressed how 1920s movie palaces, as glamorous venues of urban film consumption, turned the film experience into something safe, pleasant, and even luxurious.[9] In a decade welcoming and celebrating these large, airy, and brightly lit "temples of classness," mainstream narratives about Americans' moviegoing have long maintained that the "formal and privatized mode" of 1920s film reception had replaced immigrants' "residual interactive sociability" associated with the dark nickelodeons and small storefront theatres of earlier times.[10] Overlooking the major immigration restrictions of the period, commentators have long posited that the standardization of Hollywood's production and exhibition practices tamed the diversity of reception American audiences. The critical implication was that immigrants had finally learned to consume cinema properly by relinquishing their ethnic, and highly socialized, attachments, thereby surrendering to an individualizing Americanization. "Darkness further enforced the silence," Richard Butsch has recently repeated, "and made the experience less collective and more a dialog between individual viewer and film." In that regard, the question of movie audiences' social and cultural difference became in the 1920s a "nonissue."[11]

This overall assessment presents two major problems. First, only a fraction of American movie theaters in the 1920s were movie palaces. The vast majority consisted of neighborhood theatres, aimed at working class patrons, including immigrant groups. Such venues still offered opportunities for social gatherings and loud, communal exchanges informed by Hollywood fare but not devoid of ethnic lore, whether contemporary observers cared to notice or not. In these sites, different forms of film consumption and experience, linked to a variety of cultural and political urgencies, complicated individual films' singular address mode.[12]

Second, a multinational dimension of American film culture was not just evident in the nationality of film patrons crowding movie theaters, but it also belonged to what was projected on screen. The expression "transnational America," to adopt Randolph Bourne's felicitous 1916 phrase, ought to be both considered in conjunction with Hollywood's post–World War I domestic and international domination and associated to broader currents in American public life.[13] Hollywood hegemony and cosmopolitanism walked parallel tracks. The Great War, in fact, had impaired the ability of European film industries, including the Italian one, to compete both in the American market and in their own. In the early 1920s, film periodicals were quite aware of the Americanization of US and foreign film cultures. "Wherever one goes the world over," one *Photoplay* article read, "from the interior of China to South Africa or from Australia to Iceland, [the traveler] finds the American movie, for ninety per cent of the motion pictures of the world are American."[14] Parallel to this, however, was an opposite dynamic: The crisis of the melting pot ideology provided American culture with multiple opportunities to open itself up to transnational influences. Whether projected at home or abroad, American films were contributing to a starkly diverse film culture. "The Iowa lad is learning that the French aren't frog-eaters, nor are the Italians 'Ginnies,'" *Photoplay* had written in 1918, before adding, "Likewise, the men of Europe are discovering a land of fellow-beings—not an imaginary continent of bad manners, red Indians and financial savages."[15] Far from an isolated observation, *Photoplay* was articulating ideas about a post–melting pot America that a few progressive intellectuals had voiced a few years earlier. If in 1915 Horace M. Kallen had argued that "Americanization has not repressed nationality [but] has liberated nationality," a year later Randolph Bourne had maintained that America was "not a nationality but a transnationality."[16] By 1923, *Motion Picture Classic* identified the phenomenon as Hollywood's "European complex" by reporting that "nearly every production now filming, or in immediate prospect, has a foreign setting."[17]

According to a strategy that made cultural and commercial sense, after World War I mainstream American culture intensified the commodification of foreign cultures and national differences rather than striving for their erasure. In an epoch of expanding mass entertainments and urban tourism resulting in quasi-ethnographic visits to ethnic enclaves, Italianness solidified its broader commodifiable appeal as charmingly anti-modern, authentically exotic, and even romantic. Stories of slumming in the Greenwich Village, next to Bohemian communities, are well known.[18] Yet, what occurred inside "the colony," as the Italian neighborhoods were often referred to, is less well known. In the midst of rising and ambitiously homogenizing consumerism, at a time when the memory of immigrants' transatlantic journey had not yet become a glorious repository of fictionalized mythologies and when Italian American culture still bore the marks of dissonance and inadequacy, Italian Americans' film consumption underwent significant changes. Close examination of *Il Progresso* reveals the extent to which in the 1920s the Italian American public discourse did not hail the consumption of Italian and American films as two opposing cultural practices that signaled conflicting national loyalties. Instead, through a series of modes transatlantic engagement, the ethnic press discourse engaged in efforts to transnationalize film culture and, in the process, deprovincialize Italian film consumers.

No Island Is an Island

The film coverage in *Il Progresso* displayed three such modes of power-laden relationship between Italian and American cultural constituencies. Accounts of new and reissued historical epics informed a first and initially quite dominant mode that relied on Italy's celebrated past and that insisted on national difference—whether superiority or inferiority, but not equality—between Italian and American film cultures. This *passatist mode* unfolded in the conceited name of Italy's spiritual kinship with its glorious artistic past against America's modern consumerism, or in the self-effacing one of Hollywood's technological and commercial preeminence. A second, *vernacular mode* relied on the nostalgic marketing of filmed *sceneggiate* and on vernacular theater and music. Through reissues of old southern melodramas or the distribution of new ones, this mode operated through an interpellation of proud backwardness and picturesqueness that divorced immigrants and their descendants from all other groups. As the passatist mode, it also relied on *difference* by hailing regional culture as a sign of national distinction and isolation. The Italian American response to Enrico Caruso's fame, however, including his widely covered sickness and death, constituted the strongest counterexample to this second mode. Finally a *dialogic mode* stressed transnational parity and exchange, and was predicated not on hierarchy, but on equality, eagerness for exchange, and mutual appreciation. It was a cultural stance that was not particularly visible in the early to mid-1910s, but that in the 1920s emerged out of a variety of news reports that included coverage of Hollywood stars visiting Italy, Italian films distributed in the United States, American films relying on Italian dramatic sources and filmmaking settings, and Hollywood personalities speaking highly about Mussolini and Italy in general. This mode had a profound and lasting impact, affecting in the 1930s Italian American film productions.[19]

While variously embodying these transatlantic modes, film culture in New York's Italian America mostly revolved around few sites of consumption, although there were significant exceptions. By the 1920s, long gone were the nickelodeons, the storefront shops turned into improvised movie houses, and almost gone, too, were the many neighborhood theaters offering live shows and moving pictures. According to the newspaper's coverage what remained were three key venues for Italian Americans' film culture: the Acierno's Thalia Theater, located at 46–48 Bowery, in the heart of the Italian enclave of Lower Manhattan and for a century the center of theatrical life in the Lower East Side; the 14th Street Theatre, also known as Teatro Italiano, located between Fourteenth Street and Sixth Avenue; and the Teatro Italiano (143 East Fourteenth Street), located near Union Square, on the north side of Fourteenth Street between Irving Place and Third Avenue. The multinational functionality of this latter location was evident through the variety of its bilingual names—Nuovo Teatro Italiano, Teatro Olympic, and Olympic Theatre.[20]

All three venues exhibited rereleased Italian epics, which included *La Gerusalemme liberata* (The Crusaders; Cines, 1911), *Quo Vadis?* (Cines 1913), and *Jone o Gli ultimi giorni di Pompei* (The Last Days of Pompeii; Pasquali 1913).[21] New Italian productions were exhibited at more upscale Broadway theaters, as we shall see. An exception to this rule was *Cabiria* (Itala Film, 1914), rereleased in the summer of 1921 and screened not at a neighborhood venue, but at the lavish Strand Theatre (West Forty-First Street and Broadway). The popularity of the film explains this unique circumstance. Differently from its first 1914 American release, its 1921 advertisement relied on the aura of three by then exceptionally famous names, which the ads promoted in capital letters (figure 4.3). The decadent poet Gabriele D'Annunzio, who had famously collaborated on the film's intertitles, had made headlines in the previous months. Italian and American newspapers alike had covered his defiant paramilitary leadership at Fiume (Rijeka since the end of World War II, now in Croatia), which he defended as an Italian outpost militarily won in the Great War.[22] As *Cabiria*'s Nubian slave-turned-hero, the character of Maciste had been cast since 1915 as a white, bourgeois and patriotic Italian strong man in a series of successful films, partially reedited and serialized for the American market in the late 1910s.[23] Finally, *Cabiria* had by then achieved cult status as master example of Italian art film in American cinematic culture.[24] Titles aside, the advertisement stressed the proud achievement of national recognition by positing, in a rather redundant manner, that the "three great names . . . added splendor to the Italian name [and] granted Italian dramatic art the enthusiastic admiration of all the world." The image of

Figure 4.3. "D'Annunzio, Maciste, Cabiria."
Il Progresso Italo-Americano (July 2, 1921): 4.

the patriot D'Annunzio in military outfit on the top right corner of the flier celebrated a militarized Italianness that may have been appreciated, but that was not in dialogue with the host country.

New film releases were mostly of grand historical epics—the genre that in the 1910s had had give the Italian film industry the largest success in the American market. Their introduction to *Il Progresso* readers relied on a passatist and rather insular rhetoric. Consider *La nave* (The Ship, 1921), from Gabriele D'Annunzio's eponymous tragedy (1908), and *Teodora* (Theodora, 1922), adapted from Victorien Sardou's theatrical work, *Théodora* (1884). First screened on October 14, 1921 at the Astor Theatre (West Forty-Fifth Street and Broadway), *Teodora* emerged as Italian cinema's long-awaited repeat, seven years after the triumph of *Cabiria*. *Il Progresso* invited all Italians to join state representatives and local authorities to marvel at "what Italy had been able to create," amounting to "a miracle not only of the Italian talent, but of the national film industry."[25] In 1921, *Il Progresso* covered the Italian release of *La nave*, distributed in the U.S. only three years later, by publishing a long interview with the film's director, Gabriellino D'Annunzio, the son of the celebrated writer. The younger D'Annunzio praised the producer and distributor UCI (Unione Cinematografica Italiana), Italy's film trust, for supporting a production that had celebrated the Italianness of settings and locations.[26] Similarly, the Rome-based interviewer underscored the "rigorous exactitude of the staging, the authenticity and picturesqueness of the locations" to emphasize the production's "singular nobility and efficacy" and thus to challenge "Teutonic competition" or "Anglo-Saxon rivalry" in the name of two exclusive materials: the sun and the landscape. In the same paragraph, the display of haughtiness only anticipated the foreseeable recognition of glaring narrative shortcomings, explained as a "lack [of] full discipline."[27] Similar patriotic echoes informed the promotion ("every Italian's duty") and reviews of *Messalina* (The Fall of an Empress, Cines, 1923)[28] and the release of *Dante, nella vita e nei tempi suoi* (Dante Alighieri, V.I.S. Florence, 1922).[29]

As noted earlier, the ancient past did not exhaust the major facets of Italian film culture in 1920s America. A competing experiential form of self-segregation, one that privileged regional identity and vernacular culture over national and monumental history, accounted for the rerelease of such classic vernacular melodramas as *Capitan Blanco* (1914) and *Assunta Spina* (1915).[30] Their promotion relied on the performances of their stars, the Sicilian Giovanni Grasso and the Neapolitan Francesca Bertini. If Bertini had by then almost retired from public life, Grasso was a familiar feature in the colony's cultural scene. Together with fellow Sicilian performer Mimì Aguglia, he regularly performed roles in Neapolitan and Sicilian dramas at the Acierno's Thalia Theatre. An international star since the early twentieth century, his presence in New York in the 1920s coincided with the intermedial institutionalization of *sceneggiate*—staged and filmed adaptations of famous songs. The pervasivess of Neapolitan *sceneggiate* across the Atlantic consolidated a market of films, plays, and consuming habits that a few Italian companies effectively exploited. In 1921 alone, for instance, *'O Festino e 'A Legge* (Dora Film, 1921) and *Santa Lucia Luntana* (Eliocinemagrafica, 1921) brought an air of uniquely authentic Neapolitanness to the 14th Street Theatre and the Winter Garden (Houston Street and Second Avenue).[31] The latter film took its name from a famous eponymous song, also known as *Partono i bastimenti* (The Ships Leave), written in 1919 by E. A.

Mario, turned into a one-act *sceneggiata* the same year, and associated with southern Italian immigrants' actual and imaginary travels. At a time when the Fascist regime was opposing regional and vernacular culture, the success and longevity of these shows in New York throughout the 1920s signaled their heightened geocultural situatedness and seemingly discouraged a broader address. Only in theory, in fact, the story of *Partono i bastimenti*, whether on stage or on screen, could have become an Italian master script for immigrant narratives shared by the many European groups who had experienced the sorrow and nostalgia associated with a transatlantic relocation. Instead, *Santa Lucia Luntana* remained a profoundly intranational, even regional, affair, that was promoted in the colony without inviting much of a communality with America's mainstream migration narratives.

Enrico Caruso mobilized a very different consumption strategy. Since the early twentieth century, the coverage of his life and accomplishments catalyzed discussions about his broad interclass appeal and universal cultural capital *beyond* his native Neapolitanness or Italianness.[32] Caruso's performances may have been an Italian commodity, but they were not for Italian only. In the 1920s his status continued to be that of a supreme "divo," an "incomparable artist whom all the world, without distinction of language, nationality or faith, adores as opera houses' undisputed sovereign."[33] When his health deteriorated during his residency in New York, President Wilson telegraphed his well wishes, yet, as *Il Progresso* noted, so did humble and anonymous workers in an "imposing *plebiscite* of loving admiration."[34] Differently from the proud regionalism infusing the public discourse about vernacular stage melodramas and films, Caruso's talent constantly emerged in the press as "peerless in his art and adored by all."[35] A few years earlier, in 1918, Paramount had translated his uniquely broad democratic allure into a film, *My Cousin*, that told the story of two Carusos—an indigent sculptor named Tommasso (*sic*) living in the Lower East Side and a cosmopolitan opera tenor named Caroli who resides uptown. The two cousins are united by both ancestry and physical resemblance to the point that Caruso played both roles with just a minimum of costume and makeup adjustment. Rereleased after his death on August 2, 1921, the film celebrated a broad interclass and international *communality* and as such anticipated a number of other, significant occurrences.

Italy in Silent American Cinema

A few years after the end of World War I, the exhibition of a few Italian and American films began to elicit a novel, more inclusive, type of response. Repeatedly *Il Progresso* published advertisements that stressed how Italian film narratives (and settings) had become humanity's patrimony, not just the pride of a single nation. The promotion for the colossal *Dante's Inferno* (Fox 1924) emphasized the universal value of the *Divine Comedy*, which "nations all over the world have translated in all existing languages." It was produced in Hollywood, but it was "the film the world was waiting for"[36] (figure 4.4). A comparable tone of transnational communality infused the speech given by *Il Progresso*'s director, Carlo Barsotti, on the third anniversary of the erection of a monument to Dante Alighieri. Addressing the city's mayor on behalf of all Italians, many of whom were his devoted readers, Barsotti promised to contribute "with our minds, hearts,

N. 10 "DANTE'S INFERNO"

Il film che il mondo aspetta

Le fotografie delle scene dell'"Inferno", il Prologo e l'Epilogo sono completati nello Studio di Fox, Los Angeles, il 2 Agosto 1924.

Il dimostrare agli uomini il sentiero divino che conduce alla salvezza era la mira di Dante.

(Continua)

CENTRAL Broadway alle 6.30 **COMINCIANDO LUNEDI' 29 SETT.**

Figure 4.4. "Dante's Inferno." *Il Progresso Italo-Americano* (September 27, 1924): 5.

and arms to wellbeing and prosperity of this noble nation. Long live America, long live Italy!"[37]

Similarly, *Il Progresso* reviewed the 1925 screening of the remake of *The Last Days of Pompeii* as "a true miracle performed by the Italian genius," but at the same time did not register any contradiction when attributing the film's "lively reconstruction of the most tragic episode of Roman and Latin life" to the truthfulness of its literary source—Edward Bulwer-Lytton's historical novel. Instead it noted that "never before had historical accuracy been so wonderfully respected."[38] While the story's human tragedy had occurred in Italy, the force of its reenactment insisted on a universal value that defied national differences.

Several news items conveyed a similar rhetoric. Rather than confining "things Italian" to a matter of national (or neighborhood) interest, they placed Italy and Italians at the heart of American film (and political) culture. The range of news, advertisements, and even film reviews included also references to nonfilmic events although the intersections with film culture were frequent. *Il Progresso* discussed American films shot in Italy that were endorsed by Fascist authorities, American film stars visiting Italy or simply playing Italian roles, Hollywood directors praising Italy and its political leadership, and even beauty contests organized to identify future Hollywood stars among Italians in America.

Through these reports, *Il Progresso* exhibited a nationalistic emphasis, by commenting on the need for a thorough reorganization of the Italian film industry along the lines of the Duce's economic reconstruction plans and against foreign competitors.[39] But it also exhibited a transnational approach by articulating a mode of address—a sort of consumer's guide—for American films made in Italy or with a clear Italian resonance.

Consider J. Gordon Edwards's *Nero* (Fox, 1922), praised for its grandiose scenes, "shot in Rome, in the Alps, and the feet of Vesuvius and inside Villa d'Este in Tivoli—featuring characters wonderfully played by Italian artists."[40] The advertisement for the film, exhibited at the prestigious Lyric Theatre on West Forty-Second Street, also included an open letter signed by William Fox (figure 4.5). In it the producer emphasized the degree of cooperation between the American film studio and Italy's best artists. The letter concluded with homage to a notion of relational, rather than insular, nationality. "*Nero* has been produced entirely in Italy, in the world's best scenic sites," the advertisement read, "and given that its participating artists were Italian, both Italians and Americans ought to be rightly proud of this grandiose filmmaking result." Another major film was *Ben-Hur: A Tale of the Christ* (MGM, 1925), the costly superspectacle that the Goldwyn Pictures Corporation began shooting in Italy but that, due to labor disputes, set construction delays, and filmmaking maladroitness, was completed in Hollywood under a new director (Fred Niblo) and the supervision of the newly formed Metro Goldwyn Mayer. *Ben-Hur* opened at the George M. Cohan Theatre (Broadway and Forty-Second Street) on December 30, 1925, and *Il Progresso* boastfully advertised it as an Italian American production featuring Ramon Novarro and "shot in Rome, Livorno, and Los Angeles with a price tag of $4,000,000."[41] A similar proud claim of equal partnership for an American production shot in Italy was reserved for *Mare Nostrum* (Metro Goldwyn, 1926), adapted

Figure 4.5. "Nero." *Il Progresso Italo-Americano* (May 27, 1922): 4.

from Vicente Blasco Ibáñez's novel, and exhibited at the Criterion Theatre (Broadway and West Forty-Fourth Street). *Mare Nostrum* combined Hollywood production values, associated with the talented Rex Ingram who—as *Il Progresso* noted—had directed Valentino's breakout film *The Four Horsemen of the Apocalypse* (1921), with authentic Italian settings: it "featured scenes from Naples, the Neapolitan Bay, Mount Vesuvius, Pompeii, and Venice" photographed with permission of the Ministero delle Belle Arti (Ministry of Artistic Heritage).[42] Whether associated with actors or directors, stardom represented throughout the 1920s a major vector for the modernization of Italian American film culture and for the development of an aspiration of equivalence and reciprocity between consuming Italianness and Americanness.

Consuming Transnational Stardom

In and of itself, an Italian-accented American stardom was no news in American public culture or in the colony. In addition to Caruso's domestic and global fame, American actor George Beban had carved a special place as impersonator of Italian characters first on stage then in such celebrated films as *The Italian* and *The Sign of the Rose*. By the early 1920s *Il Progresso* described him as the "greatest American artist endowed with Italian character."[43] His stardom anticipated the American fame of Italian actors and historical figures, namely Valentino and Mussolini, variously associated with Hollywood, but it also publicly signaled a new phenomenon: Italian immigrants' craze for Hollywood stars. Douglas Fairbanks was among the most notable ones. *Il Progresso* often expressed admiration for his films (among them *Three Musketeers, The Thief of Bagdad,* and *The Black Pirate*), but it also showed special attention to Fairbanks's triumphant trip to Italy in 1926 in the company of his wife, the even more famous Mary Pickford. In Florence, *Il Progresso* reported, they were welcomed by Fascist authorities, visited a local film company, and inaugurated a movie theater devoted to Italian cinema.[44] The two Hollywood royals enjoyed a much-advertised meeting with dictator Mussolini, heralding a convergence of transnational celebrities that operated according to Hollywood's publicity practices. In his presumption of grandeur, for instance, Mussolini treated Fairbanks and Pickford as *his* fans and offered them a Hollywood-like gift: his autographed photograph.[45] Mussolini's sense of entitlement was not misguided, however. Following their meeting with Mussolini, *The New York Times* reported excerpts of the conversation between the dictator and Fairbanks. After communicating how "impressed [he was] by the progress and modernity of Italy," Fairbanks allegedly told the dictator, "I have seen you often in the movies, but I like you better in real life." To which Mussolini "smilingly" replied: "I don't know whether I like you better in the movies or in real life, but I certainly do both. I admire the movies tremendously, because the action is so precise and rapid, which is one of the finest things in all life."[46] Whether it had actually occurred or not, the publicized exchange revealed a kinship between the two iconic figures based not only on their *celebrity status*—a key consumeristic vector—evident in the inevitable comparisons between exceptional personal charm and celebrated fictional self, but also on the political import of transatlantic celebrity culture. Both Mussolini's and Fairbanks's comments, in fact, verged on the political, with the latter even more explicitly aligning the novelty of Italian star-dictator with "the progress and modernity of Italy." Similarly, *Il Progresso* continued to emphasize publicly the mutual admiration between Fairbanks and Mussolini as a synecdoche of the two nations' newly established equal partnership, and used their shared celebrity to highlight Mussolini's Hollywood-like fame as a political leader and cultural icon—an unprecedented circumstance for an Italian politician.[47]

Mussolini's fame in American politics is well known thanks to the pioneering work of John P. Diggins, which first appeared in the late 1960s and culminated in *Mussolini and Fascism: The View from America* (1972).[48] What is less known is the range of his public visibility beyond political and scholarly coverage that, as *Il Progresso* reported, involved Italian and American newsreels, recorded speeches (commercialized by Victor Records), newspaper coverage, and even biographies and book reviews. The Duce's interweaving of media and political coverage supported and informed discussions of his policies, political stance, and national representation. The nationalist *Il Progresso* participated wholeheartedly in his exploitation as a hot news commodity and in the process raised awareness about the legitimacy of propaganda and the importance of publicity. On one day *Il Progresso* publicized Mussolini's intention to pay in full Italy's war debts to the United States; on another it offered a preview of the positive coverage about the Duce about to appear in William Randolph Hearst's *New York American*; on an another again it criticized the archenemy of Hearst's paper, the *New York World*, for its attacks against its bestselling news icon.

The widespread marketing of the star Mussolini contributed promoting Italy in a way that had purchasing appeal for both American and Italian consumers. *Il Progresso* aligned the Duce's American fame with the dawning of a *New Italy*, defined by such all American values as youth, discipline, and work ethic, capable of producing utterly new stage and film works.[49] Perhaps one of the most explicit proclamations of new national identity came in mid-April 1924, on the wave of news about the approval by the U.S. Congress of new immigration restrictions known as the Johnson–Reed Act. *Il Progresso* reported how Mussolini, wanting to defy old stereotypes about Italians' inefficiency and lack of work ethic, stressed that Rome, and Italy in general, "was not made of antiquarians and antique dealers, but of workers."[50] The marketing of a new Italy as an industrial and hardworking nation quickly reached Hollywood's upper echelons. On May 1924, *Il Progresso* published an interview with the much-celebrated director D. W. Griffith, who identified in the Duce's iconic youthfulness the emergence of a new Italy and, in the process, an implicit justification of his regime's authoritarian rule. "Mussolini is a great man because of his alliance with young people," the American director noted before making a broader reference to history: "He will do great things. I do not know what exactly he will be doing, but I would not be surprised if, like Napoleon, he were to conquer the world." In his view, Mussolini embodied a new national narrative of industriousness and efficiency, quite different from past accounts, for no other reason than his American-like character. "Italy is no longer a backward nation, moving at a slow pace," he noted, "the Duce has American ideas and he applies them to his country." Griffith even legitimized the Duce's forceful political style through a comparison with the then world heavyweight champion, Jack Dempsey, and even by praising the cinematic quality of his energy: "[Mussolini] is a young governor. He is not even forty years old and his physique is like that of Dempsey. . . . I would love to put into a film of mine this great Fascist spirit."[51]

A similar rhetoric of novelty, modernity, and transnational purchase accompanied Rudolph Valentino's exceptional fame. *Il Progresso* treated Valentino as an iconic representative of proud Italianness, at once attached to old tropes of Latin charm and confidence, but also capable of transcending them toward new, modern expressions.[52] Differently from Mussolini, however, his *Il Progresso* coverage revealed a range of conflicting positions. Valentino's success in Italian America presented significant challenges as passatist formulations of an idealized Latinity could not seamlessly be reconciled with the modern materialism associated with the Hollywood star system.

On the euphoric side, *Il Progresso* devotedly covered Valentino's career by regularly reporting on his newly released films and his private life, including his first divorce from Jean Acker, his tumultuous marriage to Natascha Rambova, and his second, final divorce.[53] The narratives and the advertisements that celebrated his rise to fame often described his success and celebrity not as unique and inimitable, but as a model for others to aspire to. In the early 1920s, *Il Progresso* began to publish advertisements for full-service talent agencies, that is companies specialized in training individuals as professional actors and models in introducing them to Hollywood agents and producers. A comparable operation, one that allegedly guaranteed immediate notoriety, was the beauty contest. Valentino was certainly not the first celebrity to preside over such competitions, but his version, known as the Mineralava Beauty Pageant from the name of its sponsor, Mineralava Beauty Clay, attracted enormous publicity. Visiting eighty-eight cities throughout American and Canada in the company of his wife, with whom he performed in tango dances, Valentino selected as many beauties. He then descended to New York's City Hall, paraded along Fifth Avenue, and participated in a final contest held at the Madison Square Garden for the selection of "America's Queen of Beauty." A young David O. Selznick made a short, surviving film of the contest, entitled *Rudolph Valentino and His 88 American Beauties* (1923). *Il Progresso* played a role in the contest. Potential applicants were to send their pictures to Valentino in case of *Il Progresso Italo-Americano* at 42 Elm Street, New York. At first, *Il Progresso* framed it as an opportunity for young Italian women to gain notoriety, but the event had a broad all-American appeal, involving judges and a well-promoted formula that a year earlier had launched the career of actress Clara Bow, later known as America's It Girl.[54]

On a dystopian side, there was a pressing question of cultural reconciliation. For Italian film productions, as noted above, the vectors of fame were the transcendent tropes of "History" and "Art" versus New World consumerism. Searching for a solution, *Il Progresso* depicted Valentino as a romantic and spiritual figure against the materialistic backdrop of Hollywood's dream factory, for instance by describing his heroic contractual extrication from Famous Players Lasky Corporation as a regained "artistic freedom."[55] A few articles also complained that too many young Italian women, while dreaming of actually being able to make it in Hollywood, were willing to spend fortunes in recitation courses, most of which were either ineffective or a sham.[56]

Still, amid denunciations of the Hollywood dream as a juvenile fad, the paper kept glorifying Valentino and interpellating Italian star consumers into becoming American stars themselves.[57] *Il Progresso's* sensationalist reportages of popularity contests and its advertisements for Italian talent agencies boasted their improbable Hollywood connections and relied on an alleged popular demand (*"Tutti vogliono entrare nel*

CANO — Giovedì 4·Settembre 1924

RODOLFO VALENTINO - NITA NALDI
DOUGLAS FAIRBANKS -- MARY PICKFORD
e moltissimi altri hanno raggiunto fama e fortuna nel cinematografo.

VOI POTETE FARE LO STESSO

Venite ai nostri uffici per una intervista. — Scrivendo inviate 4 soldi in francobolli e riceverete il nostro opuscolo e complete informazioni.

MAIDINA PICTURES, Inc.
987 - 8th AVENUE   NEW YORK
Comm. F. ALBERINI, President — BURTON KING, Direttore Artistico
(2432) — a.x)

Figure 4.6. Casting agency advertisement: "You can do it too." *Il Progresso Italo-Americano* (September 4, 1924): 10.

cinematografo!"—everyone wants to get into the pictures).[58] In such cases the link with Valentino was often overt. On September 4, 1924, one such company, Maidina Pictures, released a new ad (see figure 4.6) explicitly pairing Valentino with other Hollywood superstars, Nita Naldi (whose real name was Mary Dooley) and Fairbanks and Pickford. What the paper could not avoid marketing was the notion that any Italian of talent and determination, just like any comparable American, could legitimately aspire to become an Italian celebrity. If economic struggles and even discrimination had deterministically followed racial and national lines, individual success did not have to. Choice was seemingly the difference, including the opportunity of "behaving Italian"—a choice that many non-Italians found appealing for the first time. Obviously, for Italian immigrants this novel option of embracing their own racial identity, as opposed to viewing it as an inevitability, was the most remarkable difference from the past. The slogan "You can do the same" ("*Voi potete fare lo stesso*") spoke to Italians' new alleged equivalency with any other American groups in terms of aspiration to personal celebrity. Whether this path to celebrity as Italians was historically real is somewhat secondary to its emergence as a cultural possibility that did not exist before. Furthermore, Valentino's involvement in modern practices of studio publicity and marketing, including the countless interviews, public relations appearances, and the nationwide Mineralava Beauty Pageant tour, showcased strategies of self-invention and ethnic agency that contributed to articulating the notion of a modern, proactive, and well-adjusted Italian immigrant. Such novel articulation of Italianness held profound experiential consequences, particularly in terms of Italians' national stance within a media environment that was looking at transnational differences as constructive personal resources in dialogue with mainstream America and not just as inescapable traits leading to prejudice.

The polemics around Valentino's request for American citizenship emerged against the background of the tension of national insularity and exclusivity versus dialogue and interchange. By opposing what for many was the actor's wish to cut his ties to his native land, *Il Progresso*'s reaction was fascinating. The reports that Valentino wished to take Italian citizenship made headlines toward the end of 1925, a few months before the actor's sudden death on August 23, 1926. The Italian press and, initially, a few local authorities solicited a boycott of his films. *Il Progresso* reported that the Italian government was not officially endorsing either the boycott or the popular charge that Valentino was a national traitor ("*rinnegato*")—even though as late as January 1926 Mussolini's newspaper, *Il Popolo d'Italia*, was still calling him just that.[59] The matter could have had significant diplomatic ramifications given the episode's polarizing nationalistic tones. Yet, the Italian American press articulated the most interesting response. In late December 1925 and through its chief editor, I. C. Falbo, *Il Progresso* took the opportunity to shed old prejudices and embrace a new form of transnational affiliation beyond the singular passport allegiance. Falbo summarized the content of a letter that Valentino had allegedly written to Mussolini about his desire to acquire American citizenship.[60] According to Falbo, the Italian actor adopted the argument that the Duce had often made about Italian immigrants' most appropriate conduct in America. "Mussolini had decisively opposed old prejudices," Falbo recounted, "recommending instead that immigrants gain American citizenship in order to protect both their personal and collective interests more effectively in the country where they live, work, and accumulate wealth."[61] What the *Il Progresso* editor was indicating was a way out of the model of *exclusive* national allegiance and belonging, and toward one based on a *relational* Italianness beyond the legalism of citizenship status. "You can be an excellent American citizen without forgetting your homeland," he noted, "and actually keeping its memory alive in your heart and educating your America-born children to the same memory."[62] The link with the homeland, for *Il Progresso*'s editor, had such deep and widespread roots that no piece of paper could threaten it.

Conclusion

The laying of transatlantic telegraph cables linking Rome to New York in the early 1920s was both a historical instance and a emblematic illustration of Italian Americans' dynamic relationships with both Italy and America. Italian Americans' film culture underwent significant changes in the 1920s in the direction of transnational equivalence and exchange. Differently from forms of reception and consumption that insisted on proud exceptionalism and national solipsism, whether associated with glorious Italian history or distinct Neapolitan culture on one side and Hollywood might on the other, the 1920s saw the emergence of a dialogic mode of film experience. A whole range of film-related news items and editorials linked Italy to America in novel ways through such cinematic vectors as film genre (such as the historical epic) and stars from Caruso and Fairbanks to Valentino and Mussolini.

When American cinema began making Roman epics either in its studios or in Italy, it prompted *Il Progresso* critics and their readers to recognize the transatlantic bridging of two traditionally separate cultural domains: *Romanitas* and Hollywood. When Fairbanks and Mussolini traded starlike gestures and compliments about public and fictional roles, the Italian American film consumer experienced a new cultural synapse linking Hollywood fare with the larger-than-life Mussolinian character. Finally, the willingness to accept Italian-born Valentino's intention to become an American citizen, without denouncing a betrayal of national allegiance, spoke about a new ability to consume *at once* "things Italian" and "Italian Americans." Rather than convey uneasiness and anxiety over the Italian actor's and, more in general, immigrants' Americanization, *Il Progresso* articulated a new confidence in dynamics of partaking and alliance between Italian and American cultural citizenships beyond nation-states' traditional sovereignties. Thus the 1920s, particularly its early years, inaugurated a short period of transatlantic connectedness that strikingly contrasted with later periods.[63] Years before the forced request of exclusive loyalty to the United States during World War II, when the transcontinental cables signaled a problematic umbilical cord with the motherland, radical changes had already being occurring in America. The effects of the new immigration restrictions, the sudden death of Valentino in 1926, and the decline a year later of old silent film stars—but, most radically, the shifting fortunes of Fascism in America after the mid-1930s—altered both the demographics and the spirit of this brief but significant "telegraphic moment" in Italian American film culture.[64]

5

Consuming *La Bella Figura*

CHARLES ATLAS AND AMERICAN MASCULINITY, 1910–1940

Dominique Padurano

In many ways, Charles Atlas (1892–1972) makes an unlikely case for inclusion in a volume on Italian American consumption. Most Americans today associate him with mid-century kitsch—and thus white-bread Americana—famous for hawking his twelve-week mail-order fitness course, *Dynamic Tension*, from the back pages of comic books in the legendary advertisement, "The Insult that Made a Man Out of 'Mac'" (figure 5.1). With the exception of a few Italian American men born between 1930 and 1950, most people today have no idea that "Charles Atlas" was only the public moniker of the Italian immigrant born Angelo Siciliano.[1] The fitness entrepreneur abandoned his given name completely by 1925, and made no effort to recruit a specifically Italian American clientele. Indeed, according to his son, Atlas harbored a lifelong antipathy for his birthplace and the privations that he had suffered there as a boy. After leaving Calabria at age eleven, he never returned, preferring to vacation close to his adopted home of New York City.[2] So why, then, include him in this book?

First, though he regretted his impoverished Italian youth, Charles Atlas filled his private life with countless "acts of Italianness," many of which involved consumption—a luxury that had been denied him as a child. The food he ate, the clothes he wore, the car he drove, the way he related to his family and friends: all bear traces of his Italian origins. Once in the United States, these private acts of consumption testify to an individual creating an identity that was neither Italian nor American but a unique hybrid of the two. Like many other Americans of Italian descent, Charles Atlas chose consumption as an important means through which to construct an Italian American identity.[3]

Figure 5.1. Charles Atlas, Ltd., "The Insult that Made a Man Out of 'Mac.'" *Physical Culture* (August 1932): 11.

As a public figure, Atlas's acts of consumption did not only shape his own identity. His celebrity induced others to consume in distinctly Italian ways, thus helping to shape American culture. When Atlas recommended that students rub olive oil into their skin, for example, he might have done so without a conscious link to *Italianità,* but such "Italianisms" pervaded Atlas's public work as much as they did his private life. As a consequence, since it debuted in 1923 *Dynamic Tension* served as a conduit for consuming *à la italienne* for millions of readers worldwide.

Ironically, only when Atlas shifted *away* from associating himself with *Italianità* could he do so successfully. During the early 1920s, Atlas—who until 1924 used both "Angelo Siciliano," "Charles Atlas," and permutations of the two names interchangeably— was frequently portrayed in the popular press as Italian and represented visually as an erotic (or homoerotic) figure. Centuries-old stereotypes of darker-skinned people as hypersexualized found new expression in the modern media of photography (as in the homoerotic images taken by Wilhelm von Gloeden in Sicily) and film (silent screen icons Rudolph Valentino and Ramón Novarro) in the 1920s. Material abundance and the cosmopolitan environment of large American cities during that decade absorbed and diffused the racial, gender, and sexual tensions that bodies like Atlas's tended to provoke.[4] By the beginning of the 1930s, however, the socioeconomic dislocations of the Great Depression made many Americans less tolerant of the gender bending that Valentino,

Atlas, and others had committed during the previous decade. American consumers soon found images of "beautiful" male bodies less appealing and instead sought "strong" models of ideal masculinity. Since then, photographs of and words about Atlas's body accordingly attempted to convey its power, the new *sine qua non* for American "he-men."[5] But despite his own public embrace of hegemonic notions of 100-percent Americanism in *Dynamic Tension* and advertisements from the 1930s onward, Atlas continued to engage in private acts of consumption that reflected his Italian origins. *Dynamic Tension* inadvertently continued to teach other men how to "consume Italian" in order to become like its corporate icon. In the process, Charles Atlas helped to alter dominant conceptions of what it meant to be an American man, ensuring that he would be a little more Italian for decades to come.

Working the Italian Male Body

Angelo Siciliano was born on October 30, 1892, in the small hilltown of Bisignano, Calabria. He lived with his mother, Francesca Fiorelli, until he was six years old; she then sent Angelo to a nearby larger town to apprentice as a leatherworker while attending school. Angelo's father Annunziato had traveled twice to the United States—in 1893 and 1896—to work as a rural laborer. Like half of the millions of southern Italian migrants from Italy, Annunziato probably returned permanently to Calabria after his second sojourn in America. Annunziato and Francesca never seem to have married, a situation that perhaps made it easier for Angelo's mother to decide to join her brother in New York to improve her own life chances—and those of her illegitimate son, Angelo. On February 5, 1904, Angelo and Francesca sailed from the port of Naples on the S.S. *Lahn*; exactly two weeks later, they passed together through Ellis Island.

Until the age of fifteen, Angelo lived with his uncle, a tailor, and mother at 82 Front Street in Brooklyn. After spending a couple of years in third and then sixth grades because of his initial lack of literacy in both Italian and English, he left school sometime around 1908 to contribute to the family income, a practice common among Italian families of the period.[6] Using the leatherworking skills that he had acquired in Italy, Siciliano soon rose to the position of supervisor in a ladies' handbag factory, where his mainly Irish co-workers allegedly resented working for a "guinea."[7]

A worker by day, Angelo soon learned other ways to become American by night, but took pains to cast these experiences as equally "productive" early in his career. Sometime around 1906, young Siciliano joined the Italian Settlement School, a settlement house not far from his home and public school on Front Street. Pioneered by reformer Jane Addams at Hull House in Chicago, settlement houses functioned as places where immigrants could learn ways to acculturate to the United States. According to Siciliano's 1921 autobiographical piece in the fitness magazine *Physical Culture*, his settlement house teacher, "Mr. Davenport," one day brought Angelo's class to the Brooklyn Museum of Art. "While the other boys were wandering about looking at other things," Siciliano recalled, "I remained studying the magnificent bodies of Hercules, the Dying Gladiator, the Wrestlers, the Discus Thrower, the Boxer and the rest of the splendid specimens of manhood" immortalized in plaster in the galleries of ancient art.[8] Siciliano framed his initiation into the cult of physical culture (a contemporary term that included any type of exercise) as a transformation narrative. "I couldn't believe that such men had ever really existed," Siciliano remembered, but Davenport taught young Angelo "that the ancient Greeks had worshipped a well-developed body.... All this fired my admiration and roused my ambition," he rhapsodized, prompting him to ask Davenport, "I suppose ... that no one could get to be as strong as that in these times?" Playing the role of archetypal American instilling the nation's work ethos into the young immigrant, the teacher replied, "Most anybody can be strong.... Anybody who is willing to work for it can obtain the same muscular development." The incredulous boy then allegedly asked, "Do you think I could develop myself to be like one of these men?" Davenport assured him, "If you were willing to work hard enough, you could."[9]

After this mythical metamorphosis to physical culture devotee, Angelo Siciliano reinterpreted Davenport's traditionalist inculcation of hard work as assimilation strategy: the object upon which he would productively toil would not be a printing press or sewing machine, but rather, his own body. Unsure of where or how to begin to change his body, he asked his teacher, "How can I learn the way to go about (becoming strong)?" Davenport recommended that Angelo join the gymnasium at the YMCA. Siciliano recalled that although "I was amazed and delighted with what I saw when I went to one at the very first opportunity.... I was too poor to join." Adopting a tone that recalls *The Autobiography of Benjamin Franklin* or Horatio Alger's Ragged Dick, Siciliano chose that moment of financial hardship to highlight his ingenuity and tenacity: "I was too much in earnest to be turned from my purpose on that account." At home, he began to practice the squats, toe raises, chin-ups, push-ups, and forward, backward and side-to-side bends that he had seen others perform at the YMCA. Moreover, Siciliano wrote, "I made myself a bar bell with a stick and two stones, weighing about twenty-five pounds each. I tied the stones to the end of the stick and made a bar bell, which if not pretty to look at was just as good to use as a better looking one would have been.... I contrived a set of pulleys and weights ... and used them regularly.... In fact whenever I heard of a new exercise for development I was not satisfied until I had tried it."[10]

Atlas's apocryphal tale of resourcefulness suggests that immigrants hoping to Americanize during the early 1920s needed to beware of claiming to have done so through consumerism.[11] According to cultural historian Jackson Lears, Americans harbored ambivalent attitudes toward the market. Alternately drawn to and repelled by the notion of abundance that consumer capitalism flaunted, advertisers offered products that promised the contradictory ability to take control of self-fulfilling rationalist, Protestant desires and simultaneous release from that self-control. Though becoming a physical culturist did involve a great deal of consumption—as Atlas's own future career proves—twenty-nine-year-old Angelo Siciliano framed his youthful initiation into the physical culture lifestyle as an adoption of the values of discipline and hard work. Indeed, a common, present-day term for the verb "to exercise"—that is, "to work out"—first appeared in 1927, incorporating the connotations of laborious production, perhaps to obfuscate its actual lack of productive value in the traditional sense. In a decade during which Americans began to consume (radios, automobiles, fan magazines) more conspicuously than ever before, many regarded the shift away from puritanical values of thrift and productive work with skepticism. Just as early bodybuilders frequently posed as ancient statues as a way to render their nearly nude bodies more acceptable to supposedly prudish

Americans, so too did Charles Atlas's adopted tribe need to paint bodybuilding as productive to a populace allegedly wary of consumption for its own sake.[12]

But Americans' initial ambivalence toward consumer culture only partially accounts for Siciliano's framing physical culture as a productive enterprise. In the nativist climate of the post–World War I era, an immigrant with such a recognizably Italian name derived other advantages by appearing to emulate Benjamin Franklin and Horatio Alger's Ragged Dick. After U.S. Attorney General A. Mitchell Palmer deported foreign-born labor leaders, the U.S. Congress passed restrictive immigration laws in 1921 and 1924 targeting Eastern and Southern Europeans just like Siciliano. Publicly aligning himself with such "American" values as thrift, discipline, tenacity, and resourcefulness enabled Angelo Siciliano to be seen by the American public more credibly as Charles Atlas, the icon that he created during the 1920s. Yet, despite his tale of transformation, Siciliano retained many aspects of his Italian past, both in his private life and public work. By incorporating such Italianisms into his corporate persona and mail-order fitness course, Siciliano sold ways of being Italian to native- and foreign-born Americans hoping to become "real he-men." In the process, he changed Americans' notion of what a *real* man was: in essence, he made him more Italian.

Seeing and Buying *La Bella Figura*

As the United States absorbed millions of immigrants between 1890 and 1920, its entire culture and the notion of what it meant to be "American" reflected their influence. Angelo Siciliano first contributed to this changing American culture by playing a role in what historian Kathy Peiss has called the "culture of amusements." A new, heterosocial world comprised of dance halls, nickelodeons and amusement parks, the culture of amusements catered to and was created by the largely young, working-class, immigrants who toiled by day in urban centers and sought relief from this drudgery in the few hours of their days not devoted to working or sleeping.[13] This consumer culture of amusements functioned on a currency of images. From Lower East Side nickelodeons to Coney Island's fabulously illuminated Luna Park, New York's early twentieth-century immigrant world of amusements delighted Americans' eyes as a means to open their wallets.

As New York City and the nation's most numerous immigrants, Italians uniquely contributed to the ocular turn that consumer culture took around the turn of the twentieth century. As Gloria Nardini explains, Italians' particular preoccupation with aesthetics, "looking good, style, appearance, flair, ornamentation, (and) illusion"—which they call *far bella figura*—"is a central metaphor of Italian life." Certainly, many of the New York City immigrants of Peiss's study were Italian. Instead of promenading in the piazza before the dinner hour, they—especially men, who were given much greater freedom of movement than young women—may have strutted their stuff in the city's dance halls and performed their public selves on the shores of Coney Island. In this way, immigrants like Siciliano made seeing and being seen central to the culture of amusements that began to flourish by the early twentieth century. By starting his own career in physical culture in this milieu, Siciliano contributed to its visual emphasis. Nardini notes that the word *"figura"* refers to "the exterior of something, especially the human body."[14] Who better to introduce Americans to the concept of *bella figura*, then, than Angelo Siciliano, someone who had been cultivating his own body for years? Moreover, by offering his body up to viewers for a price, Siciliano transplanted the Mediterranean "notion of self as a social presentation for the consumption of others" to American soil. By turning his own body into a commodity, Angelo Siciliano taught others to do the same, infusing Italian customs like *far figura* into twentieth-century American life.

Turn-of-the-century amusement culture escorted Angelo Siciliano into the nation's burgeoning consumer culture. His conversion to physical culture occurred sometime before 1908; by seventeen—he recalled years later—"I was getting around pretty fair."[15] For the next several years, he continued to work by day in the handbag factory and, by night, in his homemade gym. But by the outbreak of World War I Angelo Siciliano had entered professionally into the culture of amusements, earning money based on the beauty of his body, for the enjoyment of and consumption by others. In 1914, his photograph appeared on the front cover of the British version of *Physical Culture*, a magazine devoted to exercise and healthy living published by Bernarr Macfadden.[16] Around the same time, Siciliano demonstrated a chest-developing pulley by standing in a storefront window on lower Broadway, performed as a strongman on Coney Island, and toured in a vaudeville stage act entitled "Weston's Models" with fellow physical culturist Earle Liederman.[17]

Images of people held particular sway over the American imagination. The often eroticized pleasure that Americans took in looking at bodies—or photographic images of bodies—informed *Current Opinion*'s now infamous 1913 proclamation, "It's sex-o'-clock in America." Eight years earlier Sigmund Freud remarked upon the ocular engine driving the ticking clock: "Visual impressions remain the most frequent pathway along which libidinal excitation is aroused." Many of those who saw Siciliano in the store window, on Coney or a vaudeville stage, or on the front cover of *Physical Culture*, also were likely titillated by what they saw.[18]

At the same time, witnessing images of others' bodies set a new standard by which Americans judged their own forms. Men as well as women increasingly felt the need to cultivate their physical appearance as a way to heighten their own sexual attractiveness after viewing the new standards set by Atlas and others in the visual culture of amusements. Often, onlookers turned to the market to purchase the tools for such corporeal cultivation. By the 1920s, women bought lipsticks and brassieres to conform to new standards of femininity, while men consumed Arrow collars and courses like Atlas's to achieve the broad-shouldered, trim-waisted silhouette considered the masculine ideal. Though looking at bodies became a form of entertainment, for many, it was merely the first step in a process that required consumption to produce a desired effect in one's own body.

To Angelo Siciliano, providing American men with a marketable product to effect such a change involved commodifying his own body as visual spectacle. Shortly after World War I, Siciliano's ideal masculine physique secured him a series of jobs posing as a model for artists living around Washington Square. Yet his body appealed to these sculptors and painters for another reason: his name, physiognomy, and skin and hair color, were all recognizably Mediterranean. The artists' neighborhood, located in the heart of in New York's Greenwich Village, had attracted bohemian types for its association with the "picturesque" Italian immigrants who resided there. For these avant-gardes, the name "Angelo Siciliano" only rendered his body more attractive. One of his first patrons, Mrs. Harry Payne Whitney, circled around a bare-chested young Siciliano upon their first meeting, declared him "a knockout," and asked him to model for her. Posing for sculptures of American allegories such as *Patriotism* in the Elks' National Memorial Headquarters in Chicago, as well as Founding Father Alexander Hamilton in front of the Treasury Building in Washington, Atlas claimed that soon he was earning $100 per week as an artist's model, at a time when most models made fifty cents per hour. Throughout his brief stint as a model, artists likened him to the ancient mythological heroes that sprang forth not far from where the real Angelo Siciliano had been born. "When I used to walk into a studio on MacDougal Alley in Greenwich Village, the [artists] would holler, 'Here comes the Greek God,'" Angelo recalled. Sculptor I. S. Filcher wrote of him, "He is Apollo and Hercules moulded into one," while Duncan Smith professed, "His supple and powerful limbs immediately suggest the living embodiment of a Greek God, although the Apollo and Hermes seem weaklings beside him."[19] The artists praised an ineluctable Mediterranean quality that Siciliano's name and appearance undoubtedly fostered.

Angelo Siciliano survived the competitive world of 1920s professional physical culture by cultivating an explicit connection to the Greco-Roman world and the beauty that it connoted to Americans of the day. Scores of immigrant and ethnic entrepreneurs, such as George Hackenschmidt (also known as the Russian Lion), Lionel Strongfort (né Max Unger), Antone Matysek, and Earle Liederman, an early mentor to Siciliano, dominated the field during the 1910s and 20s. By selectively highlighting his *Italianità* early in his career, Siciliano was one of the first of his compatriots to achieve success in the field. For contemporary artists and physical culturists, the ancient world in which Italy played a key role connoted beauty, grace, and sensuality, and for a culture in the midst of sexual and consumer revolutions, possessing such qualities added to one's marketable allure.

But as a budding entrepreneur, Angelo Siciliano also understood the need to market his beauty explicitly. As Nardini explains, *fare bella figura* also necessitates close attention to exterior form. Able to manipulate and exploit surface appearances, photography was the perfect tool for those hoping to *fare bella figura*—and to make money from it, especially in the highly visual culture of amusements flourishing by the 1920s. Angelo Siciliano's career thus increasingly hinged upon the circulation and sale of photographs of his *bella figura*. In 1921, he likely commissioned a series of portraits of himself from New York's leading photographer of dancers and bodybuilders, Edwin F. Townsend. Like the artists for whom Siciliano had worked, Townsend elicited his model's link to Greco-Roman antiquity by rendering him as Polyclitus's spear bearer. Atlas then sent that image to *Physical Culture*'s competition to find the world's "Most Handsome Man"—a contest "judged both from photograph and measurements." When he won the 1921 and 1922 contests, *Physical Culture* proclaimed him, "Like a Greek God" beneath the spear bearer portrait, and entitled his autobiography, "Building the Physique of a 'Greek God.'" The magazine then printed several full-page and other large photographs of Siciliano posing clad in short togas as "the Apollo Belvedere redivivus" in its monthly photographic column, "The Body Beautiful."[20] Certainly, Atlas's thick, wavy, dark hair, black eyes and olive skin—combined with his identifiably Italian name—helped him to *fare*

la figura of the beautiful, southern Mediterranean god that *Physical Culture* and its readers seemed so eager to consume in photographic form. Atlas's first course materials,
printed in 1923 and 1924, repeatedly refer to his body as "beautiful." His first promotional brochure, entitled "Secrets of Muscular Power & Beauty," reported that he regarded "health and a beautiful physique of far more value than mere strength." Not only
did Atlas fail to discourage this association with beauty, heightened by an explicit textual and iconographic connection to the ancient world, he consciously exploited it for
commercial and professional gain.

Although rampant nativism forced Angelo Siciliano to refrain from using his given
name by the mid-1920s, he did not abandon incorporating elements from his southern
Italian culture into his work. In 1925, Atlas and several partners opened the summertime Physical Culture Camp in the Catskill Mountains. Affectionately called "Camp
Atlas" by its juvenile attendees, the upstate New York facility promoted healthful living
through sports, dance, and proper nutrition, implicitly defined by Atlas as a diet along
Mediterranean lines. Towards that end, Atlas placed a "help wanted" advertisement in
the *New York Times* in the summer of 1925 seeking a "gardener and poultry man" to
grow fruits and vegetables. Moreover, similar to the Italian practice of incorporating
non-blood relatives into the family as "aunts" or "cousins," "the campers all . . . called the
counselors Uncle." Perhaps unsurprising for a man who had himself suffered privations
as a child in Italy, Atlas, according to a former camper, "would roam the mess hall, making sure we ate the foods that would help build our bodies. When one boy left his bread
crust on the plate, Atlas picked it up and ate it. 'It's the best part of the bread,' he told the
kid."[21] Atlas's attention at the camp to fresh produce, bread crusts and lean meats, while
not exclusively an Italian trait, suggests the lingering imprint of a Mediterranean diet
on his ideas of healthful living. The importance of food in Charles Atlas's fitness regimen
is even more striking when one compares his mail-order course to those of his contem-
poraries. The first iteration of *Dynamic Tension*, called the "Atlas System of Health,
Strength and Physique Building," appeared in 1923. Though Atlas's first company went
bankrupt during the late 1920s, Charles Atlas, Ltd., the company he co-founded with
adman Charles P. Roman and that still exists today, resurrected *Dynamic Tension* in
largely the same form in 1929. The exercises that Atlas recommended resembled those
of his peers; *Dynamic Tension* was exceptional solely in that it only endorsed isometric
contractions, static positions in which the student presses the force of one muscle
against another. Most other courses of the 1920s advised lifting weights or pulleys in
conjunction with performing isometric exercises. Relative to these competitors, *Dynamic
Tension* stands out primarily in its close attention to diet and overall care for the surface
of the body (as opposed to simple muscle building). While Liederman and Matysek, for
example, devoted merely a couple of sentences of their written courses to diet, Charles
Atlas spent numerous pages instructing his students about nutrition, and hair and skin
care throughout several lessons of his first course. His advice amalgamates southern Italian folk remedies and recent scientific discoveries. Atlas counseled students to consume
"vegetables, fruits, milk, eggs, and lean meats . . . to supply your scalp and hair with all
the B vitamins needed for buoyant health" and to "eat enough foods containing . . . vita-
min [A]" such as "green leafy vegetables (and seafood)" to maintain youthful eyes. He
suggested that they "gently massage with pure olive oil . . . to remove any tendency to

soreness and stiffness" in the muscles and recommended that students wash their hair and scalp "about once a week" with "a pure castile soap (made from olive oil)." Finally, "to keep the skin young," Atlas cautioned, "eat wisely. You must eat plenty of fresh fruits and vegetables, lean meats and eggs. Don't forget your lemon juice, orange juice, grapefruit juice and tomato juice. Avoid overly rich food. . . . Don't overeat."[22]

Atlas continued to endorse the value of a Mediterranean diet throughout the 1930s. The *Dynamic Tension* course offered by Charles Atlas, Ltd., expanded upon its predecessor's advice, collecting advice on diet and nutrition into its entire second lesson, consisting of nine pages. In it, Atlas not only recommended consuming water, lean meats, and vegetables but also condemned sweets, white rice, and caffeinated beverages. By twenty-first century standards, his nutrition counsel seems visionary. He did not spare the larger public from his Mediterranean diet advice. When he joined Jack Dempsey on the latter's radio show on May 15, 1936, for example, he answered a question about proper foods to eat by saying, "I eat plenty of vegetables . . . and I like my soup."[23] In his dietary counsel itself, as well as for its impact on the aesthetics of the body, Atlas incorporated *Italianità* into the commodities he offered the public.

Just as Charles Atlas publicly encouraged his students and campers to embrace Italian habits of personal hygiene and diet, he retained traditionally Italian ways of being in his private life. While working as a strongman on Coney Island in the late 1910s he met first-generation American Margaret Cassano, the daughter of immigrants from Avellino. Margaret and Angelo married in January 1918, and by December of the same year, they welcomed into the world their son, Charles Jr., whom they nicknamed "Hercules." In November 1919, daughter Diana (also called "Francesca," after Siciliano's mother) was born. The elder Francesca continued to live for about fifteen years with the Sicilianos, who moved frequently from one rental apartment to another throughout Brooklyn until they bought their own home in Dyker Heights. Like many other Italians, home ownership was of paramount importance to Angelo Siciliano, amounting to what Simone Cinotto has called "the Italian American Dream."[24] Purchasing a brand-new home in Brooklyn sometime around 1930, Atlas crafted an Italian American identity through consumption.

Other, less costly but still significant purchases helped Atlas to continue to cultivate *la bella figura*. Embracing the Italian penchant for fine fashion, Atlas was photographed frequently in well-tailored, light-colored, three-piece suits. He also drove the most expensive convertible sold by the Paige Detroit Company, even when payments on that car helped to bankrupt him in the mid-1920s.[25] In these ways, Atlas followed native-born Americans, who during this decade both enthusiastically bought automobiles *and* began to purchase more and more items on credit. Yet, Atlas's love of beautiful cars also typified Italian American men of this time.[26] Finally, Atlas's Italian heritage inspired his generosity with friends, family and the Church. Roger Roman, son of Atlas's business partner Charles P. Roman, recalled fondly how Atlas slipped a $20 bill into his hand every time he visited his father's office as a child. The younger Roman also recounted how Atlas donated much of his money to the Catholic Church after Margaret's death in 1966. Finally, Atlas's own son, Charles Atlas Jr., remembered that during the 1930s, his father fed dozens of relatives each Sunday, sharing his own abundance during this time with his extended family: "We always had a couple of uncles over or an aunt or a cousin and every weekend there were an army of people we had to feed."[27] The meal that Atlas Jr. could remember eating as a child more than any other? That staple of southern Italian cuisine: eggplant.

As Angelo Siciliano encouraged Americans to change the way they ate, moved, and related to their bodies by introducing them to selected Italian practices, American culture as a whole increasingly incorporated the body as a crucial site of consumption. As Jackson Lears explained, American consumer culture since the 1890s had been growing "therapeutic." Advertising arose in part to encourage Americans to consume new products designed to remedy previously unnamed "illnesses." Listerine mouthwash was marketed to counteract the newly minted scourge of halitosis. Not every consumable item of the 1920s fit into the therapeutic model, but a surprising number of new products (Kotex, the first brassieres, men's girdles, and anticonstipation medicines) did respond to Americans' heightened concern with their bodies. Though Lears's study investigated primarily native-born and middlebrow sources, it is interesting to note that Americans developed a therapeutic culture of consumption at exactly the same moment that millions of immigrants from poverty-stricken regions of Europe arrived on their shores. Did immigrants' own experiences of physical deprivation fuel Americans' "fables of abundance"?[28] While scholars have tended to describe the shift to a therapeutic-oriented culture of consumption as a purely white, Protestant, middle-class elaboration, it is clear that Angelo Siciliano survived the 1920s (and his own poor business instincts) because the products that he offered Americans jibed well with the nation's needs during this era. On one hand, Siciliano developed and marketed his own body as a product of ancient Italy, disseminating eroticized photographs of his body into the modern American visual culture of amusements. On the other hand, Siciliano's teaching efforts, both at Camp Atlas and through *Dynamic Tension*, reaffirmed traditional Italian ways of nourishing and showcasing *la bella figura* at a time when native-born Americans themselves fretted with unprecedented intensity about the health and appearance of their bodies. As the 1920s drew to a close, Siciliano did not abandon such teachings, but his new company did radically alter the way his body was marketed. During the 1930s, Charles Atlas, Ltd., severed its spokesperson's public ties to *Italianità*, highlighting instead his Americanness and strength, two traits that his customers could emulate while they strived to survive the Great Depression.

"Italian Beauty" to "Husky He-Man"

The 1930s altered much more than the numbers of guests at the Atlas family's dining table. A sea change occurred in the ways in which Charles Atlas's body was presented to and consumed by the American public, catapulting him onto a national stage. He became the nation's leading fitness entrepreneur, sailing beyond the bevy of ethnic competitors shipwrecked amidst the shoals of the times. Atlas's new image as powerful rather than beautiful—an impression cultivated both iconographically and textually—enabled him to flourish during that most difficult decade.

The man primarily responsible for that change was Atlas's new business partner, Charles Roman. A 1928 graduate of New York University, Roman had worked on the Atlas account at Benjamin Landsman, an advertising and marketing agency, before the two founded Charles Atlas, Ltd., in 1929.[29] The business of Charles Atlas, Ltd., soon sky-rocketed thanks to both Roman's intuitive ability to sense the emotional needs of male consumers during the Depression, and Atlas's physical ability to embody on film and reflect back to them the type of man that they wanted, and even needed, to become—to *fare figura* of strength, as it were—in their darkest hour. Many American men who had lost their jobs grew depressed and even emasculated by their inability to provide for their families, long a traditional marker of manliness. Sociologist Mirra Komarovsky documented one of her subject's poignant testimonies:

> The hardest thing about unemployment, Mr. Patterson says, is the humiliation within the family. It makes him feel very useless to have his wife and daughter bring in money to the family while he does not contribute a nickel. He would rather walk miles than ask for carfare money. His daughter would want him to have it, but he cannot bring himself to ask for it. He feels more irritable and morose than he ever did in his life. He doesn't enjoy eating. He hasn't slept well in months. He lies awake and tosses and tosses, wondering what he will do and what will happen to them if he doesn't ever get work anymore. He feels that there is nothing to wake up for in the morning and nothing to live for.[30]

Sometimes a man's unemployment changed his wife or children's attitudes towards him. Though it is unlikely that diminished food intake significantly altered men's physical size, several Depression-era wives remarked how unemployment somehow had rendered their husbands smaller. "Mrs. Garland said that her husband seemed a bigger man to her when he was employed and was making good money." Likewise, "in the words of (another) wife, 'I still love him, but he doesn't seem as 'big' a man." Komarovsky explained that "the humiliation within the home dr[o]ve some men to seek compensation outside it"; one man, for instance, "became a leader of the church and spent a good deal of his time in church activities" after a year of unemployment. Some of these men—emotionally and possibly physically diminished and lacking productive labor—might have sought refuge in *Dynamic Tension*, a consumer item that Atlas had constructed as "work" and promised to magnify their bodies and thereby restore their manhood.

But first, Charles Atlas, Ltd., needed to present *Dynamic Tension* as the product that could bolster manhood and muscles better than any other on the market. *Dynamic Tension's* actual content differed little from other fitness courses; its sole difference—that it did not include any weights or other "apparatus"—in actuality *hampered* its ability to help men increase the size and bulk of their muscles. (Isometric contractions, the sole focus of *Dynamic Tension's* exercises, firm muscles' tone rather than significantly increase their size.) Nevertheless, since Charles Atlas, Ltd., sent through the mail only the paper upon which *Dynamic Tension* was written, rather than weighty barbells, its potential for profit was great: less money going to the postal service meant more of it for Atlas, Ltd., Roman only needed to convince consumers that the methods of *Dynamic Tension* effectively built muscle and strength by changing the way that he marketed Atlas's body, photographs of which functioned as proof that the course worked.

As we have seen, during the 1920s, Charles Atlas marketed his body as beautiful and erotic. One important way in which he highlighted his body's beauty was by assuming iconographic conventions of femininity in photographic images. He appeared in his ad-

BE A HUMAN DYNAMO!

Radiate Energy! Inspire Confidence! Attract others to you—and you literally compel SUCCESS. Brain Power depends on pure blood, steady nerves, a perfect digestive system, an unclogged body. To have a mind alert, to be able to match your brains against other better brains, to be *popular* and *win quick promotion* in business and the social world you MUST have Sound Health, you MUST have a Dominating Personality, you MUST have a Splendid Physique—for then, and then only will you COMMAND the respect of others.

BE A BATTERY OF HUMAN POWER!

CHARLES ATLAS
twice pronounced the World's MOST PERFECT Man, receiving $1000.00 FIRST PRIZES and a Diploma for Physical Perfection
96 Fifth Avenue   Dept. 4   New York City

CHARLES ATLAS   P. O. Box 4,
Dept. 4,   96 Fifth Avenue,   New York City

Name ....
Street ....
City .... State ....
(Please write or print PLAINLY)

Moles   HOW TO BANISH THEM

My Regime

Figure 5.2. Charles Atlas, "Be A Human Dynamo!" *Physical Culture* (August 1923): 96.

vertisements without clothes despite the fact that in the art historical tradition of European oil painting, nudes were always women. As John Berger noted in his famous *Ways of Seeing*, "*men act* and *women appear.* The surveyed female . . . turns herself into an object—and most particularly an object of vision: a sight." Since "the spectator in front of the picture . . . is presumed to be a man," the very act of appearing before the consuming eyes of other men rendered Atlas more feminine.[31] Moreover, in these early advertisements Atlas rarely gazed into the camera's lens, underscoring a submissive—and thereby feminized—position. The most frequent photograph that adorned Atlas's advertisements of that decade featured him looking away from the camera, both arms raised languorously above his head (figure 5.2)—a pose reminiscent of odalisques of nineteenth-century Orientalist paintings, not to mention the sexually transgressive, erotically charged *Barberini Faun* and *Dying Slave* by Michelangelo.

At the same time, however, public figures like Benito Mussolini circulated a different vision of Italian masculinity. Though Mussolini, like Rudolph Valentino and Atlas, embodied the Italian tradition of *fare bella figura*, his aggressive style eschewed the feminizing tendencies that theirs did. Instead, Il Duce promulgated a vision of himself as virile and strong. In the logic of fascism, male bodies needed to be hard and impenetrable to achieve the "dreamt-of metalization of the human body" necessary for the constant modern warfare that would feed the ever-growing state.[32] Mussolini therefore made it a point to have himself photographed shirtless, hard chest bared, engaging in athletic activities such as skiing or flying airplanes. Like Valentino and Atlas, Mussolini exploited photography to disseminate the spectacle of his body, but not to commodify it for individual gain. Rather, he hoped that the visual spectacle of his body could "sell" the Italian people on fascism. Mussolini's heroic image corresponded more closely with hegemonic notions of maleness in the United States than did the erotically charged, gender-bending images that Valentino and Atlas popularized during the 1920s—one reason, perhaps, why Il Duce garnered a significant following in the United States during that decade.[33]

Ultimately, the hard times of the Depression forced Charles Atlas to adopt the hard, virile masculinity that Mussolini also embodied. In Atlas's case, an overtly masculine style also corresponded to advertising's changed tone during the Depression. As Roland Marchand points out in *Advertising the American Dream*, ad copy and images—in particular, what he terms "the image of the clenched fist"—grew much more aggressively masculine in the 1930s relative to those of the preceding decade: "In conformance with the mystique of sweaty, hardboiled virility with which the advertising trade responded to the depression, the image of the clenched fist was a thoroughly masculine icon. It symbolized the ad men's self-conscious reaction against the 'effeminacy' of the soft, overly pretty advertising they imputed to the late 1920s."[34] Likewise, Charles Atlas, Ltd., abandoned photographs of its spokesperson posed with his arms raised sensuously above his head or captured in artistic soft focus by Townsend's aestheticizing lens. Beginning in the 1930s, Atlas posed much more assertively, either with legs planted and arms akimbo, pointing and staring directly at the viewer, or hunched over and pounding a desk with his clenched fist (figure 5.3). In this way, Atlas commodified his body as representative of the product, *Dynamic Tension*, that would bestow strength. At the same time, he taught men how to *far figura* in a new way, highlighting the male body's ability to radiate strength rather than beauty through the consumption of *Dynamic Tension*.

The texts of Atlas's promotional materials from the 1930s also emphasized strength over beauty. The company's brochure that had been titled *Secrets of Muscular Power & Beauty* during the 1920s was now called *Everlasting Health and Strength*. Rather than spend time and space convincing prospective consumers that his body was beautiful, Atlas's new brochure featured photographs of him bending steel bars in Bermuda, "showing strength of his hands and teeth" and asking customers to consider, "How Strong Are you?" And while an *illustration* of the old, "sexy" photograph of the 1920s did appear, the actual photographs of Atlas in "Everlasting" replicated the finger-pointing and fist-clenching ads of the 1930s. In all, Atlas made an effort to leave behind his sexually transgressive image from the 1920s to recruit new customers during the Depression.

During the 1930s, Charles Atlas also publicly cultivated relationships with boxers to prove his bona fides as a "husky he-man" himself. He appeared on Jack Dempsey's radio show and was photographed alongside the most famous pugilists of the era, from Max Baer to Joe Louis. Atlas's love of the ring became so legendary that cartoonist Sam Leff even featured him ringside in a comic strip from 1945: a silhouetted character said to his companion, "Look, Harry—there's Charles Atlas, th' famous strong man!! He never misses an important bout!!"[35] No such publicity images exist from the 1920s. Roman went out of his way to have such connections photographed and published in the local

Figure 5.3. Charles Atlas, Ltd., "Give Me Your Measure." *Physical Culture* (March 1932): 73.

and national press, suggesting that he determined that Atlas's association with boxers possessed commercial potential.

The marked shift in Atlas's image would remain mere iconographic analysis, though, if it did not correspond to a change in his company's fortunes. Actual sales figures are hard to obtain, since Charles Atlas, Ltd., was a privately owned company, not required to make public its tax filings. However, contemporary press accounts and other evidence suggest that despite the challenging economic environment, Charles Atlas, Ltd., not only achieved financial solvency during the 1930s, but as early as mid-decade it had also surpassed all competitors to become one of the nation's most successful mail-order fitness companies. In 1937, *Time* reported that since launching his first mail-order company fifteen years earlier, Atlas "has started a total of 500,000 puny people on the road to potent health." The next year, *Fortune* claimed that Charles Atlas, Ltd., annually budgeted $200,000 toward advertising alone, and that the company charged "$20 cash or $25 in installments" for *Dynamic Tension*. By 1939, the trade publication *Mail Order Journal* stated that the company's total sales had reached $10,000,000.[36] By the mid-1930s, that gaggle of fitness entrepreneurs against whom Atlas vied during the 1920s had almost completely stopped advertising in *Physical Culture* and other traditional fitness advertising venues like *Popular Mechanics*.[37] While countless businesses—including most of Atlas's competition—withered during the 1930s, Charles Atlas, Ltd., grew big and strong.

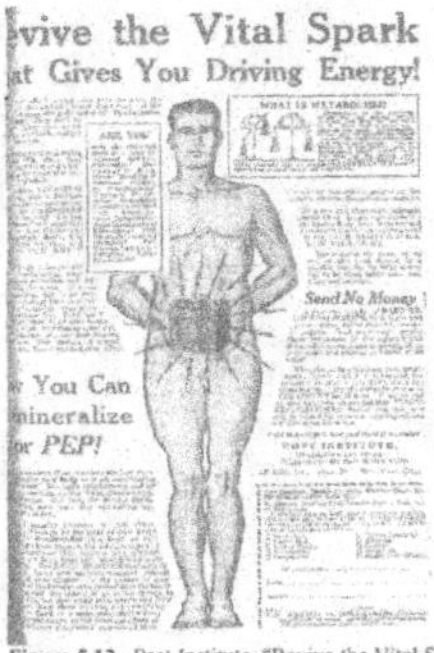

Figure 5.12. Post Institute. "Revive the Vital Spark That Gives You Driving Energy!" *Strength,* September 1927, p. 57.

Figure 5.4. "Striking Likeness." Binghamton, N.Y. *Sun* (January 27, 1936). Unprocessed boxes 9–11, Charles Atlas Collection, National Museum of American History, Smithsonian Institution.

Several events that took place in 1936 showed that the company's new advertising strategy effectively embodied the burgeoning national zeal for strength. On January 30, Atlas played the figure of "Manhood" in a pageant at New York's Waldorf Astoria Hotel in honor of the president's birthday. The sole fact that the party's organizers chose Atlas from among scores of other fitness celebrities to appear in front of Franklin D. Roosevelt himself suggests Atlas's prominence during the mid-1930s. Even more significantly, a publicity piece for the event, "Striking Likeness," ran in newspapers around the country several days before the bash. Showcasing Atlas's smiling visage alongside that of the commander-in-chief, the caption beneath the photographs read, "A more than passing resemblance between the faces of Charles Atlas, the world's most perfectly developed man, and President Roosevelt (right), is shown clearly here" (figure 5.4).[38]

The dubious comparison helped both men to promote a publicly useful image. On one hand, Roosevelt, paralyzed from the waist down by polio more than a decade earlier, used the link to the nation's leading strongman to promulgate an image of his own body as healthy and vital—and thus "man" enough to lead the country through its tough times. On the other hand, Atlas's link to the president bolstered his crafted persona as "one-hundred percent American"—and thus honest and trustworthy. As this piece appeared in the nation's newspapers, the Federal Trade Commission was preparing to impugn Atlas's integrity, investigating whether he had used weights to build his physique and questioning his right to use the name "Charles Atlas." A connection to Franklin

Roosevelt, the country's top blue blood *and* a man adored by many Americans for his perceived integrity could only benefit Atlas, who stood on the precipice of national dominance in his field during the spring of 1936.

Whether the public comparison to the president played a role in the FTC's eventual decision against Atlas's competitor, Bob Hoffman, is unknowable, but 1936 appears to have been another crucial turning point in Atlas's career and, indeed, in the history of physical culture in the United States. Unable to bring down Atlas, Hoffman returned to York, Pennsylvania, and continued to manufacture the barbells still used today by millions. Serious bodybuilders acknowledged the efficacy of weightlifting to build muscle mass and by the end of World War II, these practitioners engaged in multiple efforts to organize the sport along these lines. Canadian brothers Ben and Joe Weider established the International Federation of Bodybuilding, helped secure Olympic recognition of bodybuilding, and founded the Mr. Olympia competition and a publishing empire. Meanwhile, Charles Atlas, Ltd., was left alone to capture the imaginations of others.[39] These "others" were, increasingly, boys. Throughout the 1930s, Atlas continued to publicly associate his business with children, building on the experience he had gained running "Camp Atlas" during the previous decade. In 1936, he served as a judge in a "Best Baby" competition on Coney Island and in a "Best Boy" contest among Boy Scouts in the New York City area. Three years later, the Boy Scout Foundation of Greater New York appointed him "a merit badge counselor in personal health and physical development." Atlas also helped adjudicate the "super boy" and "super girl" contestants at the World's Fair on July 4, 1940.[40] While Atlas held a genuine affection for youngsters, boys had also grown to become an important segment of the buying public since at least the 1910s. Since *Dynamic Tension* alone would not dramatically increase a student's size, Atlas relied on another element that only young adolescents possessed: the promise of puberty. If Atlas's advertisements could reach boys before the start of natural changes to their physique and they enrolled in *Dynamic Tension* at the beginning of or during puberty, it might appear that *Dynamic Tension* changed their bodies. Although FTC investigators acknowledged this clever strategy as early as 1938, Charles Roman denied the centrality of Mother Nature in the boys' altered states.[41] Nevertheless, by hooking boys early on promises of physical transformation, Charles Atlas, Ltd., gambled on reaping big future profits.

Perhaps boys' relevance to the company's fortune was the reason that Charles Roman decided to narrate *Dynamic Tension*'s possibilities in comic strip form (figure 5.1). Appearing for the first time in 1938, comic books provided an important venue for Atlas's advertisements. Playing upon adolescent fears of humiliation in front of peers and, especially, female friends, "The Insult That Made a Man Out of 'Mac'" is remembered today not just because it was so ubiquitous but also because it resonated so deeply with boys' greatest fears. Indeed, Atlas's juvenile consumers often framed their own narratives of transformation in terms that echoed the ad. Youngster "R. B.," for example, wrote Atlas: "As for the friends who used to laugh on (sic) you and your course, I can plainly state that they even try to avoid me, because they have no more face to come to me and speak against you. REMEMBER, I HAVE A REMEDY FOR STOPPING THEIR VOICES. THAT IS BY SHOWING THEM MY *BICEPS, TRICEPS* AND *CHEST*. Thank you again, for changing me from a weakling into a strong fellow." By the late 1930s, almost one-quarter of the company's customers were boys under the age of eighteen; fifty percent were under twenty-one; and three-quarters were younger than thirty years old.[42]

But boys were not the only ones who read comic books during the genre's first decade and a half—and Charles Atlas, Ltd., did not limit advertisements to the comics. Since its inception, the company marketed *Dynamic Tension* to adult men and boys in publications that enjoyed a largely male readership, such as *Popular Mechanics* and *Popular Science*, and scores of pulp magazines like *Action Stories*, *All Star Detective*, *Black Mask*, *Clues*, *Cow Boy Stories*, *Ranch Romances*, *Science and Invention*, *Screen Book*, *Sky Riders*, *Sport Story*, *True Detective*, and *War Stories*.[43] Roman helped "Charles Atlas" to become a name synonymous with strength because he changed Atlas's image to correspond with that trait—and then bombarded the public with that image. Roman eventually drove home a few essential facts: a fit, strong body made you a real man; Charles Atlas possessed the ideal fit, strong body; to obtain a fit, strong body like Atlas's you had to purchase *Dynamic Tension* and practice its methods. This deceptively simple formula helped make Roman and Atlas wealthy men. In the process, they helped to change the way millions of Americans would view the male body and relate to their very selves. Though they may have done so by jettisoning Angelo Siciliano, important elements of *Italianità* remained in the ideal man that Charles Atlas came to represent. First and foremost, immigrant and ethnic performers from Atlas and fellow fitness entrepreneurs to film stars Rudolph Valentino and Ramón Novarro made a stylized presentation of the body central to Americans' conceptions of what constituted the "ideal man." Italians' native culture valorized self-presentation as a way to acquire social status through the practice of *far figura*; thus, Atlas was particularly well situated to introduce Americans to the importance of the well-maintained body to the modern notion of the self. Second, Atlas and others helped popularize the notion that the stylized male body could become a marketable commodity, especially when aestheticized by a camera lens, during the 1920s. While the particular masculine style that Atlas helped make appealing in the 1920s might have been too transgressive for the 1930s, the idea that masculinity was an embodied style, able to be manipulated in the marketplace and appropriated through consumption remained. Photographs of Atlas's body helped to sell *Dynamic Tension*, the product that convinced American men to rub olive oil into their skin and to skip meat and potatoes in favor of fruits and vegetables not just during the lean years of the Great Depression and World War II, but into the abundant postwar era. Last but not least, by inflecting modern masculinity with the notion of *bella figura*, Atlas helped break down the notion of a private, "sincere self" distinct and apart from the public self with which one might have to interact with the market, which, in the Protestant imagination, required artifice and dissimulation.[44] If, as Nardini asserts, "the 'real person' is *in* the *bella figura*," Atlas helped Americans overcome their discomfort with surface appearances and embrace the self as inextricable from that appearance. From our twenty-first-century vantage point of virtual realities and online personae, it is easier than ever to see that Charles Atlas, Ltd., helped ensure that Angelo Siciliano became a little part of *all* Americans through his *bella figura*.

6

Radical Visions and Consumption

CULTURE AND LEISURE AMONG THE EARLY
TWENTIETH-CENTURY ITALIAN AMERICAN LEFT

Marcella Bencivenni

On July 7, 1906, *La Questione Sociale*, one of the most important Italian-language anarchist newspapers published in the United States, announced a "libertarian" picnic sponsored by the Circolo di Studi Sociali (Social Studies Club) of Hoboken, New Jersey, the following Sunday. For twenty-five cents, participants would enjoy "five drinks or snacks," "appropriate music," and an abundance of entertainment. The ad also noted that the entire revenues would go to the benefit of the anarchist press, urging readers to attend and bring along families and friends.[1]

Similar announcements filled the pages of Italian-language radical newspapers until the Second World War. As photos of crowds of men, women, and children holding musical instruments, food baskets, and copies of radical newspapers attest, picnics became a regular feature of Italian immigrant life and a beloved working-class family event (figure 6.1). Typically held on Sunday or on special holidays like May Day, the Fourth of July, and Labor Day, they had long and elaborate programs. As another ad published in 1927 illustrates, they featured, along with plentiful food and wine, concerts, dances, performances, and games such as sack races, target firing, and bingo. A raffle typically concluded the program bestowing the lucky winners with special prizes such as cameras, books, pens, yearly subscriptions to radical newspapers, and even revolvers (figure 6.2).

Like other leisure activities and cultural institutions that I will discuss in this essay, picnics were part of a distinctive "movement culture" that helped shape, sustain, and

Figure 6.1. This photo of a crowd of Italian immigrants attending a picnic in July 1911 was published in *La Parola del Popolo*. Note the presence of women and children and the display of radical newspapers and musical instruments.

spread an alternative lifestyle, or, to use Maurice Halbwachs's famous term, a *genre de vie* within the Little Italies. They were key occasions for political propaganda and fundraising, but they also became "forms of consumption that gave a sense of collective life" to Italian immigrants, reinforcing their working-class and ethnic identity.[2] Indeed, as labor historians have noted, picnics were a popular form of working-class leisure—a cherished opportunity to escape the boredom, toil and strains of day-to-day life.[3] Workers, as Simone Cinotto reminds us in the introduction to this volume, had their own priorities, tastes, and values, determining what they purchased and consumed and how they spent their budgets. While "disgraceful," "wasteful," and "offensive" in the eyes of middle-class reformers, these boisterous outings were for workers crucial occasions of community building and fun. For Italian immigrants, who were largely from the south and the countryside, picnics also represented a transnational link to their native peasant cultures and places, providing an occasion to spend a day outdoors immersed in nature, forgetting the sordidness of industrial life, and reconnecting (if only imaginatively) with the land they had left.

Events like the picnics exemplified an important relationship between radical cultural production and consumption; they were the expression of a leftist subculture that ideologically rejected mainstream capitalist values and mass culture even as it exploited

Ottavo Pic-Nic Internazionale

Sotto gli auspici delle Unioni della

I. W. W.

DOMENICA, 21 AGOSTO

dalle 10 A. M. alle 10 P. M.

HARMONY PARK

GRASMERE, STATEN ISLAND

a totale beneficio de

"IL PROLETARIO"

Organo, in lingua italiana dell'I. W. W.

-- *PROGRAMMA* --

1. — INTERNAZIONALE	ADOLFO DEGEYTER
2. — CAVALLERIA RUSTICANA — SELEZIONE —	P. MASCAGNI
3. — STELLA MARINA — VALTZER —	A. A. EGIDJ
4. — BANDIERA ROSSA	
5. — TRAVIATA — SELEZIONE —	G. VERDI
6. — MARCIA	A. A. EGIDJ
7. — POETA E CONTADINO	VON SUPPE'

Orchestra di undici professori, diretta dal MAESTRO ARMANDO A. EGIDJ.

-------- **BALLO** --------

NEL PARK

1. - Corsa nel sacchi (per uomini, donne e bambini). — 2. - Tiro della fune. — 3. - Tiro a segno. — 4. - Corsa degli aghi. — 5. - Pesca "reale". — 6. - Il nuoto delle mele. — 7. - La padella misteriosa. — 8. - Corsa degli spaghetti. — 9. - Gli snelli fortunati. — 10. - Le pallottole giapponesi — ed una infinità di altri divertimenti.

I biglietti costano appena 50 soldi e ai ha diritto ai seguenti premi i quali verranno consegnati al fortunati alle ore 6 P. M.

1. — UNA MACCHINA FOTOGRAFICA DA $18.	4. — CINQUE DOLLARI IN ORO.
2. — DIECI DOLLARI IN ORO.	5. — LIBRI PER IL VALORE DI $5.00.
3. — UN OROLOGIO DEL VALORE DI $10.	6. — Abb. annuo a qualsiasi giorn. dell'I.W.W.

Come andare sul posto : - Prendere qualsiasi treno che va a South Ferry, New York City. Di li prendere il "ferry" di Saint George, Staten Island. Poi prendere il "Tottonville Train" e scendere a Grasmere (dopo due fermate).

Figure 6.2. "Eighth International Picnic." *Libertas* (August 1927). Like similar announcements of radical picnics, this ad offered detailed information on the program and specific directions on how to reach the park—in this case Harmony Park at Grasmere, Staten Island, N.Y. The ticket cost fifty cents and the entire revenues were used to fund *Il Proletario*.

entertainment and commercial leisure to promote class consciousness and mobilize the working class.

Starting with Werner Sombart's 1906 classic, *Why Is There No Socialism in America?*, historians have generally seen mass culture as a powerful homogenizing and assimilating force that eclipsed working-class consciousness and tamed militancy, eventually leading workers to integrate into mainstream middle-class America.[4] But as historian Rosanne Currarino has written—and as this volume suggests—"consumption could also be political and transgressive, a site of struggle or assimilation, and the source of social identities that might incorporate and move beyond narrowly defined juridical rights."[5] Echoing Currarino and other scholars such as Lizabeth Cohen and James Barrett who have challenged the "embourgeoisement thesis," I argue that during the early twentieth century consumption was more fluid than generally thought, reinforcing in some cases working-class and ethnic values rather than eroding them.[6] Italian immigrant radicals, for one, put forth a fierce critique of American consumerism and materialism, offering an alternative way of life and culture that drew on working-class values as well as distinct Italian cultural practices, traditions, and amusements. By attempting to incorporate cultural traditions and commercial culture into their political activities, in Cohen's words, they "put the market power of the consumer to work politically."[7]

Looking at what Italian immigrant radicals produced—how they articulated their individual and collective ethnic selves—and what Italian workers consumed—their choices and behaviors—offers an important doorway into how Italian culture and ethnicity were made in the United States, showing that radical leaders and workers were main actors in the different stages of this process. The institutions, culture, and lifestyles they created are in fact an important reminder of the radical, working-class, and transnational roots of the Italian immigrant experience.

Contrary to their present conservative image, Italian Americans, as many scholars have documented, have a vibrant, if "lost," radical past.[8] As early as 1882, an Italian Socialist Club was founded in Brooklyn, New York. Three years later, a group of anarchists began to meet in the basement of a building on 108 Thompson Street in Manhattan, launching, in 1888, the first Italian-language radical newspaper, *L'Anarchico*.[9] Many other radical organizations and newspapers soon followed. By 1900 there were thirty official Italian sections of the Socialist Party along the East Coast and countless independent anarchist and revolutionary circles throughout the nation.[10] After *L'Anarchico*, nearly two hundred radical Italian-language newspapers were published in the United States (see figure 6.3 for samples), making Italian immigrants the third most prolific radical ethnic group after the Germans and Jews.[11]

Distinct Italian radical communities quickly emerged in large urban cities like New York, Boston, Philadelphia, Chicago, and San Francisco; in smaller industrial towns such as Lawrence (Massachusetts), Paterson (New Jersey), Barre (Vermont), Buffalo (New

Figure 6.3. A sample of the mastheads of some of the most important Italian-language radical newspapers. Italian radicals eventually published 189 newspapers in the United States from the late nineteenth century through the Second World War.

York), and Ybor City (Florida); and in mining settlements in Pennsylvania, Ohio, West Virginia, Illinois, Montana, and Iowa. New York City's Lower East Side, the largest and most active of such radical settlements, epitomized the heart of Italian immigrant radicalism with a multitude of political organizations, affinity groups, unions and, of course, newspapers.[12]

From its outset, the movement had a strong transnational bent, which was reflected in the leadership, culture, and ideological composition and sequential evolution of the movement, with the early dominance of anarchism and syndicalism, then socialism and, after World War I, communism. The driving force behind its flourishing was a group of Italian radical expatriates—known generically as the *sovversivi*—who emigrated to escape the ruthless governmental repression that followed the uprisings of the Fasci Siciliani and the infamous Fatti di Maggio (May Events), a series of riots and labor protests during the late 1890s violently suppressed by the army.[13] This early radical chain supplied a steady flow of men, ideas, and contacts back and forth between Italy and the United States, helping spread anarchism and socialism and establishing close transnational ties among comrades on both sides of the ocean.

This transatlantic political connection continued for most of the twentieth century as a new generation of anarchists, socialists, communists, and social democrats flew the repression unleashed by Mussolini's Fascist regime after World War I. Unfortunately, radicals brought with them not only their traditions of militancy and protest, but also their ideological polemics and divisions, seriously weakening the movement.[14] Their political disagreements notwithstanding, the *sovversivi*, as even their collective noun suggests, shared a distinctive oppositional culture: a set of common values, beliefs, and practices firmly rooted in Europe's left-wing political and cultural traditions. Their vision, for instance, lay deep in the century-old Enlightenment struggle for democracy, equality, liberty, scientific rigor, and education. Pursuing an internationalist vision of global humanity and egalitarian universalism, all *sovversivi* were also firm antinationalist, antimilitarist, and anticlerical. Perhaps more importantly, they all shared the same dream, what they called the "Beautiful Ideal"—the revolutionary hope of working-class emancipation and social justice for every man and woman on earth.[15]

The *sovversivi* also had the same enemies and goals. As other radicals committed to social justice and economic change, they saw capitalism as the root of human oppression and vowed to eliminate it, using armed retaliation and insurrectionary violence if necessary. But economic change, they believed, should be accompanied by a change of ideas, for capitalism reflected not only a major form of production but also a hegemonic mode of social organization and control. Like the later theorists of the "Frankfurt School," particularly T. W. Adorno and Herbert Marcuse, the *sovversivi* essentially viewed the "culture industry" that emerged under industrial capitalism as an instrument of mass enslavement, alienation, and domination that effectively promoted the interests of the capitalist class at the expense of the workers.

The communist newspaper *Alba Nuova*, among others, illustrated this view in an article on the presumed "humanitarianism" of American capitalism. While noting that workers in America tended to live better than workers in other parts of the world, a fact exemplified by their ability to go to theaters and dance halls, it argued that their higher "standard of living," and particularly their increasing participation in various forms of mass culture, effectively depoliticized them. American capitalism was not "better"; it was just more successful. By conceding higher salaries and providing cheap amusements, American capitalists, wrote the editors of *Alba Nuova*, "had managed to brainwash and blind the workers to the point that they do not think any more about their problems or the profound injustices that dominate bourgeois society."[16]

The *sovversivi* tried to counter the negative impact and effects of consumerism on the workers by exposing the myth of "the American dream" and attacking "the American way of life" and its ethic of profit, individualism and self-interest. American culture, wrote the socialist Vincenzo Vacirca in 1927, in an article of great relevance still today, "is purely individualistic. There is the myth that every American boy can become President of the United States and that any ragged immigrant can become richer than Henry Ford." As a result, "the American youth strive towards the individual conquest of power, wealth, and pleasure. Ideals are mocked, idealists scorned: material success becomes the only measure of a man's success." Industrialization, sadly concluded Vacirca, further exacerbated this mentality: Consumed by "a devastating fever of immoderate riches" life becomes "dehumanized"; "the spirit dies of frostbite"; and the brain is transformed itself into "an icy machine to coin money."[17]

The American educational system was a particular focus of radical criticism. "The shame of America," read a 1911 article in *Il Prolerario*, "is the university." The article accused American colleges of serving the needs of dominant corporate interests and enforcing and justifying the prevailing political ideology and power structure. Instead of promoting rational debate and discussion, universities were factories producing submissive and passive citizens. Their goal was to create not intellectuals but middle-class experts who carried out the day-to-day administration of the capitalist infrastructure. "The American student," the article commented sarcastically, "goes to school like the worker goes to the workshop: to learn a trade, not to educate himself. Besides football, baseball and sports in general, he has no interests in life." The article ended with a comparison between the old and new world educational systems, noting, with a touch of nationalistic pride, that in Italy students concerned themselves with a little of everything—politics, arts, literature—whereas in the United States they are interested "only in its Majesty the dollar."[18]

Echoing Alexis de Tocqueville's observations on American "exceptionalism," a theory that would be further developed by the "liberal consensus school" in the 1950s, the *sovversivi* believed that the aridity of American culture and apathy of American people stemmed from the lack of social contrasts. As an editorial in the radical magazine *Il Fuoco* put it, "America has managed to create the millionaire without creating the corresponding dynamiter." Effectively marketed as "a diabolic European invention" by the media, the schools, and the entire cultural apparatus of capitalist power, class struggle in America had been meek and ineffective. The idea of class itself had become "un American," thereby suppressing the human strive for social and political change.[19]

But the *sovversivi*'s struggle in the United States was not directed against American capitalism and consumer culture alone. With equal, if not greater, intensity they fought against the Catholic Church and the established political and business elite of their own immigrant community, the so-called *prominenti*: "prominent" men who ran the immigrant banks, employment agencies, mainstream organizations, clubs, and newspapers, in effect controlling the Little Italies. In their view, the *prominenti* and the priests were an extension of Old World politics: instead of using their power and influence to advance the interests of Italian immigrants, they perpetuated a system of ideas and values that kept the masses enslaved. Therefore, one of the main goals of Italian radicals was to liberate their compatriots from their servility toward the boss by fostering education and knowledge.

Striving "to awaken the mind first and then unchain the wrist," the *sovversivi* essentially sought to refashion Italian culture according to their moral and political values.[20] "Let's renew our colonies," declared Arturo Giovannitti, the movement's poet laureate: "Let's set fire to all remnants of the ancient regime. . . . Let's disintegrate all the crockery and rubbish of philanthropists, housemasters, protectors, well-to do and respectable people, illiterate rich, pigs in white peplum, asses in black cloaks, and mandrills in purple. . . . If we must promote patriotism, let's do it properly. Respect for the old Italy in the young America should not be imposed through *baccalà*, preserves, pecorino, *soppressata*, and citrate of magnesia. Let's import talents and wills, wrathful ambitions and deranged passions. . . . If we have to affirm here our language let's do it through our illustrious culture: through theater, meetings, and dignity of thought."[21]

While rejecting the American capitalist ethos, the *sovversivi* sought to modernize Italian immigrant life, embracing middle-class and progressive views regarding nutrition, clothing and health. In stark contrast to the photos of downtrodden peasants circulated by Jacob Riis and Lewis Hines, radicals like Carlo Tresca and Arturo Giovannitti, for instance, enthusiastically embraced the bohemian fashion and flamboyant lifestyle of Greenwich Village, wearing broad-brimmed hats, Byronic collars and flowing cravats, sporting Van Dyke beards, and smoking fancy pipes.

Significantly, radicals covered in their newspapers not only articles about political theory and political news but also day-to-day issues of immigrant life such as hygiene, birth control, and children's education. As the editors of *Il Proletario* pointed out, "we don't simply want to launch a socialist paper" but also "a paper that, beyond the politics of parties and class struggle, carries out a daily act of purification and moral recovery."[22]

Radical newspapers, for instance, regularly featured a column called *Alfabeto igienico del lavoratore* by Simplicio Righi, a socialist physician and poet who directed *Il Proletario* from 1901 to 1902. In it, Righi offered detailed information organized in alphabetical order on healthy norms of life and problems like alcoholism and smoking. Under the letter B, for example, he discussed the importance of the *"bagno,"* urging Italians to try to live in a home with a bathroom and to take a bath at least twice a week. He also stressed the importance of using soap, but warned to not buy perfumed soaps, which contained alkaline ingredients harmful to the skin, and advised those at higher risks of skin infections, such as sanitation workers, to use sulfur and salicylic acid soaps.[23]

It was in this same spirit of wellness that a group of concerned physicians, including Ettore Tresca, Carlo Tresca's older brother, founded *La Parola del Medico* in 1916. Devoted entirely to health education, the paper featured articles on diet, medicine, and diseases in an effort to instruct immigrants about proper medical practices and thwart the influence of fraudulent doctors.[24]

Besides encouraging immigrants to implement healthier habits of life, the *sovversivi* also sought to alter their consumer practices. Like American middle-class reformers, they bitterly criticized immigrants for spending large sums of money on religious family events such as baptism, confirmations, weddings, and funerals. They especially detested the fact that Italians would spend thousands of dollars on fireworks, banners, and other decorations for religious festivals or nationalistic parades instead of using this money for more serious and urgent needs. For the *sovversivi*, such practices were unacceptable reminiscences of a medieval world, the product of ignorance, fanatical bigotry, and superstitions that perpetuated and reinforced passive perseverance, effectively distracting workers from their true struggle, namely overthrowing capitalism.

Aspiring to provide Italian immigrants with an alternative vision and lifestyle to both industrial capitalism and "colonial bossism," the *sovversivi* created a rich web of political organizations, educational institutions, and leisure activities that, they hoped, would change the way people lived *and* thought. On Sunday, public lectures provided a substitute for religious Mass. Revolutionary holidays replaced nationalistic and religious celebrations. Instead of Christmas, Columbus Day, and Easter, Italian radicals, like other radicals, celebrated May Day and commemorated the anniversary of revolutionary events like the Paris Commune on March 18, the Haymarket executions on November 11, and the Russian Revolution on November 7. Every year, hundreds of meetings and feasts were held in every part of the country, and special newspaper issues, often embellished with poems and drawings, were published on these occasions.[25]

Immigrants were also encouraged to supplant religious rituals with secular ones. Radical newspapers regular featured articles on "free love" and published ads of men and women looking for anticlerical soul mates. Under a column called "Examples to Emulate," they proudly announced the civil unions of "rebel couples" and anarchist and socialist christenings where newborns were baptized to the rhythm of revolutionary songs and given the names of popular working-class heroes (a favorite was Spartacus) or libertarian names such as Libero (Free) and Alba (Sunrise).[26]

Alternative schools were also formed to counter the "perverted education of the priests," and help children become "champions of free thought."[27] Inspired by the Escuela Moderna, created by the Spanish anarchist educator Francisco Ferrer in 1901, the *sovversivi*'s schools aimed to promote a rational, secular, and libertarian education, in contrast to the dogmatic parochial and public schools of the time.[28] As the syndicalist poetess Bellalma Forzato-Spezia, one of the movement's most interesting women, argued in one of her popular lectures, conventional schools rather than enlightening and elevating the minds of future generations, had become a powerful "instrument of domination and enslavement," another way for the bourgeois state "to fabricate docile citizens, respectful of laws, authorities, and pre-established orders." True education, she insisted, should free children "from the shackles of dogmatic education" and create a revolutionary milieu fit to preparing "a new generation of conscientious, free, and innovative men." Her educational plan included, among other things, "the demolition of religious, patriotic, militaristic, and capitalist dogmas," as well as the promotion of a "compassionate rationalism" conducive to fighting all social injustices and creating a better future.[29]

By World War I, the *sovversivi* had established at least three Modern Schools in the United States—in Paterson, Boston, and Philadelphia, along with hundreds of other free-thought and working-class schools.[30] Particularly successful was the *università po-*

polare, an informal network of schools that provided instruction on a variety of subjects to working men and women. Born originally in Great Britain during the 1870s as part of an international socialist campaign to make higher learning accessible to everyone, the *università popolare* was launched in Italy in 1900 and reproduced in the United States in 1903. As in Italy, its curriculum did not focus exclusively on politics, but covered history, science, art, and literature. Like the other educational initiatives sponsored by the *sovversivi*, its main goal was to counter the influence of the Catholic Church and the *prominenti* by advancing scientific knowledge and combating ignorance and religious bigotry.[31]

Special libraries and bookstores formed another important part of the *sovversivi*'s world. Virtually every radical group had its own "*libreria rossa*" (red bookstore), which featured hundreds of titles, ranging from social novels to famous political and anticlerical treaties and works written by local *sovversivi*. Sold at a few cents, these books served as a schoolhouse for the movement's members while, in turn, their sales helped fund radical activities. Bartolomeo Vanzetti, in his autobiography, tells us that in America he "studied the works of Peter Kropotkin, Gorki, Merlino, Malatesta, Reclus." He "read Marx's *Capital*, the political *Testament* of Carlo Pisacane, Mazzini's *Duties of Man*, and many other writings of social import." His list included also books of history, science, and literature. "I studied Darwin and Spencer, Laplace and Flammarion," he noted. He also read Italian literary classics like the *Divine Comedy* and *Jerusalem Liberated*, the novels of Hugo, Tolstoy, Zola, and the poetry of Leopardi, Rapisardi, and Carducci.[32] We may assume that it was thanks to the *librerie rosse* that he and many other workers were able to gain access to such a rich collection of books and attain a far-reaching self-education.

Theater was also effectively used to refashion Italian immigrant working-class culture and leisure time. Starting from the late nineteenth century, the *sovversivi* created revolutionary dramatic societies known as *filodrammatiche rosse*, which put on hundreds of performances of Italian and European classics as well as plays written by local radical intellectuals like Arturo Giovannitti and Ludovico Caminita (see figures 6.4–6.6). Their primary role was to provide an opportunity for socialization and entertainment, but, as in the case of other radical theaters, the stage was also seen as an important shaper of public opinion and crucial catalyst in the making of social consciousness. As Colette Hyman and other drama scholars have recognized, the workers' theater reflected essentially an effort "to use working people's leisure hours as a terrain for political education," and "to develop and sustain among working people and their allies the solidarity necessary for bringing about social and political transformation."[33]

Attempts were also made to institutionalize the radical stage beyond its use at social and political events. In 1918, Arturo Giovannitti and other Italian radicals in New York launched the *sovversivi*'s most ambitious theatrical venture: the Teatro del Popolo. Conceived by its founders as an alternative theatre to "the banal and frivolous commercial stage," it was meant to invigorate the culture of Italian immigrants, by promoting "critical thinking instead of just fun."[34] Its mission was to cultivate a specifically revolutionary aesthetic and create an authentically "popular" theatre, made by the people for the people, combining art and politics, education and entertainment, thought and action.[35]

Utilizing the auditorium of the socialist People's House, a large hall that could accommodate five hundred spectators, the Teatro del Popolo operated for about a year,

SERATA D'ARTE
all'Accademia di Musica di Brooklyn
(LAFAYETTE AVE. & ST. FELIX STREET)

Venerdi', 5 Dicembre, alle ore 8,15 P. M.

Verrà presentato al giudizio del pubblico un nuovo lavoro drammatico del nostro Direttore
ARTURO GIOVANNITTI

"IL RIVALE DI DIO"
Un Prologo e tre atti.

I nostri lettori già conoscono in parte la trama del lavoro che Giovannitti ci presenta nell'interpretazione dei migliori attori di lingua italiana. Sarà una serata di arte e di studio poichè la tesi, che l'autore svolge magistralmente, interessa vivamente quanti si occupano di questioni sociali.

I Biglietti possono essere prenotati presso gli uffici della Camera Italiana del Lavoro (231 East 14th St.) o comprati al Botteghino del Teatro. Prezzi: $1.10, $1.65, $2.20, e $2.75 (inclusa la tassa di guerra).

Figure 6.4. "Evening of Art." This ad, published in the antifascist *Il Veltro*, announced the opening of *Il Rivale di Dio*, a new dramatic work by Arturo Giovannitti, the laureate poet of Italian immigrant workers. The performance was held at the Brooklyn Academy of Music on December 5, 1924 at 8:15 P.M. Sold through the newly launched Italian Chamber of Labor, the tickets ranged from $1.10 to $2.75.

running weekly performances from January 1918 through 1919. It is unclear why it came to an end, but one can easily guess that, like many of the *sovversivi*'s educational projects, the financial cost could not be met on a long-term basis.[36]

Immigration scholars have long noted the tendency of Italian immigrants to establish insular and stable communities with their own ethnic stores, markets, restaurants, and professional services. Reflecting this distinctively Italian sense of "togetherness," "commensality" and "belonging," the *sovversivi* had their own cafes and restaurants that served as important social, political, and intellectual centers, similar to the nineteenth-century *osterie* in Italy, the *goguettes* and *marchands de vins* in France, and the Anglo-Saxon saloons. As a number of international scholars have argued, it was often in these informal social settings that working-class politics and revolutionary movements began to develop.[37] Though seen as a site of corruption and depravity by the middle class, working-class taverns were places where people gathered not only to drink and have fun but also to share information, problems, hopes, and dreams. "It was 'man's social nature,' and his 'craving for companionship,' rather than a desire for strong drink," writes Roy Rosenzweig, that led workers to the saloon.[38]

In fact, as Tom Goyens has argued, social space and radical politics were intimately connected. Beer halls and saloons helped build a "sphere of free action" for a dissident culture and alternative lifestyle. They were not just taprooms but served as a principal forum for political meetings, public lectures, discussion circles, fundraising events, and

```
┌─────────────────────────────────────────────────────────────┐
│  MUSICA  RIBELLE  ANTIFASCISTA  RIVOLUZIONARIA              │
│                                                             │
│           OFFERTA  STRAORDINARIA                            │
│     Questa straordinaria offerta avrà la durata dell'anno in│
│  corso, fino a tutto il primo gennaio prossimo.            │
└─────────────────────────────────────────────────────────────┘
```

MUSICA RIBELLE ANTIFASCISTA RIVOLUZIONARIA

OFFERTA STRAORDINARIA

Questa straordinaria offerta avrà la durata dell'anno in corso, fino a tutto il primo gennaio prossimo.

M. 1 - Bandiera Rossa
M. 2 - Salutiamo l'Umanità
M. 3 - Inno Antifascista
M. 4 - Inno a Matteotti
M. 5 - Stornelli d'Esilio
M. 6 - L'Internazionale
M. 7 - Addio, o Lugano Bella:
M. 8 - Primo Maggio
M. 9 - Inno dei Lavoratori
M. 10 - Amore Ribelle
M. 11 - La Rivolta degli Schiavi
M. 12 - Inno dei Pezzenti
M. 13 - I Gladiatori
M. 14 - Canto dei Malfattori
M. 15 - Canto dei Lavoratori
M. 16 - Canto dei Sofferenti
M. 17 - Canzone Sacco-Vanzetti
M. 18 - La Morte di Caserio
B. 501 - L'Uultima Canzone
A. 5 - A Song of Separation

Oggi l'International Music Roll Co. offre a prezzi di costo i seguenti rolls con parole e musica italiana:

L'intera collezione di venti rolli si spedisce assicurata franca di porto per la somma di quindici dollari. Sei rolls a scelta si spediscono per cinque dollari. Un singolo rollo costa un dollaro. Ogni rollo e garantito e si spedisce assicurato e franco di porto.

Inviate le ordinazioni oggi stesso. Il numero dei rolls è limitato. Non aspettate che siano esauriti. Inviate le ordinazioni accompagnate dall'importo alla

INTERNATIONAL MUSIC ROLL COMPANY
199 Broadway (Room 523) New York City

Figure 6.5. "Rebel, Antifascist, Revolutionary Music." *Il Nuovo Mondo* (November 19, 1925). This ad announced the "extraordinary offer" of a collection of twenty famous revolutionary Italian music rolls, such as "Bandiera Rossa," "Addio, o Lugano Bella!" and "Primo Maggio," for $15. Six rolls were sold for $5 and one single roll for $1. Orders were to be submitted by mail to the International Music Roll Company in New York City.

---

performances.[39] Similarly, in his study of Italian weavers, Franco Ramella shows that the *osteria* played a crucial role in promoting socialization and politicization: mutual-aid associations, political decisions, and, more important, class solidarity took place there. The *osteria* represented, in the words of another Italian scholar, Renato Monteleoni, "a family, sometime the only available; a confidential refuge from solitude; a comforting and almost endless reservoir of speakers and listeners who exchanged sentiments and ideas in a fecund debate often otherwise unthinkable anywhere else."[40]

In the United States, the *sovversivi's* most popular hangout was John's Spaghetti House on East Twelfth Street in New York City (now simply John's), which was commonly advertised in Italian radical newspapers "as the favorite meeting place of free thinkers of all nationalities." Established in 1908 by John Pucciatti, an immigrant from Umbria, its menu offered an appetizer, main dish, dessert, and cup of coffee for under a dollar. Carlo Tresca, Arturo Giovannitti, and other famous *sovversivi* regularly ate there, often holding special radical banquets at John's private apartment upstairs.

Another favorite place on East Twelfth Street was the Ferrer Tea and Lunch Room, "a modest little place in the heart of New York where good food is served at popular prices." Pasta, noted an ad, was not served there, since the aim was "not so much to make money as to cultivate plain living and high thinking."[41]

Radicals also founded cooperative grocery stores that sold inexpensive home goods and food. For example, William Gallo, who grew up in an Italian anarchist family in Paterson, New Jersey, recalls that Italian anarchists there started a *cooperativa* on Park Avenue with a club upstairs where they met "every Saturday and practically every evening" to play cards and have a glass of wine or beer. Similarly, *Il Proletario* informed its readers that the "Union Cooperative Store" of Barre, Vermont, located on the "socialist block" at Granite Street, was "well stocked with all kind of groceries of the best quality at low prices, including meat." All sympathizers of Barre and surroundings, noted the ad, should go there to shop: "It would not only be in their best interest but they would also support a good cause."[42]

PER-I PRIGIONIERI POLITICI

Il 24 NOVEMBRE avra luogo al
MANHATTAN   LYCEUM
66 East 4th Street. New York City.

sotto gli auspici dello
Italian Defense Committee

U N

Grandioso Ballo

a beneficio dei prigionieri politici.

Il 24 sarà giornata di festa   Thanksgiving Day - e quindi non ci sarà ragione d'assentarsi per tutti coloro cui sta a cuore la causa di quelli che languoro nelle galere per il solo delitto di essere stati fedeli alle proprie idee ed ai proprii principii.

Tutti dunque al Manhattan Lyceum il 24 Novembre. alle 7 p. m. Vi sara una eccellentissima orchestra.

THE ITALIAN DEFENSE COMMITTEE.

Figure 6.6. "Grand Ball for Political Prisoners." *Alba Nuova* (October–November, 1921). This ad urged Italians to participate in a dance organized by the Italian Defense Committee to raise funds for Sacco and Vanzetti and other political prisoners of the Red Scare who "are in jail for the only crime of being faithful to their ideals and principles." The dance was held at the Manhattan Lyceum in New York City on November 24, 1921, starting at 7:00 P.M. and lasting all night.

Identifying culture as a fulcrum for social change, Italian immigrant radicals also spawned a vigorous associational life which entertained workers all year-round with traditions and practices such as picnics, concerts, dances, and theatrical performances. Drawing on both working-class and Italian popular culture, these events were the principal way to spread radical ideas beyond the confines of the workplace into the larger immigrant neighborhoods. More important, they helped reinforce working-class styles of consumption and keep alive Italian folk traditions in the face of increasing Americanization.

Music occupied a central role in the *sovversivi's* efforts to incorporate Italian cultural traditions into their political activities. Plays, parades, festivals, picnics, and other public and political events all featured concerts by radical groups' orchestras, such as La Simpatica or Il Circolo Corale Figli del Lavoro.[43] The repertoire included famous opera compositions, often reset to new words honoring the socialist revolution, international working-class hymns like the "Marseillaise" or "Internationale," and Italian revolutionary folksongs like "Primo Maggio," "Addio Lugano Bella," or "Bandiera Rossa."[44]

Music, perhaps more than other cultural forms, exemplified the transnational connection of Italian immigrant radical culture, leading back to Italian backgrounds and working-class rituals. Italian opera, for instance, was a symbol of national identity, arousing the immigrants' visceral attachment to their homeland, and holding immigrants from different regions together. In the 1920s and 1930s, radios and gramophones helped

Figure 6.7. Front cover of *L'idea cammina!,* a drama written by Michele (alias Ludovico) Caminita in 1905. Born in Palermo, Sicily, Caminita came to the United States in 1902, becoming, according to American authorities, "one of the most dangerous Italian anarchists." A draftsman by trade, he wrote several sociological books, a biography, a novel, and two plays and also composed cartoons, drawings, and posters. Arrested in 1920 and threatened with deportation under the Red Scare, Caminita eventually collaborated with the police, providing crucial information on anarchist groups.

keep Italian culture alive, allowing immigrants to hear and sing along their favorite operatic arias and popular songs.

The importance of music in the cultural world of the *sovversivi* is also reflected by the fact that their libraries included songbooks with titles such as the *Canzonieri dei ribelli, Canzoniere rivoluzionario, Canti anarchici rivoluzionari*, and *Nuovo canzoniere sociale* (figure 6.7). Similar to the famous pocket-size *Little Red Song Books* of the Industrial Workers of the World, they were sold to workers for a few cents or given as presents to new members of radical groups or subscribers of radical newspapers. Not only were these lyrics one of the main weapons used to popularize revolutionary ideas, but they were also extremely successful.

Richard Brazier, a songwriter and member of the Spokane branch committee that put together the first IWW song book in 1909, admits that what first attracted him to the IWW "was its songs and the gusto with which its members sang them." "Songs are easily remembered but dull prose is soon forgotten," argued the supporters of the first red songbook. "Our aim and principles," they added, "can be recorded in songs as well as in leaflets and pamphlets—in some cases even better. For songs will be more apt to reach the workers than dry-as-dust polemic."[45]

Dances, as evidenced by the numerous ads published in radical newspapers, were also extremely frequent and popular. Like other radicals, the *sovversivi* held smaller, local dances on a weekly basis and larger, more formal ones in occasion of major holidays, such as the Fourth of July and New Year Eve, or to commemorate important revolutionary anniversaries. William Gallo recalled that the Piedmont Club of Paterson organized a dance "every Saturday, with music played by a little orchestra." He played the guitar, his brother Henry the violin, and his brother-in-law Spartaco Guabello the mandolin, while his mother acted in the plays, which were all "about the life of the poor and how they were oppressed."[46]

Local unions also had their own separate annual galas and concerts. Radical papers announced these *serate speciali*, as they called these special entertainments, in their last page, giving often specific information about the evening program. Tickets for these concerts and balls cost about twenty-five cents and were typically free for women. According to newspapers' reports, as many as five hundred people regularly attended these events, dancing, drinking, and playing all night.[47]

Another standard event that drew large crowds was *la festa della frutta*, a traditional Italian peasant harvest festival that was held annually at the end of the fall to celebrate the season's harvest. Like the picnics, it lasted the whole day and included music, games and raffles with fruit trophies symbolizing a better and healthier future.

This rich cultural life was of course not unique to the *sovversivi*. In fact, a similar "culture of entertainment" could be found among other radical and labor groups of the early twentieth century. Roy Rosenzweig, for example, has described the rich leisure culture of industrial workers in Worcester, Massachusetts, particularly the vibrant life of the saloon—"a separate and largely autonomous cultural sphere" where workers spent most of their free time.[48] Focusing on Detroit, Richard Oestreicher found an intense "subculture of opposition" embodied in ethnic and working class institutions such as concerts, balls, and parades.[49] And Bruce Nelson and Tom Goyens have documented the vibrant social life of Chicago's and New York's German anarchists, which bore remarkable similarities to the *sovversivi*'s subculture.[50]

Indeed, by the end of the nineteenth century, the demand for "eight hours for what we will" had become a central quest of the labor movement that moved past simple monetary concerns. As the famous slogan of the Lawrence Strike of 1912 implied, workers wanted not only "bread" but "roses too"; they demanded not only higher wages, shorter hours, and better working conditions but also "all that was essential to the exercise and enjoyment of liberty."[51]

Samuel Gompers, the President of the American Federation of Labor, for example, insisted that America's workers wanted and deserved "more"—"more leisure, more rest, more opportunity . . . for going to the parks, of having better homes, of reading books, of creating more desires." Greater leisure time for the workers, he noted, would mean not only more social welfare but it would also translate in direct benefits for the economy by expanding the market and social participation.[52] Similarly, Ira Steward, the most prominent leader of the movement for the eight-hour day, argued that working class consumption was a necessary pre-requisite for industrial democracy. As Lawrence Glickman noted, Steward put forth a distinctively working-class vision of consumerism centered on decent wages and leisure as the roots of social progress.[53]

The *sovversivi*, too, recognized the importance of leisure in the life of workers, but their premises were radically different from American mainstream labor leaders. For Gompers and Steward, consumerism was a "natural and absolute" right to citizenship, a measure of material success and "standard of living." The *sovversivi*, instead, rejected high-level consumption as well as consumer values and practices. Consumerism for the *sovversivi* meant not so much the pursuit of amusement as open support for the revolution. They condemned entertainment per se, arguing that it would make the masses too complacent, undermining political resistance and class collectivity.

What they envisioned was a "socialist commercial culture" that served their members, from the food they bought to the schools they attended, the books and newspapers they read, and the holidays they celebrated—an alternative culture and way of life through which workers would educate themselves and socialize. Not only would workers work together and organize together, but they would also play together, dance together, and eat together. For the *sovversivi*, working-class clubs, family picnics, May Day parades, and dance halls essentially defined the socialization of workers, families, and immigrants within the labor culture, serving several important functions. First, they created a rich social and cultural life inside the ethnic communities with distinct institutions, interests, and forms of socialization that offered an alternative to capitalist values. They were crucial occasions of entertainment and fun—but also, as Victoria De Grazia suggested, a way to reinforce working-class subcultures, promoting a sense of collective belonging and building solidarity.[54]

In addition to their symbolic functions, working-class *divertimenti* fulfilled practical "materialistic" needs, serving essentially as the movement's primary form of fundraising. Virtually all Italian immigrant radical groups relied on these events to finance their newspapers and other radical activities. Anarchist Attilio Bortolotti remembered that "almost every Saturday there was a dance and a *recita* [performance] to send a few dollars overseas."[55]

Figure 6.8. Front cover of *Come era nel principio*, an antiwar play written by the famous socialist poet Arturo Giovannitti during World War I. First performed on October 10, 1916, at the People's Theatre of New York with the famous Sicilian actress Mimì Aguglia in the leading role, it became an instant success, and a year later it was also performed in English on Broadway. *L'idea cammina!* and *Come era nel principo* are examples of the vibrant theatrical culture that enlivened the lives of Italian immigrant workers.

Besides financing the movement's activities, cultural events, such as the "Grand Ball" organized by the Italian Defense Committee, paid sickness and death benefits as well as legal expenses of arrested political prisoners, war victims, or widows and orphans of fallen comrades (see figure 6.8). The defense campaigns of Italian radicals such as Arturo Giovannitti, Carlo Tresca, and above all Sacco and Vanzetti were all funded almost entirely through the revenues of picnics, dances, and dramatic performances. Similarly, after Gaetano Bresci was executed for killing King Umberto in 1900, the *sovversivi* were able to raise thousands of dollars on behalf of his wife and two daughters through the organization of benefit feasts, despite repeated attempts by the police to stop them.[56]

Cultural activities also helped transcend the radical movement's divisions, allowing large and diverse crowds to mingle together in ways otherwise impossible. Unlike union and political meetings, which tended to be homogenous, recreational events were open to all. Women were welcome, and radical papers regularly stressed their participation. Indeed, while apparently absent from the political movement, which was male-dominated, women were a vital presence in the cultural events, playing a key role as community and labor organizers, fundraisers, and writers. As Jennifer Guglielmo has written, the cultural world offered them "a sanctioned way to move somewhat freely beyond their families" and participate into the movement's life. Nicola Sacco's wife, Rosina, regularly acted in the plays put on by anarchist theatre in Milford, Massachusetts, and so did many other *sovversive*, such as Fiorina Rossi, Ernestina Cravello, Ersilia Cavedagni,

Jeanne Salemme, and Ninfa Baronio. Women even formed their own separate clubs, orchestras, and theater groups to bring forth the emancipation of women.[57]

Finally, culture also operated as a base for propaganda and recruitment, providing an opportunity for people who sympathized with socialist ideas but did not necessarily belong to any political group to be active participants (that is, consumers) in the movement. In fact, while only a tiny fraction of the Italian immigrants were official members of parties and organizations, thousands of immigrant workers partook in radical cultural activities on a regular basis—buying radical newspapers and books, attending lectures and schools, socializing at parties, picnics and dances, and protesting at rallies.

Knowing that Italians participated enthusiastically into these events is one thing; assessing their reactions to them is of course another. Did going to a radical picnic, attending a radical play or dance, or buying radical songs and books effectively radicalize Italian immigrants? Did these commercial practices change their political and cultural orientation?

While it is impossible to know how Italian workers responded to radical activities and recreational events, or the meanings they ascribed to them, there is evidence suggesting that the *sovversivi*'s campaign bore important fruits. Lizabeth Cohen has showed that even in the 1920s, when ethnic workers came to share more in the new consumer goods, they did so "in their own neighborhood and in their own way," continuing to reinforce ethnic and class allegiances. Buying a Victrola or a radio, for example, allowed Italian immigrants to play Italian records and listen to Italian news. Despite the growth of chain stores, the Italian workers remained loyal to local merchants, continuing to shop in their local neighborhoods and to buy bulk goods from barrels and crates rather than packaged items. Even the increasing popularity of movies, Cohen concluded, did not erase ethnic cultures.[58]

Interestingly enough, cultural practices were the last aspect of Italian immigrant radicalism to die. Although the *sovversivi*'s political world completely vanished after World War II, traces of their distinctive culture survived well into the 1950s and 1960s. Two anarchist papers, *Controcorrente* and *L'Adunata dei refrattari*, were published until 1967 and 1971, respectively, while the socialist *La Parola del Popolo* lasted well into the 1980s. As the late Nunzio Pernicone, whose father was active in New York's radical theater, noted, the *sovversivi* "still went to plays, dances, picnics, and lectures, although the frequency of these activities diminished with each passing year as did the number of individuals attending."[59]

The *sovversivi*'s "invented traditions" served an important source of class and ethnic identity that provided an alternative organizational focus for the lives of Italian workers in America, giving them a shared basis of experience—a similar lifestyle, or, in the words of Benedict Anderson, "an imagined political community" with distinctive values and norms of behavior.[60] But while it rejected the American way of life, their vision ultimately did not, or could not, challenge capitalist consumerist practices and Americanization. As changing cultural and political climate, particularly governmental repression and forced Americanization, disempowered radicals, Italian immigrants gradually began to be integrated into "the Nation of Immigrants"—the mainstream flow of American life, values, and commercial leisure.

PART TWO

The Politics and Style of Italian American Consumerism, 1930–1980

7

Italian Americans, the New Deal State, and the Making of Citizen Consumers

Stefano Luconi

Italian Americans were a pivotal component of the New Deal coalition of voters from diverse ethnic minorities that elected Franklin Delano Roosevelt to the presidency for his unprecedented four terms at the White House.[1] In particular, after deserting the Republican Party in 1932, they cast 88 percent of their ballots for the Democratic candidate in 1936, 75 percent in 1940, and 64 percent in 1944, when the repercussions of World War II—a conflict that pitted the immigrants' adoptive country against their motherland—significantly cut into Roosevelt's plurality in the Little Italies.[2]

Research on Italian Americans' political mobilization during the great depression of the 1930s has addressed primarily how patronage in the distribution of jobs and relief as well as recognition in terms of candidacies and appointments to public offices affected the electoral behavior of this immigrant group and consolidated its Democratic allegiance after many voters of Italian ancestry had defected from the ranks of the GOP in the wake of an economic crisis that they blamed on sitting Republican President Herbert Hoover. Conversely, scholarship has paid relatively little attention to Italian Americans' shift into the Democratic column in support of the welfare programs of the Roosevelt administration. Furthermore, next to nothing has been written about the implications of consumer policies for Italian Americans' partisan allegiance and political involvement in the 1930s and early 1940s.[3]

This brief chapter investigates these heretofore overlooked dimensions of Italian American politics during the New Deal era against the backdrop of both the spread of consumerism in the Little Italies and the rise of the Italian newcomers' offspring as consumers in the early decades of the twentieth century. Indeed, like other immigrant groups, Italian Americans, too, came to conceive participation in consumer culture in the adoptive country as a significant part of their American dream.[4] Moreover, consumerism was not only a field for a confrontation between parents, who cherished savings, and children, who wished to partake of the pleasures of spending.[5] It can be argued that consumer culture helped set the stage for community activism as well. For instance, Buffalo's Socialist Italian Americans encouraged the creation of consumer cooperatives in the early twentieth century in order to force wholesalers and retailers to lower prices.[6] Their fellow ethnics rioted in Providence in 1914 in the wake of an increase in the cost of macaroni.[7] Likewise, Tampa's Italian Americans resorted to boycotts in the early postwar years to protest against a sudden jump in the cost of living.[8] It can also be reasonably suggested that a steep decline in consumption during the great depression had political implications because the members of the Little Italies suffered from it and, consequently, were likely to express their ensuing resentment at the polls.[9]

Scholarship has hardly followed such clues, but in the last few years a growing literature has begun to deal with Roosevelt's at least vocal commitment to the consumers' interests during his presidency. This essay focuses on the response of Italian Americans to the president's economic policies as well as on the impact of the consequent legislation on their lives and identity.[10] In addition, this chapter highlights how campaigns for social equity playing on the language of the citizen consumer became a means to claim a voice in politics on the part of such a theretofore marginalized minority as Italian Americans.

The Vote of the Purse

Roosevelt and his circle of advisors maintained that underconsumption was at the roots of the depression that had been affecting the United States since 1929. In their view, therefore, a rise in consumption was the centerpiece of the strategy to stimulate the economic growth again and to reestablish prosperity. Spending became the administration's mantra and replaced the traditional celebration of saving as a national virtue. Consequently, enabling consumers to spend money by increasing the purchasing power of the people—namely the workers—seemed more important than channeling new investments into business activities. The primacy of the consumer in the New Deal programs substituted the predominance of the producer resulting from classical economic theory. Moreover, the emphasis on consumption was not confined to market recovery only, but it also implied calls for the protection of consumers' interests.[11]

Mercurial Roosevelt's actual and consistent commitment to consumption-oriented policies is a matter of scholarly controversy.[12] Yet, even such historians as Alan Brinkley who have contended that rhetoric rather than substance characterized the president's approach to these issues have nonetheless acknowledged that the new stress on consumption shaped a innovative vision of economic life and came to share the center of the political debate.[13]

The federal regulation of maximum hours and especially minimum wages, as provided for in the 1933 National Industrial Recovery Act (NIRA), was intended to pave the way for a significant increase in the purchasing power of the average American. A ceiling on the number of work hours aimed at enabling more people to earn a living, while the stipulation of the lowest acceptable level of pay was devised to let workers earn extra money.[14]

These requirements not only met with the favor of Italian American mainstream newspapers, such as the New York City-based *Il Progresso Italo-Americano*, which had long aligned themselves with the Democratic Party.[15] The provisions were also endorsed by the radical Italian-language press. For instance, *La Stampa Libera*, a Socialist-oriented daily published in New York City, initially warned that the minimum wages were likely to become the maximum income for laborers.[16] Nonetheless, it soon considered the measure as an achievement for workers because it gave the latter's representatives seats on the local commissions in charge of setting salaries in the various industries.[17] Appreciation for the NIRA as for its attempts at giving ordinary people a voice extended to the establishment of a Consumer Advisory Board with the function of protecting the interests of consumers in the elaboration of the codes of fair competition that entrepreneurs were encouraged to elaborate in order to prevent disastrous overproduction.[18]

Remarkably, Italian Americans eventually appropriated the consumer-related arguments underlying the New Deal approach to the economic recovery. As late as 1936, *Il Messaggero*—the leading Italian-language weekly in predominantly working-class Passaic and Berger counties, New Jersey—proclaimed that "more workers means more buying power."[19] Likewise, on the eve of the 1936 presidential election, *Il Progresso Italo-Americano* gave Roosevelt the credit for placing "more money in the buying of consumer goods."[20] Even when it discussed the problems of grocers resulting from a steep decline in the price of macaroni, *Il Progresso Italo-Americano* drew upon the Roosevelt administration's rhetoric in order to criticize "unfair competition" and to call for the harmonization of interests among producers, retailers, and consumers.[21]

After all, the early reservations about the NIRA found expression by means of worries about its effects on the actual purchasing power of workers.[22] Moreover, after dropping its initial skepticism about the minimum wage provision, *La Stampa Libera* agreed that the main asset of such a piece of legislation would be "strengthening the people's capacity of consumption without which there could be no end to the economic and industrial depression."[23] Casting aside the jargon of class struggle and embracing the language of consumerism, the newspaper also suggested that enhancing the purchasing power was an antidote to the instability of manufactures caused by underconsumption.[24] One of its readers even stressed that a thirty-hour workweek would not only create new jobs and reduce unemployment but also benefit entrepreneurs because more workers would mean more consumers and, thereby, better opportunities to sell products on the market.[25]

Beyond what emerged in the columns of newspapers, the benefits that many Italian Americans actually drew from the minimum wages provision of the NIRA and the ensuing weighty political debt they owed Roosevelt can be easily perceived in their recollections about the contribution of that piece of legislation to the improvement of their living conditions. A jewelry worker in Providence remembered that "we were only getting about fifteen, twenty cents an hour until the NIRA came in during the Roosevelt presidency. When this bill was passed . . . we started with thirty-five cents an hour."[26] In the same city, the NIRA was also responsible for an increase in wages to $13.50 a week for retail workers such as Antonetta Filippone.[27] As another jewelry worker concluded, "everybody loved it (the NIRA)."[28] Actually, to strike a sensitive chord within the Italian American electorate, Democratic activists emphasized the contribution of the New Deal to the increase of consumers' purchasing power while campaigning in 1936.[29]

By the time Italian American voters contributed to Roosevelt's 1936 landslide reelection, other consumer-oriented pieces of legislation had added to the NIRA in benefitting the members of the Little Italies. To them, a key field of federal intervention was that of home ownership because Italian immigrants coveted a living place of their own, a longing that historian Virginia Yans-McLaughlin has explained "as the wish of former peasants to possess—even at great sacrifice—something which had been denied to so many for generations."[30]

The march of Italian American families out of the tenements had already begun in the 1920s, but the Depression had severely impaired this achievement. For instance, in New York, by the early 1930s worsening economic condition had forced back to shared housing in East Harlem a few Italian Americans who had left this neighborhood for better residential areas during the previous decade.[31] In addition, both there and in other district of the city foreclosures and evictions threatened Italian American residents.[32] "People were losing their homes"—recalled Elvira Adorno—"when my father lost his business I was unable to pay the mortgage."[33] Similarly, a Brooklyn resident of Italian descent remembered that "My family always liked to own their own home. We only lost our home once, when we had to go on relief during the Depression."[34] Analogous problems affected the Italian American community in Providence, Rhode Island.[35] Likewise, according to a 1933 report, in Philadelphia's main Italian American section, "thousands have lost their property for non-payment of interests and taxes. They've been having sheriff's sales at the rate of 1,300 a month."[36] In particular, 52 percent of the houses in the heart of South Philadelphia's Little Italy were mortgaged.[37] Yet, the Home Owners' Loan Corporation, the federal agency that was formed in 1933 to prevent foreclosures by refinancing mortgages in default, helped numerous Italian Americans save their homes.[38] For example, according to a sample by Amy E. Hillier, Italian immigrants were the largest group among the recipients of assistance from the Home Owners' Loan Corporation in Philadelphia throughout the 1930s, while a significant number of the city's U.S.-born beneficiaries of federal loans were the children of Italian newcomers.[39] Therefore, it is not by a chance that the efforts of the New Deal to shield homeowners from foreclosures bulked large in the Democratic propaganda in the Italian-language press during the 1936 presidential campaign.[40] Of course, Italian American voters were appreciative of the endeavors of the Roosevelt administration for their houses and pledged to express their gratitude to the president at the polls.[41] As Ida Y. M. Antonelli observed, "My home has been saved from foreclosure and my morals have been restored. I shall always as long as I live hold most devotedly sacred the name of Mr. and Mrs. Roosevelt. . . . I am now able to rear my four children in utmost decency and as honorable American citizens. . . . Every right and sane thinking person will know what to do when November comes."[42]

The New Deal not only endeavored to protect the existing homeowners. It also encouraged tenants to purchase dwelling units. Specifically, the establishment of the Federal Housing Administration in 1934 helped numerous Italian American families fulfill their long-cherished desire to acquire homes. Since this agency insured lending institutions against loss, it made it easier for working-class consumers, such as Italian American laborers, to obtain low-interest loans in order to buy houses. As a result, for instance, Italian Americans' rates of home ownership in Chicago's newly created neighborhoods in the late 1930s and early 1940s spanned between 43 percent and 61 percent, as opposed to 25 percent to 30 percent in the city's districts that predated the founding of the Federal Housing Administration.[43] Likewise, in the prevailing Italian American Eighth and Twelfth wards in Pittsburgh's Bloomfield and East Liberty districts, the percentages of the families that owned the houses in which they lived rose, respectively, from 47.2 percent and 31.0 percent in 1930 to 60.2 percent and 48.8 percent in 1940.[44]

Roosevelt's further emphasis on consumers' entitlement in both his 1937 second inaugural speech and 1944 State of the Union address, which called for an economic bill of rights guaranteeing every citizen a decent living, contributed significantly to curbing Italian Americans' defections from the Democratic Party in the wake of World War II.[45] Not only did his words win acclaim in the Italian-language press on both occasions.[46] The New Deal policy also determined the partisan alignment. For example, on the eve of the 1940 presidential election, assessing Roosevelt's record as opposed to the platform of his Republican challenger, Wendell Willkie, Pittsburgh's Italian-language weekly *Unione* remarked that "After considering the history of the Republican party with its depression, soup lines, food riots, bank failures and general misery, no Italian will consciously vote to return to the system which made that national disaster possible.... Willkie . . . will reduce relief, assistance on mortgages, social security, unemployment insurance, low-rent housing, and all the other activities which made it possible for America to get back on its feet."[47]

Similar appreciation of Roosevelt's commitment to the protection of citizens' welfare was widespread in the Little Italies on the occasion of the 1944 presidential campaign.[48] New Orleans' *La Voce Coloniale* even called the president's housing policy "a blessing."[49]

The Power of the Purse

Lizabeth Cohen has pointed out that "citizen consumers were made from the top down as well as the bottom up."[50] Actually, Italian Americans were not only passive beneficiaries of the new attention of the Roosevelt administration to the consumers' interests. Such a change in the economic perspective by policymakers in the U.S. government and Congress also made the Italian immigrants and their children more conscious of their role and needs as consumers so that members of this ethnic minority began to voice their claims and demands. Against the backdrop of the efforts of the federal government to empower theretofore underrecognized groups, Italian Americans mobilized not only as workers, who profited from the rights to unionization and collective bargaining in section 7A of the NIRA, but as consumers, too. The New Deal's commitment to consumers' interests offered the frame to advocate safeguard against frauds and gave new momentum to campaigns, for instance, against adulterated olive oil, a sensitive issue in the Little Italies, for the sake of quality and consumers' health.[51] The latter operations reached a climax in late 1938, when New York City's Mayor Fiorello H. La Guardia—an Italian American himself—ordered the raids of suspected retailers and secured the conviction of a number of grocers who sold counterfeit olive oil.[52]

Although such initiatives played on consumers' protection, they were also the result of pressures from producers and importers of genuine food. Therefore, in the field of consumers' activism, housing offers once again a better case in point for the mobilization of the rank-and-file members of the Little Italies. Italian Americans did not confine themselves to complain about foreclosures with Roosevelt.[53] In the late spring of 1933, for example, threatening crowds of unemployed took to the streets in New York City to prevent the eviction of families that had lost their homes for failure to keep up their mortgage payments or, more simply, brought back the furniture of those who had been evicted to the latter's houses as acts of defiance.[54] Other Italian Americans appealed directly to the president and asked for amendments to the Homeowners Refinancing Bill that would be friendlier to consumers, such as an increase from 50 percent to 80 percent of the assessed value of properties covered by federal loans.[55] As late as 1938, tenants still joined forces under the auspices of the Communist-inspired Workers' Alliance in order to fight against high rents and to force proprietors into enhancing the conditions of the apartments they leased.[56]

After the passing of the 1937 Wagner-Steagall Act, which provided grants for the operation of local public housing agencies so as to build low-rent homes and to improve the existing dwelling units in poor urban districts, Italian Americans also lobbied for better housing in their own neighborhoods.[57] In 1939, for example, Providence's only Italian-language weekly—the *Italian Echo*—adhered to a movement to establish a municipal housing authority that would apply for federal funds to clear the city's slums and other blighted areas in the hope that the program would benefit Federal Hill, the site of the local Little Italy.[58]

East Harlem's Italian Americans launched a similar campaign in New York City. In January 1938 they participated in the founding of the East Harlem Housing Committee, under the auspices of the Communist-leaning Harlem Legislative Conference, and resorted to the former organization—along with petitions bearing thousands of signatures, as well as other public and personal appeals—in the following years to call on Mayor La Guardia and the New York City Housing Authority to appropriate funds for low-cost housing projects that aimed at benefitting the district's tenants. Community leader Leonard Covello, the principal of Benjamin Franklin High School, had called for the rehabilitation of the dwelling units in East Harlem since the mid-1930s. Specifically, Covello was instrumental in promoting a housing committee at Benjamin Franklin High School as early as 1935 and presided over a few initiatives of the East Harlem Housing Committee in 1938 and 1939.[59]

In spite of its top-down initial stimuli, the movement developed at the grass-roots level, too. In particular, it gained momentum in March 1939 in the wake of a series of fires that swept old apartments killing several children.[60] Ordinary Italian American women were very active in the lobbying efforts for better housing in the district. For instance, they took the lead in a parade through the streets of East Harlem that was held on March 25, 1939 in response to the casualties of the previous days, under such slogans as "We refuse to die like rats in dirty old tenement flats!" and "Make East Harlem a model town, tear the old-time tenements down!" By identifying themselves only as mothers—exploiting, thereby, maternity as a political tool—and claiming the right to decent housing not just for themselves but also for their own children and families, these women added a maternalistic approach to Italian Americans' struggle as citizen consumers.[61] Their mobilization on this specific issue reflected a larger nationwide rise in American women's consciousness as consumers during the Roosevelt presidency, which reached a climax with the attempts of the National Consumers' League at using consumption to improve wages and labor standards.[62] Furthermore, such activism not only involved typical maternal needs such as the demand of a playground and a supervised nursery for childcare.[63] It also aptly endeavored to play on the New Deal's gendered vision of rights, which implied special protection for mothers and children, although the Roosevelt administration treated males and females unequally in welfare programs.[64] Therefore, at least in the field of housing, within East Harlem's Little Italy women fulfilled the role that Lizabeth Cohen has identified for American female citizen consumers, namely the function of "protectors of the public interest."[65]

Congressman Vito Marcantonio—a supporter of Roosevelt's social legislation who had been reelected to the House of Representatives on the ticket of the American Labor Party in 1938 and was the chairperson of the Harlem Legislative Conference—became a major spokesperson for Italian Americans' demands for slum clearance and low-rent housing.[66] For instance, in 1939, stigmatizing the delays in the appropriation of funds for the construction of low-rent new apartment buildings in East Harlem, he emphatically sympathized with the residents of the district's tenements who, "when the siren of the fire truck is heard . . . wonder as to which relative, whose brother, whose sister, whose mother, whose child is going to be the next victim on the funeral pyre of a slum fire."[67] Marcantonio also made a point of advocating the extension of the benefits of the broader existing federal legislation on housing.[68]

While the efforts of Federal Hill's Italian Americans were to no avail, the mobilization of their fellow ethnics in East Harlem came to a successful outcome in mid September 1939, when the New York City Housing Authority received a loan from the Roosevelt administration for a public housing project in lower East Harlem.[69] Mayor La Guardia presided over the ground breaking for what would become the East River Houses providing apartments for more than 1,100 families on March 2, 1940.[70] The first 115 low-income families moved into their new homes a year later.[71]

New York City's Italian American female consumers were not active in the movement for better housing only. A handful also participated in the campaigns against the high cost of living. The latter initiative reached a climax on May 22, 1935, when housewives started a four-week boycott against retail butcher shops to protest allegedly inflated meat prices.[72] Other Italian American women took on excessive expenses for food in letters they sent to their ethnic newspapers.[73] Such activism enhanced Italian Americans' consumer consciousness and stimulated mobilizations in additional fields.

At the time of the meat strike, for instance, *Il Progresso Italo-Americano* carried readers' appeals against the one-dollar monthly minimum rate that New York State's Public Service Commission intended to enforce for electric power on the grounds that such a provision was detrimental to the purse of consumers.[74]

The Identity of the Purse

In the struggle for better housing, East Harlem's Italian Americans always remained the larger and leading cohort of the campaign, determining its goals and strategy. Nevertheless, they also reached out to and joined forces with a few residents from other ethnic backgrounds living in the district, especially the growing Puerto Rican community that was also active in the Harlem Legislative Conference.[75] Furthermore, Jewish Women were the backbone of the Communist-inspired United Council of Working-Class Housewives that promoted the 1935 meat strike and a significant number of Harlem's African Americans also adhered to the boycott.[76] These attempts at interethnic activism, however, hardly meant that the fight for consumers' rights and access to an American standard of living in the depression years contributed, among several other factors, to the demise of Italian Americans' national insularity or helped the development of an awareness rooted in their progressive Americanization, as Lizabeth Cohen has conversely implied in her study of Chicago's steelworkers.[77]

As soon as Italian Americans realized their political role as consumers, they also exploited such a function to support initiatives that clearly demonstrated the failure of the immigrants' assimilation within the U.S. society. The response to the Italo-Ethiopian War offers an illuminating example of the retention of strong connections to the native country on the part of Italian American consumers at depression time. The Italian-language press and radio programs, as well as organizations such as New York City's Italian Chamber of Commerce, launched a nationalistic crusade to encourage consumers in the Little Italies to purchase Italian products in the aftermath of the 1935 Fascist invasion of Ethiopia. They argued that a significant increase in the sale of imported Italian goods in the United States would help the Fascist regime offset the damages to Italian exports resulting from the economic sanctions that the League of Nations had passed against Italy in retaliation for her unprovoked attack on the African country.[78] Specifically, the president of the Italian Chamber of Commerce, Pietro P. Carbonelli, stated that "by consuming Italian products, not only will you make your own interest, but you will also contribute to the final victory of your brothers who are fighting to secure the Italian people a better position in the world."[79] Likewise, addressing Italian American consumers, another official of the same organization, Carlo Bertolaia, pointed out, "you can serve your motherland even by purchasing a gallon of Italian olive oil, a can of Italian tomatoes, or a piece of Italian cheese."[80]

As Italian Americans collected more than 700,000 dollars in New York City alone to support the military machinery of their native country in the colonial conflict in eastern Africa, such appeals did not fall on deaf ears.[81] Actually, after undertaking a steady decline since the inception of the economic crisis, the imports of Italian food products to the United States grew by 2.8 per cent between 1935 and 1936. Although the rise was relatively modest, it was a significant countertrend to the fall of all other Italian exports in the same period. Indeed, it was food that let the overall value of all Italian imports to the United States increase by sixteen million lire in the first five months of 1936.[82]

After all, even if one sets aside the resort to the purchase of Italian stuff as a means of political warfare, the early stages of access to the consumer society did not prove to be an Americanizing experience for most Italian immigrants and their offspring in the interwar years, contrary to the dynamics that scholars have suggested for other minorities.[83] Little Italies were usually impervious to the penetration of department and chain stores carrying nationally advertised brands with wide but standardized consumer appeals that helped the assimilation of other immigrant groups by turning the latter's members into shoppers of U.S.-made products that bore no resemblance to the ethnic merchandize available at neighborhood retailers within their respective community. Instead, Italian American consumers continued to patronize independent mom-and-pop shops in the Little Italies where they could find Italian goods or items produced in the United States but appealing to the Old World tastes of prospective customers. As a result, the practices of consumption on the part of a majority of Italian newcomers and their children revealed the survival and cultivation of these people's ethnic identity into World War II.[84]

The exploitation of the political power of Italian American consumers to support the goals of their mother country was not confined to the experience of the Italo-Ethiopian War only. For instance, in response to the vocal protest of the American Jews against the anti-Semitic turn of the Fascist regime in 1938, a number of Benito Mussolini's supporters in the Little Italies threatened an Italian American boycott of Jewish businesses in the United States.[85] In particular, Giuseppe Genovese admonished organizations such as the American Jewish Congress that appeals against the purchase of Italian products as an act of retribution for Fascist anti-Semitism was not advisable because "Italian Americans are so numerous that their counter-boycott of Jews will be much more harmful for the latter's economy."[86] *Fair Play*, an English-language newspaper for the immigrant second generation, issued a similar warning.[87]

Moreover, the discovery of consumers' leverage for political purposes crossed the ideological divide in the Little Italies. For example, Luigi Antonini—the secretary general of the Italian-language Local 89 of the International Ladies' Garment Workers' Union and a prominent opponent of Mussolini's dictatorship—urged Italian American workers to join their Jewish comrades in the boycott of Italian exports in the fruitless effort to coerce the Fascist regime into repealing its anti-Semitic measures.[88]

Conclusion

The politics of consumption, including its welfare provisions, failed to Americanize the Italian immigrants and their progeny into the late 1930s. Members of this ethnic group did turn to the Democratic Party in order to defend and to claim their rights as consumers along with other minorities, but they retained an identity based on their motherland that they expressed in other fields of consumerism. It was only during World War II that Italian Americans' practices of consumption disclosed a sense of affiliation that began to go beyond their national ancestry. The planting of victory gardens to reduce the pressure on food supply as well as the involvement in scrap drives and campaigns to save rationed materials in order to cope with wartime shortages pointed to Italian American citizen consumers as individuals who were fully aware of the military priorities of the United States and, therefore, revealed their own patriotism and attachment toward the adoptive country.[89]

In the postwar years, Italian American consumers' demand for and access to the American standard of living further contributed to the acquisition of an American self-perception. To this effect, a significant boost came from the passing of the 1944 Servicemen's Readjustment Act (or G.I. Bill), which expanded the veterans' purchasing power and facilitated their upward mobility toward the American mainstream by subsidizing college and university tuition fees, by granting low-interest loans for home purchases, and by providing capital to start businesses. The experience of Angelo Gualdaroni, a Pittsburgher of Italian extraction who served as a radio operator during World War II, offers an example of how such a piece of legislation contributed to making his fellow ethnics' American Dream come true. As Gualdaroni recalled, "I was thirty-nine years old when the war ended in 1945, and I had basically nothing to show for my life. But then all those G.I. benefits kicked in. I was able to buy a home in Bloomfield and enroll in the Robert Morris School of Accounting. . . . I landed a solid, long-term job. . . . Meanwhile, my brother, [who] had also served in the military . . . was able to purchase a house near mine and to open Gualdaroni's Grocery."[90] Indeed, home ownership among the families living in Pittsburgh's Italian American enclave of Bloomfield increased from 60.2 percent in 1940 to 89.8 percent in 1960.[91] Another working-class veteran, Samuel R. Sciullo, remembered that he "had entered law school in 1947—taking advantage of the G.I. Bill," which later enabled him to become a successful attorney.[92] More generally, Italian Americans' college attendance nationwide doubled from 15 percent in 1940 to 30 percent in 1954.[93] Higher education paved the way for inclusion in the middle class. By 1950, for instance, in San Francisco 27 percent of the Italian immigrants over forty-five years of age held a white-collar job. So did 40 percent of their children aged between twenty-five and forty-four . Furthermore, 14 percent of the former and a quarter of the latter earned at least $4,000 per year.[94]

The federal subsidies let Italian Americans use a noteworthy share of their increased earnings at wartime and in the postwar years for larger consumption.[95] The participation in the white flight from the inner city neighborhoods to the suburbs epitomized the new material affluence of the immigrants' second and third generations. A Bostonian of Italian origin recalled that the benefits of the Servicemen's Readjustment Act "made it possible to live in a house that had (at least) three cubic inches of grass and assured status. If you moved to the suburbia, you would finally find the recognition from the larger America that the people in the old neighborhood had always wanted."[96] As many residents of San Francisco's Little Italy in the North Beach left it for new homes in Santa Clara, San Mateo, and Marin counties, the concentration of the population of Italian ancestry in that ethnic enclave dropped from 25 percent to 10 percent.[97] Likewise, in New York City's metropolitan area, Italian Americans significantly strengthened their preexisting presence in Glen Cove and Inwood in Nassau County by doubling the number of residents in the Long Island region, as their concentration in the suburbs rose from 10 percent in 1930 to 24 percent in 1960.[98] They also relocated from the working-class ethnic district of Corona in Queens to the middle-class area of Flushing, where they intermingled with residents of different national extractions.[99] Suburbanization affected even a few Italian American former cigar makers of Ybor City's Little Italy in Tampa, as they contributed to the doubling of West Tampa's population between 1945 and 1955.[100]

In many cases the move to suburbia resulted not only from upward social mobility, but also from the influx of African Americans into the old Italian American neighborhoods. Paul Pisicano, a New Yorker of Sicilian descent, admitted that "We went to college. Our whole neighborhood became professionals. . . . Everybody started to get a piece of the rock. Everybody wanted to have a house away from the niggers. Now guys were talking about niggers: I gotta move out or my kids."[101] Conversely, for those who remained in the old neighborhoods the priority became the efforts to prevent blacks from moving into their own districts. For instance, in spite of earlier efforts to involve other minorities, consumers who had campaigned for low-rent public housing in East Harlem before World War II subsequently mobilized in the fruitless attempt at keeping African American and Puerto Rican residents out of the project.[102] The case of East Harlem was only an instance of the fight against residential integration that characterized other public housing projects Italian Americans had previously advocated such as the Frances Cabrini Homes in Chicago.[103]

This stand had political implications once more time. As Roosevelt's recognition of consumers' interests had helped consolidate the Democratic affiliation of the Little Italies in the prewar years, the dissatisfaction of East Harlem's Italian Americans with the influx of Puerto Ricans weakened Marcantonio's electoral following. After six consecutive reelections to the House of Representatives from 1938 through 1948, Marcantonio lost its seat in Congress in 1950 in the wake of growing but controversial accusations that he had stimulated the arrival of Puerto Ricans from their native island in order to secure their votes and to strengthen his own following at the polls.[104]

Marcantonio's 1950 defeat epitomized the demise of the progressive stand of many Italian American voters that had shaped their participation in the New Deal coalition in the 1930s and in its revitalization in the 1948 presidential race.[105] In addition, Italian Americans' rejection of black residents made their activism as consumers acquire a racial overtone that contributed to revealing the eventual shift of the immigrant's offspring to an identity as white Americans.

8

Italian Americans, Consumerism, and the Cold War in Transnational Perspective

Danielle Battisti

Historians generally view World War II as a watershed moment for Ellis Island immigrant groups and their children. By midcentury, Italian Americans, and other "new" immigrant groups, had achieved unprecedented levels of social integration in the United States and could legitimately lay claim to "mainstream" status in the United States.[1] Yet many Italian Americans continued to feel the pains of ethnic discrimination and exclusion in the postwar period. Despite the Italian American community's overwhelming rejection of Mussolini and Italian fascism by the late 1930s, and its wholehearted support for the American war effort, some Italian Americans believed that their group's fitness for democratic citizenship remained in question.[2] With the onset of the Cold War in the late 1940s these anxieties intensified. In the first years of the Cold War, it was not clear whether Italy would embrace democracy and ally itself with the West or adopt communism and turn toward the East. Many Italian Americans felt the need to prove that Italians were not in some way predisposed to favor totalitarian over democratic regimes. For these reasons, many Italian Americans became ardent anticommunist crusaders in both Italy and the United States.

Other concerns emerged as well. If Italian Americans were indeed members of the mainstream, on par with older-stock Americans, why then were they still stigmatized as a less desirable immigrant group in American immigration laws? Italians had been largely barred from immigrating to the United States since the 1920s with the country's adoption of the National Origins System, which regulated immigration based on a preference system of racial and ethnic hierarchies. In 1952, Congress largely reaffirmed the ideology behind the National Origins System in keeping allocations for Italian immigrants and other less desirable groups at levels that did not drastically depart from quotas that had been in place since the 1920s.[3] In response to this situation, hundreds of thousands of Italian Americans mobilized in the postwar period to campaign for an overhaul of American immigration policies, to repeal the legalization of racial and ethnic hierarchies, and to prove that Italians were indeed desirable immigrants and, by extension, American citizens.

Italian Americans made great efforts to combat both of these stigmas associated with their ethnic group in the postwar period. In particular, they appropriated the ideology and culture of mass consumption that so embodied the "American way" during the first decades of the Cold War to recast their group's public image and ultimately to claim full membership in the American mainstream. Americans had long believed that political and economic freedoms were mutually reinforcing phenomenon.[4] During World War II, President Roosevelt had promised the American people that victory would help ensure "Four Freedoms," which included not only political and religious freedoms, but "freedom from want" as well. So Italian Americans engaged in a widely publicized letter writing campaign in 1948 to encourage Italians to embrace a democratic government, follow American economic models, and adopt the culture of mass consumption that American policymakers believed would foster economic growth and international peace. These beliefs became central to American domestic and foreign policies during the Cold War. Arguing that all democratic citizens should have the opportunity to achieve a high standard of living, American policymakers outlined their vision of a postwar order based on democratic principles, free market capitalism, and international peace facilitated in part by free trade and material abundance. Americans promoted the development of institutions and programs to achieve those ideals at the end of the war. Along with the United Nations, the International Monetary Fund and the World Bank were created to help stabilize war-torn economies and to promote economic development and free trade throughout the world. Likewise, direct American aid was an essential tool in promoting economic recovery, free trade internationalism, and democratic ideals, particularly in Europe. From an American perspective, the European Recovery Program, better known as the Marshall Plan, played an important role in European economic recovery and the stabilization of liberal governments in the West. It solidified the political, military, and economic links between Western Europe and the United States. Finally, it contributed to the transmission of American-style mass consumption patterns and consumer culture across the Atlantic.[5]

Second, Italian Americans involved in organizations that worked to repeal the National Origins System quotas and reform American immigration policies set out to prove the fitness of Italians as both immigrants and citizens in the 1950s and 1960s. One way they did so was to demonstrate that Italian immigrants who came to the United States after World War II adopted lifestyles that reflected the culture of mass consumption that prevailed in the United States. Mass consumption had become a powerful expression of domestic anticommunism during the Cold War. In 1959, Vice President

Richard Nixon and Soviet Premier Nikita Khrushchev faced off in the now-famous "Kitchen Debate." Nixon argued that the suburban American home, complete with modern appliances, automobiles, and other consumer goods, epitomized freedom, opportunity, and the superior "American Way."[6] Many Italian Americans enthusiastically embraced these ideals and took part in American consumer culture, thereby helping to construct the suburban environments and middle-class families that Nixon and other Americans extolled during the Cold War.[7] By ensuring that Italian immigrants adopted these consumption patterns, Italian Americans solidified their ethnic group's inclusionary status in American society. They also suggested that Italian immigrants, who adopted American lifestyles and values with ease and rapidity, should also be accorded opportunities to immigrate and become American citizens.

Communists of the Stomach

At the end of World War II, conditions in Italy were bleak. The nation had suffered a political collapse. The war had physically destroyed portions of the country's infrastructure, industries, and countryside. The bombings and invasion of the country had dislocated millions from their homes and livelihoods. Finally, the nation faced an economic crisis as government officials struggled to maintain a viable currency, control inflation, and come up with a plan for economic recovery and growth.[8] Many Americans were intent on intervening in Europe by providing long-term political and economic assistance to Italy and other war-torn nations. But even before long-term plans for European reconstruction could be addressed, Americans stepped in to provide immediate war relief. Ethnic Americans, concerned about their homeland and their people, were at the forefront of war relief efforts.

War relief campaigns, undertaken during and immediately after the war, were the first attempt by Italian Americans to provide Europeans with large-scale material assistance and consumer goods. In 1944, State Department officials and ethnic organizers began working together to form relief committees for European war victims, including American Relief for Italy, Inc. (ARI). From 1944 to 1946 ARI collected money and material donations from the National War Fund and Italian American individuals, ethnic organizations, labor unions, and religious groups all over the country for distribution to Italians in need.[9] The organization received widespread support and publicity from *Il Progresso Italo-Americano*, the largest Italian language newspaper in the United States, which cosponsored ARI drives in 1946 and 1947. Throughout 1946 *Il Progresso* printed articles soliciting monetary contributions for Italian war relief. News of sizeable donations was accompanied by stories and pictures about the continued devastation, suffering, and need in the country. Every other day, the paper featured stories detailing the activities and donations of organizations or individuals who contributed to ARI.[10]

Under the auspices of ARI, millions of dollars' worth of food, clothing, household goods, medicine, and other materials were sent to Italy in the years after the war. In 1945 alone ARI collected nearly ten million dollars' worth of goods, including approximately seven million pounds of shoes and clothing and more than two million pounds of food. Shipments that year also included medicine, vitamins, personal hygiene products, blankets, needles and thread, bolts of cloth, automotive parts, and toys.[11] These donations were humanitarian in nature; they provided some small relief to a war-torn people. They served other purposes as well. Shipments of clothes, shoes, foodstuffs, and the occasional luxury item reminded Italians of the consumer goods and heartier diets they had enjoyed before the war. They also suggested a promise that these goods would soon become available in Italy and could be reincorporated into daily routines. These shipments, as well as other aid packages, such as United Nations CARE packages, were intended to help encourage Europeans to return to prewar consumption patterns that were disrupted by the war.[12]

In studying displaced persons in World War II and its aftermath, Franca Iacovetta has argued that relief packages, including food and household goods, were particularly important for helping women return to earlier models of household production and consumption. The disruptions of war had created a lack of food and household materials, disrupting domestic routines. It not only inhibited regular food preparation and consumption patterns for the entire family, but it had also kept a younger generation of women from learning those consumption and preparation patterns from their mothers and other older women. Thus, food and other household goods not only provided material relief, but they also helped create conditions where Europeans, especially women, could relearn previous behaviors of household management and consumption.[13]

Italian Americans continued to send war relief aid to Italians in the years after the war through formal organizations or as private gifts and remittances to family. By 1947, as the battle lines of the Cold War became more firmly drawn, such aid took on new meaning. Material conditions in Italy and elsewhere in Europe became increasingly important to many Americans as the United States and Soviet Union vied for political, economic, and military dominance on the continent. From the onset, Cold War conflicts were driven in large part by economic concerns. President Truman and his advisors were just as concerned with protecting American access to open markets, maintaining viable trading partners in Europe, and ensuring a high standard of living for Americans in the process, as they were in halting the spread of communism. Therefore, Truman's call for American support for the European Recovery Program, or the Marshall Plan, illustrated the link between economic recovery and political stabilization in Europe.[14]

Arguably, the single greatest concern for postwar Italy was the nation's ability to achieve a full economic recovery and thereby improve the social and material welfare of its citizens. However the process of recovery was slow in 1946 and 1947. By 1948 many Italians had lost confidence in the pro-Western Christian Democratic (DC) government that had been in power since 1946 to achieve this goal. National elections that year brought this issue to a head as the Popular Front, a coalition of the Italian Communist Party (PCI) and the Italian Socialist Party (PSI), threatened to expel the DC government and potentially steer the county toward an alliance with the East. In the spring of 1948 the struggle in Italy commanded international attention. Americans feared a PCI-led victory would put Italy on the road to communism and into the hands of Moscow. The much-vaunted elections thus became a referendum for the Italian people to choose between democracy and communism, American and Soviet leadership, capitalism and a command economy.[15]

Certainly political and foreign policy concerns were of paramount importance as Italian political parties positioned themselves in the campaign. But, both sides made economic and material concerns central elements of their campaigns as well. Each party outlined a program that they believed would lead to a higher standard of living and greater quality of life for the Italian people. For its part, the PCI promised land reforms to Italian peasants and the nationalization of key industries to urban workers. Conversely, a vote for the DC carried with it the promise of large-scale economic aid from the United States, plans for long-term modernization and growth, and trade with the West.[16]

Italian voters were acutely aware that their vote not only reflected a political position, but a choice between two competing ways of life. If there were any doubts, Americans reminded them of the stakes at every opportunity. In the months preceding the Italian elections, American diplomats, government officials, and the media bombarded Italians with propaganda denouncing the Soviet Union, communism, and command economies. At the same time, Americans portrayed the United States as an ideologically just ally and as an economic and social model for Italy to emulate. Just to be sure American intentions were understood, in March 1948 the State Department threatened to withdraw Marshall Plan aid to Italy in the event of a PCI victory.[17]

Many Italian Americans were willing participants in the campaign to promote democratic and capitalist lifestyles in Italy in 1948.[18] In the spring of that year, hundreds of thousands of Italian Americans engaged in a movement that came to be known as the "Letters to Italy Campaign," in which they wrote to their Italian family members and friends encouraging them to vote for the Christian Democrats in the elections of April 18.[19] These letters made many of the same basic arguments that could be found in general discourse about the elections. They denounced the Soviet Union, its ideological underpinnings, and its aggressive foreign policies. They further implored Italians to protect freedom, liberty, and world peace by halting its spread. Likewise, they represented the United States as a friend to Italy and to all the "freedom-loving" people of the world. But along with extolling democratic values and a political alliance with the West, they did much more. In the Letters to Italy Campaign, Italian Americans reminded Italians of Italy's central role in fostering the cultural construction of the West—from the Renaissance to Columbus to the Vatican—and argued that this flow of ideas, culture, and people must be kept open. Finally, they addressed economic and material concerns as well.

Italian American letter writers made significant arguments for capitalism, free trade, and the higher standard of living that such an economic system could offer Italians in their correspondence. One way they did so was in their focus on the importance of Marshall Plan aid. Countless letters from the campaign discuss how the absence of Marshall Plan aid would hurt the ordinary Italian worker and consumer. Letters commonly reminded Italians that American raw materials and financial aid had already begun to revitalize Italian industries. It was this process that would soon lead to improvements in wages and standards of living. In addition, letter writers warned their readers that not only would long-term economic recovery and growth would be halted without American aid, but immediate material conditions would deteriorate as well. Without the Marshall Plan, they cautioned, much-needed basic foodstuffs and in-demand manufactured goods would disappear almost immediately.[20]

Italian Americans also argued that the higher standard of living promised by the PCI, and that the Soviet Union boasted its citizens enjoyed, was a farce.[21] Moreover, letter writers not only denounced "false promises" for material wealth that were made by communists, but in her study of the Letters to Italy Campaign, Wendy Wall argued that "no aspect of the 'American Way' received more attention than America's material plenty."[22] Letter writers spoke of the abundant jobs in the United States, the high wages, and the unrationed supply of food, clothing, and other consumer goods. Wall even points out how letter writers also sent American newspapers along with their letters so that even those who could not read English could see the many advertisements and images that showed the wide array of products readily available to consumers.[23]

Testimonies of American abundance found in the Letters to Italy Campaign could be found in a variety of other exchanges as well. As previously discussed, Italian American individuals and organizations had been providing relief money and materials to Italians since the end of the war. The very presence of such goods in Italy suggested that material surpluses existed in the United States. Moreover, Italians with relatives in the United States were certainly aware of their family members' relative material wealth before the Letters to Italy Campaign. Since the late nineteenth century, remittances and returnees from the Americas had remade Italian landscapes, diets, and patterns of consumption.[24] Regular flows of information, goods, and people had been disrupted by the war but had resumed with relative speed after 1945. In 1948 alone, Italians sent nearly $30 million in remittances to relatives in Italy.[25] Also by 1948, Italian Americans had begun to take trips back to their homeland to visit relatives and reconnect their ancestral roots.[26] Most important, the regular correspondence that had long existed between family members resumed with regularity.[27] In private letters and personal networks, Italian Americans shared news of their lives and successes to their loved ones back home. Indications of material abundance could be found throughout these exchanges. Enclosed in a letter might be a photograph of a well-dressed, well-fed family standing in front of their new automobile or home (see figure 8.1). Images such as these carried great meaning on both sides of the Atlantic and required no lengthy explanations.[28]

All of the activities Italian Americans took part in certainly impacted the outcome of the Italian elections, even if pressure from the Vatican and threats to rescind Marshall Plan aid from the Truman administration were more persuasive in influencing Italian voters.[29] In the Letters to Italy Campaign, regular correspondence and exchanges, visits to Italy, and in their remittances and charity, Italian Americans helped convince Italians that American political and economic models generated prosperity, a high standard of living, and a better way of life. Under these circumstances, Italians could more fully understand the consequences of losing American aid, guidance, and trade. In short, by the end of the 1940s, Italian Americans had helped raise Italian expectations about appropriate standards of living and consumption patterns. The Letters to Italy Campaign was therefore part of a wider project in which Italian Americans, even if unconsciously, were instrumental in fostering the development mass consumption in postwar Italy. By helping to change Italian worldviews about mass consumption, Italian Americans contributed to the transformation of Europeans into mass consumers in the decades that followed.[30]

But Italian American intervention in Italian reconstruction was meaningful not only abroad. The collective efforts of Italian Americans in these campaigns were enormously significant in refashioning their group identity in the United States as well.

Figure 8.1. Manlio and Rina Battisti, ca. 1955. Personal collection of the author. Although this photograph is from a later date, it reflects similar images and sentiments conveyed in earlier postwar correspondences as well.

Italian Americans made sure that the American public was aware of their campaigns. Throughout March and April of 1948 national and local newspapers in the United States provided regular coverage of Italian American efforts. Moreover, when the Christian Democrats had won, Italian Americans received a great deal of praise in the press for their efforts.[31] Following the elections, an American correspondent in Rome reported to the Associated Press, "probably no single factor weighted the scales as heavily as [the letters]. Whole villages read these letters. They were discussed in cafes. They were the witnesses that a confused and groping people believed." The reporter editorialized further, "there is something very moving in the way these immigrants of yesterday rose to the opportunity of testifying for America and American intentions. In an hour of rest, this the best gauge of the strength of the great union we have made out of the people of Europe."[32] Such commentary was telling. In their campaign, Italian Americans had gained domestic recognition as immigrants "of yesterday" and rose to the rank of a full-fledged American citizens with their efforts.

As Wendy Wall has argued, in becoming anticommunist crusaders, Italian Americans had found "a short-cut into 'mainstream' American society."[33] Wall is certainly correct in this assessment. In their campaigns, Italian Americans tried to convert Italians into democrats and capitalists by proclaiming their own commitment to those institutions. In doing so, they laid a firm claim to an anticommunist identity that was quickly becoming part of the national political consensus. But the Letters to Italy Campaign went beyond a simple appropriation of the emerging anticommunist ideology and the rhetoric employed by other Americans in order to become part of the "mainstream." Italian Americans also tried to recast the nature of Italian communism itself in the Letters to Italy Campaign, and in their characterizations of Italian communism in American media sources. Many Italian Americans were fearful that Americans would view all Italians, or worse yet Italian Americans, as potential communist sympathizers or fifth-column agents. In supporting Mussolini, Italians had embraced a totalitarian regime and ideology in the past. The strength of the Italian Communist Party in Italy suggested to some Americans that Italians possessed values that made them especially prone to support totalitarian governments. Many Italian Americans were concerned that perceptions of Italians in this manner stigmatized the group as "undesirable" Americans. Italian Americans therefore tried to mitigate American perceptions about the nature of Italian communism itself in the Letters to Italy Campaign. Arguments about consumption played a central role in Italian American efforts to recast the nature of Italian communism.

Italian Americans were careful to argue that although the Popular Front coalition reputedly had the support of nearly 40 percent of Italian voters in the months before the election, few Italians possessed a genuine ideological commitment to communism. Instead they portrayed Italians as a people who were weary and worn down by years of war and deprivation. They were therefore easy prey for the communists, who promised the masses food and immediate material improvements. In the press, from the pulpit, and on the radio, Italian Americans argued again and again that the majority of Italians were not in fact communist ideologues, but were only "communists of the stomach."[34] In a press release on the subject, George Spatuzza, the head of the Order of the Sons of Italy in America (OSIA) argued that the "hungry people" of Italy were "no match for the tireless propaganda and activity of a well-fed Communist organization." He went on to ask the American people to send food, clothing, and medical supplies to Italians so they would have "the physical strength to oppose communism."[35] In OSIA newsletters, letter writers were instructed to remind Italians that goods were not rationed in the United States, that there was a surplus of food and clothing in the country, and that consumer goods abounded. Thousands of Letters to Italy therefore included not only written pleas but canned goods, consumer baubles, and cash as well.[36] These enclosures served as symbols that democratic regimes could also deliver immediate material aid that Italians would need to resist communist promises and appeals.

One New York Times article chronicled the travels of an Italian immigrant priest who had recently visited a rural town in southern Italy reported how communist agents "walk into the peasants' homes and . . . ask whether the roof of the house is leaking or the barnyard needs repair, and what agricultural implements they can use." He added that these agents go on to tell these impoverished peasants, "it is up to you now to have these things." Later in the article, the priest summed up the situation in Italy by declaring how difficult it was for people in this condition "to resist the materialist appeal of the communists."[37] By spinning the appeal of communism in Italy in this manner, Italian Americans distanced themselves, and all Italians, from the stigma of being communist sympathizers. Italian Americans tried to cast Italians as a desperate people duped by promises of material abundance rather than a people who possessed a firm ideological commitment to communism.

In making these arguments, Italian Americans were not only fighting communism in Italy. They were making a case to the American people that Italians were no less capable of becoming democratic citizens than anyone else, given adequate economic support. This line of reasoning reinforced anticommunist rhetoric, emerging in the United States, which linked political and economic freedoms. It lent support to the Truman administration's call for large-scale economic aid to Europe and reinforced the idea that by fostering material plenty abroad, Americans could protect their own security and material wealth at home. Finally, Italian Americans were reshaping their own group's public image. Italian Americans attempted to head off public perceptions that Italians were prone to sympathize with totalitarian regimes. Instead they attempted to show that, just like Americans, Italians were primarily concerned with achieving "freedom from want." In their quest to export American-style democracy as the means to ensure improvements to Italian standards of living, Italian Americans demonstrated their own commitment to democratic ideals in America.

Postwar Immigrants and "a New Standard of Living"

Italian American efforts to promote mass consumption and to recast their group's public image in the process did not end with the Letters to Italy Campaign. However, in the 1950s and 1960s, Italian Americans turned their attention closer to home as they used displays of material abundance to solidify their own membership in the American mainstream and to claim a place for Italian newcomers there as well. Italian Americans active in immigrant-aid organizations and groups that worked to reform American immigration policies were deeply concerned with the successful resettlement of recently arrived Italian immigrants and their ability to adopt American values and lifestyles. Although Italians were rapidly becoming modern mass consumers, whose behavior and lifestyles increasingly mirrored American standards of living, many Americans in the 1950s and 1960s continued to perceive of newcomers as traditional peasant migrants, with few resources to their name, and a desire to bundle away their wages to send to family members back home.[38] These perceptions were likely compounded by the stigmas Americans associated with refugees and displaced persons, two categories that represented a fair share of the Italians who immigrated to the United States after the war. Italian Americans who promoted postwar Italian immigration therefore engaged in a variety of activities aimed to combat those views. Most notably, they worked to ensure the successful economic and cultural resettlement of recent immigrants. Moreover, they encouraged recent arrivals to appropriate American styles of family organization and material consumption. In doing so, ethnic advocates hoped that Italian immigrants would demonstrate their cultural compatibility, their fitness for citizenship, and compel American observers to abandon discriminatory immigration policies regarding Italians.

As previously noted, World War II was a watershed moment in the social, political, and economic integration of Italian Americans and other "Ellis Island" immigrant groups in the United States. The war had significantly changed American attitudes regarding race, ethnicity, and religion. Wartime tolerance campaigns urged pluralism and unity for all racial, ethnic, and religious groups at home to preserve national cohesion and defeat enemies abroad. The war also revealed the horrors of pseudoscientific racial ideology, while cultural models for explaining racial and ethnic categories became the dominant paradigm. Moreover, service in the army and work in wartime industries created demographic shifts that increasingly led to upward mobility for whites and ethnically, if not racially, integrated neighborhoods, schools, and workplaces.[39]

The trend toward ethnic inclusion and cultural pluralism continued in the postwar period. As suggested by the Letters to Italy Campaign, earlier calls for "100-percent Americanism" gave way to the idea that ethnic Americans could be valuable Cold Warriors with the ability to influence political decisions in their homelands when properly mobilized. Fears that Catholic and Jewish Americans were less fit for democratic citizenship also dissipated when contrasted with the image of communist atheism. And finally, "Ellis Island" immigrants continued their move out of ethnic neighborhoods into American colleges, universities, and suburbs in the postwar period. Aided by the G.I. Bill and the postwar economic boom, Italian Americans and other ethnic groups experienced upward mobility and unprecedented rates of social integration with older-stock Americans in the postwar period.[40]

Perhaps more so than any other characteristic, homeownership in middle-class and working-class suburbs was an indication of the new social position of Italian Americans. Like other Americans, not only did Italian Americans purchase new suburban homes in record numbers, but they bought cars, household appliances, and other consumer goods as well. They likewise embraced middle-class domesticity and traditional gender roles in their personal lives. In the postwar period Americans put a new emphasis on the nuclear family, fulfillment in the home, and family-centered household consumption.[41] In achieving both social and physical mobility in such ways, Italian Americans could increasingly lay claim to "whiteness" in the United States.[42] Residence in ethnically heterogeneous but racially exclusionary suburbs was a powerful and visible badge of whiteness for Italians and other "new" ethnic groups in the postwar period.[43]

However, despite the significant upward mobility and social integration Italian Americans had achieved in the postwar period, many ethnic Italians recognized a glaring indication that they were still considered cultural outsiders or social inferiors by other Americans. As late as 1952 Congress reaffirmed barriers to Italian and other southern and eastern European immigration in the Immigration and Citizenship Act of that year by upholding national origins quotas that kept the immigration opportunities available to these groups at extremely low levels. In doing so, Congress and the public continued to rank immigrants by racial and ethnic hierarchies, and Italians continued to rank as a less desirable group.[44]

Following the passage of such legislation, hundreds of thousands of Italian Americans banded together to push for the abolition of National Origins quotas and greater immigration opportunities for Italians, which they believed would better reflect their group's status within the nation. They created new organizations to achieve these goals, the most important of which was the American Committee on Italian Migration (ACIM).[45] With a national office in New York City, nearly 130 chapters nationwide, and more than 300,000 active members, ACIM was the most important Italian American group in the postwar period that worked to promote Italian immigration and reform

American immigration policies. Along with ACIM, other Italian American organizations already active in the community, including immigrant-aid societies, fraternal organizations, labor unions, and Catholic lay groups joined in the fight.

One early goal that ethnic crusaders achieved in their campaign to liberalize opportunities for Italian immigrants was the passage of the Refugee Relief Act in 1953.[46] The Refugee Relief Act provided for the entry of more than 200,000 refugees and traditional migrants outside of National Origins quotas. Through the lobbying efforts of ACIM and like-minded organizations, Italy received the greatest share of these spots: sixty thousand visas for refugees and relatives of American citizens.[47] Its passage was a boon to Italian American activists because the legislation opened back-door channels through which Italian immigrants could circumvent normal restrictions to their entry. Moreover, it demonstrated the inability of the National Origins System to effectively regulate immigration to the United States and deal with real-world foreign policy concerns. But for all of its benefits, the Refugee Relief Act presented Italian Americans with concerns and challenges as well. If many Italian Americans still believed themselves to be subjects of discriminatory attitudes in the United States, the passage of refugee relief legislation now added the additional stigma of "refugee" to the group's image. In the early postwar period, the term refugee was often associated with the term displaced person. A refugee was unable or unwilling to return to one's home due to potential political, economic, or cultural persecution. A displaced person (DP) had been displaced from his or her traditional home or place of business, often as the result of war. Both terms carried connotations of economic loss and impoverishment.[48]

Postwar legislation regulating refugee and DP entry into the United States reflected these stigmas. American policymakers allowed a number of displaced persons and refugees entry, but they included a series of mandates in the new legislation to insulate Americans from the potential economic and social threats refugees posed. American immigration laws had long contained certain minimum economic requirements for immigrants. Throughout the most of the twentieth century, immigrants had to prove that they were "unlikely to become a public charge." But the political climate of the postwar period and added concerns about the impact of Europe's most destitute classes on the U.S. economy compelled lawmakers to include strict economic provisions in both the Displaced Persons Act (1948) and the Refugee Relief Act. Under new requirements, a citizen had to sponsor an immigrant by guaranteeing the prospective immigrant housing and employment insurances. Sponsors further had to guarantee financial support to the applicant to so that he or she would not become a public charge. To demonstrate this last requirement, a sponsor had to undergo a thorough vetting process in which he or she disclosed bank statements, real estate holdings, and other assets to prove his or her ability to personally support an applicant.[49]

The unprecedented economic safeguards written into postwar immigration legislation not only reflected a strong nativist impulse in Congress and the nation, but they compounded the challenges new immigrants and the ethnic groups they represented faced in the postwar period.[50] Italian American organizations made a calculated effort to combat the stigmas associated with both refugees and Italians by proving to the American public that Italian immigrants were valuable producers and consumers who added to America's economic growth in the postwar period.[51] The American Committee for Italian Migration, the National Catholic Welfare Conference, the Italian Welfare League, the Italian American Labor Council, and other ethnic and religious organizations therefore assisted Italians who immigrated under the Refugee Relief Act in securing immigration visas, finding sponsors, houses, and jobs, and resettle in the United States.[52] These groups were particularly concerned that Italian immigrants embrace lifestyles that reflected postwar domesticity, gender roles, and consumption patterns. In doing so they hoped to demonstrate the desirability of Italian immigrants, even if they were refugees.

One of the most fundamental ways ACIM shaped the newcomers' resettlement and consumption patterns was by encouraging family migrations under the Refugee Relief Act. ACIM representatives constantly counseled refugee relief applicants to bring their entire families to the United States despite the financial concerns and practical difficulties that constrained them.[53] In part, this advice reflected constraints in American immigration laws. But promoting family migrations accomplished ACIM's broader goals in shaping the public image of Italian Americans during the Cold War. In the 1950s and 1960s, the nuclear family carried with it cultural connotations that reflected Cold War cultural values in the United States. All over the country Americans embraced the nuclear family as the primary bulwark against communism. The home provided a protective environment in an insecure world. It reinforced Western and capitalist gender roles that idealized male providers and female consumers within a family household economy.[54] By encouraging family migrations, ACIM encouraged Italian immigrants to conform to this form of social organization and to adopt these cultural values. In addition to conforming to these norms, the Italian immigrant families that would eventually occupy suburban homes and fill those homes with household goods would contribute to mass consumption patterns in the United States that fueled both postwar economic growth and the nation's Cold War credo. They would not be sending remittances back to Italy, nor would they relentlessly save their wages to finance the future migrations of family members. These families would become American producers and consumers—fueling the economy and symbolizing the material abundance that an American way of life offered.

Once individuals and families arrived in the United States, ACIM and its partner organizations continued to shape immigrant experiences. ACIM provided economic and social assistance to immigrating families, thereby encouraging their successful resettlement and integration in American society in a variety of ways. The organization began by helping immigrants secure jobs, which was mandated in the provisions of the Refugee Relief Act. However, whenever possible ACIM attempted to secure skilled work and relatively high wages for immigrant heads of households. They were most successful in doing so by developing programs with American companies to sponsor Italian custom tailors and shoemakers who filled a labor shortage in the United States.[55] By securing skilled work and competitive salaries for immigrants who came to the United States with limited resources, ACIM was attempting to provide newcomers with opportunities for upward mobility in the United States.

ACIM also helped refugees secure affordable housing when a sponsor was unable to do so. ACIM and partner organizations were often able to provide free temporary housing, were able to negotiate reduced-rate housing, or temporarily subsidize rent for immigrant families in need. These efforts kept immigrants from turning to substandard, low-cost housing in poor neighborhoods. With ACIM help, immigrants were exposed to better neighborhoods, social opportunities, and American abundance. ACIM and other Italian American organizations also provided refugees with donations of clothing, groceries, and household goods to help newcomers get on their feet. Large furniture items, kitchenware, bedding, tools such as sewing machines, radios, and other luxury items were given to refugee families to help ease the resettlement process and expose recent arrivals to American material culture. In addition, ACIM made loans to immigrant families so they could make important household purchases within the first months of their arrival.[56]

Finally, Italian American volunteers provided social assistance to newcomers with the end goal of encouraging the social and economic integration of Italian immigrants. Female volunteers in ACIM and the Italian Welfare League visited immigrant homes and where they helped teach Italian women English so they could better secure jobs and navigate American marketplaces. This service was especially important in the postwar period as fewer immigrants settled in Italian-dominated neighborhoods where one could get by with little knowledge of English. They likewise provided childcare for mothers so that they could attend English language or citizenship classes. Volunteers also brought immigrant women to their churches so that they could socialize and learn from Italian American women in those communities. In all of these ways, ACIM and other organizations encouraged refuge families to adopt American models of family organization, living, and consumption. If newcomers could be shown to assimilate quickly and smoothly to American lifestyles, ACIM hoped they would buttress Italian American claims for social quality and immigration reform.[57]

Whenever possible Italian American organizations publicized stories that demonstrated the Italian immigrant's fitness for immigration and citizenship opportunities in the United States. In March 1959, ACIM published an article in its monthly newsletter entitled "A New Standard of Living."[58] The article featured two Italian families, the Tuiachs and the Giurins, who had recently immigrated to the United States under the 1953 Refugee Relief Act. The article and accompanying photographs depicted the two families, who had previously been living in refugee camps, now enjoying "a well-furnished home with all the modern equipment and appliances owned by the average American family." The article even drew special attention to four-year-old Fabbio Tuiach as the proud owner of a brand-new camera.[59] In less than five years since their arrivals, the Tuiachs and Giurins had made the transition from "refugees" to middle-class Americans. Nowhere was this clearer than in the immigrants' household consumption patterns. It was the two families' embrace of American consumer culture that most seemed to mark their assimilation and their transition into the American mainstream. The featured immigrants did not seem appear to be destitute "refugees" who burdened American taxpayers. Neither were they migrant men without women, squirreling away their wages to send back home, who so characterized earlier waves of Italian immigration in the United States.[60] They were families, firmly resettled in the United States, embracing postwar American family and gender norms and buying modern appliances for their American homes, fashionable clothing to wear to work and school, and automobiles for travel in their suburban neighborhoods.

The Tuiachs and the Giurins were not the only immigrant families receive public attention. Armedo Vasari's voyage from Trieste to the United States in 1958 was likewise chronicled by the press. He and his wife, both former DPs, had resettled in a suburb of Chicago. There Vasari worked in manufacturing, earning a wage that afforded his wife the luxury to stay at home and raise their twenty-month-old daughter. The article also featured a photo of Armedo in his home garage working on the nineteen-foot cabin cruiser he had recently purchased.[61] Within only a few short years, the Vasaris had become homeowners, had adopted gender and family roles typical for American Cold War families, and had become model consumers. Likewise, in 1962 the *Chicago Tribune Magazine* ran a three part series, "From Italy to Chicago: the Dramatic Success Story of Our Italian-Americans," similarly noting the smooth transition from immigrant to "American" Italians had made.[62] But no story received more coverage than the arrival and assimilation of the Italian refugee tailors and shoemakers that ACIM sponsored. For months, Chicago-based newspapers chronicled the arrival and integration of these families in their new workplaces, homes, and neighborhoods.[63]

When immigrant families failed to "properly" assimilate, ACIM stepped in and tried to minimize the damage. The case of the Merola family, handled by ACIM's Detroit chapter, illustrates this point. Giuseppe Merola, his wife Angelina, and their three children immigrated under the RRA in 1956. They moved to Detroit to join Giuseppe's oldest daughter from a previous marriage, who had married an American soldier, Roy Jenkins, and immigrated under the War Brides Act a few years earlier. After their arrival in 1956, relations between the Jenkins and Merola families quickly broke down. Despite pledges of support and housing assurances, Roy evicted his wife's family within only three months of their arrival. At that point, ACIM representatives stepped in to aid the Merolas and noted in their files the need to keep the police away from the family's turmoil and the local media unaware of the situation. ACIM-Detroit workers provided the family with free housing for six months, a temporary job for Giuseppe, and tuition-free schooling for the children at Santa Maria parochial school. They also supplied the family with donations of furniture, household goods, groceries, clothing, and medical care to help the Merolas get back on their feet. Yet despite providing what ACIM caseworkers characterized as "assistance beyond their obligation" the Merolas were unable, or unwilling, to conform to ACIM's expectations. Giuseppe failed to provide for his family, and the family could not afford proper housing and other consumer goods. With a great deal of disappointment, ACIM workers ended their involvement with the Merolas by helping the family apply for public housing in the Detroit suburb of Hamtramck.[64]

Recent immigrants like the Merolas certainly felt pressure from other Italian Americans to assimilate and succeed in their new environment, as seen in ACIM's records, public accounts of immigrant success stories, and the accounts of immigrants themselves. Dozens of interviews collected from the "Italians in Chicago" oral history project reflect the importance that postwar Italian immigrants assigned to their material success in the United States.[65] All of the interviews of postwar immigrants in this collection reflect the centrality of material culture in their lives. This process began in the immigrant's homeland. In Italy, the decision to immigrate to the United States almost always reflected the family's desire for better diets, homes, consumer goods, and opportunities for upward mobility. Once in the United States, material abundance was an indication of one's success. Respondents frequently commented on the importance of large meals as an important marker of their success in the United States. Sam Ori, who immigrated with his family at the age of twelve in 1946, remembered his family's struggle to "keep up with the Joneses." Ori noted how his family always felt pressure to want more and have more in the United States, even though they lived in a predominantly Italian neighborhood. According to Ori, material acquisitiveness was a central part of his experience growing up in an ethnic neighborhood in the United States at midcentury.[66]

In displaying economic success, material abundance, and acquisitive consumption patterns, Italian immigrant families were helping to solidify the "mainstream" image of Italian Americans in the United States. Even Italians who came to the United States as "refugees" appeared to rapidly assimilate by embracing American lifestyles and standards of living. Such displays had enormous significance in the postwar period. Italian Americans who campaigned for changes to American immigration laws would capitalize on changing perceptions about Italian immigrants to argue that Italians were indeed desirable citizens and should therefore be accorded greater immigration opportunities.

Conclusion

In both the Letters to Italy Campaign and the strategic incorporation of postwar Italian immigrants into American society, Italian Americans played upon American cultural values regarding consumption to reconstruct their group's public image and its place within the nation.

By extolling and embracing American consumer culture, Italian Americans buttressed their claims to mainstream status in the United States. These claims were particularly important during the Cold War, as ethnic outsiders became American ambassadors, and during ethnic campaigns to achieve social equality, reflected in American immigration laws. But these campaigns were significant in other ways as well. In their personal networks and public appeals, Italian Americans played a significant role in influencing their Italian kin to embrace American political, economic, and cultural values as well. In both the Letters to Italy Campaign and in their relationships with migrants, Italian Americans helped raise Italian expectations about appropriate standards of living and consumption patterns as well. These exchanges had long-lasting effects in both shaping the development of postwar consumer culture in Italy and remaking Italian American ethnic identity in the United States.

9

Italian Doo-Wop

SENSE OF PLACE, POLITICS OF STYLE, AND RACIAL
CROSSOVERS IN POSTWAR NEW YORK CITY

Simone Cinotto

The Work of Place and Race in the Age
of Mechanical Reproduction of Music

Right at the opening of his 2009 anthemic ode to New York City, "Empire State of Mind,"
top-selling rapper Jay-Z introduces two iconic Italian American artists, ostensibly celebrating the uncompromising attitude and grace with which they have reached their
popularity: "Yeah, yeah, I'm outta Brooklyn, now I'm down in TriBeCa; right next to De
Niro, but I'll be hood forever; I'm the new Sinatra, and since I made it here; I can make
it anywhere, yeah, they love me everywhere."[1] Robert De Niro's and Frank Sinatra's styles
clearly resonate to Jay-Z with authenticity and familiarity. When he raps that he is going
to "make it" in the city like "the new Sinatra," Jay-Z endorses the significant common aesthetic ground Italian and black American popular artists have walked, and, at a deeper
level, the affinities of and mutual fascination for certain features of the life and culture of the other that Italian and African Americans have—more or less clandestinely—
shared.[2] Besides dramatically adding to the catchiness of the song, the lyrical vocal
work of African/Italian American singer Alicia Keys (née Alicia Augello Cook) further
hints at bridges between artistic cultures, while offering a bodily evidence of emerging
postethnic black Italian American identities at the millennium's turn.

Indeed, throughout the last century American popular music provided a particularly
important site for representations of Italian and African diasporic identities to contami-
nate and become reciprocally meaningful. The influence of turn-of-the-twentieth-century
Italian immigrant musicians, opera singers, and musical instrument makers on black

163

artists still needs to be ascertained, but *canzone napoletana*, a form of song extremely popular both in Italy and in American Little Italies, was clearly a cross-racial invention rooted in transatlantic commercialism. Immigrant musicians, many of whom had become recording artists in America by catering to the large immigrant enclaves in New York, brought back to Naples rhythms like the Charleston, rumba, and shimmy (a dance form originating in Nigeria), which were quietly appropriated and incorporated in *canzone napoletana* after World War I.[3] Since then, other examples have ranged from New Orleans Sicilian musicians Nick La Rocca and Louis Prima, some of the most successful popularizers of jazz in the interwar years, to contemporary Italian hip hop acts reelaborating the original black style with vernacular influences, as part of a conscious musical project aimed at "unmask[ing] the hidden negritude of the *Mezzogiorno* (Southern Italy)."[4]

Black/Italian musical crossovers are especially important to read in the light of the history of conflict between Italians and people of color that has otherwise been the dominant tale of the Italian racial experience in the United States.[5] On one hand, the story of these diasporic musical encounters speaks of the particular racial territory that dark "Latin" or "Mediterranean" Southern Italians inhabited in the United States, as a group that at the beginning of the twentieth century was considered barely "white," and by the end of the century seemed to many to epitomize white ethnic bigotry; on the other, it illustrates how commercialism and popular culture have been critical arenas for black/Italian exchanges to develop.

This chapter aims at shedding light on the role of consumerism in shaping the modern racial drama of Italians in the United States by making sense of the leading role Italian American performers played in a black musical genre—doo-wop—in late 1950s and early 1960s New York City. Doo-wop was one of the strains of early rock and roll as it emerged from the confluence of rhythm and blues and country music after World War II. A quintessentially urban and working-class form of expression, doo-wop traced its roots in gospel, urban blues, and the barbershop a cappella singing of the 1930s and 1940s. It typically consisted of a vocal quartet (lead tenor, second tenor, baritone, and bass) harmonizing on simple love lyrics, with the support of little or no instrumentation, the sound of instruments mimicked by nonsense syllables (hence the name "doo-wop").

In the early 1950s, proto-doo-wop black groups like the Ravens and the Orioles sang mostly for black audiences. In what is considered the classic era of vocal group R&B, from 1954 through 1958, younger black male groups (the Cadillacs, the Crows, Frankie Lymon and the Teenagers, and many others), reached an emerging record-buying and concert-going market of white teenagers with their up-tempo songs.[6] Between 1958 and 1962, finally, in the wake of the notorious payola scandal, which seriously reduced the interracial ground rock and roll had created up to that point, "white" doo-wop groups became predominant in terms of record sales and visibility.

So overrepresented were young working-class Italians among the makers of this substyle that music historians have called it interchangeably "Italo-doo-wop" or "Italo-American rock."[7] New York was the undisputed capital of Italian doo-wop, with every borough represented by successful recording bands: the Crests (Manhattan's Lower East Side); Dion & the Belmonts, the Regents, and Nino & The Ebb Tides (the Bronx); the Elegants (Staten Island); the Capris (Queens); the Mystics, the Neons, the Classics, and

Vito & the Salutations (Brooklyn). Italian doo-wop was as short-lived as it was intense: it faded, along with the entire vocal group scene, with the advent of the Beatles and the "British invasion," socially conscious soul and folk music, and a more mature age of rock. Chronologically, it was situated at a dramatic turning point in Italian American history, at the onset of the civil rights era and at the peak of the unprecedented migration of people of color from the American South and Puerto Rico into New York City that decisively framed the Italian American descent into whiteness.

In mid-1950s New York, Italian teenagers were hardly alone among "white" ethnic youth in consuming R&B vocal group music as the most exciting new thing with which to articulate their generational identity and desire for cultural difference. Why, then, did they emerge as the most credible performers in this black musical style?

The convergence of distinctive cultural and social factors that created Italian doo-wop first stemmed from the fact that music had always been central to self-representations of Italians in America and their diasporic nation-making. Between 1899 and 1910, musicians represented by far the largest segment of the "skilled and professional" category of Italian immigrants in New York.[8] From collective singing on the job to vaudeville, band playing in ethnic parades, and church hymns performing, music continued to be a vital form of expression for diasporic Italians in the city—and as significant a part of Italian children's upbringing as it was for their African American or Puerto Rican peers—well into the postwar years. Italian American children grew up listening to radios and gramophones playing everything from Neapolitan song; Enrico Caruso and opera; *bel canto* singers Mario Lanza, Jimmy Roselli, Jerry Vale, and Julius La Rosa; crooners Perry Como, Tony Bennett, and of course Frank Sinatra.[9]

These influences would reverberate, often unconsciously, in Italian renditions of doo-wop, making them the original product of a diasporic sonic encounter rather than mere copies of the black archetype. Discussing Dion DiMucci's (of Dion & the Belmonts) hit record "The Wanderer" (1961), historian George Lipsitz noted that, "the song . . . was inspired by 'I'm a Man,' by blues musician Bo Diddley, and the lyrics certainly show an affinity between the two songs. The infectious groove of 'The Wanderer,' however, comes from the tarantella, the traditional Italian dance frequently played at weddings and other festive social occasions. Pietro di Donato's Depression-era novel *Christ in Concrete*, published [in 1939], the year Dion DiMucci was born, uses the tarantella as the key symbol of continuity in Italian life, as part of the Italian past that persists within Italian immigrant communities."[10]

Indeed, the cultural centrality of music in New York's Italian enclaves resulted in widespread social approval for musical personal performance, be it amateur or professional. While working-class Italian parents generally discouraged artistic pursuits and studies in liberal arts, they (like black parents) incited their children (particularly, but not only, their sons) to use their bodies and voices in order to achieve fame in the world of entertainment. In his late-1950s ethnographic survey of an Italian American working-class community in Boston, Herbert Gans noted that "Although an interest in art is considered effeminate, there is nothing wrong if boys wants to become singers of popular music, for this is an opportunity for self-display. In fact, most of the successful white singers today are Italians, and it is no accident that they are much creators of a distinctive personal image as they are purveyors of songs. Italians have done well in contemporary popular music because it emphasizes the development of an individual image and style more than technical musical skill."[11] This approach was particular relevant for doo-wop, a do-it-yourself musical style that did not require any formal training (and, notably, no equipment), but was based on relentless practice, emulation, and competition among the practitioners with a premium put on authenticity rather than formal accuracy.

However, what Italian doo-wop exactly did was to locate these cultural elaborations and specificities in a particular strategy of production and commodification of race and place. On one hand, in the outer boroughs of New York City, young Italian Americans' street-corner interpretation of the black musical form of vocal-group rock and roll helped to create an *actual* place—the "Italian neighborhood"—which was emotionally, socially, and economically valuable for Italian residents over time. On the other hand, Italian doo-wop situated in, and could blossom because of, a *deterritorialized* space— the space of commercially performed, recorded, and broadcasted music—that widely transcended the segregated racial boundaries that the very creation of the "Italian neighborhood" entailed, opening up new grounds for listening to, imagining, and consuming the other.

Italian doo-wop was a productive force in each of these two seemingly disjointed geographies of consumption. It was at the *crossroads* of these two spaces that Italian doo-wop rearticulated a racially complex Italian American identity; an original urban working-class style that Italians and African Americans alike have since loved to endorse and consume, whether infused in the forms of music, fashion, food, or film.

Defenders of the Neighborhood

At the peak of Italian mass migration, 1890–1915, most Italian immigrants to New York congregated in distinct areas of first settlement: a few dozen blocks around Mulberry Street in the Lower East Side, across Broadway in the West Village, uptown in East Harlem, and other low-rent tenement districts in Manhattan. They did so out of discrimination as well as their own preference for living among fellow Italians and close to their jobs in the construction work and garment industries. These usually overcrowded communities were lived by residents and recognized by outsiders as "Little Italies" less because Italians represented the overwhelming majority of the population (that was a rare occurrence) than because they filled the public space around them with a proliferation of "Italian" colors, tastes, odors, words, objects, and performances.[12] Since the 1920s, immigrants and their children began to move out these neighborhoods and regroup into newly developed areas outside Manhattan, where they were able to fulfill the true essence of the Italian American Dream—homeownership.[13] As early as 1930, a full third of the households with an Italian-born head of family owned their homes (nearly all of them in the city's outer boroughs).[14] This process was not smooth and painless, however. The Italians who left the original Little Italies in Manhattan for their new homes in Brooklyn, Queens, or the Bronx between 1930 and 1950 did so in a frantic climate of ethnic and racial succession, as recent rural migrants of color (blacks from the American South and Puerto Ricans) often filled the voids created by departing Italians.

In the 1950s, the influx became a flood: between 1950 and 1960, New York City lost 997,657 white residents in the flight to the suburbs (in Brooklyn only, almost half a million whites left). At the same time, the city's nonwhite population grew by 169,364, with a particular geographical distribution—while Manhattan actually *lost* almost 40,000 nonwhite residents, the black population of Brooklyn, Queens, and the Bronx increased by 93,091, 74,608, and 38,425 respectively. In 1960, 613,000 New Yorkers—or 8 percent of the population—were either born in Puerto Rico or had Puerto Rican parents. By that time, for Italians resettling in second-migration areas, resuming the work of place-making that their parents and grandparents had done earlier in the century consisted mostly of keeping their neighborhood segregated. As Italians perceived any influx of African Americans and Puerto Ricans into their residential area to dramatically lower property values and bring physical and cultural decay to it, "making community" meant jealously guarding the enclave borders against "blacks."

"This is all Italian inside this area," Rev. Mario Zicarelli of Mount Carmel Church explained to the *New York Times* reporter who interviewed him about the frequent racial incidents occurring in the Belmont section of the Bronx. "We're not the kind who move. The Irish left when the Negroes came, but Italians don't move."[15] Because of their relative insularity, class interests, and distinctive racial experience, Italians emerged from the rapid process of urban change with the label of the toughest "defenders of place" and most passionate "lovers of place" among white ethnic groups, uncompromisingly, and even violently, upholding their ethnic-inflected working-class community life.[16]

These sentiments were articulated in different strategies. One was indeed the exercise of violence: Organized crime and youth gangs patrolled Italian neighborhoods against anyone who looked different or acted suspiciously.[17] Before opting for music, all of the original Dion & the Belmonts (Dion DiMucci, Carlo Mastrangelo, Fred Milano, and Angelo D'Aleo) had been members of gangs in the Belmont section of the Bronx, where they all grew up. DiMucci would later note that "one reason he and the Belmonts didn't sing together earlier was that he was in the Fordham Daggers while Mastrangelo and Milano hung out with the Imperial Hoods."[18] Even success would not wash away such an early imprint. As Dion would at some point grow to cultivate ambitions of making more elaborate music and reach to an upper level in the music business, he had to recognize that "For Carlo, Freddie, and Angelo, it was different. . . . We'd roll into town and after a show they'd want to go down to the local hangouts, have a few drinks, and break anyone's face that bothered them. The old gang attitude."[19]

In fact, Italian doo-wop and gang culture were embedded in the same lower-class urban culture, so much that Italian doo-wop was, in effect, the soundtrack of gang life at the time. Both gang membership and street-corner harmonizing provided adolescents alienated from school, work, or the family opportunities to articulate their feelings of estrangement in the displaying of their masculine identity, posturing, and acting out. Prestige, power, and admiration from girls similarly descended on local gang leaders and talented singers. Gangs and vocal groups shared especially important similarities, including rootedness in place (candy stores in Italian neighborhoods served both as gang headquarters and as practice rooms for vocal groups)[20] and the determination to protect their turf, albeit with different weapons.

Indeed, more important than violence in producing and defending the "Italian neighborhood" was culture: from the Italian spoken in the streets, to the public reverberation of family and religious life, to a racialized style of dressing, talking, eating, and acting, in certain areas of Brooklyn or the Bronx an idiosyncratic Italian taste imbued urban spaces with distinctive and meaningful signs.[21] While racism made a black musical style like doo-wop an unlikely candidate to contribute to this work of place-making, street-corner vocal harmony, performed by groups of young local males gathering in landmark neighborhood spots like candy stores, hallways, or subway stations, was consistent with the other varied cultural tactics Italians set out to turn portions of the city into "Italian neighborhoods" and preserve them as such. In his autobiography, DiMucci suggests time and time again that his approach to music was just an unmediated expression of his embeddedness in a specific historical environment: "Being in a studio never really made me nervous. My approach to cutting records was simple: don't fake it. Standing in front of that microphone, I could shut my eyes and see the street corner where we'd first started singing. I could hear everyone joining in, the girls clapping hands, and someone banging on a cardboard box. Sometimes it would be winter, bitter cold, but we'd still be out there, stamping our feet by an oil barrel fire."[22]

Younger Italians largely consumed and performed doo-wop to mark their difference from their parents, and the latter's apparent dull contentment with the relative security and material abundance the postwar years had finally brought to them. Italian parents in turn looked suspiciously at the racial mixing and rebelling potential that the music their children liked implied. But the fact that vocal harmony seemed to fall in the Italian tradition of *bel canto* and personal display in music, and, most importantly, the shared attachment to "the neighborhood" as an entity to endorse and defend, overcame any

Figure 9.1. Dion & the Belmonts, 1958. Dion Di Mucci is at the right.

generational difference. When the radio played for the first time Dion & the Belmonts' hit single "I Wonder Why" (1958), pride and excitement pervaded the entire Little Italy of the Bronx.[23] "It was more than local boys making good," Dion recalled. "It was like we proved that our turf was the best. It was something we all shared: Joe the groceryman, the boys down at Tally's, Willie the janitor, Mike the stonecutter, all our girlfriends and brothers and sisters and everyone who'd known us since knee pants."[24] An underdog at that, in places like Belmont Italian doo-wop and its handful of home-grown successful musicians came to symbolize and embody larger narratives of migration, settlement, working-class life, and community-making.

Historian Herbert Gutman famously proclaimed culture a "resource" for subaltern groups to resist oppression and assert their identities.[25] Vocal-group rock and roll was likewise an important resource for working-class Italians in postwar New York. Based on spontaneity and embeddedness in the local community of purveyors and consumers of the music, emphasizing "image and style more than technical musical skill," being and appearing true to their historical experience, Italian doo-wop created *locals* at the same time that it created *place*.[26]

Through the Barriers of Sound and Color

The second pillar of the geography of consumption that constructed doo-wop as an Italian American culture was the shaping of another *immaterial* and interracial new context—the consumer market of popular music and its evolving technologies.[27] It was the emerging seven-inch 45 RPM record, rock and roll live concert, and radio and television broadcasting industries that first brought black doo-wop to New York's Italian teenagers to inspire them, provided them with the opportunity to actually record what they have been doing on the street corners, and disseminated their original form of ethnic working-class cultural expression—Italian doo-wop—among fellow Italian, black, and other New York youths. The deterriorialized arena of radio airwaves, records, and live concerts drew together white and black teenagers who would have otherwise remained in their own neighborhood and it formed a buffer space of commodification and consumption of music and style that transcended the boundaries between the segregated communities that racism built.

The defining event that started it all was the arrival in New York of disk jockey Alan Freed (1921–1964) to launch his show *Rock and Roll Party* on WINS radio in September 1954. A Jewish-Welsh American from Cleveland, Ohio, also known as "Moondog," Freed was a shrewd and unscrupulous show-biz entrepreneur who matter-of-factly copyrighted the enticing label of rock and roll. Freed was far from being an advocate of racial tolerance or a civil-rights activist, but in a logic of profit maximization (he actually thought that rock and roll would not last long), he almost single-handedly introduced the most exciting mix of loud and fast rhythm and blues available at the time to a just emerging white teenage audience with a disposable income.[28] Technology was a decisive factor in the success and social and cultural impact of Freed's radio show in New York. With its 500,000 watt power, WINS—a commercial, strictly for-profit radio—brought this most modern form of black music, which up to that point had been put irregularly on the air by a few small left-leaning and minority local stations in Manhattan, into all boroughs in unison.

There was no way to segregate the airwaves or to stop the excitement that rock and roll enticed. "I was hooked!" Philip Groia, an Italian American teenager growing up in Long Island City, remembered about the experience of first listening to Alan Freed's *Rock and Roll Party* on Halloween 1954. "Hooked on honking horns, rocking piano sets, and electrical sound accompanying male falsetto vocalists who sounded like nothing I had ever heard before, women whose vocalizing was equally outstanding, lyrics I didn't understand, and bass singers who confused everything with their 'bop-bye-oh's' and 'doe-doe-doe-doe's.' This was my music, something new and refreshing, that I had discovered, cherished, and worshiped."[29] One of the most talented and popular Italian doo-wop singers, Johnny Maestro (née Mastrangelo, 1939–2010), also became interested in R&B vocal harmony by "listening to Alan Freed. That's when I got into harmonies, listening to the Flamingos, Harptones, and Moonglows. It was such a great sound and I wanted to create that for myself."[30] Mastrangelo would in fact go on to form the Crests, the most important interracial "Italian" vocal group, with Puerto Rican Harold "Chico" Torres and African Americans J. T. Carter and Talmadge "Tommie" Gough.

A further technological and consumer-market innovation to spur the interest of young New Yorkers like Groia and Mastrangelo in music, transistor radio was also introduced in 1954, making recorded music portable and transforming listening from a family to an individual experience—thus separating the consumer generations.

Skillfully mastering the support of media to promote his products, Freed organized live concerts in which both the stage and the ballroom were integrated. Events like the "Rock 'n' Roll Jubilee Ball" at the St. Nicholas Arena in Harlem in January 1955 and the "Rock 'n' Roll Easter Show" at the Brooklyn Paramount Theater on Flatbush Avenue in March–April 1956 attracted enormous crowds of teenagers.[31] In Freed's world of rock and roll, Italian doo-wop was not a more acceptable "white" alternative to original black doo-wop, but an exciting complement to it. Both the Crests and Dion & the Belmonts performed for the first time in front of a large audience at Freed's "Christmas Jubilee of Stars" at the Manhattan Loews' State Theater at Times Square in 1958—a show that also featured Chuck Berry, Jackie Wilson, the Cadillacs, the Moonglows, the Flamingos, Bo Diddley, and other black artists. Freed was thus instrumental in turning both the Crests and Dion & the Belmonts into chart toppers, by playing their early hits "16 Candles" (1958) and "I Wonder Why" on rotation on his radio show.

The rapid and ruinous fall of the man who had been most responsible for bringing the original black vocal group sound to young Italian New Yorkers, in fact, did not bring any good to Italian doo-wop despite the fact the changes in the record industry's policies that this ensued nearly destroyed the supposedly competing black presence in doo-wop. The carelessness with which Freed dealt with the color divide annoyed from the beginning the many conservative individuals and lobbies that saw in rock and roll the receptacle of all the wrong values that jeopardized the morality of young Americans and domestic racial order at a moment in which the United States stood as the guardian of the free world. In the summer of 1957, canceled Freed's TV show *The Big Beat* when the camera showed black teenage singer Frankie Lymon dancing with a white girl—and Freed was totally unapologetic about the incident. A few months later, the payola investigations offered the enemies of rock and roll and the racial intermingling that it entailed a convenient occasion to get of rid of Freed. The common practice of record companies to pay disc jockeys for playing their songs on music radio supported self-righteous Americans' beliefs that young people were manipulated into listening to rock and roll. In 1959, Freed was accused of accepting bribes from record companies. WABC, where he had just moved from WINS after the latter had failed to provide support for the attacks he had to suffer, immediately fired him. His career was ruined. Freed's most important competitor, *American Bandstand*'s host Dick Clark, got away with the same accusations by virtue of his cooperation with authorities, more respectable waspish persona, and much more unadventurous approach to the racial issue.[32]

The broadest and long-lasting consequence of the payola scandal and Freed's demise was the music industry's general retreat from the production of rock and roll performed by black artists. Italian doo-wop, though, was hardly a beneficiary of the "whitening" of the music; rather, this turning point marked the beginning of its end. Coed Records, the label for which the Crests had recorded all their many hits in 1958–59, by 1960 insisted that the interracial composition of the group limited their opportunities and market potential. "We were told that we could not do national TV because of that," Johnny Maestro remembered. "We did do *Bandstand*. That was the only one we did. They told us that the other major stations would not take us and because of that, record sales were going to diminish and we'd need to split the group up. They wanted me to go solo and I did for a while. I didn't enjoy it but being young we didn't understand business and we did what the record company told us."[33] Dion also split up with the Belmonts to go solo in the aftermath of the payola investigations. He reinvented himself as a more rocking and authentic alternative to the "Teen Idols," the white, nice-looking, "safe" performers of syrupy versions or rock and roll (nearly all of them also working-class Italian teenagers from Philadelphia, the home of *American Bandstand*: Fabian, Frankie Avalon, Bobby Rydell) with which the record industry tried to replace black artists.

For the time being, however, Alan Freed's radio and live shows were vital in creating a recording market for Italian doo-wop. By the mid-1950s, the demand for black rock and roll records Freed had been able to entice among teenagers was met by a skyrocketing number of independent labels taking over a market majors were uninterested or unprepared to occupy.[34] Cheap 45 records were produced on a mass scale and at a frantic pace. By 1958, after the success of the Belmonts' "I Wonder Why" on the independent label Laurie Records—which marked the emergence of the Italian sound as a definite genre in the rock and roll record market—Italian vocal groups could thus find many opportunities to record their songs. The Crests' Coed Records had offices at 1619 Broadway in the Brill Building, and the Belmonts' Laurie Records was multimillionaire Allan I. Sussel's creation. The vast majority of Italian vocal groups, though, found their way to recording in the grass-roots world of smaller labels, often the effort of single individuals who were at the same time businessmen and fans. The Regents recorded their hit "Barbara Ann" (1961), later covered by the Beach Boys, on Cousins Records, the personal label of Lou Cicchetti, the owner of Cousins Record Shop on Fordham Road in the Bronx, where the group's members used to hang out.[35]

In fact, the most successful groups were also signed to perform, usually in integrated shows for racially mixed audiences, in New York and nationwide, but, for all the acclaim it received at the top of its popularity, Italian doo-wop never emancipated from its working-class, streetwise roots. At the peak of their fame in early 1959, Dion & the Belmonts were booked to participate in the infamous "Winter Dance Party" tour across the Midwest that ended with the airplane crash killing Buddy Holly, the Big Bopper, and Ritchie Valens. Dion allegedly survived the tragedy on account of his ethnic working-class ethics. Although he was offered a chance to accompany the other program headliners on the plane, he decided to continue the tour on the bus with the rest of the musicians because the price of the flight—$35—was exactly the monthly rent of his family's tenement apartment in the Bronx, the source of so many fights between his parents when his father was unable to put the money together.[36]

The low production costs of records and the high number of groups that managed to play concerts made the distance between the audience and the (often unpaid) artists extremely thin.[37] The community aura that surrounded Italian doo-wop was the product of the common origins of performers and fans—which were quite often the same people—as well as the unprecedentedly easy access to the means of reproduction of music. As a result, commodification and commercialism barely undermined the grass-root, place-bound authenticity of Italian doo-wop, at the same time as it broke away with the parochialism and racism of the local communities it stemmed from.

In this same vein, an additional deterritorialized, desegregated, working-class inflected means of liberation from community's bounds for young New Yorkers to be deeply entrenched in doo-wop culture was the subway. The city's "incomparable subway system, with its low fare—a nickel until 1948 and only fifteen cents as late as 1966—made the whole city in all its richness accessible to everyone," historian Joshua Freeman noted. "Generations of young New Yorkers would ride the subway to arbitrarily-picked stops, just to see what was there."[38] Black and Italian vocal groups alike performed routinely on subways, taking advantage of the rumbling acoustics of cars and stations and using train seats to beat the rhythm of songs. A great number of them, among which the Crests and Vito & the Salutations, got their first recording contract after having being noted by label representatives while singing on the train.[39]

In general, Italian doo-wop came very short of interrogating white supremacy or being part of any "active antiracist struggle." But it would be reductive to diminish it to some young Italian Americans' plain appropriation, consumption, and exploitation of black popular culture for the sake of expressing their teenage angst—without the burden "to deal with the consequence of Blackness in America."[40] The commodified space of popular music provided Italian doo-wop opportunities to break through racial borders more deeply.

The first "Italian" doo-wop act to make it to the top of the pop charts were the Crests; a group formed in 1955 when Italian lead singer Johnny Mastrangelo joined schoolmates Chico Torres, a Puerto Rican, and J. T. Carter and Tommie Gough, two African Americans, all living in the Alfred E. Smith housing project on the Lower East Side. "There were Jewish, Russian, Italian, and African Americans—we all got along together," Carter recalled about the housing project where the Crests lived and started singing. "We were forced together [by economic conditions]."[41] Social class, place, and similar musical sensibilities brought the Crests together, *not* race.

Alongside Dion & the Belmonts, the Crests were the only Italian doo-wop group to line up a long and consistent list of Top 40 hits between 1958 and 1960—"16 Candles,"

Figure 9.2. The Crests with Johnny Maestro (*second from left*), ca. 1957. The first lineup of the Crests included Patricia Vandross, the older sister of R&B singer Luther Vandross. Vandross left the Crests in 1958, when the group started touring and her mother denied her permission to go.

"Six Nights a Week" (1959), "The Angels Listened In" (1959), "A Year Ago Tonight" (1959), "Step By Step" (1960), and "Trouble In Paradise" (1960)—that propelled them to national fame. As a national act, the Crests toured the Jim Crow South, thus experiencing firsthand and reflecting on the absurdity and obscenity of institutional racism. Johnny Maestro recalled that, "Some places we played, I would have to stand on the other side of the stage [than the rest of the Crests]. They would say, 'The white boy has to stand here.' Coming from New York we never saw that kind of thing. [In the South] we had colored bathrooms and colored water fountains and the audiences were also segregated." "In Dallas, they had a rope down the center of the auditorium," J. T. Carter remembered. "The white folk would be on one side and the black folk would be on the other. One time we played to a double stage. There was a curtain blocking the middle of it. In this theater, on one side there were black people and on the other side there were white people and we played to the wings. Whenever we'd go to the black people they'd start cheering and then we'd sing to the white people and they'd start cheering. That felt kind of stupid but we went through it."[42] The experience of the Crests in the South illuminates the role of popular music and commercialism in breaking down the most public and lewd manifestations of racism. The Crests' traveling helped make segregation in places of consumption—a practice that had such a critical part in the history of the civil rights movement, from diners to buses—appear not only immoral and vicious but also something that obviously limited the commodification of popular culture, hence anachronistic and residual.[43]

"The white guys in the bus had to get out at the stops to buy the black guys sandwiches and coffee from these little roadside dives," Dion echoed about a tour of the American South the Belmonts did with Sam Cooke and his band. "It was my first run-in with real racism and, being from New York, I thought it was outrageous."[44] Even back home, to be sure, Dion had to use all his ethnic knowledge and charisma to prevent fellow doo-wop superstar Frankie Lymon, who was hanging out with him on his own turf in the Bronx, from being beaten by DiMucci's childhood friends just because Lymon was black. (Dion apparently defused the situation by breaking into impromptu street singing.)[45] In New York, however, Italian doo-wop singers who had to painfully reconcile their love for black music with the prevalent racism of their home communities did find numerous opportunities for escape and actual gratification in the interracial space of commercial musical performance. The Belmonts, the Capris, and the Elegants successfully played the Apollo Theater in Harlem and other black venues, showing great pride for being treated as equals of or—and this is a recurring theme in Italian doo-woppers' oral histories—even being mistaken for the black artists they revered. Nick Santamaria of the Capris remembered the group's first appearance at the Apollo: "Clay Cole [the MC] went out and he said, 'Ladies and gentlemen, we'd like to bring you five boys from Mississippi. They have a number one hit in New York, the Capris.' And we walked out onto that stage and everybody's jaw dropped. They expected us to be black. Nobody knew we were white. But to me that was a compliment because that was the sound [we admired]."[46]

Indeed, the racial confusion that the Italian overrepresentation in doo-wop generated in working- and middle-class audiences locally and nationwide clearly made these young Italian American performers rethink their class and racial identity. As Dion remembers about the controversial first appearance of the Belmonts on *American Bandstand*, "there was something about the sight of those four Italians, decked out in city slicker clothes, snapping their fingers and acting like Negroes, that must not have set too well with the folks in the Midwest. We were kind of exotic, which meant foreign, and that, in turn, meant dangerous. . . . If only those mothers and fathers who shook their heads in disapproval *really* knew where we were from, and what we'd been up to. As it was, our strange, foreign-sounding music, our olive skin, and big city smirks were menacing enough."[47]

The angry opposition to rock and roll of conservatives across the country, in fact, was motivated by fears of racial change as well as concerns about the attack that working-class values and behaviors waged through music on middle-class morality and national youth's uprightness. Young Italian practitioners of doo-wop from the Bronx, Brooklyn, Queens, and Staten Island, however, articulated those "dangerous" values and behaviors in a distinctive diasporic musical style which resonated with authenticity and, as such, represented material for successful commodification. Thanks to technological and economic change that democratized the mass production of recorded music and the emergence of a receptive youth market, Italian vocal groups popularized their racially hybrid, community-based music to a large public, including listeners that would have never walked the streets where they grew up and lived. In the process, they changed themselves, as well as—however slightly—the worldview of the early civil-rights-era young consumers who listened to their songs, bought their records, and appreciated their style.

As George Lipsitz noted about the revolutionary potential of popular music in general, Italian doo-wop of 1958–62 was "a site for experimentation with cultural and social roles not yet possible in politics."[48]

Italian Doo-Wop and the Making of Black and Italian Identities

At the time of its release, Spike Lee's movie *Do the Right Thing* (1989) was primarily taken as a sad parable on interethnic incommunicability and the inevitability of racial hatred in late-Reaganite America. Inspired by the 1986 Howard Beach incident in which a group of Italian American and other youth brutally assaulted three black men in a pizzeria provoking the death of one of them, most of the movie is set inside the pizzeria of forty-something Italian American Salvatore "Sal" Frangione (Danny Aiello) and his two sons in the heart of the predominantly black neighborhood of Bedford-Stuyvesant, Brooklyn. The issues the movie deals with most extensively, though, are not violence, hate crimes, or police brutality, but the cultural construction of race, its irrationalities and tragic paradoxes, and the role of popular culture—music, sports, food, and dress—in facilitating the consumption—if not the understanding—of the other. Lee did not choose by chance Italians as the "whites" African Americans relate most closely in the movie—the empathies they share are as numerous as the differences. It's easy for main character Mookie (Lee) to point at blatantly racist Sal's son Pino's kinky hair, dark skin, and admiration for Prince, Eddie Murphy, and Magic Johnson to conclude that, "Pino, deep down inside I think you wish you were black." The crisis that makes the story develop sparks when black activist Buggin' Out (played by Italian African American actor Giancarlo Esposito) complains to Sal that the only photos on the pizzeria's Wall of Fame are of Italian Americans (Sinatra, De Niro, Di Maggio, and so many others in the pantheon of Italian popular culture celebrities). Sal's arrogant defense of his choice incites Buggin' Out to organize a boycott of the pizzeria, which, albeit will end in tragedy, is conspicuously unsuccessful. The black teenagers who patronize Sal's Pizzeria say they "love Sal's pizza"—an act that represents the satisfied consumption of the other; actually his embodiment. John Gennari aptly noted,

> These Italians and blacks are the most passionate of enemies: familiar enemies, others who are almost the same. . . . [They] inhabit overlapping urban style worlds marked by syncopated streetwise lingo, body posturing, and a visual vernacular of hair, clothing, and ubiquitous gold jewelry. They treat their Air Jordans and their Cadillacs as organic extensions of their bodies, using them for purely expressive purposes. They groom and they strut and they emote. And they scream. None louder or uglier than Buggin' Out and Sal in the pivotal showdown that grows into the most incendiary racial conflagration in recent American cinema.[49]

Sal's racial construction is indeed the most complex in *Do the Right Thing*. Sal loves Bed-Stuy and his black regulars, has a soft spot for Mookie's sister, and befriends the "Mayor," an old alcoholic scarred by the experience of racism and poverty few people respect. But on the wall he hangs the pictures of Italian working-class heroes and keep-ers of an original Italian New York style to mark the place as "Italian" in a clear racial hierarchy. He does not hesitate to run for his baseball bat to defend HIS place and property—the pizzeria "he has built with his own hands"—and show his determination not to leave, as Father Zicarelli of the Bronx would have put it. Why do Bed-Stuy homies still love his pizza?

It is not irrelevant that "Sal Frangione" must have been a teenager in Brooklyn in the golden age of Italian doo-wop, a fan of the music and/or a singer himself. He grew up as an Italian working-class youth "at a major pop-cultural moment in New York" when ra-cial lines were blurred. At that moment, Italian doo-wop was the quintessential sound of racial and cultural boundaries crossing in the arena of arts and consumerism. Italian doo-wop got its credibility and power from representing the solid construction of the "Italian neighborhood" in New York's outer boroughs and its distinctive cultural reflec-tions: the vocation for music and performance as a pathway to social inclusion and upward mobility; distinctive representations of masculinity and style; and effective strategies of sociocultural construction of place and community. In the 1950s, this cul-ture was embedded in and shaped by racism. But the very toughness of Italian Ameri-can life as expressed in Italian doo-wop became a highly marketable discourse when it was transformed into recorded music, live performance, and TV appearance—it spoke *truth*. The commodification of Italian doo-wop, made possible by the dramatic, sudden expansion of the teenage market and the technology to make it profitable, set it free from the narrow boundaries of the Italian neighborhood's parochialism and bigotry; it provided a sense of new possibilities and alternative worlds, while it retained its working-class unaffected feel. Even as commodification made it cross cultural boundaries, Italian doo-wop held on to the most genuine values of early rock and roll: "an innocence with respect to record industry machinations; the spontaneity of amateur performance, and a host of performers no older than their audiences."[50]

These distinctively urban, working-class, and "dangerous" traits were exactly what fascinated a black audience that would have otherwise thought of Italian doo-wop as just another music stolen from their rich cultural repertoire. Despite the racism and vio-lence that underlay its formation, the urban working-class attitude articulated in the sounds, lyrics, and gestures of Italian doo-wop produced an authentic style that black consumers deemed worthy of respect, attractive, and usable. Bobby Jay, an African American disk jockey for WCBS-FM, noted that when Dion & the Belmonts came along in 1958, as the first "white" vocal group to make it into a previously all-black territory, they "had that indescribable element that set them apart, that street attitude. . . . Dion, he had a New York swagger, a New York walk, a New York way of talking, that New York style that no one else had." After all, all of them had been in street gangs. It was commodification that made possible Italian–black encounters and made ground for identities that could be consumed across an artificially—socially and culturally—built racial line. "When I was growing up, I remember me and my friends listening to them on the radio," Jay continued, "and we weren't sure if they were white or black."[51]

Italian doo-wop coherently joined the most convincing (and economically valuable) self-representation Italians were able to craft in the diaspora—that of the spontaneous, group-oriented, and virtuous performative Italian—which dialectically mirrored white-middle-class emotional restraint at the same time that it echoed familiar overtones of authenticity and style for black, Latino, and white working-class audiences. To this, Italian doo-wop added the sense of the possibility of rewriting Italian American identity to acknowledge for the "blackness" in it—be it articulated in the love for the body and its artistic expressions, sensual primitivism, or lyrical emotionality—at an enormously important political turning point in American history.

10

Consuming Italian Americans

INVOKING ETHNICITY IN THE BUYING
AND SELLING OF GUIDO

Donald Tricarico

A Guido is an Italian who listens to disco and drives a Monte Carlo.
—SELF-IDENTIFIED QUEENS GUIDO (1987)

So if you're a loud and proud Italian, and rep the shore to the fullest, we want to hear from you!
[We] are currently seeking the proudest Guidos and Guidettes to rep the real deal.
—*JERSEY SHORE* CASTING CALL POSTED ON THE INTERNET (FEBRUARY 2009)

Although consumption has moved to the forefront of the relationship between culture and identity in late capitalism, it has sounded a minor note for Italian American
studies. It is reasonable to frame Italian immigrant ethnicity by a scarcity culture
that positioned the blue-collar second generation on the margins of burgeoning consumer markets through the Second World War. A straight-line assimilation model
predicates access to the postwar consumer affluence on the erosion of compelling
ethnic difference signaled by the exodus from urban Italian neighborhoods for
the suburbs. It is at this point that consumption becomes a construction site for
"symbolic ethnicity."[1] In this scenario, third-generation, middle-class adults pursue
"nostalgia" for a "heritage" in ways that are consistent with core middle class American
values of expressive individualism and consumerism. A symbolic Italian American
experience is mediated by commodities invested with acceptable ethnic difference
like tins of extra virgin Tuscan olive oil and occasional forays to a commodified Little
Italy.[2]

Symbolic ethnicity cannot account for Guido, a youth subculture originating in New York City's Italian American neighborhoods. This chapter understands Guido as a *collective* ethnic subject defined by a signature *consumption culture* or style. This Italian American consumption style coalesced in a particular social context and historical moment which grounds youth agency in objective ethnic difference. The first part of the chapter traces the origin of Guido to the disco movement of the 1970s; an urban Italian American youth subculture specializing in expanded opportunities for leisure-based consumption referenced to the mass media and entertainment industries is meaningful in the context of local ethnic group development or "ethnogenesis."[3] Because stylized youth identities were embedded in lived Italian American communities, consumption became an important new site for reworking ethnic cultural differences. Following Bourdieu the cultural practices that define group identities also reproduce social status; Guido is an ethnic strategy that uses consumption to struggle for "distinction" in local status hierarchies.[4]

Just as Guido symbolizes the incorporation of commodities into a new Italian American cultural identity and status, it has become a commodity that is merchandised to wider markets. Inclusion in the media spectacle brings alignment with core consumption values, although it compromises subcultural boundaries especially claims to ethnic authenticity. Guido is seen as part of a larger pattern that constructs Italian American difference in relation to American consumer culture while exposing ideological divisions inside the ethnic boundary.

Anticipating an Italian American Consumption Culture

Contemporary youth subcultures are "leisure cultures, revolving around particular styles of consumption."[5] Style-based youth subcultures are products of the post–World War II development of consumer culture referenced to the mass media. The concept of youth culture elaborated by the cultural studies perspective stresses the role of symbolic repertoires (i.e., culture) produced or performed by young people as an attempt to create identities linked to commodities like fashion and music. Contemporary youth subcultures exhibit a vulnerability to "the power of commodities" that "inevitably shapes the contours of personal and collective identity."[6] The cultural studies literature documents the capability or "agency" of young people to use consumption to realize their own interests.[7] Consumption-based youth agency supplies a meaningful alternative to status in the family, the school, and the workplace by becoming the basis for a style market that links taste to a hierarchy of social power.[8]

Youth styles of consumption are hardly prominent in the study of the Italian American experience. Leonard Covello does not even recognize youth peer groups in a depiction of Italian life in New York City before World War II "centered" on the family's "little tradition."[9] Gans's study of the Italian American West End of Boston in the late 1950s depicts family institutions that absorbed age-based sociability and thus precluded the absence of adult surveillance necessary for youth culture; a minor exception was a pattern of teen age "action-seeking" that opposed the "routines" of family-based culture and school. However, the "episodic search for action" that bordered on "delinquency" expired when West Enders "reach the end of their teens" and courtship began in earnest.[10]

Delinquent youth cultures were likewise articulated with adult controls. My research in Italian American communities in lower Manhattan and Bensonhurst points to the surveillance of delinquent youth by adult males affiliated with Italian American crime syndicates.[11]

The sociological literature does not assign a significant role to consumption in the formation of urban Italian American youth identities. William Foote Whyte's "corner boys" cultivated urban slum leisure styles during the Great Depression characterized by restricted access to consumer markets.[12] As late as the 1960s, Gerald Suttles maintained that intergenerational kinship ties isolated Italian American youth in Chicago's Addams Area from the style spectacle: "More than any other group, they ignore the fads and fashions that attest to one's place in the forefront of urban life."[13] Suttles framed local Italian American youth in terms of urban deviance reflecting a sociological disposition that Howard Pinderhughes recently applied to communities in New York City's outer boroughs that were breeding grounds for Guido.[14]

Notwithstanding gaps in the literature, youth in urban Italian American neighborhoods did turn to consumption inspired by American popular culture by the 1950s and 1960s. Into the post–World War II period, a peer group style was built around doo-wop music—a style identified with urban working-class youth in older industrial cities, especially in the Northeast. A sanitized and diffused version was broadcast at the time by the after-school television program *American Bandstand*, which featured Italian American teenagers in Philadelphia. The marketing of doo-wop to mainstream white audiences relied on urban Italian American performing artists in a genre dominated by black performers; Dion & the Belmonts, an Italian American group from the Bronx, solidified crossover authenticity as the first "white" performers to appear at the Apollo Theater in Harlem. However, while doo-wop established a prominent connection between Italian American youth and American popular culture, it did not galvanize a style of consumption identified with Italian ethnicity either on the local level or in the wider society; in contrast to *Jersey Shore*, a subculture bounded by Italian ethnicity was not performed on *American Bandstand*. The label "greaser," imposed on doo-wop-based youth style, suggests that ethnicity was vacated by class and race. Greaser was the class-based style of youth who worked on cars, anticipating adult jobs as mechanics or "grease monkeys." It marks the ambiguous "whiteness" of swarthy complexions and creates an equivalent racial status to Chicanos as the consummate greasers of the southwestern United States. The quasi-racial character of Italian American greasers seems largely a function of urban lower-class masculine toughness and delinquency. This blurs the racial distinction between lower-class Puerto Ricans and Italian Americans in New York City in the 1950s and 1960s.

Class reinforced ethnic culture to stunt an Italian American consumption pattern. The working class was only beginning to be incorporated into a burgeoning consumer culture in the post–World War II period, and the "youth culture industry" was in incipient development. In contrast to middle-class college students, the working class did not enjoy a lengthy period of leisure with little "adult surveillance."[15] Into the 1960s, consumption and leisure were compressed within the "teenage" years and truncated by early marriage. This can be read in a grainy 1966 black and white Diane Arbus photo captioned "A Young Brooklyn Family Going on a Sunday Outing." The composition portrays a young married couple, perhaps in their early twenties, with a small child and an infant in tow. The couple display a look culturally coded for greaser and Italian American ethnicity. The young man is dressed in a dark (probably black) jacket and slacks; his black hair is greased back and formed into a pompadour, with the hint of a DA ("duck ass") or flip at the nape of the neck. The wife's look features "high," teased black hair and a tight dress accented by a coat with a leopard-skin print (a motif that anticipates *Jersey Shore* hairstyles) draped over an arm that is holding the baby. The youthfulness of the married couple suggests that their fling with "teenage culture" was brief (they did not look much older than couples dancing on *American Bandstand*) and truncated by parenthood. Although they seem to be barely out of their teens, sullen facial expressions and tense postures distance them from the fun and pleasure pursued by the middle-class college students at the time.[16]

The weak structural basis of greaser subculture can be traced to restricted opportunities to consume in leisure especially as the basis of peer group solidarity. The economic resources to consume with age peers were limited. Access to automobiles that defined greaser "carheads" was predicated on investing the work needed to fix cars. Indeed, working on cars precluded leisure; young people could not cruise if they were under the hood of autos that were on blocks in the alleyway. Youth consumption was crimped by the early onset of adult jobs, a status transition signaled by a high school dropout rate for Italian Americans in New York City into the 1980s that was comparable to rates for blacks and Latinos.[17] However, opportunities for employment in trades like construction and small business like pizza parlors provided the financial capital for a consumption style. Perhaps the critical difference was the postponement of marriage, which allowed youth to live at home and cultivate some measure of personal consumption. Youth who entered the labor force instead of college may have had more discretionary income and enjoyed a higher standard of youth culture consumption, which acquired magnified importance for prestige and empowerment in lieu of academic trajectories.[18]

Restricted opportunities to consume feed the development of street gangs. Italian American neighborhoods in New York City generated formal gang affiliations like the Fordham Baldies and the Golden Guineas, which remained active into the 1960s. Gangs provided opportunities for males to construct youth identities around turf and fighting, although they were checked by adult surveillance, especially by local Mafia. As in the case of hip-hop and cholo, consumption presented an opportunity to stylize urban youth deviance. This allowed for continuity with greaser styles of consumption, including car culture, although the roads were not the key site to showcase Guido identity and status claims. By the late 1970s, an Italian American youth identity was recentered on the new dance clubs, which expanded opportunities to cultivate a distinctive style of commodified leisure increasingly scripted by the mass media. Italian American youth likely followed the black example of privileging consumption for social identity, which is a more formative influence than poaching discrete style items.[19]

Saturday Night Consumption

It is not surprising that consumption becomes a youth culture practice in outer-borough Italian American areas, specifically Bensonhurst and the other southern Brooklyn communities of Bay Ridge, Bath Beach, and Gravesend. In contrast to initial immigrant settlements in Manhattan, which were withering away by the 1970s, Bensonhurst thrived with a population of 100,000 persons of Italian ancestry in 1990. This included a mix of more Americanized families and post-1945 arrivals from a more modern Italy. The outer boroughs afforded upgraded housing opportunities; in the 1980s, Italian Americans had the highest rates of home ownership among ethnic groups in the city (an interesting juxtaposition to high rates of leaving high school). They colonized suburban areas like Howard Beach and much of Staten Island called "Staten Italy" by Goomba Johnny on "the Guido station" WKTU-FM in the late 1990s. A mix of blue-collar and lower-middle-class households facilitated possibilities for leisure and consumption central for youth culture development in the outer boroughs. While Bensonhurst supported a tough street code, urban youth became increasingly vulnerable to the pressures of commodified fun and pleasure exerted by expanding youth culture industries. Immigrant and second-generation youths turned to popular culture to negotiate their Americanization as well as upward mobility. The postponement of adulthood by virtue of extended schooling made leisure more available. Comparatively low levels of educational attainment did not preclude discretionary personal income when young people were able to secure employment in small family-owned businesses like pizzerias and in the construction trades.

"Guido" does not enter the lexicon of local youth scenes until the middle of the 1980s. However, it names a particular style of consumption that is recognizable by the middle of the 1970s as youth in the city's Italian American neighborhoods began gravitating to dance clubs referred to as discos. "Le disco" was imported from Paris in the early 1970s for economic and cultural elites, although gay men heavily imprinted the Manhattan scene. Italian Americans made noteworthy contributions to this scene early on especially as DJs and mixers.[20] However, the rank and file in outer-borough Italian American neighborhoods did not have an ideological affinity for the underground scene and were excluded from elite Manhattan clubs. The first scene crystallized in gaudy clubs in gritty outer-borough locations like the 2001 Space Odyssey in a remote industrial corner of Bensonhurst. A fictional essay by Nik Cohn in the New Yorker in 1976 embellished the scene, which inspired the film Saturday Night Fever in 1978. The commercially successful film, filmed mostly in Bay Ridge, was a watershed event for a youth culture strategy rooted in local Italian American culture. According to the VH1 documentary program Behind the Music (2001), "many of the young males" among the "thousands of fans" who watched the filming "looked like Tony Manero." In truth, "Tony Manero" looked like them, which suggests that a consumption style was already in the works. To this extent, Saturday Night Fever provided an opportunity to imagine authorship of a leisure style that was a national pop culture "movement." The film's commercial success likely recruited Italian American youths who wanted to be "in the moment." While they passed on the Beatles and the formation of rock and roll bands, local Italian American youths committed to electronic dance music and practiced new dance moves in their basements. The disco origin myth may have buttressed the confidence of Italian American youth to challenge the exclusive door policies of elite Manhattan clubs like Studio 54 and Limelight targeting "bridge and tunnel" styles.[21]

Disco provided impetus and focus for consumption as a quintessential youth culture practice. Clubs furnished a landscape where they could become somebody different, a "somebody" defined by leisure and consumption rather than school or work. Like Mexican American zoot suiters in the 1940s, young Italian American bodies "intended to look and feel good."[22] The disco became the consummate space for ritualized consumption—a veritable "cathedral of consumption." The spectacular venues of the new dance clubs promised an escape from the local routines that marked the restricted consumption choices that comprised greaser styles; it is noteworthy that doo-wop was performed on local street corners and alleys. This was achieved via a commercial hedonistic orientation that sets bridge and tunnel constituencies apart from an "underground" aesthetic and ideology of community.[23] It explains the affinity of Guidos for Manhattan clubs like Studio 54 that defined the paradigm for "excessive midtown hedonism."[24] Italian American youths have patronized these clubs because they were spaces where consumption mattered. The new youth culture practice required considerable expenditure—to purchase entrance to the dance floor, drinks at the bar and perhaps drugs in the bathroom, and the spectacular look.

At the outset, Italian American youth styles were weakly articulated. Money was likely a factor. A musician with a disco group interviewed by cultural critic and historian Alice Echols recalls that the outfits worn in local discos were not expensive: "Quiana shirts were, like $10 apiece. You'd buy one with a print, one solid." Bridge and tunnel youth were tentative about new consumption-based youth identities, which may explain why early styles were apparently conservative and adultlike. Echols's musician contends that that guys "wore suits, not because they had to but because they wanted to."[25] According to a Brooklyn DJ, Dan Pucciarelli, "The guys wore nice pants, a nice shirt, a leather jacket, collar over, collar up. The girls always wore heels, always wore a dress, always put on make-up, always had their hair done."[26] While girls are remembered wearing "Lycra body suits under either a skirt or skintight jeans," it was "always with heels."[27]

Adult influences suggest the early stages of a youth culture boundary in relation to parental ethnicity. However, disco pushed a new Italian American style of consumption toward closer alignment with the values of the media and entertainment culture. Conservative adultlike fashions were progressively eschewed for the tight bell-bottom pants and platform shoes showcased in and likely promoted by *Saturday Night Fever.*

By the mid-1980s, a Guido club style was defined by a specialized and burgeoning "repertoire of commodities."[28] The centerpiece of this style was mainstream designer brands, initially Members Only, Sergio Tacchini and Z. Cavaricci and more recently, Armani and Ed Hardy. A continuously expanding repertoire includes jewelry and cologne (Armani Exchange, Curve, and AXE), cell phones, and hair products. Previously defined by polyester, Guido style has gravitated to more expensive brand names clothing such as Polo, Chanel, and Armani.

Disco became an overarching template that organized consumption for Italian American youth. An aphorism in the late 1980s held that "No matter what the occasion, a Guido is always dressed like he is going to a club."[29] Even their cars, "Guidomobiles," were "dressed up" for disco, with miniature "disco ball" ornaments suspended from rear view mirrors and blinking electric lights on license plate frames. Like the zoot suit, disco attire became an emblem of a social transformation.[30] A new "Italian look" did not define them for crushing manual labor, like the "guinea tee," but for "work" predicated on leisure.[31] It was an escape from parental class and expressed parental aspirations for a definitive American scenario of socioeconomic mobility. A commercialized fashion aesthetic contrasted with hippie styles associated with an anticonsumerist youth culture that was based on college campuses. Males kept their hair groomed and relatively short to draw a sharp boundary against hippie influences, a countercultural stance that had little appeal for an ethnic minority struggling for acceptance in the mainstream.

Adhering to a Style Tradition

The adoption of designer fashions likely has been motivated by a desire to emulate the look of the "glitterati" and "jet set."[32] However, Guido has not simply mirrored elite consumption. This can be attributed to a disparity in financial resources. There are also cultural barriers. Elite Manhattan venues have always made it difficult to decode fashion rules that are notoriously unstated. Pressure to emulate elites may have distorted Italian American consumption given the unequal distribution of club culture capital. This can explain the tendency to excessive consumption to make up for a shortfall in aesthetic values. It is reflected in reputation for conspicuous ("flashy") display evident in big jewelry, big cars, big hair, and the like.

Rather than passively follow elite examples, consumption was folded into local youth style traditions as the foundation for selective appropriations from myriad sources. This is exemplified by the absorption of a club culture aesthetic traceable to gays that makes the body "an all-consuming project."[33] However, Guido frames this dubious sensuality in a street culture ideal much like gangsta hip-hop.[34] Street culture masculinity made the body matter for fighting, especially in the context of turf defense. Tight clothing and "muscle shirts" express this masculine tough pose.

The elevation of the body in the visual vernacular of Guido has also been promoted by the popular culture trend of bodybuilding. Weight lifting had been a working class pastime and gritty areas were dotted with small unpretentious and inexpensive gyms. The Guido gym scene that crystallized in the outer boroughs in the 1980s was predicated on increased leisure and discretionary income for memberships, stylish workout clothes, and chemical supplements.[35] It gradually became a complement to the club as a quintessential subcultural venue featuring a merger of aesthetics and performance strategies. Indeed, the gym has taken on the ambience of a dance club, with throbbing dance music pumped out by powerful speakers and shiny glass and metallic surfaces. The ascendance of a bodybuilding aesthetic quickly affected the club as the major reference for Guido style. Thus, workout fashions gym pants and "muscle shirts" were adopted for clubbing although, of course, designer quality. The signature Guido club performance has come to feature bodybuilding poses ("fist-pumping") as dancing.

While bodybuilding buttresses some facets of the performance of traditional masculinity, it has ironically led to practices that blur gender differences. A bodybuilding aesthetic subverts the working-class gender ideal of "physicality" with an ethos of "narcissistic perfection."[36] The chiseled Guido upper body is in contradistinction to the blue-collar worker's upper body mass and even girth. Guidos "escape class" by undressing the body to symbolize a conspicuous leisure style (time off from work and family obligations). The importance of "looking ripped" ("stomach-pump chic") sublimates fighting. Narcissistic themes are accentuated by routines that complement the bodybuilding regime such as tanning, which refracts light in a way that makes muscularity appear more defined. Bodybuilding has also delivered the feminine beauty regimen of depilation, countering a stereotypical Italian American body. The removal of hair from the upper and lower torso via techniques such as waxing complements an aesthetic focused on muscle definition. It also seems to be a factor in the removal of facial hair including the beard and in the sculpting of eyebrows via threading, a practice and aesthetic that is now diffused into the mainstream youth culture. The "perfection" aesthetic of the body-building culture has also led to manicures.[37]

Gangsta hip-hop brings an infusion of streetwise masculinity. Indeed, Guido has branched off into a hip-hop hybrid in certain locales, including Howard Beach, the site of a racial attack on a young black man in 2005. A background story in *The New York Times* reported the prevalence of hip-hop styles and designer brands with a soundtrack of rap artists like Eminem and Fabolous.[38] However, Guido embeds gangsta in Italian American gangster narratives. Indeed, Mafia consumption has historically furnished a style guide for youth in local Italian American neighborhoods, reflecting a capacity for cultural as well as economic and political power. It is noteworthy that gangsters not only conspicuously consumed in urban clubs, but also owned them, furnishing a bridge for local youths.[39] Conspicuous consumption made certain figures like John Gotti ("The Dapper Don") mainstream media celebrities, which reinforced their role as style leaders. Their children were privileged consumers in local Guido scenes, a status that privileged Gotti's grandsons as the first Guido media celebrities.

Consumption and Ethnic Culture

Guido reflects the agency of young people in late capitalism deployed for the creation of "common cultures" based on consumption—an informal production of vernacular subjects that manipulates the commercialized symbols and meanings that dominate popular culture.[40] However, the "consumer goods and urban lifestyles" that "have become more central elements of youth identity" became a new signifier of Italian American identity.[41] A bounded (named) Italian American youth subculture organized to consume American pop culture constitutes a collective adaptation to late capitalist New York City.

The emergence of a youth subculture embedded in the city's Italian American communities represents a structural breakthrough made possible at a particular historical juncture. Youth subcultures are collectivities defined by symbolic repertoires that address structural problems in the idioms of consumption.[42] They are a social category that exists on a higher level of abstraction than the peer groups that constitute it.[43] Thick Italian American communities like Bensonhurst accommodated and constrained contemporary youth agency. New consumption regimes were reconciled with traditional cultural idioms like the Italian American family when youths went clubbing with kin and with ethnic age-peers known as "cugines" (cousins). They also articulated with a local youth style tradition (notably, greaser) and with older consumption regimes rooted in a lived ethnic community. Thus, youth who went to discos also went to Italian cafés; consumption cultures mingled when the WKTU mobile truck showed up to play free-style records at the Santa Rosalia street *festa*, an annual event that mobilized the entire community to celebrate the ethnic heritage.

Guido signaled a collective use of commodities by local Italian American youth "to position themselves vis-à-vis others in a complex and unfolding social reality not of their own making."[44] As with urban landscapes, landscapes of consumption were coded for ethnicity (for example, an Italian "look" imprinting the identity of a dance club), regulating the relations of groups navigating the pop culture mainstream. Youth routinely link consumption to status competition and power.[45] When youths in marginalized communities maneuver for social power and access to scarce rewards like dating partners, the eroticized environment of the dance club collides with the code of the street. As with other marginalized youth subcultures in the visual spectacle of consumption, "their public presence demanded attention."[46] Although they cultivated status privilege in "Guido clubs" in the boroughs, Italian American youth crashed a stratified club culture scene that excluded styles that are derivative and distorted by insularity and insecurity. A Guido identity was definitively marked in the struggle to exclude an Italian American "bridge and tunnel" style from elite Manhattan clubs like Exit and Sound Factory.[47]

Guido has had to struggle for recognition, let alone respect, as a style of consumption in the wider public discourse. The mainstream media first became attentive to Guido in the response to a 1989 "racial killing" in Bensonhurst. However, press accounts framed an Italian American identity based on deviance rather than consumption. Moreover, Guido youth were the consummate expression of a deviant ethnic culture sliding toward an urban "underclass." Historical fears and hatreds (i.e., the dago) reconfigured Guido as a symbol for unacceptable Italian American difference, which mocked the struggle for consumption status. By embracing Guido, Italian American youth challenged a new dynamic for the production of ethnic prejudice. Indeed, opposition combined consumption with ethnic ideology. Symbolic reversal of ethnic slurs like "guinea" and "guido" restored ethnic honor to a consumption culture that was evident in the symbolic value of "cugine." Style-based youth subcultures are hardly ideologically driven "youth movements" but Guido did invoke an ethnic ideology to construct difference and even distinction on a public stage.[48] Collective consumption furnished a more meaningful alternative to local political mobilizations of "the new pluralism" era such as the Italian American Civil Rights League, the Congress of Italian American Organizations, and especially the John D. Calandra Institute, which reached out to youths, but with discourses of higher learning and a traditional ethnicity.[49] Guido deploys cultural politics that buys into the American Dream of consumption as a determinant of dignity and self-respect. It is an ethnic mobilization because it mined ethnicity for symbolic capital that made status claims in relation to certain consumer markets; consumption enhances the value of ethnicity as symbolic capital. Local Italian American organizations eschewed an interest in expressive youth culture consumption and did not engage Guido. Internal cultural differences such as age and class are evident in the failure of official Italian American organizations to publicly own or at least explain what Guido meant in the context of the Bensonhurst "racial killing" in 1989 and to flatly deny its ethnic cultural character on the Jersey shore in 2009.

The creation of a consumption culture is a far more substantive and objective outcome than what is attributed to symbolic ethnicity. A more appropriate description is available in the concept of "ethnogenesis," which Eugene Roosens conceptualizes as "the development and public presentation of a self-conscious ethnic group."[50] It is grounded in a constructionist approach to ethnic groups as "active agents" capable of "remaking" their own identities.[51] Guido uses consumption to create a culture or style that is compatible with mainstream culture. However, in contrast to symbolic ethnicity, it has been a source of tension and conflict. This is because Guido remakes ethnicity around status aspirations rather than "feelings" of "nostalgia" validated by an ecumenical multiculturalism. Consumption is designed to escape a negatively privileged ethnicity by escaping class. This makes the problem of "authenticity" a matter of enfranchisement in mainstream consumer markets rather than recovering a meaningful ethnic heritage. The struggle for status based on consumption is collective in ways that are precluded by the concept of symbolic ethnicity.

Moreover, Italian American youth agency has been adaptive over time. The appearance in the late 1990s of a chat room in commercial Internet space belonging to a major corporate Internet service provider reinforced these subcultural developments. Chat service offered a new commodity to be fashioned for youth culture identity as well as a new setting for leisure-based consumption. Online social networking aligned Italian American youth with a national trend, but a chat space was clearly demarcated as an "Italian" site; a writing culture and the relative anonymity of cyberspace promoted the efflorescence of an ideology that privileged Italian Americans in relation to other groups. A chat scene supported discourse about a consumption style that was becoming more oriented to the media and entertainment culture. In contrast to WKTU, it was a site for commodity talk *inside* the peer group—a focus group for an expanding repertoire of consumption. Chat and identity work in personal web pages (a precursor to social networking sites like Facebook) disseminated information about commodities. As with other consumerist identities, close attention was paid to arbiters of taste in the mainstream media, notably WKTU, which they listened to and discussed while online. The men's fashion magazine *GQ*, perhaps the definitive arbiter of the Guido club look, was a popular building block for a screen name (e.g., "GQGuinea.") Consumption talk was also directed at the poaching of commodities identified with other youth styles, most notably hip-hop. Chat room discourse privileged Guido over local consumption rivals, such as Albanians who were marked "uncool" for "their cologne" and cars purchased "at the Federal Auto auction."[52]

Commodifying a Consumption Culture

Like other contemporary youth subcultures, the trajectory of Guido is presently defined by commercial exploitation or commodification. This development has been led by the commercial mass media. While the Internet plays an important role, the return of the FM radio station WKTU to the air in 1998 sparked a second Guido moment twenty years after the collapse of the "disco movement." WKTU's business model cultivated ties to a new generation of Italian Americans still going to clubs and therefore not in the mainstream, as well as an older generation that listened to classic dance music songs.[53] The station built an organic connection to Guido when it hired local Italian American DJs, including the dance music impresario DJ "Brooklyn's Own Joe Causi," whose web site showcased an iconic image of "Tony Manero" (John Travolta). Anointed as "the

Guido station" and "the official radio station of all Italians," winning space in dance music radio and specifically a station that claimed to be "the Beat of New York," put Italian Americans on a par with groups—blacks, Latinos, gays—that have formatively shaped the city's dance club culture. Recognition in the commercial entertainment and media culture made it easier for young Italian Americans to imagine a youth consumption culture. It was a command center for coordinating a consumption culture organized on club dates scattered throughout the metropolitan area. The microculture of dance radio mediated a connection to the consumption space of urban dance clubs—costly cover charges, drinks, and personal overhead including clothing, haircuts, jewelry, and so on—and introduced new commodified possibilities for Italian American youth, such as a Caribbean resort aptly known as "Hedonism." A generation after *Saturday Night Fever*, Guido scenes were cropping up outside the city in suburbs that were collective destinations for the exodus from inner city. Diffusing Guido via the airwaves was perfectly suited to the suburban diaspora; a diaspora youth style relied on clubs and gyms in strip malls within a short driving distance of post–World War II housing subdivisions.

A second-generation diaspora subculture does not reflect the urgency of ethnic differences distilled in the relationship of dense Italian American neighborhood-based communities like Bensonhurst to a highly stratified urban setting. Consumption is more privileged in relatively affluent suburban settings, another factor that relaxes the need to invest in ethnic capital. Diaspora clubs kept Guidos on the "other" side of the bridges and tunnels, where they were not an immediate threat to Manhattan club culture elites. At the turn of the millennium, an organic diaspora development relied on the Internet. In 2001, *NJGuido* anointed itself as the arbiter of a second-generation subculture tilting further toward hedonistic consumption. A grassroots ideology elaborated on its web site muted Italian ethnicity in favor of "youth, beauty, and flash," which peaked in a summertime "party" scene in commercialized shore towns like Seaside Heights. By the end of the decade, a hedonistic ideology jettisoned the Guido symbol within a new commercialized entity called *Night Life Society*, a development that effectively delinked style-based subculture from its roots in urban Italian American culture.[54]

NJGuido only foreshadowed the commercial media spectacle created by the MTV reality show *Jersey Shore* in 2009. Appropriation as a mass media commodity by a subsidiary of the global communications conglomerate Viacom is an overarching event in the subcultural trajectory. It is a representation predicated on an excessive commitment to hedonistic consumption. While MTV had portrayed Guido as a "real-world" youth lifestyle in the past, *Jersey Shore* showcased Guido as a style-based youth subculture prominently identified with Italian ethnicity. Dance music subcultures like Guido were marginalized by MTV, which made rock the centerpiece of its music video rotation into the 1990s. *Jersey Shore* introduced this marginal local style to a national youth culture market as a new product; its exotic character warranted explanation in national media outlets beyond youth culture, such as *Time* and *Newsweek*. The business model of reality TV frames Guido as a "real" or authentic style of consumption presumably because it was not familiar to gatekeepers and arbiters of taste in the mass media.[55]

MTV provides Guido with pop culture credentials, validating status claims based on commercialized youth culture consumption. In particular, it reconciles a local vernacular youth subculture with a global brand of hedonistic youth culture consumption. While *American Bandstand* sanitized greaser in the 1960s, *Jersey Shore* imprints Guido with an MTV brand defined by sexualization and commodified consumption. However, the commercial success of the media spectacle goes one step further by establishing the credential of Guido as a pop culture commodity; in particular, young Italian American bodies are the latest addition to the inventory of sexualized images exploited in the expansion of youth markets in advanced capitalism.[56]

The branding of Guido by MTV can be expected to inform identity performances in the urban style spectacle now with highly visible style leaders who can figure in commercial endorsements for commodities appropriated by youth themselves like Armani Exchange and Ed Hardy T-shirts. Celebrities are enlisted to sell signature styles to young people who identify with the brands irrespective of the organic connections to ethnicity, class, and place. Merchandising contributes to the blurring of subcultural boundaries. While this is anathema to youth preoccupied with the distinction of insider membership, it might be expected that a subculture that historically wished for incorporation into the commercial popular culture is prepared to consume images of itself as a late capitalist commodity. Italian ethnicity is salient in *Jersey Shore* in order to authenticate the "reality" of a style outside the mainstream. However, this is a minimalist ethnicity that frames Guido less by ancestry and culture than by "looking Italian." Commodities are visual signifiers that can be readily marked in identity transactions; this makes it possible to read a Guido label into style surfaces. However, the visual spectacle of style overwhelms meaningful ethnic difference. A regimen of "gym, tan, and laundry" produces surface differences that explain how non–Italian Americans can also "look Italian" and authentic ancestry takes a back seat to consumption style. New Guido celebrities suggest that ethnicity can be equated with and not just symbolized by consumption. Because being Italian is about the fun of consuming, they cannot take ethnic difference seriously; the dominant motif of sexualization effectively trivializes ethnic differences indexed to traditional family values. It is also noteworthy that *Jersey Shore* Guido does not invoke Italian ethnicity for invidious distinction, a status claim that complicates the building of an inclusive brand name.

Jersey Shore also displaces Guido in relation to ethnic neighborhood culture, specifically Bensonhurst, which is stereotyped in ways that inhibit merchandising to mainstream markets (for instance, as a racist community). The symbolism of Guido has articulated with unacceptable ethnic difference and older forms of prejudice; mass media accounts in response to the Bensonhurst "racial killing" imputed the moral qualities of the "dago," which overshadowed a consumption culture. Outfitted in contemporary consumption styles, Guido symbolizes unacceptable Italian American difference further into the mainstream; a connection to historical epithets is evident in the appropriation— and symbolic reversal—of "guinea" by Guido youth. Excessive youth culture hedonism portrayed on MTV (hooking up, binge drinking) elicited moral panic in the mainstream press, which can serve to activate embedded ethnic prejudice. The MTV business model managed the noise of unacceptable Italian American difference in the interest of hedonistic consumption.[57]

Jersey Shore can be read as a narrative of nouveau riche Italian American consumption. Guido is signified by hair that is too high and slick, too much muscle mass and definition (too "juiced,") too much designer branding, too tan, lips that are too pouty, and so forth. These are the markers of a nouveau riche style insulated from a middle- and high-brow aesthetic represented by more established insiders. A rising class betrays status insecurity, which issues in overconsumption and overdependence on mass media guidance for the cultivation of taste preferences that "are not organic."[58] Established groups and their arbiters of taste waste little time in putting lowbrow consumption upstarts back in their place. Status reminders often go beyond taste shortcomings. Mass media characterizations of *Jersey Shore* Guidos as possessing "dubious intelligence and accomplishment" detract from status claims based on consumption style.[59] Status inferiority was underscored by the detection of an accent and jargon that marked a lower-class regional culture.[60] Nancy Franklin suggested to readers of the *New Yorker* that invidious status distinction was an acceptable response to Italian American difference on *Jersey Shore*.[61] The Internet is rife with blatant disparagement of Guido style.[62]

Jersey Shore reinforces an established media imaginary that stereotypes Italian Americans consumption via caricature and distortion. Arriviste Italian American families are found in the reality cable TV shows like *The Real Housewives of New Jersey* and *Growing Up Gotti*. Entire families, not just youth, are spoiled by consumption in the stereotype of the suburban diaspora. New Jersey housewives and Guidos assiduously pursue leisure, which marks them as ethnic exceptions to the American Protestant work ethic. Although there are shared consumption markers, *Jersey Shore* has so far managed to not explicitly identify Guido style with a Mafia pattern. This is well established in the mainstream media, with the commercial success of productions such as *The Sopranos*, *Goodfellas*, and *Casino* and caricatured in *Married to the Mob*. Mafia consumption turns ethnic difference into otherness, which withholds moral justification based on the perceived absence of work that has redeeming social value and the urgency of expenditures that launder ill-gotten money. Mafia stereotypes link arriviste consumption to a discourse of ethnic prejudice that frames Italian American identity in the popular culture.

Notwithstanding mass media stereotypes, there may be a structural basis for an Italian American consumption culture in more mainstream settings. Affluent Italian American families in the metropolitan diaspora can invest increased economic capital in family cohesion. This can explain expenditures to upgrade the domicile with material amenities as a setting for family gatherings and the acquisition of resort homes. Ethnic family strategies suggest that consumption is not just driven by the acquisition of mainstream status symbols but in the service of traditional family values. Elaborate Christmas decorations in the Italian American diaspora have become a showcase for the consumption-enhanced "domus."[63] Expenditures that make sense within a framework of traditional ethnic values can appear disproportionate across the ethnic boundary. A backyard patio and pool intended to add a dimension to family gatherings in the summer was "overdone," according to one neighbor.

An Italian American restaurateur on Long Island explicitly mentioned that children need to be rewarded with consumption for "staying close to the family." Although not as bounded (and named), family cohesion dovetails with youth styles when children receive spending money, clothes, jewelry, and automobiles as gifts.

Consumption linked to status competition figures as an idiom for ethnic prejudice. This is blatantly obvious at the web site www.Getoffourisland.com, which portrays Guido as a "plague" immediately recognized by visual youth style markers, situated in the rising tide of rising-class urban Italian Americans who are displacing established populations in suburban Long Island.[64] The articulation of Italian American identity with the symbolism of mainstream consumption may have originated inside the ethnic boundary as resentment of recently arrived Italian Americans that upset mobility protocols based on the immigrant queue. Ethnic animus adds a layer to status competition. Residues of historical conflict with Irish Americans who preceded Italian Americans in upscale Long Island suburbs are evident on the Getoffourisland web site; Irish ethnic identity is represented by established status group styles like lacrosse, a sport that is played at a high level in upper-middle-class public and private schools on the island. Italian American youth have responded by trafficking in their own ethnic honor as well as touting their arriviste style.[65]

The role of consumption as an idiom of ethnic prejudice was preempted in the antidefamation position staked by Italian American organizations NIAF and UNICO in response to *Jersey Shore*. The charge of "media bias" because "Guido" is an "ethnic slur" implicitly denied the existence of an Italian American consumption culture.[66] The NIAF, in particular, privileges an upper middle-class culture agenda based on higher learning and the mainstream professions and corporate business. While the NIAF agenda privileges high-brow culture (for example, Italian opera rather than electronic dance music like techno), mainstream popular culture is referred to in the form of the contributions of Italian American performers and is thus more a culture of production and work than consumption and pleasure. References to a traditional heritage including fluency in the Italian language, which can be studied at Italian universities, are another way that elite culture is identified with adults rather than the interests of young people. An ethnic ideology is predicated on a class culture that marginalizes Guido as unacceptable ethnic difference—a style identified with Italian Americans with visible roots in ethnic neighborhood culture that have not attained educational and occupational status markers associated with the middle and upper middle classes.[67]

Consumption and Italian American Group Identity

Guido signals the consumption possibilities available to second generation Italian American youth in late capitalist cities. Rather than submerge individuals within mainstream style markets, consumption occasioned a new social formation rooted in a local Italian ethnic culture. Italian American youth collectively manipulated ethnicity and commodified leisure styles to negotiate difference both in relation to other local subcultures and the mainstream popular culture and to position themselves with "distinction" in a stratified youth scene.[68] As such, consumption is fundamentally cultural production or "symbolic work."[69] In contrast to middle class, adult consumption styles that comprise "symbolic ethnicity," youth agency challenges dominant meanings of acceptable Italian American difference "from below."[70]

The assimilation model situates consumption in "symbolic ethnicity," which is characterized by "nostalgia" or "feelings" for an ethnic past mediated by the "consumption" of ethnic symbols compatible with mainstream, middle-class taste cultures such as ethnic art and cuisine.[71] Lifestyle choices or taste preferences are informed more by "individual psychology" than social structure; since the "feelings" and "the decisions of one will not be those of another," "diverse" meanings are "unlikely to sustain ethnic-group cohesion" and to prevent the individual from "mixing freely with others of different backgrounds."[72] This perspective accords little credibility to consumption as a construction site for "objective" rather than "symbolic" ethnic difference. In the case of Guido, like hip-hop and pachuco, consumption style can represent ethnic difference that sustains group "cohesion" through conflict with the mainstream and other subcultures. Guido youth style had to negotiate the complications of a lived, minority group ethnicity that was connected to a past that was valued but was also transcended, notably by consumption. This is trivialized by "nostalgia," which is a feeling of being blue about what has been lost before moving on.

Consumption maps an ethnic route to the mainstream from the margins of American society not a way to reach back to an idealized ethnic past by an assimilated middle class. It is leisure, not work, that serves as the central motif of symbolic ethnicity. Guido likewise makes consumption claims that challenge the minority group status of Italian Americans. Because minority groups buy into consumption to struggle for respect in American society, ethnicity is mobilized. However, consumption status is compromised by minority group status in the present. Arriviste style provides a contrast with constituencies associated with symbolic ethnicity. This status dynamic can explain the perception on the part of Italian American elites that Guido is an ethnic slur rather than a self-titled youth identity.

While it rescues the ethnicity of European immigrant groups from the trash heap of "straight-line assimilation," the concept of "symbolic ethnicity" glosses over the unique experiences of nationality groups, especially on the local level. The Italian American experience in New York City warrants consideration for the size and density of settlement. It is also unique because of an immigration timeline that begins in the late nineteenth century only to have another burst after 1945. More fundamentally, the classical assimilation model is blinkered by a focus on behavioral traits that foreground individuals instead of institutions. It is also fatally wed to a static measure of ethnicity that precludes the recognition that groups reinvent ethnicity to reflect changes in "objective" social positions as they move further into the mainstream.[73] While symbolic forms are clearly discernible, Italian American ethnicity that has been built into the social structure for over one hundred years warrants a radically "constructionist" perspective.[74]

As its structural basis in the urban Italian American neighborhood weakens, a style of consumption ideintified with Guido has become attached to the metropolitan diaspora and elaborated in mainstream discourse. A group position referenced to a certain kind of consumption has become an idiom for ethnic prejudice and discrimination, reworking older stereotypes like the Mafia. The transformation of a vernacular youth style into a commodity is consistent with the youth industry's commercial exploitation of marginal urban youth cultures. The reaction of official Italian American organizations exposes social divisions inside the ethnic boundary and the fundamental instability of ethnic identity in postmodern societies. Consumption choices should continue to reverberate for Italian American ethnic group development.

PART THREE

Consuming Italian American Identities in the Multicultural Age, 1980 to the Present

11

The Double Life
of the Italian Suit

ITALIAN AMERICANS AND THE "MADE IN ITALY" LABEL

Courtney Ritter

Over the past decade, there has been a resurgence of television programming centered on Italian Americans characters. In re-popularizing Italian American ethnic identity, programs such as *The Sopranos*, *The Real Housewives of New Jersey*, and *Jersey Shore* have all drawn criticism from Italian American organizations. Just as film *mafiosi* in the first half of the twentieth century could be readily identified by their wide lapels and shiny silk suits, these more recent stereotypical portrayals of Italian Americans in ostentatious shirts and gold-cross chains continue to use men's fashion as primary means through which to identify and vulgarize Italian Americans. At a time when popular culture has regurgitated old stereotypes in its latest representations of Guido culture, the "Made in Italy" campaigns of the 1980s form an historical backdrop through which to read contemporary narratives about Italian American identity and expressions of it. Contemporary representations of a geographically specific Italian American identity existing in the outer peripheries of New York City would not be possible if not for the "Made in Italy" campaigns of the 1980s. Alongside urban gentrification, "Made in Italy" campaigns inserted a host of luxury Italian goods that were intentionally distinguished from Italian Americans and Italian American neighborhoods. Examining one of the most emblematic products in these campaigns, the Italian suit, we can see not only how Italian identity became reimagined through these campaigns, but also how this new "double" identity of the Italian suit effectively re-created the old North-South divide in the United States.

An early example of "nation-branding," the "Made in Italy" campaigns of the 1970s and 1980s revamped the image of Italy in the United States. Overlooked in historical and economic research into this period, the Italian Trade Commission (ITC) was instrumental in retooling Italian business strategy abroad. The "Made in Italy" campaigns may have to a large extent revived fascist-era mythologies about Italy being a center of art and culture, but these campaigns also reorganized Italy's approach to marketing Italian-made goods. Rather than develop its traditional partnerships with networks of Italian American businessmen, as the Italian Chamber of Commerce had done in the postwar period, the 1980s witnessed a shift in which Third Italy (the small-firm industrial districts in northeastern an central Italy) looked toward new business partners to place its products outside Little Italy enclaves into the urban social spaces of America's elite. Unlike forms of ethnic branding, in which ethnic associations are employed to appeal to the group that shares these characteristics, Italian identity, through the "Made in Italy" label, was marketed primarily to upper-class Anglo Americans in metropolitans centers such as New York.[1] The ITC did not attempt to court or market to Italian Americans because it saw little thematic connection between the products coming from the north of Italy and southern Italian and Italian American identities.[2]

For Anglo American elites in the 1980s, northern Italian products transformed their social and consumptive spaces at the same time that the visual and narrative space of Italy was radically redefined to mirror their own consumptive practices. The "Made in Italy" label simultaneously cultivated an "Italian aesthetic" and an emerging class of "yuppies" keen to assert their cultural status through the acquisition of Barolo wine, Olivetti typewriters, and Armani suits.[3] While fashion shows set in art museums consciously evoked the storied past of Italy, department stores such as Barneys and Bloomingdale's constructed consumptive space around the "Made in Italy" label. Meanwhile, men's fashion magazines such as GQ and Esquire gave meaning to these experiences by producing, both linguistically and visually, a narrative through which to describe and identify northern Italian luxury. Taken together, these efforts not only effectively inserted Italian products into the spaces of high-end consumption, but they also created a new imaginary around Italian identity in the United States.

The "Made in Italy" campaigns of the 1970s and 1980s dislocated traditional concepts of Italianness in the American cultural landscape. Historically, Italianness in America has either been interpreted in terms of what Richard H. Brodhead has described the "touristic-aesthetic Italy" or as the "alien-intruder Italy."[4] The Italy envisioned through industry reports, newspaper accounts, and fashion magazines of the 1980s is a cosmopolitan space of luxury and style that consciously makes reference to the artistic patrimony of the peninsula in efforts to dissociate itself with the history of Italian emigration. The century-old split between North and South, narrativized in the history of Italy's state formation, was reemployed by the ITC in resurrecting a consumable Italian space, at the expense of southern Italian and Italian American identity. As Maria Laurino has so clearly articulated, "the promotion of the Italian brand was predicated on a glorification of certain things that are Italian. It is the country of Armani, balsamic vinegar, and for parents of infants, Peg Perego strollers—imports that all come from Northern Italy. Southern Italy, the ancestral home of most Italian-Americans, still is seen as the culture that produces Guido."[5]

Relocating the image of Italy specifically in the North, the Italian Trade Commission and American businesses were able to revive an old notion of Italy as a timeless cradle of civilization, artistic beauty, and refinement while dissociating it from contemporary southern Italian immigrants. In the process, the "Made in Italy" campaigns precariously positioned Italian Americans on a double-edged sword. In bifurcating Italy along Brodhead's aesthetic/alien dichotomy, "Made in Italy" commerce disrupted the traditional ways Italian Americans expressed their identity, both in terms of class, ethnicity and even Italian origin. Seeking to capitalize on new images of Italy, high end Italian labels worn by television characters such as Tony Soprano silently reference the Italian Americans who have used the "Made in Italy" brand to associate themselves with cultural heritage of northern Italy, instead of the corruption and economic underdevelopment of the Mezzogiorno. Yet the frequent vulgarity their personae register the gap between the *mafioso* image, perpetually flamboyant and menacing, and the northern Italian man, elegant and modern, which stems from Italy's economic power as an exporter as well as the Italian Trade Commission's success in discursively reproducing the country's North/South binaries for America's class-conscious consumers. The instability in *Italianità* produced through the influence of the "Made in Italy" label has made Italian Americans a rife location for exploring role of class, ethnicity and consumption in contemporary culture—notions which have become all the more electrified in the current economic climate of recession and crisis of consumerism.

The Third Italy Model and the Italian Trade Commission

The embrace of Italian suits by affluent Americans was foregrounded by intense efforts on the part of the Italian Trade Commission to rebrand Italy and its products as luxurious and culturally sophisticated. Yet this work was not exclusively cultural; instead, it was predicated on the profound economic changes within Italy throughout the 1970s and early 1980s. A vast literature has been generated about the productive system, known as Third Italy, which produced the successes of the Italian economy in the 1980s and its fashion brands, but little has been said about the accompanying governmental inventions of entities like the ITC.[6] Rooted in a period that was primarily interested in finding narratives that refuted the homogenizing expanse of American capitalism, these studies sought to define Third Italy as one "of the most powerful counterexamples to the once-dominant expectation that small-scale firms would not withstand the competitive pressures of modern capitalism."[7] As such, these studies viewed Third Italy almost exclusively in terms of traditional, European models of business interaction and in terms of local social networks and processes of innovation.[8]

Looking at Italy's small industrial districts, few scholars have recognized that while there was a return to old traditions, Italy also looked to new means of adjusting to global markets that followed larger trends in global marketing campaigns. Scholarship on Third Italy has failed to fully recognize two key elements. First, it has overlooked the continued role of Italian government in articulating a viable position vis-à-vis a competitive world market by pioneering the practice of "nation branding."[9] Second, emphasis on the anomalies of Italy's economy has downplayed the systematic institution of neoliberal policies that strengthened the competitiveness of Italian businesses on the world market to the detriment of the bargaining rights of collective labor. These forces have lurked in the background during this shift back to localized production, yet have not been studied within a larger context that accounts not only for local economic development in Italy, but also incorporates the role of national policy making and foreign consumer markets in the production of taste markets internationally. Understanding Third Italy as part of complex processes of globalization and flexible accumulation as outlined by scholars such as David Harvey draws attention to the challenges posed to the success of the "Made in Italy" label in the United States—primarily the existence of a large ethnic Italian population which was deemed incompatible with the high-end products coming out of Italy's North.[10]

The success of the "Made in Italy" label internationally did not rely exclusively on the efforts of Third Italy entrepreneurs. Rather, the national government, which had long relied on exports as the basis of economic development, orchestrated a well-coordinated strategy for bolstering emerging sectors of the Italian economy through policy initiatives.[11] In efforts to increase Italian competitively, the government condoned the circumvention of regulatory laws on the part of small business on one hand, while strengthening its position within networks of trade by creating centralized organizations of information, assistance, and education for developing businesses in Third Italy.[12] These organizations, which exploded in number in the late 1970s and early 1980s, were vital in filling the void in communication between local producers and international buyers.[13] They also created a highly interdependent relationship between national government and local business as the state looked to alternatives to the rigidity of Italian mass industries.[14]

The combination of de facto deregulation on issues of labor and taxes was counterbalanced by governmental support in the realm of marketing and promotion. The small businesses that comprised Third Italy could ensure the responsiveness needed in a system of flexible accumulation, but at the same time, they needed centralized promotion and marketing networks to foster the myth of the northern Italian and thereby give meaning and coherency to its wide array of products.

As the Italian Trade Commission and other governmental organizations worked to create a unified image for these products, biases in the business and socioeconomic structure of Italy replicated themselves within marketing approaches in the United States. The "dualism which exists . . . between the constant participation of Northern Italian firms in foreign trade and the sporadic and occasional nature of participation by Southern Italian firms" created a situation in which northern Italians were defining Italian identity in their own image to the exclusion of southerners.[15] Playing off existent romanticized ideas of Italy as a center of art and culture, the Italian government and its American business partners were free to recreate the boundaries that define Italy and Italians.[16]

The ITC and the Rebranding of Italy

In contrast to its position in 1990, where Italy was said, according to a former editor of *Vogue*, to have "won the battle of fashion," in the early to mid-1970s, Italian producers were unprepared to enter foreign markets.[17] Transitioning from being unknown brands to symbolizing high fashion, Italian houses such as Armani and Prada benefited enormously from the efforts of the Italian Trade Commission and other parallel organizations. In the early 1980s, most Italian designers had not yet attempted to form a direct connection between their products and the larger American consumer base. Italian producers often did not understand the importance of print advertising and promotion in American markets, nor did they have means to pay for such publicity.[18] Quite amazingly, Italian fashion houses did not start advertising themselves abroad until the mid- to late 1970s, instead preferring to promote their goods primarily through business meetings and by word of mouth.[19] Either because of incompetence or inability, Italian firms were slow to employ methods more amenable to the American market, such as print advertising. The ITC was instrumental in foraging that change in strategy.

The lack of involvement of small firms in promoting themselves abroad was recognized as a serious hindrance to global trade, and the Italian government was forced to take "measures to protect, consolidate, and further enhance the position of Italian products abroad."[20] As a result, until the second half of the 1980s, most print advertising of Italian luxury clothing was either done cooperatively, through trade organizations, the most prominent of which was the ITC, or by American buyers, including department store and luxury boutiques, which would promote all their Italian brands at once. The ITC played an indispensable role in creating the coherent marketing strategies needed to succeed in the American market. While American corporations spent a significant percentage of their total budgets on print advertising in major publications, Italians spent significantly less, targeted it more directly, and complimented it with direct promotion.[21]

Italians were involved in a very different sort of promotion that was the precursor to what the most successful brands would be doing throughout the 1990s. They were in many respects forerunners to what Naomi Klein would call the "high concept brand builders." To Klein, the companies that succeed throughout the 1990s were the ones that "saw themselves as 'meaning brokers' instead of product producers. What was changing was the idea of what . . . was being sold."[22] For Italian menswear companies, this meant creating an aesthetically cohesive look while drawing on a commonality of themes rooted in the mythologization of northern Italian identity. In promoting men's suits, there was a conscious attempt to reinforce "the 'Made in Italy' concept as a guarantee of good materials, high quality execution and *good taste,* with the *Italian look* as a status symbol of new economic power."[23] The Italian production cycle was evident in the look of the final product, a look that was coded as Italian under the "Made in Italy" label.

The ITC and the Italianization of Social Space

At the core of this shift in branding and marketing strategies was an attempt to "Italianize" the social, cultural, and consumptive spaces of American cities. Throughout the 1980s, the Italian Trade Commission sponsored fashion shows, museum exhibitions and events at boutiques and high-end department stores. These formal events would showcase Italian designers while serving northern Italian cuisine and Tuscan wine.[24] Reincarnating the *Dolce Vita* lifestyle, these events melded celebrities, wealthy guests and the paparazzi in order to project elegance and exclusivity.[25] American celebrity culture nurtured the allure of Italian brands with a whole swath of America's elite—from actors and businessmen to politicians and sports stars—publicly discussing their Armani fashions.[26] The presence of Hollywood celebrities was balanced by Italian fashion designers, who had attained a cult following uncharacteristic of their predecessors and dominated celebrity scenes in both Italy and the United States.[27] The glamour of celebrity produced through these events visually and symbolically recalled the Fellini films that had transfixed American viewers of Italian cinema.[28]

Throughout the 1980s, such events occurred with regularity, helping to make Italian products a fixture within the social spaces of wealth and celebrity. Through these events, the ITC created a public face for Italian designers that extended beyond the image created for attendees of these exclusive parties. Often doubling as charity and cultural events, these parties fostered an association between superfluous wealth, the arts and new Italian brands. The ITC would often partner with upscale New York department stores in hosting extravagant receptions. Linking the high-end department store to the museum, these events betrayed a desire to accentuate of Italy's artistic past while celebrating its indulgent present in Reagan's America.[29] By contrast, British manufacturers would only host small, private meetings for top executives, and did not engage in spectacles as a means to publicize the national brand.[30]

"Made in Italy" Labels and Consumer Spaces

Perhaps the most important step in advancing Italian luxury clothing in American markets was the successful collaboration between the Italian Trade Commission and high-end department stores, such as Bloomingdale's, Saks Fifth Avenue, Barneys and Bergdorf Goodman.[31] Since the late nineteenth century, the department store has been a site of what American cultural historian William Leach describes as "an extensive public environment of desire" which would come to differentiate classes and consumers.[32] As an emblem of middle-class and upper-class lifestyle, the department store became a key site in reinforcing the interconnection between the aristocratic past and the emerging yuppie identity of the Reagan era.[33] Barneys and Saks Fifth Avenue led the change in 1980s men's dress. Preferring Italian to Ivy League suits, the two stores dramatically changed their inventories to feature a wide array of Italian names.[34] Literally redesigning of the sales floor to highlight the presence of new Italian designers, high-end New York department stores began setting up Italian sections, using physical space to encourage the consumption of Italian suits, regardless of label, because of their country of origin. Overarching promotions, such as Italy Week on Fifth Avenue, functioned as part of the larger strategic plan developed by trade commissions and the Italian government to highlight the wide array of Italian brands as part of a shared image of luxury consumption.[35] All of these interventions gave coherency to Italian labels at the point of purchase, unifying them both in terms of their site of production and also in their shared approach to consumption. Regardless of the individual brand, the "Made in Italy" label placed luxury and pleasure fulfillment at the heart of the impulse to buy.

Magazine Culture and the Northern Italian Male

The work of the ITC created an echo chamber—spaces of social interaction, physical spaces of consumption, and the narrative space dedicated to the "Made in Italy" label in the press—all reinforced an alliance between up-and-coming Italian suit makers and the urban American elite. Magazine ads and fashion articles created a discursive space where the common elements between northern Italian and yuppie masculinities could be articulated. These narratives helped to rewrite the meaning of Italian suits, which became a symbolic marker in the construction of a new American "yuppie" class, politically, economically, and socially. The fortuitous evolution of a more targeted, narrowly segmented print culture became an ideal forum for Italian agencies and companies with limited advertising budgets. Yet the choice of publications also indicates that the young, urban professional market was the primary concern. In New York City, for example, the ITC developed relationships with magazines that targeted the young, professional, "hip elite."[36] *Spy* magazine interspersed themes of Ivy League superiority, luxury consumption, and alluring narratives about the crime and dangers of 1980s New York. *Taxi* was a publication dedicated to fashion with a strong emphasis on Italian products.[37] The ITC bought extensive ad space in both publications, where fashion articles point to the rise of Italian labels more broadly.

Newly revamped magazines targeted an urban, exclusively male audience were particularly important in constructing Italian identities alongside the lifestyle shifts offered by museum parties and newly revamped department stores. Magazines such as *Esquire* and *GQ* both changed their formats in the late 1970s in order to emphasize a new model of indulgent masculine identity. According to Kennon Breazeale's analysis of *Esquire,* the purpose of these magazines was twofold: to "constitute consumption as a new arena for masculine privilege" and to "create a comprehensive set of expectations about what constitutes a desirable upper-middle-class identity."[38] In the 1980s, the coalition between these magazines and luxury goods producers, particularly Italian designers, helped develop a culture of extravagant consumption and narcissism for urban, professional males for whom consumption was finally segregated from the traditional domain of the family and the female homemaker. *GQ, Esquire*, and the new magazines mentioned earlier provided the language for this explosion of consumption. Italian suits were symbolic markers in this change, identifying a new male who took pleasure in high-end consumption.

Both advertisements for Italian products and narratives produced by the press consciously developed an aristocratic northern Italian culture and metropolitan Italy as the locus of appeal. Advertisements fixated on the point of production, as if the northern Italian character was instilled within a suit's construction. For example, a 1984 *Chicago Tribune* article on Italian fashion in Milan replicated narratives inherent in ITC promotions by distancing southern Italy from the North. The article, recognizing Italianness as problematic for the luxury fashion industry, describes Milanese fashion scene as "full of tall, slender, attractive people, sometimes having blue eyes and light hair . . . more Middle European than Italian, more tastefully restrained than exuberant. . . . The wealthy, economic center of the country, Milan considers its difference from Mediterranean Italy as more than a matter of distance. The detachment—psychological, historical and cultural—is clearly a matter of pride."[39]

Drawing on the North/South divide, the promotion of Italian products in the 1980s often entailed the stale recapitulation of nineteenth century racial dichotomies.

Marginalizing southern Italian and Italian American identities while constructing northern Italy as a definable place, advertisements relied on three interconnected themes: Italy's artistic past, its continued artisanal production culture, and its tourist landscape. Just as Italian brands in the 1950s were able to construct a place for Italian motor scooters within British culture by distinguishing Italian design and aesthetics from its counterparts, so too did the ITC and American department stores use Italy's artistic past as a means to equate Italian suits with more exclusive, better-crafted products.[40] Italy's artistic past fit nicely within the ITC narrative where "Old World merchandising emphasized the character of the product, highlighting qualities that could be said to be intrinsic to it and closely related to the environment in which it was produced."[41] Small-scale distribution and the artisanal emphasis on the manufacture and quality of the suit overlapped with the construction of northern Italy as tourist space because of its artistic past. One of countless examples from the period, the Saks Fifth Avenue advertisement (figure 11.1) incorporates and interweaves northern Italy, luxury, and artisanal quality. The ad copy equates the quality and craftsmanship of the Italian suit and its "mastery of elegance and cut" made from the "luxury of the finest wool" with the context in which it is supposedly produced, one of the world's most historically important artistic centers. By encapsulating Italian luxury brands within the tourist landscape of Tuscany and by coordinating with Alitalia, itself engaged in campaigns to

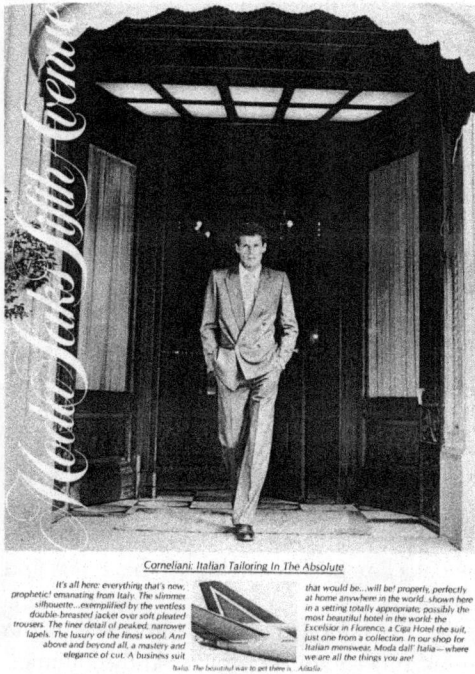

Corneliani: Italian Tailoring In The Absolute

It's all here: everything that's now, prophetic! emanating from Italy. The slimmer silhouette...exemplified by the ventless double-breasted jacket over soft pleated trousers. The finer detail of peaked, narrow lapels. The luxury of the finest wool. And above and beyond all, a mastery and elegance of cut. A business suit that would be...will be! properly, perfectly at home anywhere in the world, shown here in a setting totally appropriate, possibly the most beautiful hotel in the world: the Excelsior in Florence, a Ciga Hotel the suit, just one from a collection. In our shop for Italian menswear, Moda dall' Italia — where we are all the things you are!

Italia. The beautiful way to get there is...Alitalia

Figure 11.1. "Corneliani: Italian Tailoring in the Absolute." *Attenzione* (October 1979). A collaborative campaign among Saks Fifth Avenue, Corneliani, Alitalia, and the Excelsior Hotel in Florence, this advertisement is emblematic of the Italian Trade Commission's marketing strategy in the late 1970s and early 1980s. The ITC sought to create a broader "Made in Italy" brand by connecting the tourist landscapes of northern Italy to the high-end retail spaces of New York.

market itself as the "cultured airline,"[42] the advertisement reiterates this link between the Italian suit and the tourist landscape of northern Italy.

Italian Americans, Made in Italy

Early incarnations of Italian male fashion worn by southern Italian immigrants and their descendants have a complicated relationship with the post-1980, Italian-dominated luxury markets. The Italian suit glorified in the press and envisioned by marketers in the 1980s denied association with its troublesome antecedents while depending on their aesthetic styling and symbolism. Since the turn of the twentieth century, a series of institutional entities, including the Progressive Era reform efforts and the cinema, have defined Italian American identity for Italian Americans. In both cases, the Italian suit was emblematic of the troubled nature of Italian American identity and the failures of Italians immigrants to assimilate into mainstream society. Middle-class reformers, commenting on the living conditions of immigrant workers, often interpreted their consumptive choices, whether of food or clothing, through a discriminatory lens.[43] These accounts closely link consumptive choices, such as men's fashions, with its owner's class and *ethnic* background.[44]

In the gangster movies from the earlier twentieth century and the ethnic revival films of the 1970s, the Italian tailored, pinstriped suit came to represent criminality and the failure to adhere to bourgeois norms.[45] David Ruth argues in his study on the gangster in American culture that the "misadventures in the realm of consumption . . . marked [the gangster's] real inferiority. . . . Style continued to provide crucial information because the gangster, in his frenetic pursuit of fashion, revealingly overstepped the boundaries of good taste."[46] Yet, more important, it was considered the marker par excellence of conveying Italianness to the audience. As film historian Giorgio Bertellini recounts in *Italy in Early American Cinema*, wardrobe provided a level of authenticity otherwise unattainable in producing a realistic portrayal both in terms of ethnicity and stage presence.[47] Academic studies, governmental reports, and popular representation, therefore, all used the Italian suit as a means to explain the inadequacy of Italian Americans as citizens, both as newly arrived immigrants and within the processes of solidifying whiteness in America.

Over the course of the past century, the suit was confirmed as the point of difference in defining respectability. During the 1950s, in the Kefauver crime hearings, Italian American criminality would be delineated against the respectable businessman, the "icon of the middle-class white male—the man in the gray flannel suit."[48] Italian American urban styles were described in contrast to many of the standards of good taste and demure Anglo-American fashionability. Sociologist Herbert Gans, in his ethnographic study of an Italian working-class community in Boston's West End in the 1950s, criticized the Italian American tendency toward ostentation in their dress, describing their interpretation of the Ivy League style as being incompatible with the fashions of the counterparts attending Harvard University.[49] John Gennari argues that these codes inscribed within the Italian suit extend throughout popular culture, from Frank Sinatra and the Rat Pack to hip-hop rappers. The Italian suit has symbolized ethnic authenticity, but also hinted at a menacing Otherness.[50] Whether representing criminality or youthful rebellion, these stylistic digressions were seen as an affront to authority and represented a sort of malignant individualism, an individualism that will be interpreted as unproblematic when located within the confines of Italy's cultured northern regions or within America's affluent metropoles.[51]

However, in contrast to their antecedents, the new wave of Italian designer suits that entered the U.S. market starting in the mid-1970s were not defined in terms of garishness and social Otherness, yet relied upon and incorporated previous southern Italian traditions and understandings of the suit in reformulating masculinity in the consumer-driven 1980s. The urban masculine ideal of the 1980s maintained the feminized and rebellious feel associated with earlier versions of the Italian suit, while codifying these associations within new class boundaries. The second incarnation of the Italian suit employed the same Italian sartorial traditions, placed however within a revised vision of *Italianità*. As Nicholas Antongiavanni argues in his treatise on the suit, northern Italian designers such as Armani drew on the same sartorial traditions as the South, specifically from Neapolitan tailors.[52] Historicizing Armani's successes in 1990, one contemporary suggested that there is an unexplored underside of Armani's aesthetics, saying "never mind . . . that the cultural antecedents were suspect. . . . The wide- shouldered double-breasted Armani suits recalled an earlier era, but in many cases it was the ill taste of one's grandparents that was being mimicked. Not Henry Cabot Lodge, but Al Capone."[53] Southern Italian sartorial traditions and Armani's redesign of the suit in the 1980s stylistically share similar shapes and cuts; yet mobster fashions were mocked as failed attempts to assimilate to norms of good taste,[54] while the rise of northern Italian fashion in the 1980s saw little resistance from America's elite classes.

As yuppies shopped in the Italian sections of Barneys or Bergdoff Goodman, Italian suits were seen as the epitome of quality as well as style, and as an expression of good taste and affluence. Using the subversive appeal of the Italian suit described by John Gennari, the 1980s rhetoric around new Italian designers balanced older interpretations within a new conceptual framework. Armani's suits, for instance, became understood as a representation of the "renegade bourgeois" for incorporating elements of "flashy and opulent exhibition of luxury" within the "English matrix . . . that codified luxury in a conservative formality."[55] The redefinition of the Italian suit is closely linked with the reimagining of Italy within the artistic patrimony and the sophisticated European lifestyles to which Americans have often aspired.[56] While earlier representations of the Italian suit symbolized noncompliance with the rules of capitalism as expressed in the mafia, a refusal to work hard to gain success, and an association with hedonistic pleasures, the Italian suit of the 1980s inverted these codes to "suit" a new era centered on conspicuous consumption. For both the gangster and the yuppies, the Italian suit became intertwined with a culture that glorified the extremes of hard work and indulgent consumerism, two foundational elements in American capitalism.[57]

The new wave of Italian fashion in the 1980s, while intended for Anglo yuppies, nevertheless opened up new pathways and constructions of identity for Italian Americans, especially of the middle and upper class, for whom Italian luxury clothing came to express their upward mobility. Whereas "the positive evaluation of high Italian culture has been in direct contrast to Italian Americans as an ethnic category," Italian Americans in the 1980s had new means of incorporating the "prestige of the Italian heritage" into their own identities through a newly created Italian luxury market.[58] Italian Americans, who at various points throughout the twentieth century responded from nationalist calls from abroad, were receptive to the "Made in Italy" label. Within the context of the ethnic revival of the 1970s, these new campaigns by the ITC and its counterparts seemed to have taken on increased relevance. Just as clothing is a key point of anxiety in assimilating into mainstream culture, it could also offer new avenues of ethnic expression, which defied rote acceptance of these refashioned Italian identities.[59]

Indicative of the interest on the part of Italian Americans in the new flow of Italian-made goods is the creation of the magazine *Attenzione* in 1979. Targeted directly toward upper-middle-class Italian Americans, the publication was part of a larger trend of "subscription ethnicity."[60] Subscription ethnicity refers to the increasing number of white ethnics turning to publications focused on topics relating to their ethnic backgrounds as a means of reaffirming a connection with those suppressed identities. Articles in *Attenzione* focused on the consumption of Italy as both a producer of high quality goods and as tourist space of art and culture. *Attenzione,* in addition to its clearly consumption-driven articles, also featured numerous ads for high-end Italian products from menswear suits and shoes to wines and liquors to cars and motor scooters. *Attenzione* presented to its readers an alternative way to express Italian identity in which ethnicity and class were not defined in opposition to one another. The reappropriation of Italian styles by Italian American belies this desire to assert ethnicity on different terms than their parents or grandparents who by contrast had read publications like the daily Italian-language political and news-oriented *Il Progresso Italo-Americano*, which offered a different formulation of *Italianità* from the consumer-driven *Attenzione*.

The Italian suit, within the context of subscription ethnicity, created the means by which class gains could be expressed within a new framework of Italian American ethnicity. Instead of symbolizing the problematic path to achieve the American Dream, as it did in gangster films, the new wave of Italian suits came to represent the end goal in the American struggle by the late 1980s. A 1990 *New York Times* article interviewing businessmen across the country about their Armani suits found that for men outside the New York elites, wearing Italian suits expressed success and achievement of the American Dream. One man describes how "it's a power look that is more cutting edge. I get better tables at restaurants, I can drop into a liquor store and buy champagne, and all I need to do is pull out a check. It's like an instant credit rating. . . . I don't know what it is, but when I wear Armani, I feel better."[61] For Italian Americans, as for others, Italian luxury brands were symbolic of financial success and sophistication.

By the 1990s, the "Made in Italy" label boosted product recognition and its products became iconic pieces of an expanded luxury class of American upper- and middle-class consumers. With the democratization of luxury that would occur in the 1990s, the Italian brands became incorporated into wider subcultures as they lost their exclusivity only for American elites. Italian goods began being marketed to primarily middle-class, but also working-class consumers. Italian luxury fashion designers, including Armani, began catering to middle-class clientele as Italian Americans sought to share in newly revised Italian identities through the purchase of more modestly priced Italian fashion labels. Giorgio Armani's "Mani" brand of the mid-1980s, which specifically target Italian

American consumers, would be short-lived, but he would later gain success with amongst this demographic with his Armani Exchange outlets. The larger consumer culture that developed around Italian luxury goods provided new avenues for express-ing identity that digressed from the ethnic or class stereotypes which had often accom-panied Italian products before the 1980s boom.

The "Made in Italy" label, though couched in terms of a universal national identity, in reality expressed a very limited view of *Italianità*. In the hands of the Italian Trade Commission and its American business partners, *Italianità* was specifically northern Italian, but it was nevertheless claimed in the reformulating of Italian identity for a new generation of Italian Americans interested in material success and their own cultural capital. Throughout the 1980s, 1990s and today, the "Made in Italy" label provided a means of assimilation and gave validity to affluent Italian Americans who could now unproblematically express a connection to Italian culture. As the Italian suit became used as a marker in appealing to fashion-oriented, young, single professionals that thrived financially during the Reagan years of supply-side economics, much of its symbolic baggage—such as criminality and poor taste—became lost in the process. Immigrant, working-class stereotypes were obscured and challenged, as a new urban and bourgeois northern Italian identity emerged.

The "double" associations of the Italian suit continue to be a vital part of America's cultural understanding of itself. A product of deregulation and a symbol of the market boom of the 1980s, the presence of luxury Italian fashion labels in programming about Italian Americans now effectively speaks to the economic crisis and the cultural back-lash against working- and middle-class Americans who overburdened themselves with debt by accumulating the fashions and homes of their social betters. As Jon Kraszwski astutely points out, television programming about Italian Americans is a "cautionary tale about ethnic identity in an increasingly gentrified Northeast."[62] As the astronomical housing prices of the New York and New Jersey region continue to push out white eth-nic cultures of the New York metro area, popular discourses about the *Jersey Shore* reg-ister tones of resentment for the Italian American cast members, who refuse to conform to the mores of bourgeois society created through the revitalization of 1980s Manhat-tan.[63] Yet implicit in reports of their salary increases, fashion faux pas, and the excesses of their hedonistic lifestyles is a self-reflexive, damning critique of the culture that the "Made in Italy" label helped create. As much as their garish misuse of luxury fashion speaks to old tropes about Italian American suit, it simultaneously registers anxieties about an economic system that has pushed unsustainable consumerism while failing to create wealth across America's socioeconomic ladder. *Jersey Shore* cast member Mike Sorrentino perhaps most succinctly describes the predicament within contemporary representations of Italian American culture. "At 25, I had lost my job due to the econ-omy, and my family wanted me to become a policeman or firefighter, but I knew there were other things out there."[64]

12

Sideline Shtick

THE ITALIAN AMERICAN BASKETBALL COACH AND
CONSUMABLE IMAGES OF RACIAL AND ETHNIC MASCULINITY

John Gennari

Much to the chagrin of the ethnic pride entrepreneurs at the Italian American Sports Hall of Fame, the term "Italian American basketball star" is one we have almost no occasion to use. Not, at least, since the great Paul Arizin, on offensive force for Villanova and the Philadelphia Warriors, hung up his Converse kicks in 1962. This would change if Manu Ginobili, the lighting-quick San Antonio Spurs guard, an immigrant Argentinian of Italian descent, were to choose to self-identify as Italian American, or if we look to the women's game, where we can behold the superlative Diana Taurasi, perennial WNBA all-star.

Alas, the place for the heritage industry proselytizers to focus is the sideline of the college game. That is where we find Taurasi's coach at the University of Connecticut, Geno Auriemma, the azure-eyed, raven-haired dandy who walks with a cocky strut and has won—as of this writing—seven national championships.[1] And that is where in the men's game, for the past several decades, we have seen a parade of vowel-heavy names (Carnesecca, Vitale, Valvano, Massimino, Carlesimo, Pitino, Calipari, Martelli, and so forth) command attention for charismatic modes of dress, gesture, talk, and interpersonal intimacy that have helped engender new models of masculine sports leadership and celebrity.

As the popularity and profitability of basketball have skyrocketed since the late 1970s, the big-time college men's game has become in many respects coterminous with the professional game. College stars receive as much media coverage as their counterparts in the NBA—college coaches get *more* attention than pro ones—while the NCAA championship tournament has become a national ritual ("March Madness") that the

NBA playoffs rarely match for audience share or intensity. In so many ways, this economic and cultural phenomenon owes overwhelmingly to the labor and artistry of African American athletes. Yet, as big-time college basketball has become blacker, it also has become more Italian, even as Italian Americans have been among the white ethnic groups whose on-court athletic presence has radically diminished.

Hardcourt Dagotude

Italian American ascendancy into basketball's managerial and media elite has happened at the same time as we have seen a dual, or even bifurcated, African American basketball narrative take shape. In one storyline, megatalents like Magic Johnson, Michael Jordan, and LeBron James have become American sport plutocrats, transforming the game with their transcendent court skills while also becoming media icons and tycoons. At the same time, at the vernacular level, as perhaps best captured in the remarkable documentary film *Hoop Dreams*,[2] scenes of inner-city schoolyard basketball commingle with images of drug-dealing and struggling black families. Italian Americans have inserted themselves into both these narratives, mediated between them, and in some cases brought them together.

What is being marketed and consumed in the media presentation of big-time college basketball is nothing less than the core national mythology, the so-called American Dream. There is a breathtaking passage in *Hoop Dreams* in which Dick Vitale gives a pep talk to a group of blue-chip prospects attending a summer camp sponsored by Nike, the sports gear merchandiser. Vitale, who grew up in a working-class Italian immigrant family in Passaic, New Jersey, is a former college and NBA basketball coach who has garnered considerable wealth and fame as an analyst for the cable sports network ESPN. For better or worse, Vitale's manically exuberant broadcasting voice, one of most consumed sports media voices in history, has been the dominant sound of men's college basketball for the last three decades. Vitale fairly oozes a quality of ethnic presence the critic Pellegrino D'Acierno has dubbed *dagotude*, a style of self-presentation redolent with an extroverted charisma characteristic of many Italian Americans, perhaps especially those from the New York metropolitan area.[3] In the *Hoop Dreams* clip, Vitale's voice quivers and his body gesticulates wildly as he delivers his heartfelt homily: "While you're sitting here today, you should feel like a million dollars. You should feel so special. You are one of the hundred best high school players in this country, the United States. My mother, God bless her, she's up in heaven today. She used to always say to me, [the vocal quiver intensifies] 'This is America. You can make something of yourself.'"[4]

Here we are witnessing the machinery of corporate consumer capitalism shifting into high gear, powered by an alignment between black labor and Italian social capital. As a Nike shill, Vitale is selling the American Dream through the symbolic power of his ethnicity, an ethnicity positioned both inside and outside of the U.S. establishment, inside and outside of American whiteness. From his time recruiting inner-city players as a coach at Rutgers and the University of Detroit, through his broadcasting career at ESPN, Vitale (like the other Italian American men I am writing about here) has shown himself to be comfortable among black bodies. This is why his assimilationist pieties of family, hard work and material acquisition should not be heard as patronizing his audience in the familiar manner of those who hold up a mythical Italian American bootstrapping narrative as a model for African Americans. Vitale has made something of himself, to be sure, but he has not done it by himself; he has made himself through the American consuming public's huge appetite for the skill and beauty of the players whose performance he once managed and now narrates, interprets, and evaluates. In this sense, "Dickie V" is a trickster, a liminal, transactional figure poised at the intersection of race, economics, and culture.

The man who has best understood the commercial possibilities of this transactional space is a *gumba* of Vitale's who goes by the name "Sonny." John "Sonny" Vaccaro, a self-described "fat little dago," is proud of his mutually enriching relationships with basketball royalty from Michael Jordan to Kobe Bryant, and he is not in the least shy about his Las Vegas affiliations, including a brother slyly referred to as a "consultant to the gaming industry." Vaccaro's home office is decorated with photographs of his favorite basketball players, Rat Pack publicity shots, and Sands Hotel memorabilia. He made his fortune masterminding a scheme for marketing Nike basketball sneakers: He paid college basketball coaches to outfit their teams in the sneakers and other clothing and gear bearing the company's trademark swish, such that television coverage of their games would become, in effect, long-running Nike advertisements.

The big breakthrough came in the early 1980s when Vaccaro signed up Georgetown's coach John Thompson just as his team was emerging as a symbol of black authenticity in the burgeoning hip-hop culture. Vaccaro went on to broker endorsement deals with Michael Jordan and other African American superstars, leading to Spike Lee–directed Nike advertisements that helped make the new black aesthetic of the 1980s central to U.S. corporate consumer culture. Vaccaro then positioned himself as the single most influential force in the college recruiting process as the architect of the Nike-sponsored summer camp—the ABCD camp—where his friend Vitale colorfully channels his mother's uplift ethos.[5]

Scorned by his critics as an oily "sneaker pimp," Vaccaro fashions himself an avuncular "counselor" to young players, especially black ones from disadvantaged backgrounds. Why do inner-city kids trust the old white guy? According to sportswriter Ric Bucher, "It's for the same reason *Scarface* and *The Godfather* are on every NBA player's favorite-movie list. Any minority who has busted his or her butt to succeed and has suffered that you-must-be-crooked look can relate. Any old Italian guy with lots of friends and money must be shady. A young black kid with fresh hip-hop gear and a nice car must be a drug dealer."[6]

The black/Italian affinity here is premised on a shared experience of social stigma—of being outside the arc of traditional American bourgeois normalcy—that underwrites a shared code of style, a glamour that carries a whiff of transgression. Hollywood gangster films and sports media are among those many culture industry spectacles that have propagated powerfully influential models of masculinity that run counter to traditional WASP ideals. Basketball's inventor, Presbyterian minister James Naismith, envisioned the game as an outlet for young white men's moral education in hygiene and Christian virtue, a forge for the building of character. It has instead become, in the larger cultural framework enabled by its massive media presence, an arena for the display of personality, style, and image.

It is in this respect that sport is a generative and defining space of American capitalism, especially American consumer capitalism. The story of U.S. sports culture is the narrative of an epochal economic/cultural transition in which bodies originally built for production (bodies disciplined by and for work on the plantation, on the railroad, in the factory, and other sites of agricultural and industrial labor) became bodies groomed for consumption (bodies whose labor on the fields and courts of "play" serve as objects of spectacle, entertainment, desire, and fantasy). Sport is a space where labor and leisure, power and pleasure, muscle and grace, sweat and style infiltrate each other in ways that profoundly—perhaps singularly—shape cultural perceptions of race and gender.

Basketball has emerged as an especially fascinating consumer culture since the 1980s, as cable television, the Internet, talk radio, and other electronic mass media have enhanced the consuming public's visual, verbal, and imaginative access to the bodies that animate this sporting spectacle. Of all the major team sports, it is basketball—with the relative compactness of its stage, and with, as a result, its intensively proximate interaction between fleshly athletic (mostly black) laboring bodies and the (mostly white) bodies of coaches who clad themselves in the uniform of the professional managerial class—that most powerfully dramatizes the intermeshing of capitalism and race.

To spotlight the black/Italian nexus in men's college basketball is to illuminate a spectacle in which producers assert their identities through lavish bodily display of consumption, expressive displays of signature personal style that mass audiences then consume for themselves. Players and coaches alike construct public personae through their own performances as consumers of music, movies, clothing, and food; in turn, through the shoes and the clothes they wear, the language they vocalize, and the personality they express kinetically through their movement, the bodies of the players and coaches literally become sites of public imagination, consumable images that stoke audience desire and fantasy. Understandably, most of the attention paid to basketball as a cultural spectacle has centered on its blunt racial staging, in which exceptional, mostly black bodies meet the gaze of an ordinary, mostly white audience hungry for fantastic displays of athletically erotic beauty. I aim here to reconfigure conventional views of this spectacle by putting Italian American male basketball coaches center stage, where we see these important actors as brokers and as originators of alluringly consumable, seductively racialized and ethnicized images. I seek to unveil at the center of the mass mediated spectacle of big-time men's college basketball a story of the cross-racial fashioning of consumable African American and Italian American masculinities, a story that challenges and complicates simple black/white binaries that impoverish our understanding of American race and ethnicity.

From the 1950s to the early 1970s, the most famous U.S. college basketball coaches were men like UCLA's John Wooden, who never lost his Indiana wholesomeness and reserve while mentoring stars like Lew Alcindor (Kareem Abdul Jabbar), a devotee of John Coltrane and Malcolm X, and Bill Walton, a Deadhead and Vietnam War protester. Or they were men like Kentucky's Adolph Rupp, who grew up in rural Kansas, the son of Mennonite German immigrants, and became best remembered as a segregationist whose 1965 all-white team lost to an underdog Texas Western team that featured an all-black starting five. Wooden made his peace with the countercultural and black freedom movements, and perhaps not coincidentally won an astounding ten national championships in these years; Rupp symbolized what those movements were fighting. But both men performed their role as an act of mid–twentieth century professional middle-class, Middle American whiteness, embodying the same general masculine vocabulary and cultural idioms as small town teachers, businessmen, and clergy.

This model of white Protestant leadership is deeply rooted in U.S. sports culture. One sees its extremes of nobility and decadence in a figure like Bobby Knight, the Ohio-bred longtime coach of Indiana University. Knight trademarked a strong-on-the-fundamentals style that yielded three national championships in the 1970s and 1980s, only to see his career at Indiana end in infamy in 2000 following the public release of a videotape showing him choking one of his own players. Knight's first head coaching position was at West Point, and at his best his coaching exemplified an effective military-style approach, endowing his players with strong fundamentals and selfless team commitment. At his worst, Knight was a bully and a boor, given to embarrassing public temper tantrums. As basketball became blacker, Knight became whiter. He practiced a kind of racial passive-aggressive behavior: He recruited black players (though not as successfully as his competitors) but then became more of a close-minded traditionalist than he had been early in his career, making more of a show of his friendships with local good old boys. His arrogance expressed itself in an unwillingness to communicate with the press, except to belittle and strong-arm reporters. His white privilege revealed itself in a dress code that became more casual as he attracted more public scrutiny. While the newer breed of Italian American and African American coaches dressed in expensive tailored suits, Knight, the standard bearer of the old-school coaching ideal, took to underdressing in a run-of-the-mill college sweatshirt.[7]

Against the Middle American, rural and small-town, Protestant basketball coaching tradition stands another one—urban, immigrant working-class Jewish and Catholic. Not surprisingly, given these demographics, the capital of this coaching nation is New York City, with strong orbiting satellites in the ethnic diasporas of Long Island, Westchester County, New Jersey, southern New England, and greater Philadelphia and eastern Pennsylvania. Here, the coaches are men who toughened up in the sidewalk and schoolyard ethnic combat zones that make the so-called melting pot a decidedly treacherous and bloody space. Here, the coaches are fast and highly demonstrative talkers with stylish flair, and a warm, suffused, tactile approach to interpersonal intimacy. This is the context in which Italian American basketball coaches—and certain other figures occupying key sports media and marketing positions—have forged electronic media-friendly aesthetics of theatrical self-display derived from the cultural sensibility I am calling—with thanks to D'Acierno—*dagotude*.

The pioneers of hardcourt *dagotude* are well known even to the casual American sports fan. Lou Carnesseca, who grew up slicing salami and cheese in his immigrant father's Italian deli on Manhattan's Upper East Side, achieved renown as the coach of St. John's University in Queens (1965 to 1970, 1973 to 1992) for an expressive face straight out of the *commedia dell'arte* and a sideline shtick so acrobatic that *Sports Illustrated* described him as "jumpier than a minstrel end man."[8] Bergen County, New Jersey's Dick Vitale first established his life's goal of "being the most enthusiastic guy about everything"[9] while coaching at the University of Detroit (1973–1977); there, the only thing louder than his mouth were his clothes, garish checked-slacks and glaucoma-test shirts that stood out even in the outré polyester 1970s. Queens-bred Jim Valvano, whose entertainer chops exceeded the combined talents of Lou Carnesseca, Lou Monte, and Lou Costello, first pioneered his postgame press conference as Vegas lounge act while head coach at Iona College (1975–1980); later he became the virtual personification of "March Madness" the night his underdog North Carolina State Wolfpack won the 1983 NCAA championship on a spectacular last second play, as CBS cameras followed him frantically running around the court looking for someone—anyone—to hug. Rollie Massimino, whose smelly DeNobili stogies and Frank Sinatra/Jimmy Roselli soundtrack (standard issue cultural equipment from his central New Jersey upbringing) brought a vivid, not entirely welcome cultural tone to Villanova University's Mainline Philadelphia suburban idyll, achieved sports immortality the night he took down heavily favored John Thompson and Georgetown for the 1985 national championship, to the great delight of a middle-aged white sportswriter corps mortified by the Black Power overtones of "Hoya Paranoia."[10]

That 1985 NCAA championship game (and the whole Final Four weekend) in many ways marked a watershed in the shifting culture of college basketball. As such, it provides a vivid snapshot of Italian American ethnicity being framed within the racial politics of post-1960s America. That year's Final Four also included Lou Carnesecca's St. John's, which came, as did Villanova and Georgetown, out of the Big East conference, the institutional formation most responsible for driving the cultural changes I am mapping here. A close reading of that game (one of the most consumed spectacles in recent American sports history) and its cultural surround paints an especially vivid picture of black/Italian masculinity in a complex, transitory dynamic.

The Brothers vs. The Joeys

The Big East, founded in 1979 as a made-for-TV basketball conference of schools from the major urban markets of the Northeast, originally was comprised mainly of Catholic schools (St. John's, Providence, Boston College, Seton Hall, Georgetown) as well as Syracuse and Connecticut. (Villanova, also Catholic, joined the league in 1980, while non-Catholic Pittsburgh joined in 1982). The league's founders recognized that most of the best players on the Eastern seaboard were leaving the region for other major conference schools in the Southeast, Midwest and beyond. To keep them closer to home, the Big East promised not just major television exposure (lucrative contracts were negotiated first with CBS and then ESPN), but also a gritty, blue-collar style of play. This required, above all, a special kind of coaching sensibility: Whereas many coaches in the South, Midwest, and West recruited urban players but then tried to leach the "city" (that is, black) element out of their game, Big East coaches encouraged and embraced many elements of the urban schoolyard game.

A generation earlier, on the neighborhood courts of New York City, black players like Earl "The Goat" Manigault—the schoolyard legend featured in Pete Axthelm's *The City Game* (1970)—introduced a soulful and spectacular improvisatory aesthetic of self-expression that finally killed off any vestigial sense of the sport as a white man's game of late nineteenth-century Scottish Calvinist inspiration. Basketball had come to be associated with both the expressive styles and the social problems (among them Manigault's drug addiction) of the post-1960 black ghetto. And yet, throughout the so-called urban crisis of the 1960s and 1970s, basketball, in both organized leagues and playgrounds, became one of the few remaining urban spaces of interracial, interfaith contact. "In the 1960s," writes historian James T. Fisher, "sports became the main conduit for interaction between urban [white] Catholics and blacks; by the late 1970s, sports talk was providing grounds for the preliminary stages of reconciliation made possible by the profoundly democratic mysticism of the streets and the school yards."[11] As inner-city public schools deteriorated, and as more and more black families opted to send their children to parochial schools, certain of these parochial schools' basketball teams began to operate like college or even semiprofessional programs.[12] Many of the best Big East players were recruited out of these schools.

Remarkably, six Big East teams reached the NCAA Final Four in the 1980s; even more remarkably, four of the six (all Catholic schools) were coached by Italian Americans: Massimino at Villanova, Rick Pitino at Providence, Carnesecca at St. John's, and Irish-Italian P. J. Carlesimo at Seton Hall. One of the others, Georgetown (also Catholic), the marque team of 1980s men's college basketball, was coached by the most visible African American coach of the era, John Thompson. This meant that when sports media trained their focus on these major northeastern Catholic schools—schools whose hierarchies, like the other institutions of the U.S. Catholic Church, continued to be predominately, even tribally, Irish—the most visible authority figures were Italian American and African American.

Thompson, an imposing six-foot-ten, three-hundred pound man who had been backup center to Bill Russell on the Boston Celtics in the mid-1960s, had turned Georgetown into a national power in the late 1970s and had assured Georgetown's preeminence in the early 1980s by landing the most prized recruit of the era, center Patrick Ewing. Georgetown made it to the NCAA championship game three of Ewing's four college years, winning the championship in 1984. Thompson introduced a new style of play—defensive-minded, rigorously disciplined, physically and mentally aggressive to the point of intimidation. His team projected an aura of purpose, intensity, and menace never before seen in college basketball. "Georgetown has the panzer divisions and the swift tanks and the Luftwaffe and the long bombs," said Lou Carnesecca in a deft spin on the military analogy that became a commonplace of Georgetown commentary. "They just completely destroy people, and, yeah, they scare the hell out of you."[13]

Thompson's hulking body, mean stare, and profane street language enabled him to commandeer the sidelines; he carried a white towel over his shoulder, making him look more engaged in the sweaty labor of the game, his body and his aura another physical force thwarting the opposing team's will. His players, in a tactic new to the sport, used dead-ball time to huddle up on the foul line and other spaces in a way that signified both territorial sovereignty and all-for-one-one-for-all team unity. Georgetown *owned* the court and the sidelines; opposing players and coaches lined up to take their beating.

Either that, or they proved their manhood by standing up to the Hoyas. When Rick Pitino was trying to win respect for Providence, which had been languishing in the lower reaches of the Big East, a key turning point came when he refused to back down from Thompson in a midcourt shouting match. Thompson called Pitino a "young punk." "Fuck you," Pitino fired back. Pitino later said he wanted to send a message to his team:

"No more being intimidated by Georgetown. No more being patsies for the Big East teams."[14]

Georgetown University, otherwise best known for training young diplomats for careers in the State Department, had become perhaps the most visible and assertive public symbol of masculine black power since the Black Panthers. Georgetown jackets and caps became de rigueur among urban b-boys and b-girls. The team was celebrated in rap lyrics and counted Grandmaster Flash and the Furious Twelve among its aliases. To their admirers, John Thompson's Georgetown Hoyas stood for dignified, unapologetic self-determination; to their detractors, they looked like thugs and hustlers.[15]

The media framed Thompson's image as a racial warrior, an image that might have synchronized with the military, business, and religious values of Reagan-era America had it been attached to a white authority figure. But for the fact that its patriarch and his charges were black, Georgetown basketball might even have been a model for the family values rhetoric of the Moral Majority. Race changed everything, however. John Thompson's Georgetown existed in the national imagination as a symbol of black power, and for the white majority, the terms "black power" and "family" did not go together.

How very different the situation when it comes to Italians. In the American mind, Italian American ethnicity is hardly ever imagined outside of sentimentalized, stereotypical notions of "the family." The Italian family, in general, is a cultural figure shaped by myth, desire, and lack—perhaps never more so than in the United States, where tropes of Italian ethnic soulfulness, warmth, and loyalty serve as antidotes to the individualism, materialism, and capitalist instrumentality of the dominant culture. We see this in audience responses to *The Godfather* and other Italian mob films and television shows, when viciously violent men are romanticized as defenders and protectors of their families, and even as sentimental, emotionally vulnerable figures. We see it in any number of media images of Italian men tying their identities to food and fraternal intimacy.

We see it as well, not surprisingly, in the cultural memory of Villanova's win over Georgetown in the 1985 NCAA championship game. Three documents help illustrate the point. In March 2004, *Sports Illustrated* published a long article by Tim Layden, "The Upset," recounting Villanova's seismic upset and tracing the legacy of the game over the next two decades. Also published in 2004 was *Ed Pinckney's Tales from the Villanova Hardwood*, part of a series of chatty books on college basketball programs from Sports Publishing, this one seemingly written by the Villanova sports information department. In 2005, HBO aired its documentary *Perfect Upset: The 1985 Villanova vs. Georgetown NCAA Championship*. Together, these documents frame the 1985 game as a battle between two distinct value systems: Georgetown's culture of monoracial homogeneity and paranoia versus Villanova's food-and-family-centered culture of multiracial harmony and playfulness.

Villanova's coach, New Jersey-reared Rollie Massimino, son of an Italian immigrant shoemaker, went by the moniker "Daddy Mass." "Every coach has a shtick," *SI*'s Layden writes, "Massimino's was family. Come to Villanova to play basketball and you'll be part of a family. We'll eat pasta dinners together and talk about life. We'll win because you'll love one another like brothers. If it was a sales pitch, it was nonetheless heartfelt."[16] HBO's *Perfect Upset* features home movie–style footage of Villanova postgame dinners. "We'd cook, eight, nine pounds of macaroni," Massimino says. "You know how many people that feeds?" Tarantella music washes over these images, bathing the scene in the feel-good sentiment of an Italian wedding.[17] Massimino incarnated folk notions of Italian sociality: He needed people around him all the time. "Even on the road Rollie never wanted to be alone," Mitch Buonaguro, his top assistant in 1985, told *SI*. For home games, Massimino brought in celebrities like Tommy Lasorda, Mario Andretti, and Perry Como as "designated Italian" guest for the evening. "Rollie made sure I announced that 'Coach Massimino's *good friend*, Perry Como, is in the house tonight,'" remembers Al Elia, Villanova's public address announcer.[18]

Massimino's sideline demeanor was hot and passionate. "By the end of the game he looked like he'd been in a Maytag washing machine," Big East founder Dave Gavitt says in the HBO documentary. With his bulging waistline and Napoleonic stature, there was something cartoonish about Massimino pacing the sideline, erupting into a tirade, ripping off his suit coat, stamping his feet. But there was no mistaking his skills at building team chemistry, devising zone defenses, and rallying his players at critical junctures. Stories about Massimino's motivational techniques circulate like folklore. The Ur–Daddy Mass folk tale has become known as the "Pasta Bowl Speech." Earlier in the 1985 NCAA tournament, in the regional final against North Carolina, Villanova had been thoroughly dominated in the first half, scoring only seventeen points. The players were tight, lifeless, maybe scared. In the locker at halftime, Massimino tried to loosen his team up. In HBO's *Perfect Upset*, Massimino remembers starting his halftime speech: "You know what I want more than going to the Final Four? I want a big bowl of pasta with clams." The players looked at each other with puzzlement as Daddy Mass went on talking passionately about eating. Win or lose, there's always pasta, the coach seemed to be saying, so why not relax and just go out there and have fun? The speech seemed to work. In one of the most dramatic turnarounds in NCAA tournament history, Villanova came out in the second half and ran UNC off the court.

Stories of Massimino's prowess as a recruiter also saturate the memory of Villanova's championship; there is fascination with the spectacle of a short, pudgy, well-dressed man flapping his lips, flailing his arms, and baring his heart in the living rooms of prospective players, many of them from black, mother-headed households. "His family atmosphere was key," Harold Pressley recalls of Massimino's visit to his Connecticut home. "He came in, lounged around with my mother, seemed real comfortable."[19] This was the soft, sociable Daddy Mass; he could also go hard and play the role of the tough-loving father. According to the account in *Tales from the Villanova Hardwood*, when Massimino visited Ed Pinckney's home in the Monroe Housing Projects in the Bronx, he told Pinckney and his mother that Ed would not play as a freshman; he would need first to get his academic game in order. "When he left that day," Pinckney recalls, "my mom said, 'You should go to Villanova. That little Italian coach—he'll make sure you graduate.'"[20]

In the early 1980s, Massimino built a strong Villanova team around his undersized but strong, deft-footed center, John Pinone, an Italian American from the Hartford area whose mother cooked the team pasta dinners when Villanova came up to play the University of Connecticut. Pinone's toughness and intensity defined a team that often played above its talent level. His senior year, Villanova beat both Patrick Ewing's Georgetown and Michael Jordan's North Carolina. After Pinone left, Pinckney, Pressley, and point guard Dwayne McLain's became Villanova's leaders. These three black players ("The Expansion Crew," they called themselves) each had big-time quality, but none had the Big East notoriety of Ewing or Chris Mullin of St. John's. The year they won the championship, Villanova had finished the regular season with disappointing 19–10 record, and barely made the NCAA tournament. Pinckney had played several strong games against Georgetown, but critics persisted in drawing unfavorable comparisons between his languorous style ("E–Z Ed") and Ewing's fiercely intense one. In general popular perception, Georgetown exemplified the gold standard of black masculinity: everyone else's manhood was open to question. The Hoyas' stylistic affinity with urban rap culture, combined with John Thompson's anti-accommodationist posture, meant that Georgetown was the authentically "black" team, no matter how well black players on their opponent's teams performed.

During the Final Four weekend in Lexington, Kentucky, Georgetown maintained an air of secrecy and menace in the style of rap group Public Enemy. The Villanova camp, meanwhile, struck a tone closer to a doo-wop revival. "Rollie had more fun down at the Final Four than any other coach I could possibly imagine," recalled a Villanova athletic department associate.[21] Photographs of the Villanova team and their "extended family" lounging around in front of their Ramada Inn headquarters circulated through the sports media. At an open practice in front of fifteen thousand spectators, Massimino staged a team scrimmage with a cagy twist: he pitted the team's seven black players and seven white players against each other. The team came up with a name for the event: "The Brothers versus The Joeys." "The spectators couldn't believe we were cutting up like that," said backup center Chuck Everson, "but it was a terrific idea and it turned into a really effective practice session. It kept us loose and brought us even closer as a squad."[22]

In the narrative that has been forged retrospectively, Villanova's riveting upset win over Georgetown vindicates Massimino's family holiday party atmosphere and sly mockery of Georgetown's black power ideology. The first half of the game was a dead heat, with Villanova holding a narrow 29–28 lead going into the locker room. Pinckney and the Villanova forwards challenged Georgetown inside right away, making clear that they were not intimidated by Ewing. Just as important, point guard Gary McLain did an excellent job controlling the pace of the game and protecting the ball. This was the last year the tournament would be played without a shot clock—the Big East had experimented with a 45-second shot clock during its regular season—and Massimino figured this team's best chance at winning was to minimize the number of shots taken in the game, and to simply outshoot Georgetown from the field. Unable to dictate the pace and tone of the game, Georgetown seemed tentative and frustrated. At the very end of the first half, Hoya forward Reggie Williams gave Everson a rough shove to the face. Massimino raged, defiantly pumping his right fist while screaming at the Georgetown contingent as both teams ran through the arena tunnel to their respective locker rooms. Massimino used the incident to fire up his team. "Who do they think they are?" *Perfect Upset* recalls him emoting in his locker room oration. "They can't do that shit to us. That's it. We're going to kick their ass!"[23] Here was a distinct echo of Pitino's showdown against John Thompson, only now a national championship and, more, a national racial mythology were at stake. To reach right up to the edge of caricature: Rollie Massimino was now playing the same role as another iconic Philadelphia Italian American underdog—Sly Stallone's Rocky Balboa—in standing up against the fearsome black co-lossus.[24] Unlike Rocky—in the first movie, anyway—Rollie took home the crown, as his team hit nearly 80 percent of its shots and eked out a 66–64 win over Thompson's more talented and heavily favored Hoyas.

Alas, Villanova's "perfect upset" turned out to be not so perfect. Two years later came a controversy that threatened the "Daddy Mass" image and family narrative. In 1987, Gary McLain published a first-person cover story in *Sports Illustrated* revealing a co-caine addiction that went back to his Villanova playing days.[25] It was recovery memoir rich in sordid detail, a play-by-play account of major college basketball experienced through the haze of a drug habit. McLain's description of his own experience was star-tling, but he also painted a culture of deception and cover-up at Villanova. McLain claimed that he was not the only Villanova player involved with illegal drugs. Worse, he alleged that Massimino was aware of his problem but never took steps to face up to it squarely. There were denials all around, but the damage was done. The sentimental im-age of Massimino's Villanova as an old-fashioned, morally superior ethnic family had been tarnished—only to be resurrected in historical memory.

Try as Villanova might to dismiss McLain as an anomaly, the fact was that he was its team's inspirational leader, its coach on the court. He had come from a broken family and was living with his high school coach's family outside of Boston when Massimino recruited him. As much as anyone, he fit the symbolic role that licensed Massimino's reputation as a surrogate father. One of Massimino's own sons was one of McLain's teammates; he like the others had to clear his name in the face of McLain's allegations. But certain difficult questions still linger, including the biggest of all: What was the true nature of the Villanova team culture underneath the one-big-happy-family rhetoric? None of the retrospective accounts address this at all. *Ed Pinckney's Tales from the Villanova Hardwood* buries mention of the McLain episode in a wincingly credulous postscript: "The incident has not caused his teammates to replace or rethink the fond memories they have of Gary as a person and teammate."[26] *Sports Illustrated* and HBO treat the McLain incident as an afterthought, sealing it off from their general feel-good pasta-bowl narratives. HBO's *Perfect Upset*, in fact, does its best to cast the McLain story as one of forgiveness and redemption. It shows footage of Massimino and McLain em-bracing at the 2005 Villanova team reunion, and ends the segment with the words, "We're always going to be family."[27] Such, evidently, is the scandal-proof power of the sentimental Italian family image.

Before the McLain controversy, the NCAA crown had brought Massimino, as it did Valvano earlier, a much higher media profile, enticements from better-endowed univer-sities, and, in what emerged as a standard perquisite for successful Italian American coaches, flattering interest from the hapless New Jersey Nets of the NBA. Both coaches later lost their jobs (Massimino at UNLV in 1994, which had seduced him away from Villanova just two years earlier; Valvano at NC State in 1990)[28] after scandals (for ex-ample, grade manipulation and under-the-table deals with boosters) sullied their pro-grams. Through thick and thin, neither lost the folksy ethnic persona that had won them renown. After being forced out at North Carolina State, Valvano moved into the ESPN/ABC broadcast booth. Occasionally paired with Dick Vitale, the two were touted as the "Killer Vees," and the broadcasts sounded like the cacophonous Sunday dinners of their youth. Bill Cosby was among those who dug the act; soon, Valvano and Vitale showed up on *The Cosby Show* in a cameo appearance as professional movers, parlaying Italian working-class ethnic shtick on primetime television's parable of black middle-class uplift.[29]

Sideline Shtick

The emergence of Massimino, Valvano, and Vitale as celebrity ethnics came at a time when the advent of ESPN (Entertainment Sports Programming Network) permanently increased the size, scale, and cultural influence of U.S. sports media. ESPN changed the landscape of U.S. sports media in no small part through the resonance of Italian American personality and voice. According to Michael Freeman, author of *ESPN: The Uncensored History* (2000), the veteran New York sportscaster Sal Marchiano commanded one of the network's first six-figure salaries for a Thursday night boxing program and various other events because "ESPN needed a New York voice to appease rich Manhattan advertisers, and there were few broadcasters in New York better known than Sal Marchiano."[30] Through the years, sportswriters Al Morganti, Sal Paolantonio, and Mike Lupica have cut their broadcasting teeth at ESPN. When the network moved into talk radio in the 1990s, its first major personality jock was Tony Bruno, one of Philadelphia local station WIP's "morning guys" along with Morganti and Angelo Cataldi. These kind of sports talk radio programs—like the several Valvano hosted; like the *Mike and the Mad Dog* show on New York's WFAN hosted by Mike Francesa and Chris Russo until their breakup in 2008—provide a forum for pungent, ethnically accented, almost entirely male sports banter such as one might otherwise hear in the gym, on the street corner, in the saloon, and at the kitchen table.[31]

Even against the elevated standard of Italian American garrulousness, Vitale—ESPN's longest-lasting star—is in a class by himself. "For its volume of work," said *Sports Illustrated*'s Rick Reilly, "Vitale's mouth should be studied and preserved by the Smithsonian."[32] The pitch and energy of his voice would not be unusual coming from a boardwalk barker on the Jersey Shore, but it seems completely out of kilter with almost every other human vocal utterance on national television. Vitale does not analyze the action of a basketball game; he emotes and embodies it, absorbs it into his heart and moves it up through his throat and out his mouth in wacky turns of phrase often punctuated with Sinatra-like use of the snappy word "baby." When a coach has reason to be agitated, it's "Maalox Time, baby." When a quick-handed player steals the ball, he's "All-Pickpocket Team, baby." When a team hits the soft part of its schedule, it's "Cupcake City, baby."

While Vitale's manic exuberance has won him a legion of detractors—"Can I get a V-chip that specifically screens out the most unpleasant things on sports television? In other words, is there a Dickie V-chip?" quipped one[33]—his supporters claim he is one of the biggest factors in college basketball's explosive rise in popularity starting in the 1980s. There is a larger point here: when a retired college basketball coach-turned-television-sportscaster *himself* becomes the subject of extensive sports media debate and scrutiny, something significant has happened in the perception of what basketball is really all about. It is not just the players engaged in a performance; the ninety-four-foot wooden floor on which the game is played is just one of multiple stages (locker room, arena tunnel, sidelines, courtside seats, press row, television screen, network studio) for the increasingly theatrical, multimedia spectacle of the game. Starting in the 1980s, many of the elite college basketball programs no longer played their games in the sturdy brick campus gymnasiums used by all students for recreational sports; they now played in flashy professional-style arenas or even domed stadia featuring elaborate scoreboards and audio/video systems designed to incite fan response. Pregame player introductions became rituals of staged bombast using music and lighting techniques drawn from rock and rap concert productions. As ever, African Americans took the lead in exploring innovative stylistic possibilities, using the player introductions to perform the latest 'hood-certified handshakes, fist bumps, and mock strip-search riffs.

What has this meant in the last two decades for *dagotude* sideline shtick? In my reading, it has meant a shift in cultural dynamics in which a traditional ethnic image rooted in "family"-centered sentimentality and folksy humor, while by no means absent from the college basketball landscape, has to some degree been eclipsed by a newer business-centered corporate image. Lou Carnesseca, Rollie Massimino, and Dick Vitale personify the first type, Rick Pitino and John Calipari the second. Jim Valvano represents an intriguing transitional figure between the two types. Before succumbing to cancer at age forty-seven, in 1993, Valvano had done more than merely secure his reputation as one of the best—quite possibly *the* best—big game, everything-on-the-line coaches in history. He had also pioneered the concept of college basketball coach as entrepreneur. At Iona in the late 1970s, Valvano had tirelessly promoted his emerging brand in the greater New York City media market, taking on full-time TV and radio commitments, using "Theme from *The Godfather*" as bumper music for his call-in radio show. Through his JTV Enterprises corporation, he pursued restaurant partnerships, advertising spots, and after-dinner speaking engagements. Later, after winning the national championship at North Carolina State, his heightened celebrity status led to an endless stream of media opportunities. He did sports on the CBS Morning News. He hosted a cheesy sports bloopers TV show. He cut a pilot for a Hollywood variety show. He occasionally read commute-time traffic reports on a local Raleigh radio station. Valvano's comic shtick came straight out of the Jewish and Italian vaudeville tradition of Jimmy Durante, Jack Benny, George Burns, and Mort Sahl, whose routines Valvano studied with a connoisseur's zeal.[34] This kind of Italian American coaching shtick has all but disappeared. The new breed of Italian American basketball coach, as exemplified by Pitino and Calipari, has translated Valvano's entrepreneurial style into a virtually humorless, purely business-centered, corporate sensibility.

Rick Pitino, the most celebrated Italian American coach of the contemporary era, enjoys the distinction of being the first college coach to have taken three different teams (Providence, Kentucky, and Louisville) to the NCAA Final Four. (His protégé, Calipari, is the only other coach to have done so, at UMass, Memphis, and Kentucky.) Pitino has coached two of the NBA's most storied franchises, the New York Knicks (successfully) and the Boston Celtics (unsuccessfully). Raised in a working-class Italian American family in New York City and Long Island, he is now transplanted Kentucky gentry, a multimillionaire who trades in racing horses. He pulls top dollar for his Dale Carnegie–style motivational speeches at business conventions and publishes best-selling books on executive leadership bearing titles like *Success Is a Choice*. He is a fashion plate who favors gorgeously tailored dark suits with matching pocket squares and ties ("Lots of coaches don't got style like Coach P," said Louisville forward Earl Clark), but recently has taken to a once-a-year game appearance in a luminous white linen suit ("Pitino was looking very guido in the white leisure suit," ran one YouTube comment; another said he looked like "a pimp at P. Diddy's all-white Hampton's party"). One sportswriter has said of Pitino and Calipari—this was back when Calipari was coaching at Pitino's alma ma-ter, UMass—that as young men they had "become prototypes of the modern basketball coach. They were slick and good-looking. They were sultans of spin and sound bites ev-ery bit as they were Xs and Os experts. They were not father-figure coaches [of past generations], but rather the new generation of coaching genius, the gym rat gone GQ."[35]

On the Sunday afternoon of Thanksgiving weekend in 2008, while visiting my wife's family in Nashville, I snuck away to attend the Louisville–Western Kentucky game at the Sommet Center, the city's downtown arena. As I took stock of the pregame scene, I was struck with the thought that here at the crossroads of the Sun Belt and the New South, in this massive arena peopled with thousands of Kentuckians, a couple of hundred local Nashville service and security personnel, a hundred or so media workers, and possibly a handful of souls of my ilk—holiday weekend carpetbaggers escaping the in-laws—it was entirely possible that Rick Pitino, his son Richard (a Louisville assistant coach at the time), and I might be the only Italians in the house. The closest Pitino's Louisville team came to on-court Italian American representation was through a racial passing fantasy: in the team media guide, the six-foot, six-inch African-American forward Terrence Williams said that the actor who should play him in a movie is the five-foot, five-inch Al Pacino—physique evidently being less important than gangster iconicity. I chuckled at this. But a theme had presented itself and very soon would begin to resonate.

While the players came to the end of their drills and the cheerleaders started tum-bling through the air, the arena sound system pumped high volume Jay-Z, a favorite of today's players. Then, all of a sudden, the bass-heavy hip-hop throb let up, and I heard something I could hardly believe. It was the Louisville pep band, just to my left, launch-ing into "Theme from *The Godfather.*" Just at this moment, with the band's brass section miming the plaintive mandolin lines of Nino Rota's original, Rick Pitino alighted from a tunnel on the far side of the arena, striding confidently to the loud cheers of the Louis-ville fans. It was a staged celebrity-style entrance, drenched in the rituals of hero wor-ship. Impeccably dressed and coiffed, coolly poised, regal, Pitino was Michael Corleone arriving at a meeting of the heads of the five families. He was Sinatra mounting the stage at the Fontainebleau. He was Julius Caesar making his entrance at the coliseum.

It was, in short, a spectacle of such bombastic, over-the-top ethnic kitsch, so tonally dissonant from everything I had heard and seen that day, I could scarcely keep myself from doubling over in laughter. But the ritual is a serious one for Pitino and his fans, and we should scrutinize it for clues about the deeper cultural flows at work in basket-ball. One flow was captured in the arena audio track, in the abrupt shift from contempo-rary black hip hop to Italian ethnic nostalgia, a segue not nearly as dissonant as one might suppose. Jay-Z, one of those hip-hop artists who are also fantastically successful business entrepreneurs, dresses in a high-fashion corporate style very much like Rick Pitino's. His beats may not sync up with "Theme from *The Godfather*," but his aura of sovereign discipline and cool toughness echoes something of the posture of Michael Corleone, a gangster persona white America finds more safe and pleasing than its black gangsta derivatives. So, as I sat next to the Louisville pep band, perhaps I should not have felt so whipsawed by the sound cues: There was a cultural logic here, a cross-racial, black/Italian masculinity that has become so seemingly natural and seamless that it plays beautifully even here in Nashville, country music heaven.

There is a more straightforward way to hear the movie soundtrack in a basketball arena—that is, simply as the sound of sentimental ethnicity, of Italian American group memory made audible in our so-called postracial era. Usually, when I hear "Theme from *The Godfather*"—even just the signature riff blaring from the car horns of my New Jersey uncles back in the 1970s—my thoughts and feelings do not focus on the scenes of tough men smoking cigars and plotting revenge; they focus on the scenes of the vulnerable young Vito Corleone arriving at Ellis Island among his fellow Italians, steerage immigrants leaving Old World troubles, hoping for New World opportunities. I think of my father arriving at Ellis Island with one small suitcase and the salami his mother had slipped into his pocket. I think of my maternal grandparents, who met each other on Ellis Island—at their own marriage ceremony. *The Godfather* was the first movie my parents ever saw that depicted the Ellis Island experience, and watching it with them connected me to the family narrative. The movie soundtrack usually goes right to my heart. But in Nashville that day it went somewhere else—to my funny bone, as I have said, and to whatever part of me holds the irony and the snark. Maybe it was simply because the tune was being played by a college pep band, an outfit that trades in satirical burlesque. But I think it also had something to do with the crowd I was part of—southern U.S. white and black, with nary a sign of Southern European or Eastern European stock—and the incongruity of having this audience witness, in Pitino's grandiose entrance, a performance of New York-style bravura: *dagotude* incarnate. What I *heard* in "Theme from *The Godfather*" was a vestigial sound, a nostalgic audio artifact recalling a different America and perforce a different college basketball world, a world dominated by immigrant working-class Irish, Jews, and Italians, a world in which blacks were at best a token presence. What I *saw* in the Sommet Center was the reversed picture, one in which the white ethnics now are the tokens—except for one proud Italian American, who refuses to be anyone's token.

Behind such scenes, there is a form of masculinity that governs the relationships the most successful Italian American coaches develop with their mostly African American players—a rapport centered not so much on a mock-gangster code of loyalty, with its fastidious parsing of favors and slights, than on a more general style of ethnic homosociality, a schoolyard and locker room idiom of fast talk, cut-up humor, hang-loose bodily intercourse, and flowing energy. In this milieu, Rick Pitino and John Calipari have garnered reputations as master motivators and recruiters, especially adept at strategically deploying what Jack Woltz, the Hollywood tycoon in *The Godfather*, calls, in a dramatically different context, "guinea charm." Early in his coaching career, Pitino set a new standard for recruiting fervor, turning what had been merely an unseemly vocation into a full-fledged manic disorder, relishing the unrelenting travel, the fleabag motels, the happy hour free food. His disciple Calipari—now at Kentucky after a failed stint with

the New Jersey Nets and a decade at the University of Memphis—by conventional accounts has eclipsed his mentor and emerged as the best recruiter of the current era. One
of his former Memphis players, Chris Douglass-Roberts, explained to the *New York
Times* that when he was being heavily recruited out of Detroit's west side, his strategy
was to line up neighborhood friends on the front porch and watch the parade of coaches
try to engage with them. "I'm from a tough neighborhood," he said, "and I always wanted
to see how the coaches would deal with it. I had a lot of my people on that porch and
some of the coaches weren't very comfortable but Coach Cal—he handled it perfectly.
He greeted everyone, slapped five, showed he was very comfortable with where he was."
This won over Douglass-Roberts, and just as crucially, his mother. "*That* wasn't easy,"
Douglass-Roberts said.[36]

The "Godfather" trope is a colorful if imperfect metaphor for the role college coaches
like Pitino and Calipari play in the lives of their players, but certainly it works better
than the traditional image of the coach as father figure, the image most strongly associated with Rollie Massimino. In second-millennial American popular culture, many
of the defining qualities of traditional crime family patriarchy (protectiveness, discipline, "respect") have lost out to an almost purely materialistic, consumerist concept of
gangster culture. The imperial grandeur of Don Corleone is a fictional construct, and
even this mythic ideal has undergone a harsh chastening through the tortuous self-
consciousness of Tony Soprano; alas, however, the real-world mobsters who have most
decisively infiltrated the broader culture are greaseball lowlifes like John Gotti and
Nicky Scarfo. Since the 1990s, gangster rap's code of hardcore masculinity has so satu-
rated the basketball world that the NBA saw fit, prior to the 2005–2006 season, to implement an off-court dress code banning the oversized jeans, "bling" accessories, headwear,
and sunglasses synonymous with hip-hop street culture. Some see this an effort to contain and repress the influence of disorderly "bad nigga" figures like Allen Iverson and to
resurrect the image of Michael Jordan, the ultimate noble black man, an athlete of vir-
tuosic artistry and steel-willed competitiveness whose image nevertheless is safe and
pleasing to a mainstream white audience.[37]

Coaches often are cast sympathetically as victims of a degraded, egocentric, "I'm-the-
man" culture that has polluted their youthful charges. But the truth is that coaches are
an integral part of that culture, not just as enablers but also as collaborators. The prevailing Armani-clad sartorial aesthetic in the coaching fraternity symbolizes not just a welcome concern for elegant personal style, but also a bid for both legitimacy and cachet
among the business-class boosters who underwrite these coaches' gargantuan salaries.
These boosters want a return on their investment. They also crave the titillation of being
associated with men who share their capitalist values, mimic but then elevate their own
codes of appearance, and yet at the same time retain the animal vigor of the sporting
life. These boosters—and here is the point, really—are largely middle-aged white men
who like being associated with other white men who have access to young black men
and the kind of renegade young white men who masquerade as outlaw black men. Rick
Pitino and John Calipari enjoy cachet among business executives because they operate
like CEOs serving as the face of a corporate brand even as they maintain proximity to
the vital masculine pulse. They are CEOs uniquely endowed with coolness and freedom.
They slap five in the hood. They keep their jobs even after being discovered enjoying

carnal relations with younger women in restaurant booths after hours. They are coaches, in short, who are players.[38]

This is not the only model available of the contemporary Italian American big-time college basketball coach. As it happens, the game I saw in Nashville was not a good one for Rick Pitino and his Louisville Cardinals. They were upset by Western Kentucky in what turned out to be one of their only losses of the season. Later, after earning the top seed in the 2009 NCAA tournament, the Cardinals missed making the Final Four with a loss to Michigan State in the Elite Eight round. This brought more ethnic intrigue: Michigan State's coach, Tom Izzo, hails from an Italian American, working-class family in Michigan, and ESPN, ever alert to alliterative possibility, billed the game as "The Paesan Playoff." Michigan State beat Louisville the same way Western Kentucky did in the game I saw—by neutralizing Pitino's trademark full-court press and exposing soft spots in his half-court defense.

Izzo's Midwestern *dagotude* has none of the big-time flash and corporate sheen of Pitino's or Calipari's. His is a Rust Belt, meat-and-potatoes, hunting-and-fishing masculinity more common to football, Izzo's favored sport in his days as an athlete. Like Pitino and Calipari, he is demonstrative and voluble on the sidelines, an intense competitor. Unlike his *paesani*, his wardrobe never receives fawning notice, and he has never been in the headlines for on-court illegality or off-court marital infidelity.[39] Izzo has spent practically his whole life working in his home state, while Pitino and Calipari are notorious for leaving high-paying jobs for even higher-paying jobs, wherever it happens to take them. Yet Izzo, who won the national championship in 2000 and who led his team to the Final Four six times in twelve seasons, may well be the best coach of the three. He may, in fact, be the best coach working in men's college basketball today, and as such, Geno Auriemma's only true peer.

Even so, the Michigan State pep band does not have "Theme from *The Godfather*" in *its* repertoire.

You Looking at Me?

With a few exceptions, such as Angelo "Hank" Luisetti, Paul Arizin, and Ernie DiGregorio, basketball has never been a sport of Italian American male athletic achievement at anything approaching the same level as boxing (Marciano, La Motta, and others), baseball (DiMaggio, Berra, Rizzuto, to name just some of the Yankees) or football (Parilli, Lamonica, Montana, Marino, to name just some of the quarterbacks). Italian Americans also made their mark on the managerial level in these sports: witness Cus D'Amato in boxing; Tommy Lasorda, Tony La Russa, Joe Torre, and Terry Francona in baseball; Vince Lombardi, Joe Paterno, and Bill Parcells in football. It is in boxing, baseball, and football where traditional models of the tough and resilient industrial-era male body best matched the sensibility of blue-collar Italian Americans.

Basketball, too, was an inviting space for the many working-class Italian American male athletes who populated the rosters of urban Catholic Youth Organization, parochial school, and college teams through the 1960s. And yet not a single one of them came close to achieving the renown of figures like Joe DiMaggio and Joe Montana, who are considered to be among the very best ever to have played center field and quarterback.

Since the 1980s, only a handful of Italian American men have played basketball at a high level. But during this same period, Italian American college basketball coaches have excelled, hardly a year passing in which one or more of them is not competing for the national championship. Meanwhile, a "fat little dago" named Sonny Vaccaro hatched the marketing plan that transformed college basketball into a multibillion-dollar business, and a loudmouth *buffone* named Dick Vitale emceed the party.

I have suggested that this Italianization of men's college basketball at the level of management and media is correlated with changes in the nature of basketball as a cultural form, in particular its shift into a more personality-driven, style-conscious, image-making, made-for-TV consumer culture. Before they went into coaching, Jim Valvano and Rick Pitino were point guards (at Rutgers and UMass, respectively) who approached each game as if it were a street fight. This fierce pugnacity carried over into their coaching and made them winners. But it did not make them stars. *This* they (and their fellow Italian American coaches) achieved through their mastery of the basketball court as a theatrical stage, and through their understanding that players and fans alike were hungry for performances of their distinctive brands of *dagotude*.

"Image is what much of basketball is about—looking good, bad, safe, edgy, cool, tough . . ." So shrewdly asserts Jeffrey Lane, in *Under the Boards: The Cultural Revolution in Basketball* (2007).[40] Lane is talking primarily about men who play basketball, and he is thinking about the game as a text that is about more than on-court performance; he is thinking, that is, about basketball as a consumer culture. To think about basketball this way, we should consider players and coaches not just as images we consume, but as actors who work out their complicated relationships with each other through mutually constitutive protocols in which they define each other by consuming each other.

Outside of the dramatic arts, there are few if any spheres of American life in which men in positions of institutional leadership cry, hug, sing, dance, versify, or, in general, use their bodies and mouths to express deep feeling and sentiment, at least not publicly as a normal function of their occupation. Such is the enduring power in our culture of traditional Protestant norms of masculine control, rationality, and cool emotional discipline. Perhaps this is why, for many sports fans, some of the most vivid and memorable scenes in men's college basketball have involved coaches—coaching being a profession that combines the managerial and the performative—displaying spontaneity and passion through expansive physical gesture. And perhaps this is why, for many basketball players, Italian American coaches like Lou Carnesecca, Rollie Massimino, Jim Valvano, Dick Vitale, Rick Pitino, and Tom Izzo have proven to be seductively adept at the level of style, feeling, and attitude. Italian Americans who patrol the sidelines and man the broadcast booths are among the most heavily consumed bodies and voices in the U.S. sports media. As such, these colorful purveyors of sideline shtick have much to teach us about ethnicity, masculinity, and American culture.

13

The Immigrant Enclave as Theme Park

CULTURE, CAPITAL, AND URBAN CHANGE
IN NEW YORK'S LITTLE ITALIES

Ervin Kosta

"How can you propose what no longer exists?"[1] Paul J. Q. Lee, of the Chinese American Voters League, put the question to the City Planning Commission at a Board of Estimate meeting in February 1977. At issue was a bid to designate Mulberry Street's Little Italy in Lower Manhattan officially as a special zoning district. The meeting was the result of efforts by local actors to stem, and ultimately reverse, the dissolution of Mulberry Street's Italian identity. The effort was successful, yet questions about Mulberry Street's Italian "authenticity" still linger. More than thirty years later, a *New York Times* article declared, "Little Italy, Littler by the Year," noting the steady decline of Italian American residents and the constant shrinking of the neighborhood under encroachment from nearby areas of Chinatown, SoHo, Nolita (North of Little Italy), and NoHo.[2] The author attributed the mere existence of Little Italy to the "nostalgic memory" of suburban Italians and its ability to remain a must-see tourist destination.[3]

While Mulberry Street's Little Italy was being decried as inauthentic, the *New York Times* hailed the upcoming celebration of the Ferragosto (August holiday) feast on Belmont's Arthur Avenue in the mid-Bronx as "a real taste of Old World Italy" in 1997. Pointing to the prevalence of stereotypes, one of the organizers expressed the intention to "share real Italian identity and culture with New York." The festival was reportedly staged as a "correct" celebration of Italian American culture and arts that eschewed "overfried zeppole . . . rented, rusted amusement park rides, [and] chintzy carnival games," and instead featured "excerpts from popular operas . . . Shakespeare's Italian-based plays, and a rendition of 'The Adventures of the Pinocchio.'" "This is the true Little Italy [and] we want everyone to see true Italian heritage," said one of the merchants, showing off a sheet of focaccia schiacciate from the deli his father established half a century ago.[4]

Persisting differences between Mulberry Street and Arthur Avenue's Little Italies notwithstanding—it has become a cliché to point out that the former is no longer Italian, while the latter is known as "The Real Little Italy in the Bronx"—both neighborhoods share the fate of countless other former immigrant enclaves that underwent residential ethnic succession.[5] Indeed, as later generation descendants of late nineteenth-century European immigrants experienced upward mobility amidst post–World War II affluence, the central city neighborhoods that served as archetypal sites of ethnic community for half a century lost their significance as primary anchors of ethnic life.[6] Caught it the crosscurrents of "white flight," racial tension between diversifying inner city residents, disinvestment, and other ills that urban restructuring afflicted on American cities from the 1960s onward, former immigrant neighborhoods in urban areas have often transformed into sites of consumption that cater to the subsequent post-industrial affluence, offering investment opportunities for financial capital and lifestyle choices for the new creative class. The trajectory of Mulberry Street's Little Italy and Belmont's "Real Little Italy" from dissolving immigrant neighborhoods of the 1960s to successful Little Italies suggests a parallel process of revalorization of their immigrant pasts for consumption in the current ethnic marketplace. However, their location within different areas of the urban core provides an opportunity to understand how the market reproduces ethnicity—in this case Italianness—in different ways through molding the consumption landscapes of old immigrant neighborhoods.

Areas of early settlement such as Mulberry Street and Belmont are often portrayed to be on a disappearing path, as the *New York Times* article on the "Littler" Italy suggested. Alternatively, they are decried as "inauthentic" for outliving the retreat of their "original" residents. Sociologists and the media understand such places as urban ethnic theme parks that represent "Disneyfied" versions of their immigrant pasts.[7] Such characterizations often flatten the different dynamics engendered by the process of late-capitalist transformation of immigrant enclaves. The restructuring of old immigrant neighborhoods typically relies on the remaking of their consumption spaces, creating a disjuncture between the ethnicity of the stores that line up the commercial thoroughfare of the area and that of the residents above and around the stores. The reinvention of such Little Italies for consumption relies on the successful management of the disparity between commercial ethnicity and residential ethnicity. Further, as the Ferragosto article illustrates, street events can serve as powerful tools in the remaking of old neighborhoods. Their unique role in redefining street uses makes them particularly suitable in managing the neighborhood ethnicity.

Confronted with the loss of their residents of Italian origin, both "Little Italy," on Lower Manhattan's Mulberry Street, and the "Real Little Italy" of Arthur Avenue in the mid-Bronx, owe their continued significance as "Italian" spaces to the construction of commodified versions of their ethnic pasts for consumption by a variegated clientele. However, their commercial ethnicities have emerged in particular ways that reflect the geographic, economic, demographic, and ethnic and racial conditions of their local histories.

Urban Ethnic Theme Parks

Jan Lin recently noted the potential of urban ethnic places in sustaining local communities and cultures, but also the risk of becoming "appropriated by global capitalism for promoting urban redevelopment," leading him to ask "ethnic community or ethnic theme park?"[8] Lin's research on Latino, Chinatown, and African American neighborhoods centers on groups whose continuous immigration and/or marginality provides well-documented material and symbolic reasons for sustained involvement with ethnic enclaves. His question is even more prescient with regard to groups from Eastern and Southern Europe, whose earlier immigration slowed considerably after the introduction of the quota restrictions in 1924. While an earlier generation of scholars expected ethnic enclaves to wither once their inhabitants abandoned their distinctive lifestyles and joined the mainstream, Little Italies and Greektowns have become integral parts of themed downtown urban spaces.

The notion of "theming" was discussed extensively by Mark Gottdiener, who pointed to the use of popular culture symbols in the creation of consumer spaces.[9] He linked the increasing appearance of themed environments to the restructuring of the late capitalist economy and its need to maintain profit rates. Within deindustrializing urban settings, Sharon Zukin's pioneering work has pointed to the emergence of the economic importance of "culture," functioning as an asset in the case of real estate capital's ability to exploit artists' initial presence in revalorizing SoHo, as well as in the form of commodities, underlying the emergence of the "symbolic economy."[10] Ethnic culture in commercialized form can similarly serve as a strategy in the revalorization of adjacent real estate markets.[11] Within the emerging economy of consumer capitalism, ethnic enclaves have more generally served as sites where strategies of segmented marketing mesh with ethnic heritage tourism.[12] Their clientele includes not only later generation ethnics in search of a connection to their grandparents' pasts, but also international tourists who find ethnic restaurants and specialty shops both exotic and authentic, making them an important component of their overall experience.[13] From the perspective of the labor markets, the typical small-scale ethnic restaurants and specialty stores can serve to enhance the attractiveness of downtown urban areas, helping global centers of capital attract and retain the professional middle classes that associate the consumption of difference with distinction.[14]

Little Italies across the United States and Canada offer a case in point. According to Lin, Jerome Krase first used the concept of urban ethnic theme parks in relation to Mulberry Street's Little Italy.[15] Krase has similarly presented Belmont's Little Italy as an "ethnic theme park" for tourist consumption, noting recent attempts to commercialize the ethnic identity of the neighborhood for marketing purposes.[16] As noted, however, these spaces and their presumed levels of authenticity have been represented in starkly different terms, a fact obscured by the common moniker of "ethnic theme park." How do their consumption landscapes evolve, and why are some known as more "authentic" than others? Can ethnic theme parks be successful in suburban locales, or established in urban quarters with no prior residential ethnicity? In other words, how do local geographies determine the viability and trajectory of urban ethnic theme parks? Tracing the decline of residential ethnicity and emergence of commercial ethnicity in two Little Italies, I want to offer a way to unpack the "theme park" imagery into concrete analysis of the intersection of consumption and ethnicity within two spaces of the postindustrial city.

Lower Manhattan and the mid-Bronx

Mulberry Street and Belmont were working-class areas of early immigrant settlement that became predominantly Italian in the decades around the turn of the twentieth century. Both areas began to decline owing to a combination of factors related to post–World War II economic expansion and urban restructuring, which led to an exodus of later-generation ethnics to the suburbs. While many enclaves have lost their association with the immigrants they may have housed at some point—few remember the East Village as "Kleine Deutschland"—both Mulberry Street and Arthur Avenue retained and developed concentrations of Italian restaurants and specialty stores from the 1970s onward (see figure 13.1). They did so under different urban conditions, however. Belmont is located at the northern boundary of the South Bronx, where the impact of the urban crises of the 1960s was long and deep. Some of its neighborhoods were destroyed in an internationally infamous arson and abandonment epidemic throughout the late 1960s and 1970s; others were dismantled as a result of city builder Robert Moses's indiscriminating highway construction, epitomized by the Cross-Bronx Expressway destruction of the East Tremont neighborhood.[17] Belmont's Little Italy was born out of this "South Bronx is burning" atmosphere of devastation. In similar fashion to Brooklyn's Canarsie, which was an outer borough ethnic area of second or third settlement that experienced policies of racial integration as a ticket to the "abyss" of inner-city disintegration, Belmont fought against "intrusion."[18] Canarsie succeeded in remaining residentially Italian, but Belmont did not.[19] The establishment of the area's commercial Little Italy was the next logical step from the perspective of the local actors involved in retaining its association with the Italian ethnicity.

Unlike Belmont, Mulberry Street's Little Italy confronted a different scene during the urban crises of the late 1960s. The departure of manufacturing jobs from Lower Manhattan, middle class flight, the fiscal crisis of the city, and general disinvestment created a low-rent environment that was embraced by countercultural New York. Across nearby Broadway, artists were drawn to the semiabandoned manufacturing spaces of SoHo, while across Houston Street, East Village was going through waves of change: "in the 1950s, the area was the cradle of abstract expressionist art, Beat poetry, modern jazz, and off-Broadway experimental theater; in the 1960s [it] drew migrants from a new counterculture, who set up thrift shops and music stores, and smoked marijuana in the parks and streets."[20] The area surrounding Mulberry Street was subjected to waves of deinvestment and reinvestment that, as Neil Smith described, would ultimately underwrite the gentrification of Lower Manhattan neighborhoods in response to the needs of the new professional middle classes. The subsequent residential rehabilitation led to the emergence of new consumption spaces geared to professional lifestyles, such as restau-

Figure 13.1. An Italian butcher store on Arthur Avenue. Photo by the author.

rants, boutiques, and art galleries.[21] In contrast to Belmont, Mulberry Street's commercial ethnicity developed within a bustling downtown scene defined by an abundance of financial capital, wealthy residents, professional classes with disposable income and cultural capital, and a constant stream of international tourists. Lower Manhattan is a far more global space than Belmont, where local residents are nonwhite and poor, investment remains small-scale, wealthy residents must visit from Connecticut, and few tourists venture beyond Yankee Stadium and the Bronx Zoo.

Residential Ethnicity: Decline on Mulberry Street and Arthur Avenue

One of the preeminent centers of Italian life in New York for almost half a century, Mulberry Street had been in decline since the 1930s, when the relocation of jobs within the city and establishment of rapid transit to more spacious outer boroughs reduced the desirability of the area.[22] The decline culminated in the early 1970s, which appear to have been the eye of the storm: by 1975, a *New York Times* article declared Mulberry Street "a graveyard."[23] The flight of Italian Americans and disappearance of many neighborhood stores had left the area to "derelicts [that] had encroached from Bowery, taking over Louis DeSalvio Park on the southeast corner of Mulberry and Spring, and using doorways as privies and cubicles to drink and sleep." Revitalized by the post-1965 liberalization of immigration quotas, nearby Chinatown was "stretching [its] borders into

Little Italy."[24] Noting the growing "decay," a local merchant was quoted as saying: "the block died."[25]

Demographic data on the blocks surrounding Mulberry Street confirm the profound population changes in the area. Table 13.1 shows that total population declined by nine percent between 1960 and 1980, and returned to 1960 levels in 2000, at roughly fifteen thousand. (The greatest loss had occurred in the two preceding decades: as late as 1940, the same census tracts housed more than three times the 2000 population, over fifty thousand.) More dramatically, the area experienced drastic ethnic and racial turnover over the span of forty years. Between 1960 and 2000, the portion of the area residents that reported Italian ancestry steadily declined from 40 percent to under eight percent. The biggest ethnic turnover occurred during the 1960s: almost 40 percent of its residents reported Italian ancestry at the beginning of the decade, while only 22 percent were left at the end of the decade. These changes reflected the shuffling of urban populations at the onset of the post-1965 immigration, composed heavily of groups coming from Asian and Latin American countries. As table 13.1 shows, Asians constituted the majority of the residents that took the place of departing Italians on the blocks surrounding Mulberry Street (40 percent of the population by 1970; 57 percent by 1990).

Table 13.1. Demographic change on Mulberry Street, 1960–2000

YEAR	TOTAL POPULATION	PERCENT WHITE	PERCENT BLACK	OTHER RACE/ASIAN	PERCENT ITALIAN ANCESTRY	PERCENT FOREIGN BORN
1960	15,010	87.2	1.2	11.6	39.8[a]	25.5
1970	14,638	55.5	4.3	40.2	22.1	47.4
1980	13,647	44.0	1.6	48.4	17.1	53.3
1990	14,635	36.7	2.7	57.2	11.6	57.5
2000	14,907	35.9	0.9	57.0	7.8	52.1

Source: Social Explorer Tables (SE), Censuses 1960, 1970, 1980, 1990, and 2000, U.S. Census Bureau and Social Explorer. Mulberry Street consists of the following census tracts for the purposes of this chapter: 0041, 0043, and 0045. The area covered by these tracts is roughly of rectangular shape bounded by Houston Street in the north, Bowery Street in the east, Canal Street in the south, and Broadway in the west.

[a] Tables 13.1 and 13.2 present racial breakdowns of "black" and "white" for the 1960 and 1970 figures, while numbers from 1980, 1990, and the 2000 census belong to the "non-Hispanic white" and "non-Hispanic black" categories. "Hispanic" is a self-identified category introduced in the 1980 US Census as an ancestry group, including any persons with origin from the Latin American countries and Spain. The term "Latino" was added to the category in the 2000 Census. Persons in this category can self-identify with any race, but the racial categories were affected in that it is possible to now distinguish "whites" as a racial category that includes persons of Hispanic origin from "non-Hispanic whites."

In tables 13.1 and 13.2, "foreign stock" is a category that combines the foreign-born population with the native population of foreign or mixed parentage, used to determine national origin before the ancestry question was introduced in the 1980 Census. The numbers presented above were calculated by adding respondents born in Italy to those natives born of Italian parent(s). These numbers do not capture third and later generation Italians, unlike the more flexible 1980 ancestry question that counts anyone who declares Italian ancestry. Therefore, they provide conservative estimates of Italian ancestry.

Table 13.2. Demographic change in Belmont, 1960–2000

YEAR	TOTAL POPULATION	PERCENT WHITE	PERCENT BLACK	PERCENT LATINO OR HISPANIC	PERCENT ITALIAN ANCESTRY	PERCENT FOREIGN BORN
1960	31,564	97.6	2.2	–	54.7	31.3
1970	30,575	82.1	16.6	–	37.6	23.9
1980	23,163	42.4	16.8	38.4	33.9	26.4
1990	23,919	27.3	17.6	52.9	17.5	26.2
2000	26,124	15.1	20.2	59.6	9.6	30.5

Source: Social Explorer Tables (SE), Censuses 1960, 1970, 1980, 1990, and 2000, U.S. Census Bureau and Social Explorer. Belmont consists of the following census tracts for the purposes of this chapter: 385, 387, 389, 391, and 393. Since Belmont boundaries "contracted" during the 1960s and 1970s, I have chosen Bromley's (1998) conservative definition of Belmont, excluding census tracts 371/3/5/9, and 383 to its south, known as Northern East Tremont now (see also Maida, 1987). The area covered by these tracts is roughly square shaped, bounded by East Fordham Road in the north, Southern Boulevard in the east, East 182nd Street in the south, and Park Avenue in the west.

The general outline of Belmont's trajectory is similar to Mulberry Street, with a time lag of a decade or two. Known as "the Fordham area," Belmont became predominantly Italian at the turn of the twentieth century, as the arrival of rapid transit spearheaded the explosive transformation of the borough from farmland to a dense urban fabric of working-class neighborhoods. Postwar affluence opened new horizons for the young generations, who were leaving Belmont's non-elevator tenements for the expansive suburbs. Demographic data shows that the blocks surrounding Arthur Avenue experienced the highest population loss during the 1970s (table 13.2). Belmont lost over a quarter of its population between 1960 and 1980, though a portion of that decline (one third) had been restored by 2000. The area also experienced dramatic, if gradual, ethnic and racial turnover. Between 1960 and 2000, the portion of area residents that reported Italian ancestry declined steadily from nearly 55 percent to just fewer than 10 percent. Table 13.2 shows that residents of Latino descent and African Americans (60 and 20 percent of the 2000 population, respectively) replaced departing Italians. While Mulberry Street had lost Italian predominance by 1970, Belmont remained predominantly Italian until 1980. Both areas had undergone an almost complete residential de-Italianization by the turn of the millennium.

Commercial Ethnicity: Change on Mulberry Street and Arthur Avenue

Population decline and residential de-Italianization might lead one to expect parallel changes in the commercial scene, such as declining business numbers and de-Italianization. Precisely the contrary has happened in both areas. If the early 1970s marked the low point of Mulberry Street, they also signaled the beginning of its commercialization as Little Italy. Local merchants mobilized to turn the neighborhood around; they "themselves cleaned up DeSalvio park," began locking it at night, and hosing the gutters and sidewalks of their storefronts each midnight.[26] Community leaders formed the Little Italy Restoration Association (LIRA) in early 1974, in order "to preserve the character of Little Italy and stem the exodus of its residents."[27] Collaborating with a responsive Department of City Planning, local leaders devised a plan for the *"risorgimento"*— resurgence—of Mulberry Street, which involved neighborhood upgrading through restoration of historic storefronts, refurbishing of DeSalvio Park, and rehabilitation of the tenement housing stock, among other measures.[28] A plan for the *"pedonalizzazione"*— pedestrianization—of Mulberry Street over the weekend went into effect in late 1974, closing three blocks of Mulberry Street to traffic to create a mall atmosphere and give shoppers "an unobstructed view of the cafés, groceries, and pastry shops that characterize the old Italian neighborhood."[29] To "enhance the special character" of Little Italy, the area was granted a special district designation, which essentially restricted ground-floor space to restaurants and specialty shops and limited the size of buildings and stores from surpassing the intimate scale of the old immigrant neighborhood.[30] Building facades were restored, street lightning improved; by 1977, Lombardi's Restaurant reopened after a five-year hiatus, and *New York Times* reported the opening of eighteen new restaurants and the restoration of four others.[31] The foundation for the future of Mulberry's Little Italy was set.

The subsequent development of Mulberry Street bears witness to the success of this strategy. Figure 13.2 presents a decennial count of the *total number of businesses* on Mulberry Street and Arthur Avenue between 1971 and 2010.[32] The chart documents an overall increase of 81 percent on Mulberry Street, particularly during the 1990s and onwards. Arthur Avenue shows an overall increase of about 18 percent between 1971 and 2010, most of which occurred in the last decade after an initial decline. Mulberry

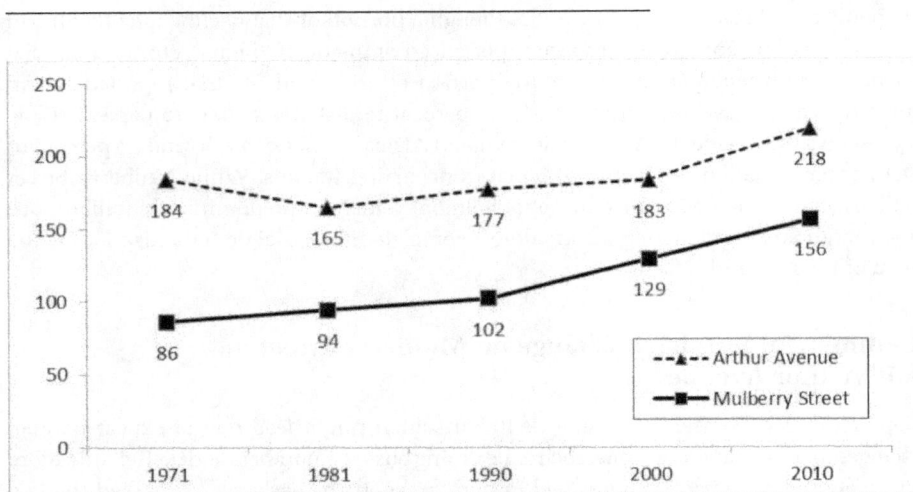

Figure 13.2. Store totals on Arthur Avenue and Mulberry Street, 1971–2010. *Cole's Cross Reference Directories: Manhattan and the Bronx.*

Street's more sizable increase may be due to faster growth, earlier commercial decline not captured by the chart, or a combination of both. What is clear is that the population decline experienced in both areas has not been paralleled by commercial decline or empty storefronts.

The residential de-Italianization discussed above has similarly not led to commercial de-Italianization. Both area restaurants and stores remain overwhelmingly Italian, in stark contrast to their residential makeup.[33] Further, both areas appear to cultivate an *Italianità* that is deliberately more pronounced nowadays, illustrated by the glossy storefronts that display prominently Italian cultural symbols. A shoemaker in the 1950s would see little need for a large storefront display with Italian symbols such as flag colors; his clientele likely lived in the neighborhood and knew him personally. In other words, the quantitative measuring of the commercial ethnicity of each area may be missing qualitative inscriptions of ethnicity beyond the store name, signaling an even *more* Italian scene in response to demographic change and diversification of clientele.

If the residents have changed, how have the businesses adapted? What kinds of businesses serve Mulberry Street and Arthur Avenue, and to what clienteles do they cater? Donna Gabaccia has recently pointed to the connection between Little Italies and food, noting that "well over half of Little Italy webpages [in a Google search] . . . take readers to information about restaurants or food."[34] Restaurants, pizzerias, and specialty food stores have come to define the commercial strips of Little Italies such as Mulberry Street and Arthur Avenue. "You can get a good espresso here, or Italian soccer shirts," mused a reporter recently, "but the reason you go [to Arthur Avenue] is to eat."[35] If the eye of the storm in the early 1970s was epitomized by the disappearance of "the old butcher . . . a grocer, a barber, a drugstore, a leatherworker's shop, a Singer sewing-machine store, an ice-cream parlor, a clothing store and the Spring Lounge [bar]," it was the reopening of Lombardi's that led the *New York Times* to point to a turnaround, declaring "miracle on Spring Street."[36] Continuous mid-1970s coverage of the area in the *Times* enthusiastically noted the opening of additional restaurants on Mulberry Street, leading a reporter to conclude that "the seemingly endless variety of restaurants is the true lure of Mulberry Street."[37]

Just how important were restaurants to the reemergence of Mulberry Street? How did other forms of consumption play into it? Food consumption in a Little Italy can take many forms, of course, uniting a cornucopia of consumers and modes of consumption. Tourists may go to a restaurant for a taste of New York, food aficionados may chase the latest restaurant sensation, students living nearby may go to a café for pastries, while former neighborhood residents may go to the cheese store for the fresh mozzarella prepared daily (see figure 13.3 for an example of a typical specialty food store). Typically inscribed in the business name, the Cole Directories allow the identification of store types. An analysis of food-related businesses revealed that while their numbers increased over the decades, their percentage to the total number of businesses remained relatively constant, at around 25 percent on Mulberry Street and 40 percent on Arthur Avenue. Many factors may account for the distinct rate of each area, such as the earlier dissolution of the residential enclave surrounding Mulberry Street, the relative accessibility of other food shopping areas in the vicinity, and so on. But to determine the relative weight of restaurants vis-à-vis other forms of (food) consumption in each area, it is necessary to

Figure 13.3. An Italian specialty food store on Arthur Avenue. Photo by the author.

look at the changing composition of businesses within the food category. To that end, food-related businesses were divided into three main categories: restaurants, cafés and pizzerias, and food stores.[38]

A story of differentiation between Mulberry Street and Arthur Avenue emerges when food-related businesses are counted accordingly. Figures 13.4 and 13.5 present graphs based on a count of these categories over four decades of available Cole data. The graphs indicate a central difference between the two areas in 1971: While the categories of restaurants and cafés are comparable, Arthur Avenue has a much higher number of food stores (fifty-three, compared to Mulberry Street's six). As we saw above, Mulberry Street had largely de-Italianized by 1970, while Belmont was still predominantly Italian until 1980. Neighborhood ethnic consumption explains the remaining food stores on Belmont and their relative paucity on Mulberry Street. Vinny Vella Sr., an old-time resident of nearby Elizabeth Street, decried their disappearance: "this block used to have everything . . . a dry cleaner, a candy store, a butcher, a steakhouse, a fruit market, and the whole block was Italian. You never had to leave."[39]

The main trend in the commercial transformation of Mulberry Street has been the spectacular increase in the number of restaurants. Figure 13.4 shows that their numbers jumped from five to thirty-three between 1971 and 2010, increasing their share to the overall food-related businesses from 24 to 79 percent. The commercial Italianization of

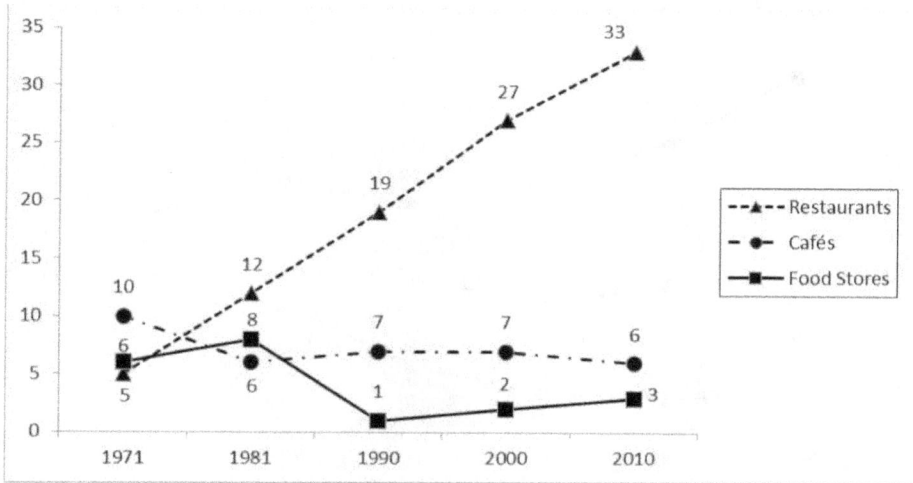

Figure 13.4. Food business categories on Mulberry Street, 1971–2010. *Cole's Cross Reference Directories: Manhattan and the Bronx.*

Mulberry Street therefore relied on the emergence of a concentration of restaurants that constitute a successful Little Italy. As early as 1993, the trend was clear: "very little of Italy [may] be left in the neighborhood. [but] Mulberry remains the symbolic main street . . . with its thriving Italian restaurants [and] sidewalk cafés."[40]

By contrast, the already low number of cafés and food stores declined even further between 1971 and 2010. Among the disappearing food businesses on the Cole Directories are a fish store, a bakery, and a liquor store, all carrying Italian names. The few remaining ones have had to adapt, as an interview with the owner of an Italian specialty food store reveals. Opened in 1903 and run by fifth-generation family members, Di Palo's is located on Grand Street, halfway down the block from the Mulberry Street corner. Lou di Palo explained: "We're still a neighborhood store, but we took the initiative to make our shop a destination. It went from an immigrant store to an Italian American store focused on authentic products of Italy. We don't expect customers to come on a daily basis. A great customer we'll see once a week, a very good customer we'll see once a month."[41] The store relies on its ethnicity to attract customers no longer living in its vicinity.

How did Arthur Avenue change during these decades? We noted that Arthur Avenue had a significantly higher number of food stores in 1971, which defined the commercial scene of Belmont. Figure 13.5 shows two trends in its subsequent transformation. On one hand, the originally distinguishing high number of food stores has seen a steady decline, from fifty-three to thirty-seven. On the other, both categories of restaurants and cafés have seen their numbers increase from six to nineteen and fifteen to thirty-seven,

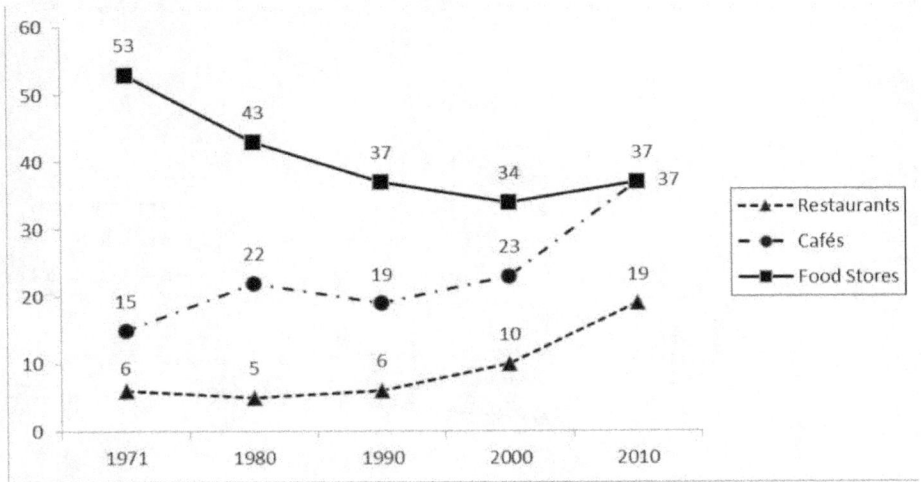

Figure 13.5. Food business categories on Arthur Avenue, 1971–2010. *Cole's Cross Reference Directories: Manhattan and the Bronx.*

respectively. In short, while Mulberry Street relies almost exclusively on a concentration of restaurants, Arthur Avenue retains a more balanced mix of restaurants, cafés, and food stores. Both areas have been successfully reinvented as Italian-themed urban spaces, but the revalorization of their commercial corridors has followed distinct trajectories, as the Cole numbers demonstrate.

Tracing the shifting composition of food-related businesses raises other important questions. What are the implications of the increase in certain types of food businesses, such as restaurants and cafés, and the decline of others, such as traditional food stores? Are restaurants and food stores "ethnic" in distinctive ways? Do such forms of consumption embody new ways of ethnic belonging, or do they simply commercialize ethnicity for broader cultural consumption? Moreover, what are the implications of these transformed landscapes of consumption for the places they "inhabit" and redefine? A closer look at the transformation of festivals in both areas offers suggestions in pursuing these questions.

The Transformation of Street *Feste*

Few communal events were more prominent than church-organized religious fests in early Italian immigrant neighborhoods. Typically celebrating saints associated with southern Italian towns where the immigrants originated, these annual events provided "site[s] for the construction, elaboration, and performance of the various emergent meanings of 'Italian American' by the immigrants and their children."[42] Given their centrality to the social life of the neighborhood, changes in street *feste* provide an important lens in understanding the transformation of Italian neighborhoods from immigrant ethnic enclaves into urban ethnic places. Festivals occur on the *streets*, making them important tools in managing the divergent ethnicities of the consumption spaces and residents around them. How do they fulfill that function? How have street festivals responded to the specialization of the commercial scenes in both areas?

BELMONT

Religious feasts were important social events of neighborhood life throughout much of the twentieth century in Belmont. In a memoir about growing up in "the Fordham town" during the 1920s and 1930s, Rocky D'Erasmo notes that "Italian festivals honoring different patron saints were the big events of the summer months."[43] An ethnographic account of Belmont from the mid-1980s, as well as a more recent memoir, affirm their continued importance to the community.[44] The feats have undergone significant change in the intervening decades. For one, the number of the festivals has dropped over time. Belmont residents originated from many towns in southern Italy, and many of their patron saints were celebrated in the early decades. D'Erasmo mentions Saint Joseph and Madonna di Monteverde, both no longer celebrated in Belmont.[45] A pastor who grew up in Belmont and served at Our Lady of Mount Carmel Church for twenty years confirmed the decline in the number of feasts: "In the early days of our [neighborhood] history there used to be six or seven festivals. [I remember] Saint Mark, [Madonna di] Monteverde . . . Now there are only two [left]." The pastor was referring to Saint Anthony and Mount Carmel, which take place in mid-June and mid-July respectively. Held since the establishment of Our Lady of Mount Carmel Church in 1908, they are the only religious festivals still celebrated in Belmont.

The remaining feasts have also undergone changes. Attendance has been steadily declining for decades, as ethnic and racial turnover has accelerated. In recent years only three blocks of 187th Street have been cordoned off from traffic and lined up with food vendors and games, in contrast to accounts of earlier decades when the feasts stretched for over eight blocks.[46] The route of the procession that concludes each feast has been shortened, reflecting contracting neighborhood boundaries, while their duration has increased from the typical two to three days in the Italian towns they originated to about two weeks in Belmont. The increased duration may have its origin in church efforts to maximize feast-generated income for the financial benefit of the parish school.[47] More important, the feasts appear to have undergone a continuous decline in their religiosity. The procession of the saint statue around the streets of Belmont on the concluding day of festivities remains important, even though more research is needed to establish whether it is preceded by the kind of communal effervescence Orsi documented in the case of Italian Harlem's Madonna of 115th Street. But the procession appears somewhat disconnected to the street festivities, and for most attendees little is evidently religious in nature.

The changing logistics of the festivities suggest a clear trajectory of decline, which is to be expected given the steady residential de-Italianization of the neighborhood. Ethnographic fieldwork during the late 2000s in the area revealed that merchants, community leaders, and attendees share the feeling that the present feasts are but a shadow of their former selves. In recent decades, merchants and community leaders have engaged in various efforts to transform the street *feste*, striving to adapt the celebrations in conjunction with the commercial re-Italianization of the area. Continuously critical of the lengthy duration of the feasts, for example, community and business leaders invested in the future of the Little Italy have time and again attempted to wrestle some organizational control from the Church. Their vision of the feasts as a potential element of valorizing Little Italy differs from the church vision. Long-lasting feasts generate more income for the church, do not affect the spirituality of the procession of the saint statue during the concluding day of the festivities, and provide an extended opportunity to engage and include the residential community of Belmont, whose predominantly Latin American origin makes them natural constituents for the expansion of the local Catholic Church. In contrast, a two-week long feast presents organizational challenges that work against the area merchant and business leaders' vision of a successful Little Italy. Weekday festivities fail to draw the typically white, middle-class suburban crowds that the merchants hope to lure into the area restaurants and specialty stores. The carnival games that line up the sidewalks of the designated blocks, such as Whack-a-mole and Drown the Clown, draw children, families and youth from nearby residential blocks, who lack the disposable income to be potential clients to the commercial establishment of Arthur Avenue. Furthermore, from the merchants' perspective, the local residents' minority status may impede the area's image as Italian. As a result, rarely do Arthur Avenue merchants "come out" to serve the crowds, though some pizzerias and cafés on or near 187th Street stay open. The feasts are mainly served by nonlocal vendors who attend street events across wide geographical areas and serve typical festival fare.

The mismatch between the actual residential community of Belmont and the symbolic community envisioned by Little Italy's boosters has led local actors to attempt transforming the street *feste* in line with the particular needs of Little Italy. Business leaders have introduced various new elements into the religious feasts intended to affect the composition of attending crowds, increase the involvement of area merchants, and ensure profits for participating merchants and the church. For example, a makeshift stage hauled by a New York City Department of Parks and Recreation truck is positioned at the Arthur Avenue intersection, the eastern edge of the designated feast area. Successive bands playing on the stage provide continuous live entertainment, constituting the only official "program" of the evening. In contrast to the carnival games that create an atmosphere with few ethnic markers, the stage performances are typically Italian-related, and the master of ceremony is an Italian American merchant and community leader that continuously remarks on the Italianness of Belmont.[48] Crowds congregate in front of the stage, sitting on the skirts of the sidewalk, on rows of street chairs placed in front of the stage, or by the tables of the large corner café that carries the last name of its Italian owner. The organizers hope that the entertainment will appeal to former residents, who will drive to Belmont to meet up with friends and reminisce. Whether by design or accident, the crowd lined up in front of the stage turns its back on the rest of the designated feast blocks, creating a somewhat divided feast where a relatively mature crowd may be listening to a singer performing old Neapolitan songs on the stage, while less than two blocks away African American youth are performing an impromptu Michael Jackson talent show driven by the boom-box music of the small

Puerto Rican store selling theme T-shirts. In short, the merchant and community leaders seek to negotiate this ethnic and racial diversity by sustaining a vision of the neighborhood as ethnically Italian.

The efforts of community and business leaders to influence the religious feasts are inherently limited by their long tradition and the organizational control of the church, whose priorities do not always mesh with those of the merchants. A clearer representation of the leaders' vision of Little Italy, and the role street *feste* can play, is offered by Ferragosto, Belmont's third and last summer festival. A mid-August short holiday in Italy, its celebration in Belmont was initiated in 1997, under the leadership of a community leader and the combined efforts of several local merchants and organizations. The main features of the Ferragosto celebrations contrast with the religious feasts, representing symbolic choices on the part of its organizers that work to enhance their particular vision of Little Italy. To maximize attendance, enthusiasm, local merchant involvement, and profits, Ferragosto is held as a one-day event, in contrast to the lengthy Saint Anthony and Mount Carmel feasts. While the latter are held in early summer and midsummer, when people tend to go on holidays, Ferragosto takes place on the Sunday after Labor Day in early September, to ensure maximum attendance of former residents, but also to coincide with the beginning of the new academic year at nearby Fordham University. Place symbolism also comes into play. The religious feasts are held on 187th Street, where the church is located, while Ferragosto is held on the southern portion of Arthur Avenue, where the majority of the core Italian businesses are located. 187th Street is heavily residential, while Arthur Avenue has a very low number of residences and is considerably less frequented by minority residents. The makeshift stage is placed at the entrance of the "Enrico Fermi" Belmont branch of the New York Public Library, facing the intersection of Arthur Avenue and 186th Street, a central corner flanked by some of the most prominent Little Italy businesses. The program is Italian-themed and defined by neighborhood nostalgia; nationally recognized local notables often make appearances (actor Chazz Palminteri, who played "Sonny" in *A Bronx Tale*, singer and actor Dominic Chianese, who played "Uncle Junior" in *The Sopranos*, and the like). As the *New York Times* article cited at the opening of this chapter explained, there are no carnival games; virtually all restaurants and cafés put tables out (figure 13.6), and people enjoy food, drinks, and music in a festive atmosphere on a typically balmy September afternoon. Actors dressed in *commedia dell'arte*–inspired costumes (figure 13.7) perform and walk throughout the crowd all day, and a local butcher selling fresh sausages teases the hungry crowds with two slowly rotating pigs on a spit in front of the Arthur Avenue Retail Market (figure 13.8).

The emergence of Ferragosto in the last decade has provided an example of what street events can do for Little Italy. Beyond its immediate success as a daily feast, Ferragosto has become a yardstick for measuring the performance of the religious feasts by area merchants and leaders. Its atmosphere is less religious and more festive, celebrating the "neighborhood" as epitomized by area businesses. Its target clientele comes from outside the neighborhood, and includes former residents, their friends and family, and people affiliated with area institutions such as Fordham University, Saint Barnabas Hospital, and the Bronx Zoo and Botanical Gardens—in short, a crowd of a higher socioeconomic status that the Arthur Avenue businesses hope to lure on a weekly basis. The

Figure 13.6. Patrons dining *al fresco* during Ferragosto celebrations on Arthur Avenue. Photo by the author.

festivities of Ferragosto represent a skillful commercialization of the Italian past of the neighborhood, shifting focus from the current minority residents of the area to the businesses that reframe the "authentic" past of Belmont. Such strategies make the feast profitable not simply in the financial sense, but help maintain the area as ethnically Italian, raise the neighborhood cache, and increase its commercial potential. The continuous negotiation of the Little Italy managers with the church to add similar elements to the religious feasts points to their potential in remapping the street as an extension of Italian businesses, not the apartment buildings of 187th Street. In this sense, festivals serve as links to an "authentic" past that mark the commercial ethnicity of present Little Italy as a surviving outpost of Europeanness in a borough that "lost" its ethnic enclaves to the suburbs (such as Jewish East Tremont).

SAN GENNARO ON MULBERRY STREET

Street festivals on Mulberry Street have similarly transformed from celebrations of immigrant faith to instruments used for managing the disparity between residential and commercial ethnicity. San Gennaro, one of the biggest street festivals in New York, takes place yearly in mid-September. The feast dates back to 1926, when Italian residents began to celebrate the patron saint of Naples. As the sole Italian festival on Mulberry Street, San Gennaro combines elements of each of Belmont's three feasts, such as the long duration of the religious feasts with the popularity of Ferragosto. The feast has

Figure 13.7. *Commedia dell'arte* actors entertain crowds during Ferragosto on Arthur Avenue. Photo by the author.

changed over the decades in ways that parallel the transformation of the commercial scene: the residential de-Italianization of surrounding blocks seems to have only increased its popularity. For example, table 13.1 shows that residents of Italian ancestry dropped from 40 to 22 percent during the 1960s, and declined further to 17 percent by the end of the 1970s. During the same period, San Gennaro's duration increased steadily from five days in 1960, to nine in 1962, ten in 1969, and reached the current eleven-day duration in 1976.[49] The number of street stands doubled from 150 to 300 during the early 1970s, and attendance kept up with the increased duration; based on sales count, organizers estimated that the feast attracted a total of three million people in 1979. Predictions of attendance routinely exceed the one million mark, averaging over 100,000 people a day.[50]

If San Gennaro's popularity grew in the wake of the residential de-Italianization of the area, it can also feel out of place for the same reason. Despite the "giant crowds" it draws, inconvenienced Nolita merchants have asked for its abbreviation, given the younger, more fashionable crowd that shops at the boutique stores that now dot the northern blocks of the Mulberry Street area.[51] Similarly, citing wide resident discontent with the disruption caused by the event, a subcommittee of the local Community Board

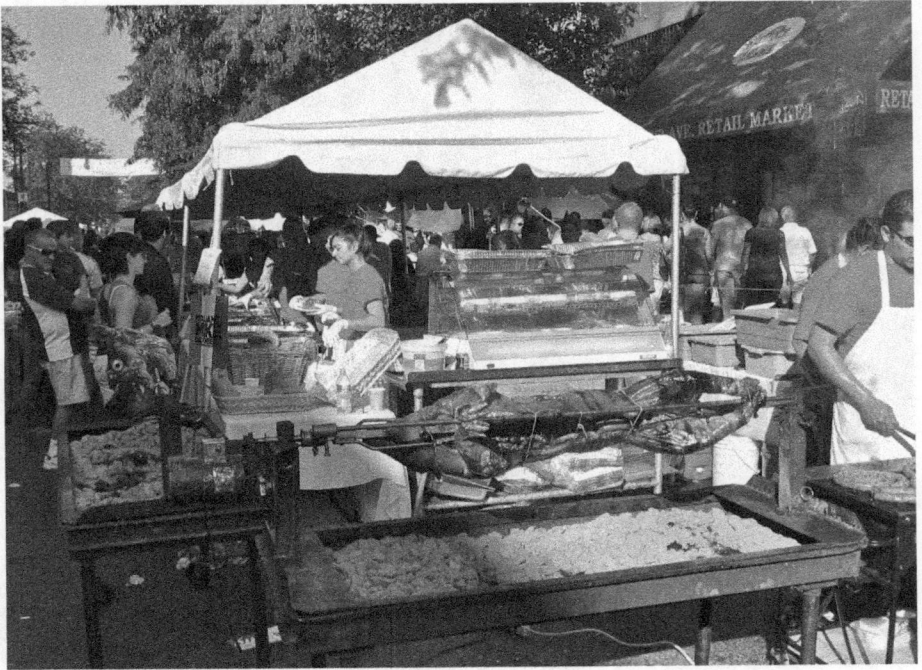

Figure 13.8. A slow-roasted pig will be served to Ferragosto crowds on Arthur Avenue. Photo by the author.

2 issued a nonbinding recommendation that the permit application for the upcoming fair be denied in 2007.[52] Festival attendees with strong connections to the past may feel out of place too. The niece of an old-time vendor who had sold "homemade nougat and cookies" with his horse and wagon for twenty-six years, recounted her alienation in this way: "Growing up, a feast was mandolins and dancing to me. Now it's trailer, trailer, trailer. Everything's commercial. When you get Thai and Filipino and Greek setting up trailers . . . they don't even know who San Gennaro is."[53] Said another attendee: "when I was a kid, the feast was about family, religion, and food. Now it's about CDs and three socks for $10."[54]

It should come as no surprise that, through its transformation, San Gennaro's religious character has declined, if not rendered marginal to the festivities. Similar to the "secular" merchant involvement in the religious street feste of Belmont, San Gennaro is organized by a nonreligious, civic entity. Figli di San Gennaro (Children of San Gennaro), a nonprofit organization who currently runs the feast, describes its role as "dedicated to keeping alive the spirit and faith of the early Italian immigrants."[55] Despite its religious origins and the saint statue procession on the concluding day of the festivities, San Gennaro shows a greater resemblance to Belmont's secular Ferragosto, in that it produces a symbolic version of past Italian presence for wide cultural consumption. Aware of the spiritual deficit, the organizers summarized San Gennaro's character in this way: "Although this is an annual celebration of faith, the Feast of Saint Gennaro is known the world over for its festive atmosphere . . . featuring religious processions and colorful parades, free musical entertainment every day, a wide variety of ethnic food delicacies, charming restaurants and cafés and even a world-famous cannoli-eating competition!" The webpage reminds readers in more than one occasion that "this is really a religious celebration" despite "the party atmosphere that permeates the Feast," and note its growth "from a one-day street festival to a gala 11-day event." In all likelihood, the religious aspect of the feast will be lost on most of the million-strong people expected to attend.

Despite the similar commercialization of their respective Little Italies, the celebrations of San Gennaro differ from celebrations on Belmont in a crucial sense. In addition to the million-strong additional tourists Mulberry Street enjoys, Lower Manhattan never became home to minority resident populations in the same way that South and mid-Bronx did. The position of Mulberry Street within the downtown urban scene ensured that San Gennaro did not have to contend with the racial markers of nonwhiteness. For that reason, San Gennaro has not evolved as a representation of a "fortress neighborhood" holding against succession. Its work lies in managing the image of a Little Italy as a spectacle of food, entertainment, and history, representing the immigrant past in the light of a joyous, good life. When Mulberry Street was closed to traffic on Saturdays and Sundays to become a "weekend mall," one of the founders of the local Little Italy Restoration Association involved in the effort explained: "What we're doing is much more reflective of the people's life-style. Without a Little Italy . . . what's New York City?"[56] If Belmont street festivals conjure a symbolic "fortress" community that befits Little Italy, San Gennaro reenact the Italian past as the embodiment of a pleasurable lifestyle.

Conclusion

When Paul J. Q. Lee assumed that Little Italy no longer existed in that meeting in 1977, he was referring to an immigrant neighborhood that had outlived its usefulness as "home" to immigrants from Southern Italy. In the intervening decades, intersecting global flows of culture and people have joined late-capitalist transformations in creating new opportunities for the expression of ethnicity in former ethnic enclaves. As a result, places like Mulberry Street have been reinvented as ethnic-themed urban spaces that commercialize their immigrant pasts for the cultural consumption of a variety of consumers. Much like residential ethnicity took a multiplicity of forms, the ascendance of commercial ethnicity is shaped by a variety of factors that constitute the local histories and geographies of such areas.

14

We Are Family

ETHNIC FOOD MARKETING AND THE CONSUMPTION OF
AUTHENTICITY IN ITALIAN-THEMED CHAIN RESTAURANTS

Fabio Parasecoli

A group of young people, who we can tell get together regularly by the way they interact, play and drink around a coffee table. They are a group of cousins that take time to have their own special moment during family reunions. They clearly enjoy each other's company, so when the same festive atmosphere moves to a restaurant, the banter and laughter continue while they pass the bread and eat. The restaurant is spacious and well lit, with a big wooden table that allows everybody to sit together. We see exposed bricks in the shape of an arc, parts of the walls are in stone, and the lighting fixtures appear to be wrought iron. The environment gives an organic, natural vibe. The table is loaded with drinks and many different foods in colorful dishes, some apparently meant to be shared. After a handful of seconds, we see a sign made of white tiles with a bunch of grapes painted on it: The scene is taking place at a restaurant belonging to the Olive Garden chain. We are immediately introduced to some menu items like chicken scaloppini, Asiago-filled tortelloni, and unlimited breadsticks. "This is like being back at the kids' table," exclaims one of the smiling cousins. We feel we can all share their experience, their delight, and their excitement by sitting at a family table where laughter and affection are as important as the meal. In case we did not get the message, the commercial drives it home with the slogan: "When you're here, you're family."[1]

Family values, tasty and abundant fare, passion for food, as well as relaxed atmosphere, are presented as core values of the restaurant chain promoted by the ad, and of the Italian traditions it is inspired by. This chapter applies a semiotic approach to the communication material produced by three restaurant chains—Maggiano's Little Italy, Bertucci's, and Olive Garden—all very different in terms of image, marketing strategies, and price point. The goal is to explore how a limited set of recognizable cultural traits has come to represent and at times to stereotype Italian and Italian American culinary customs, both for the members of the very communities from which they originate and for the public at large. In contemporary consumer cultures, Italian ethnicity and its aspects related to food have acquired relevance as a marker of distinction. As such, they are incorporated in commodities, experiences, and services that constitute commercially viable objects of desire. These dynamics are particularly interesting because those very customs—and the material culture that comes with it—are the results of century-old negotiations with U.S. consumption patterns, which exerted great influence on the construction of racial and social identities of immigrant communities. Elements that until recently were perceived as working-class and tainted by ethnic backwardness are now embraced as acceptable components of the middle-class ethos and its symbolic and material expressions in the market.

Furthermore, this analysis will assess the strategies of the three restaurant chains that refer to traditions from Italy, its past, and the nostalgia it often elicits to promote a recognizable brand to large audiences and market a specific aspect of contemporary American popular culture: casual dining chain restaurants. The popularity of these establishments, their relevance in terms of business volume, and their impact on the collective imagination, make them an intriguing object of study and offer a so far unexplored vantage point to analyze the complex relationship between Italian American material and symbolic culture, corporate business, and media in America. The culinary symbols, behaviors, and values—first elaborated by early immigrants and then shaped and given changing meanings by generations of Italian Americans—are now experienced and presented as heritage. As performance theorist Barbara Kirshemblatt-Gimblett aptly pointed out, "heritage is a mode of cultural production in the present that has recourse to the past play."[2] It generates value-added industries that do not simply reflect objective realities but actually construct them. From this point of view, Italian American culinary heritage is invented—or at least recreated—as a marketable experience to respond to contemporary preferences. Charged with relevant emotional and symbolic connotations, food heritage plays an important role for the imagination and the cultural capital of the modern—and postmodern—consumers.

Casual Dining and Corporate Branding

The recognition enjoyed by the restaurants discussed in this chapter also feeds off the repute, the unprecedented status, and the worldwide diffusion that Italian food has gained over the past few decades. In addition to being the domain of family-style eateries, ice cream parlors, and pizza shops, high-end Italian restaurants are now listed among the most prestigious establishments in world-class cities, receiving equally heartfelt accolades from both critics and patrons.

As the diffusion and success of Italian food is turning into a true global phenomenon, Italian American culinary habits are also eliciting growing attention in the USA and abroad, partly due to the visibility of Italian Americans and their cultural practices in various forms of popular culture, including fashion, movies, television, and a growing numbers of books and cookbooks, presenting both traditional and innovative recipes.[3]

The origins and development of the rich and multi-layered Italian American foodways go well beyond the extent of this chapter. A vast literature is already available on the topic, which is often approached within larger discussions about immigrant culinary traditions in the United States.[4] Furthermore, a growing number of scholarly texts have focused on specific aspects of Italian American food and wine culture, which has evolved and generated very diverse manifestations in different places and throughout history.[5] Numerous recipe collections for general audiences that underline the connection with significant places in Italian American culture have been published, from New York's Arthur Avenue to Boston's North End and Louisiana, while numerous cookbooks showcase well-known restaurants and other culinary institutions, including social clubs.[6] Interestingly, a few among these make direct reference to mafia and the mobsters' love for food and family, as portrayed in popular culture: the dark side of those same traditions that highlight the importance of tight knit social ties.[7]

While the interest in private performances of food production and consumption and their connection with family and community have generated a solid corpus of research, the more commercial aspects of Italian American food culture—and in particular casual dining chain restaurants—have so far elicited less scholarly attention. To achieve a better understanding of the topic at hand, it can be useful to assess the research on ethnic themes used in franchises and to examine the specific studies on Italian-inspired establishments.

Analysis of chain restaurants has been conducted in connection with tourism, hospitality, and the foodservice industry. Together with food quality, service quality, price, and location, the restaurant ambience has been indicated as one of the main factors influencing the customers' experience.[8] Lighting, aroma, soundscape, temperature, cleanliness, design, décor, the overall atmosphere, the comfort of the seating arrangement, the physical performance of the staff, and their interaction with the patrons have been pointed out as relevant factors. Recent research has started taking stock of the relevance of online marketing for chain restaurants, focusing on elements such as functionality, information, aesthetics, and communication.[9]

Among these strategies, the adoption of themes referring to ethnic traditions has been identified as a marketing tool that restaurants employ to provide customers with unique experiences and to differentiate themselves from the competition. The elements that are taken into consideration usually include design, décor, music, costumes, and other signifiers that in the United States have come to be associated with the culture from which the cuisine originates.[10] The use of foreign culinary terminology on menus, although it has become familiar through frequent use, also contributes to an increase in the titillation of the controlled displacement and estrangement that make dining in an ethnic restaurant interesting.[11]

Nevertheless, when the business-related literature refers to the concept of "authenticity" and its relevance in "theming" strategies, it often does so without a critical assessment of its meaning and connotations. Also when attention is paid to the cultural and contextual nature of "authenticity," the main focus remains on the practical usefulness of theming in allowing patrons to enjoy the illusion of a different environment, exotic but not threatening."[12] For instance, Claus Ebster and Irene Guist establish a difference between "authentic and themed ethnic restaurants," with the goal of better "identifying the target customer and adapting design elements to meet customers' expectations."[13] According to this distinction, patrons are classified as culturally experienced or culturally naive based on their familiarity with the restaurant's supposedly "authentic" ethnic inspiration, but what differentiates authentic from nonauthentic elements remains unclear. On the other hand, anthropological and ethnographic literature on food, consumption, and tourism, pays greater attention to cultural aspects, such as engagement in culinary tourism,[14] cultural awareness, cross-cultural interpretation,[15] and nostalgia, as well as the entrepreneur's understanding of his or her own ethnic identity.[16]

Italian Goes Ethnic

These preliminary explorations need to be integrated with more specific inquiries about the motivations behind the selection of specific textual, visual and aural elements (as opposed to other possible signifiers) from the culture of a specific community to mark the restaurant as connected to that ethnicity, and how these choices may participate, reinforce, or contest widespread perceptions and representations of the ethnicity involved as part of highly marketable commodities. A semiotic analysis of these elements offers interesting insights about the processes that regulate their functioning in specific cultural contexts and symbolic systems and their transformation into shared and recognizable signs that affect the customer's perception, interpretation, and evaluation of the restaurant experience. Interestingly, one of the first examples of semiotic analysis of food-related communication—Roland Barthes's reading of an advertisement for Panzani pasta in France—focuses specifically on an Italian dish as a signifier of the whole ethnic identity as well as manufactured authenticity.[17]

Applying this kind of analysis to the communicative strategies of the chain Fazoli's, David Girardelli argued that they "serve the ultimate goal of commodifying the Italian ethnic identity and promoting its symbolic consumption" through a set of themes that indicate "an unobtrusive use of stereotypes, a mass phenomenon of identity construction, and the depletion of a cultural capital."[18] Through a close reading of décor, menu, website, radio ads, and TV commercials, defined as a "hodgepodge of authentically fake Italian artifacts," the author identifies a specific set of signifiers, including family, rusticity, nostalgia, slow-paced lifestyle, genuineness, openness, expressivity, and romance. The commodification of these elements reify Italian American identity but at the same time point to the widespread desire in American society for human relations, romance, passion, and family values that Italian American culture is supposed to embody and make available through consumable culinary experiences.

An intriguing example of this sort of packaging and commodification is offered by "Saucy Balls," the project proposed by contestant Joey Galluzzi in the 2011 NBC reality show *America's Next Great Restaurant*. To get funding for their projects and have them launched in three U.S. locations, contestants competed to convince investors about the validity of their restaurant concept in terms of menu, visual design, feasibility, appeal to large audiences, and communication potential. In the first episode, aired on March 6, 2011, we see Galluzzi introducing his restaurant concept and preparing his grandmother's "three meats meatballs" for the judges. After zooming in on his hands shaping the meatballs, the camera cuts to an old picture of his grandmother smiling while cooking at the stove. "One of the first memories I have of my grandmother—the contestant says—is watching her grinding the meat, and I believe with every bit of my heart and soul that this idea is a winner and I can't wait to present it to them." Looking for a simple, marketable concept to put behind a new chain of fast-casual restaurants, Galluzzi digs into his own background and into his family tradition to choose an iconic comfort food in Italian American cuisine. Galluzzi then proceeds to serve the judges the dish he has himself prepared for the first challenge: meatballs in red sauce with ricotta cheese on the side—"Saucy Balls." "Every Sunday I make my sauce and my balls . . ." The judges burst out laughing, and Bobby Flay says: "By the way, you have balls for naming it this, for the record." He explains that his seven-year old daughter came up with the name. Chef and judge Curtis Stone says, "Joey, I can't believe I am going to say this, but I love your balls." The theme of masculinity and its complex role in Italian American culture lurked behind the jabs, but eventually the name was changed to Brooklyn Meatballs Co.

In the second episode, aired on March 13, 2011, the contestants need to prepare their dish for a thousand eaters, work with a graphic designer on a logo to brand their restaurant concepts, and choose a chef to work with. As Galluzzi enters a room full of chefs he could potentially collaborate with, he yells, "Who is passionate about Italian food and loves *Goodfellas*?" The loudness of the contestant, his food choices, and his references to mafia movie icons all underline his *Italianità*. His "humble beginnings" and his affection for his family—two recurring elements of the Italian immigrant narrative—are powerfully evoked in the contestant's rhetoric, to the point that Galluzzi asks his graphic designer to include his grandmother, whose picture he carries with him, in the logo design. He later explains to the judges that the logo suggests nice home-cooked meals.

In the fifth episode, aired on April 3, 2011, the participants have to design their uniform to complement the image of their restaurants. Causing consternation in the judges, Galluzzi decides to go for a supposed "old time Brooklyn gangster" look with black shirt and pants, white thin tie, white winged shoes, and guns, "something fun that people could get a kick out of." During the photo shoot, he holds a six-foot loaf of bread, another phallic innuendo. The contestant's unfortunate meddling with visual elements continues in the following episode, aired on April 10, 2011, when the participants design their food trucks and a mobile billboard. Galluzzi wants to display a busy image that includes a white, red, and green theme, the Brooklyn Bridge, his grandmother silhouette, pictures of a dish of meatballs and of a salad, to show that "the restaurant has healthy options." It is interesting how the judges did not question the use of the Italian stereotypical images per se, almost acknowledging their obviousness and their reflectivity of reality, but that the way the contestant used them did not succeed in conveying the experience of eating good food at grandma's house.

Galluzzi's clumsy attempts to claim and perhaps reclaim Italian and Italian American stereotypes as a communication strategy to connect with a mainstream clientele (who participates in creating and reinforcing these clichéd markers in the first place) can be interpreted as either a lack of self-reflexivity or a misperception of the cultural consequences of this kind of "branding," which contests the very notion of cultural authenticity that stereotypes are supposed to reflect. Galluzzi's choices reveal the ambivalences that often linger around Italian American tables: On one hand, food is a reminder of the well-deserved abundance attained after the hardships of migration. It expresses the nostalgic connection with the past and the land of origin, as well as the relevance of family ties and affection. These are values that Italian-inspired restaurant chains aim to capitalize on, by commodifying a living (and contested) tradition into a marketable food experience. On the other hand, the table is also the arena where all the dysfunctions of the family life that is projected as the core of Italian values become glaring: Meals can catalyze tensions that can explode in actual fights. Popular culture seems to thrive on these dysfunctions, in the form of fascination with mafia and with a self-proclaimed "guido" lifestyle. Movie hits like the *Godfather, Goodfellas,* and *Moonstruck* (and less famous movies like *Dinner Rush*), TV fiction series like *The Sopranos,* and reality shows such as *Jersey Shore, The Real Housewives of New Jersey,* and *Mob Wives* all seem to feed on these ambivalences, turning the dynamics that develop around food gatherings— from the Sunday meals to celebrations on special occasions—into a media spectacle.[19] These traits point to a darker side of the Italian way of life that contemporary popular culture has made visible and amplified, at times exploiting it in a quite tongue-in-cheek manner. This seems to involve theatrical manners, excessive styles (both in terms of fashion and home décor), rambunctiousness, vindictiveness, the ability to hold a grudge for inordinate extents of time, and a certain penchant to an unbridled physicality that at times can turn into violence. The very traits that under certain circumstances can be heartwarming and endearing constantly point to some lurking danger. These tensions, although ignored and erased in the theming of chain restaurant, are arguably very much present in the minds of the customers, due to their prevalence in popular culture and shameless exploitation, like in the case of the Godfather's Pizza chain, whose motto "A pizza you can't refuse" echoes a famous line from the movie *The Godfather.* It is arguable that precisely these elements, although made invisible and ostensibly ignored in Italian-themed restaurants, may turn a visit to a casual dining venue into an exciting foray into a potentially dangerous Exotic Other. However, the fact that these encounters take place in a commodified environment turn them into controllable forms of culinary tourism, which allow patrons to selectively consume only those ethnic traits that in their comfort zone.

Italian Goes Corporate

These ambivalences and the complex history of the Italian American community, which looms large in Galluzzi's concept, are accurately concealed in the communication strategies of established chains such as Maggiano's, Bertucci's, and Olive Garden. As a matter of fact, the redundancy and exaggeration of elements highlighting family, warmth, celebration, and all that is positive in the stereotyped image of Italian Americans would seem directed not only to define each chain's branding, but also to eliminate any acknowledgement or reference to the less congenial and marketable aspects of that culture. The three chains, while apparently building their public image on similar elements, hint to very different versions of the Italian and the Italian American experiences.

Maggiano's was founded in Chicago on November 11, 1991, by Brinker International, the company that also owns Romano's Macaroni Grill and Chili's Grill & Bar, another major casual dining chain whose most immediate competitors are Appleby's and T. G. I. Friday's. Maggiano's boasts forty-five locations in twenty-one states and the

District of Columbia, while one restaurant was opened in Jeddah, Saudi Arabia. The food is made daily from scratch on the premises. Brinker, whose stocks are traded on the New York Stock Exchange, does not provide data for each chain, but in total it posted revenues for $3.6 billion in 2009, $2.9 billion in 2010 and $2.8 billion in 2011, showing a decline probably due to the economic crisis.[20] As the brand name clearly indicates, the source of inspiration for Maggiano's theme is not Italy, but rather New York's Little Italy. All communication refers to a rather nostalgic past that, from the visual and textual cues inside the restaurant and in all marketing material, seems to go back to the first decades of the twentieth century. The décor is quite sober, with dark wood fixtures, tables, and chairs. The walls are decorated with antique-looking mirrors with dark wood frames, and with memorabilia that includes somebody's old black and white family pictures and portraits, which are still likely to be kept and cherished as part of family heirlooms. The images are meant to remind us of the stories and lives of the first Italian American immigrants, who sent pictures back to Italy to show that they were doing well and that they could actually afford to pay for professional photographs. However, Maggiano's does not cater to the nostalgia for the old country, but rather expresses a longing for the values and lifestyles of the first immigrants, who had to struggle to start new lives but at the same time, as the pictures suggest, could count on the love of their families, strong social connections, and solid cultural values. However, these cultural elements, although crucial for the brand and very present visually, are not explicitly conveyed in any verbal narrative. The home page of the Maggiano's website does not carry any story or description of the restaurant's spirit and philosophy.[21] Through changing banners, it showcases instead special offers and new initiatives. At the time of the writing of this article, the website promoted a "small bites" menu: small appetizers available in the bar and lounge areas. "The portions and prices are perfect for after work or a light dinner before a fun evening out," specifies the webpage. The chain is introducing small dishes, which would seem to go counter the abundant portions and family style service often ascribed to the Italian American tradition, in order to respond to new trends and the growing health awareness among its customer. However, these new forms of consumption are kept apart from the main space, as if the Italian dining experience risked losing some of its "authenticity" if challenged by small bites. As a matter of fact, the restaurant still features a separate "family style" menu for parties of four or more, but even here we see that three choices are offered, including a "light" menu with a smaller number of dishes, a "classic" with two appetizers, two salads, four main course selections, and two desserts, and a "chef's choice" that includes premium items.

Through the language used on the menu, on the website, and in other promotional material, the communication seems to purposely blur distinctions between Italian and Italian American food. For instance, on a card used to market the new online ordering page on the chain's website, the copy reads: "Want to experience true Italian dining at home? Start talking with your hands." While ironically connecting a stereotypical trait often attributed to Italians and Italian Americans to the computer savvy, marketers identify the food as Italian, without any further specification, and by underlining its "true nature," they highlight its value as experience, almost in terms of participation in another culture. On the menu, we find two categories of pasta dishes: "Classic pastas," which feature Italian American mainstays such as spaghetti and meatballs, baked ziti, and fettuccine Alfredo, and "specialty pastas," showcasing more creative dishes, inspired to both Italian and Italian American traditions, which include seafood linguine (*linguine di mare*, written in Italian on the menu), a lobster carbonara, crab and shrimp cannelloni, and chicken and truffle manicotti. More than in other sections of the menu, the very names of the pasta dishes mix Italian and English, seemingly to draw attention to their *Italianità* while reaffirming an element of comfort by making the menu clearly readable for customers, and additionally through ingredient descriptions after each dish. Other sections of the menu also mix Italian American classics like chicken parmesan and shrimp scampi with dishes that interpret recipes from Italy such as bruschetta, flatbreads with various toppings, Tuscan sausage and orzo soup and chicken saltimbocca (but served with angel hair aglio-olio pasta, in Italian American style).

Maggiano's seems to be aiming to position itself as a classy casual dining chain. The atmosphere is sober, the lighting discrete, with simple light fixtures. Tables in some areas of the restaurant feature white tablecloth, while in others have red and white checkered tablecloth (but with white tablecloth on top), one of the recognizable visual elements usually identified with Italian American restaurants. Reinforcing its connotations of sobriety, black seems to be the dominant color in the faux-leather cover of the restaurant menu, as well as in the waiters' uniforms, and the website uses a palette of restrained colors like tan, brown, and maroon. The website displays tasteful food pictures taken in the style now commonly referred to as "food porn": close-up shots, sometimes with a depth of field that focuses only on a detail of the dish while the background fades into a blur that suggests other elements of the dish and the environment. The pictures tend to be taken at eye level, suggesting the perspective that the eater might enjoy, with soft lighting that accentuates the glistening and succulent visual elements of the dishes.[22] Maggiano's seems to be engaged in a complex balancing act that uses food to nostalgically connect its brand with the Italian American experience, while refraining from the use of excessive stereotypes or explicit textual narratives referencing it, in order to present itself as tasteful, upscale, and open to new trends in Italian cuisine.

Bertucci's casual dining chain takes a different approach in negotiating between the commodification of Italian traditions in the restaurant's theming and the need to develop an identifiable and distinctive brand. The chain is privately owned and operates ninety-three restaurants with more than two thousand employees from its Northborough, Massachusetts, headquarters. It was started by Joseph Crugnale, born in Sulmona, Italy, who moved to Massachusetts when he was young and immediately became involved in the restaurant business.[23] All Bertucci's communication seems intent in capitalizing on the warmth and hospitality that is often considered a typical trait of Mediterranean countries. These values immediately come across in the restaurant's décor, with its prevalence of light brown color bricks, light brown wood, and warm colored textiles. Walls are painted in a light sage color, brick-lined arches decorated with wrought iron separate various eating areas, and terracotta tiles and wood cover the floors. The restaurant space is decorated with rustic ceramic platters, wooden rural tools like forks and pails, old-looking earthenware jars, wooden flour sieve, and bottles. The reference to the old country is recognizable also in poster size and smaller antique photographs of rural and urban scenes from the past of Italy, together with old-school portraits of people that are meant to pass for somebody's ancestors.

The warm and Mediterranean connotations are reinforced also in the lively colors of the plasticized menus (which, unlike Maggiano's, carry color pictures of the dishes), in terracotta or white dishes with lips in bright yellow and orange, and above all in the open kitchen with its visible brick oven to make pizzas. The wood fire looms large in the chain's marketing strategy. Its website's home page is dominated by a slideshow of dishes accompanied by the following text: "What's so special about the brick oven? Our signature brick oven has an intense heat that locks in freshness and enhances the natural flavors of everything from our pizza and pasta to our vegetables and seafood."[24] The importance of the presence of a brick oven in each restaurant in underlined also in the "about us" section of the website, which describes the brand of the chain:

> It's not just what happens inside the brick oven, it's what happens around it: the celebrations, the laughter, the energy. The wide-eyed wonder of looking at the dancing fire, the sweet anticipation of watching one of our brick oven chefs prepare your meal in our open kitchen, and of course, the tantalizing aroma. To us, our guests are like family, and we treat each one just the way we'd like to be treated—with open arms, warm smiles, and delicious food.[25]

Some elements emerge as particularly relevant in the marketing strategy of the company: the vitality and the celebratory nature of Italian culinary traditions, which express themselves through laughter and energy, and the emotional value of those traditions, based on close relations and the affectionate physicality that is often identified as typical of Italians and Italian Americans.

The brick oven is the star both on the website and in the restaurant printed menus, with a whole section dedicated to the oven-made items. Accordingly, pizza plays an important role in the Bertucci's brand. The menu offers three categories of pizza: brick oven classic ("our original pizzas, once flavorful rebels, are now beloved classics," each marked with the year in which it was introduced in the restaurant); Roman ("More toppings and more slices—perfect for sharing," with a choice among meatball, pepperoni and sausage, eggplant, mushroom, chicken, and veggie); and brick oven artisan pizza ("Try our creative combinations of fresh ingredients and taste why these are destined to be classics"). Rather than overplay the Italian identity card, it would seem that the first category underlines the pride in the restaurant's own past and its most popular items, which have become part of the brand image since it started creating new pizzas as far back as 1981 and that the. The second category includes more familiar (almost bland) Italian American pizza toppings, aiming to satisfy that segment of the clientele that is not interested in exploring new flavors, while the last category would seem to respond to the recent "foodie" trends in U.S. consumption culture, which include a preference for a wider variety of ingredients that are explicitly praised for their freshness and that are often relatively unusual.[26] Although arguably the least traditional in terms of stereotypical Italian American ingredients, the latter category highlights the connection to the customs of Italy, skilled labor, and artisanal specialties, all valuable elements in the contemporary American "foodie" discourse. At the same time, reminding the customers that these new pizzas might be destined to become classics, the restaurant locates itself firmly in the American history of creative and evolving traditions that might have been inspired by the Old World but that suffer from no sense of inferiority.

Confirming this overall approach, the menu offer Italian American mainstays from fettuccine Alfredo to spaghetti with meatballs and chicken parma; American items with an Italian twist such as Tuscan chicken wings (spicy wings with lemon and rosemary) and Caesar salad that offers the option of Italian cheese and anchovies; and dishes that claim a more direct connection with the culinary present of Italy, including focaccias, an *antipasto misto* of roasted vegetables, and tiramisu. Both the menu and the website avoid any stereotypical visual signifier of *Italianità*. For example, they do not employ a white, red, and green palette, but rather different tones of red (possibly a reference to the heat of the brick oven and to the warmth and passion that Italian food is supposed to provide). Unlike on the Maggiano's website, the food pictures are taken from above, allowing the customer to have a better sense of the ingredients and the composition of the item; also, when pictures are taken from a perspective closer to eye level, they tend to include the entirety of the dish. In Bertucci's case, effective communication is the priority, allowing the chain to juggle the restaurant's Italian theming, which ranges from easily identifiable elements to the more sophisticated traits of the "foodie" culture, its reliance on the values connected to it, such as warmth and hospitality, and its clear identity as a modern, entrepreneurial American business.

The reference to the Italian traditions gets more controversial in the case of Olive Garden, probably the largest, the most popular, and also the most visible among the three chains examined in this essay, due to its frequent TV marketing campaigns. The company, founded in 1982 and now boasting over 750 locations, is a subsidiary of the Orlando, Florida-based, Darden Restaurants, which is publicly traded on the New York Stock Exchange and a competitor to Brinker in the corporate restaurant business. The Olive Garden is one of six restaurant chains owned and operated by Darden, including Red Lobster, Capital Grille, Longhorn Steakhouse, Bahama Breeze, and Seasons 52, which together occupy more than 1,900 restaurants throughout the United States and Canada. The Olive Garden had total sales of $3.5 billion in 2011, up 5.2 percent from 2010. Darden's predicts a 7 percent revenue expansion for the Olive Garden through 2016, half of which is expected to come from new restaurants (including expansion for the first time in the Middle East), and the other half from same-store revenue increase.[27]

The motto of Olive Garden is "When you're here, you're family." This core brand value, based on its Italian theming, reverberates throughout the entire corporate communication. On the website, the motto appears on top of every page, next to the logo. Family values and solidarity are central also on the "My Olive Garden" webpage, which features various charities and solidarity activities in which the company is involved, such as "Pasta Tales," a national essay-writing contest for students in grades 1–12, and "Italian family reunions," special celebratory meals offered to families that may be going through hardships.[28] The company's motto provides the rationale for these initiatives: "Olive Garden was founded on the belief in the importance of family and the special experience families have when they gather around a table to share delicious food."[29] The constant reference to family values as reflected in Italian culinary traditions are also reinforced through the TV commercials. The promotion for Parmesan polenta chicken features a young boy who, asked to choose between two male members of his family, decides to show his affection to both by giving them the famed Olive Garden breadsticks. In one commercial we see mother and teenager son spending time together, while in another three generations of women ("just us girls") share a meal in an atmosphere of affection and happiness. The chain obviously aims at presenting itself as the antidote to the tensions that allegedly affect many modern families. The commercials are so heavy-handed that they have generated a great number of spoofs on TV and over the Internet.

A whole section of the company's website is dedicated to "Connections with Italy," which states that chain's chefs learn how to cook "authentic Italian foods" in the Olive Garden's Culinary Institute of Tuscany. "In a quaint 11th century Tuscan village, more than 1,200 of our chefs and managers have been inspired by the art of authentic Italian cuisine so that they can share their knowledge and passion with you."[30] The website offers videos of the chefs engaged in all sorts of food-related activity, from the visit to a market in Florence to wine education. However, doubts circulate about the school, adding to the debate about the alleged "authenticity" of the Olive Garden.[31] The actual existence of the learning institute is actually beside the point. What is relevant is that Olive Garden fully embraces Italian culinary heritage and the cultural practices that are built around it, while at the same time banking on the traits commonly attributed to the Italian American experience as perceived in the American context (good and abundant food, family, hospitality). However, the Italian American heritage is never fully acknowledged. Unlike Bertucci's, which proudly makes references to its own past as a business, Olive Garden prefers to float in a time without history, where Italian traditions appear unchangeable and are impervious to reality.

The same tension transpires from the menu. Some dish choices are inspired to food from contemporary Italy, including bruschetta, flatbreads, minestrone, and grilled sandwiches (correctly called panini). At the same time, the menu is also strongly rooted in the Italian American culinary repertoire, as suggested by dishes like ziti al forno, chicken parmigiana, and fettuccine Alfredo in the section called "Cucina Classica" (classic recipes). Many recipes appear to be the result of the company's own entrepreneurship. While incorporating a few elements of Italian cuisine, the lasagna fritta ("Parmesan-breaded lasagna pieces, fried and served over Alfredo sauce, topped with parmesan cheese and marinara sauce"), chicken and gnocchi ("a creamy soup made with roasted chicken, traditional Italian dumplings and spinach"), and steak gorgonzola-Alfredo ("Grilled beef medallions drizzled with balsamic glaze, served over fettuccine tossed with spinach and gorgonzola-Alfredo sauce") venture into new and unexplored directions.

The desire to assemble as many ingredients as possible in the same dish, with no preoccupation about calories and fat, seems to respond more to the logic of the fast food industry than to any Italian inspiration. The appeal of food served in huge quantities is also revealed by the specials that, it needs to be underlined, are not served family-style. At the time of the visit, Olive Garden had two special promotions in place: the Never Ending Pasta Bowl for $8.95 ("7 pastas. 6 sauces. 42 combinations to explore. Enjoy unlimited breadsticks and salad or soup with every combination. Add unlimited Meatballs, Italian Sausage or Roasted Chicken for just $2.95!"), and the new Half Panini Lunch for $6.95 ("with unlimited breadstick and soup OR salad"). In apparent contradiction, however, Olive Garden and Darden, together with other chains such as Red Lobster, pledged to implement improvements such as fewer calories, less sodium, and better children's menus during a public appearance of First Lady Michelle Obama on September 15, 2011.[32]

Conclusion

The analysis of the Italian-themed casual dining restaurant chains suggests that specific traits from Italian culture, and more specifically Italian American culture, are exploited to establish recognizable corporate brands of casual dining. To differentiate themselves from similar businesses, the marketing and communication for the three chains reinforces narratives built on objects, practices, and principles stereotypically perceived as Italian. Family values, traditions, shared meals as an expression of affection and commensality, as well as warmth and vitality, appreciated as nurturing and comforting, are commodified and made available to customers. Dining at an Italian-themed corporate restaurant suggests the possibility to access and partake of these very practices, and is proposed as an antidote to the anonymity and trivialization of food that corporate culture has contributed to create in the first place.

However, behind the apparently naturalized and hegemonic representations of Italian culture embraced by these chains, various forms of anxiety are lurking. At times, nostalgia seems to be rooted in references to the Old World and its culinary tradition, often expressed in the language of contemporary food appreciation that gives relevance to elements such as freshness, authenticity, and artisanal skills. Other forms of nostalgia appear to refer to the loss of aspects of the Italian American experience that appear exiled to the good old days of the past. However, the historical dynamics and the ongoing social and cultural negotiations that have shaped Italian Americans as both producers and consumers of food are largely ignored. Due to the visibility in popular culture of objectionable aspects of this very past, it is a sterilized and often bland version of *Italianità* that the corporate marketers favor and commercialize through their restaurants located all over the country, many in places where Italian Americans never even lived in substantial numbers.

Notes

Introduction. All Things Italian: Italian American Consumers, the Transnational Formation of Taste, and the Commodification of Difference SIMONE CINOTTO

1. Victoria De Grazia, *Irresistible Empire: America's Advance Through Twentieth-Century Europe* (Cambridge, Mass.: Harvard University Press, 2005); Mary Nolan, *The Transatlantic Century: Europe and America, 1890–2010* (New York: Cambridge University Press, 2012). See also Christopher Endy, *Cold War Holidays: American Tourism in France* (Chapel Hill: University of North Carolina Press, 2004); Penny Von Eschen, *Satchmo Blows Up the World: Jazz Ambassadors Play the Cold War* (Cambridge, Mass.: Harvard University Press, 2004); Robert W. Rydell and Rob Kroes, *Buffalo Bill in Bologna: The Americanization of the World, 1869–1922* (Chicago: University of Chicago Press, 2005).

2. Transnational constructions of domestic U.S. material culture and consumerism have prevalently been studied as part of late nineteenth-century nascent American imperialism: Kristin L. Hoganson, *Consumers' Imperium: The Global Production of American Domesticity, 1865–1920* (Chapel Hill: University of North Carolina Press, 2007); Mona Domosh, *American Commodities in an Age of Empire* (New York: Routledge, 2006). *British Geographers* 29, no. 4 (2004): 453–467. Post–World War II and post–Cold War examples have distinctly dealt with non-European transnational consumer cultures; see Purnima Mankekar, "'India Shopping': Indian Grocery Stores and Transnational Configurations of Belonging," *Ethnos* 67, no. 1 (2002): 75–97, and Inderpal Grewal, "Traveling Barbie: Indian Transnationality and New Consumer Subjects," *positions* 7, no. 3 (1999). The closest available perspective to this book's, Alexis McCrossen, ed., *Land of Necessity: Consumer Culture in the United States-Mexico Borderlands* (Durham, N.C.: Duke University Press, 2009), explores the historical formation of a transnational consumer culture in the liminal territories between the United States and Mexico.

3. Andrew Heinze, *Adapting to Abundance: Jewish Immigrants, Mass Consumption, and the Search for American Identity* (New York: Columbia University Press, 1990); Hasia R. Diner, *Hungering for America: Italian, Irish, and Jewish Foodways in the Age of Migration* (Cambridge, Mass.: Harvard University Press, 2001).

4. Virginia Yans-McLaughlin, *Family and Community: Italian Immigrants in Buffalo, 1880–1930* (Urbana: University of Illinois Press, 1982); Josef J. Barton, *Peasants and Strangers: Italians, Rumanians, and Slovaks in an American City, 1890–1950* (Cambridge, Mass.: Harvard University Press, 1975); John W. Briggs, *An Italian Passage: Immigrants to Three American Cities, 1890–1930* (New Haven: Yale University Press, 1978); Gary Mormino and George E. Pozzetta, *The Immigrant World of Ybor City: Italians and Their Latin Neighbors in Tampa, 1885–1985* (Gainesville: University Press of Florida, 1998); Donna Gabaccia and Fraser Ottanelli, eds., *Italian Workers of the World: Labor Migration and the Formation of Multiethnic States* (Urbana: University of Illinois Press, 2001); Donna Gabaccia and Franca Iacovetta, eds., *Women, Gender and Transnational Lives: Italians Workers of the World* (Toronto: University of Toronto Press, 2002); Samuel L. Baily, *Immigrants in the Lands of Promise: Italians in Buenos Aires and New York City, 1870 to 1914* (Ithaca, N.Y.: Cornell University Press, 1999); Philip Cannistraro and Gerald J. Meyer, eds., *The Lost World of Italian American Radicalism* (New York: Praeger, 2003); Jennifer Guglielmo, *Living the Revolution: Italian Women's Resistance and Radicalism in New York City, 1880–1945* (Chapel Hill: University of North Carolina Press, 2010); Marcella Bencivenni, *Italian Immigrant Radical Culture: The Idealism of the Sovversivi in the United States, 1890–1940* (New York: New York University Press, 2011).

5. For examples of the production of Italian American lesbian and gay identities via consumption, see the memoir by Annie Rachele Lanzillotto, *L Is for Lion: An Italian Bronx Butch Freedom Memoir* (Albany: State University of New York Press, 2013); the novels by Mary Cappello, *Night Bloom: An Italian-American Life* (Boston: Beacon Press, 1999) and Rachel Guido deVries, *Tender Warriors* (Ann Arbor, Mich.: Firebrand Books, 1996); and different essays in the collections by Denise Nico Leto, Giovanna Capone, and Tommi Avicolli Mecca, eds., *Hey Paesan: Writing by Lesbians and Gay Men of Italian Descent* (Oakland, Calif.: Three Guineas Press, 1999) and Louise DeSalvo and Edvige Giunta, eds. *The Milk of Almonds: Italian American Women Writers on Food and Culture* (New York: Feminist Press, 2002).

6. Mary Douglas and Baron Isherwood, *The World of Goods: Towards an Anthropology of Consumption* (New York: Routledge, 1996); Michel De Certeau, *The Practice of Everyday Life* (Berkeley: University of

California Press, 2002); Pierre Bourdieu, *Distinction: A Social Critique of the Judgment of Taste* (Cambridge, Mass.: Harvard University Press, 1987).

7. Arjun Appadurai, ed., *The Social Life of Things: Commodities in Cultural Perspective* (New York: Cambridge University Press, 1988).

8. Jennifer Guglielmo and Salvatore Salerno, eds., *Are Italians White? How Race Is Made in America* (New York: Routledge, 2003).

9. Matthew F. Jacobson, *Roots Too: White Ethnic Revival in Post–Civil Rights America* (Cambridge, Mass.: Harvard University Press, 2008).

10. Herbert J. Gans, "Symbolic Ethnicity: The Future of Ethnic Groups and Cultures in America," *Ethnic and Racial Studies* 2, no. 1 (January 1979): 1–20. Figures on the socioeconomic conditions of Italian Americans in support of Gans's thesis were provided by Richard Alba, *Italian Americans: Into the Twilight of Ethnicity* (Englewood Cliffs, N.J.: Prentice-Hall, 1985). A theoretical critique of the symbolic ethnicity paradigm is Yiorgos Anagnostou, "A Critique of Symbolic Ethnicity: The Ideology of Choice?" *Ethnicities* 9, no. 1 (2009): 94–122.

11. David Bell and Joanne Hollows, eds., *Historicizing Lifestyle: Mediating Taste, Consumption and Identity from the 1900s to 1970s* (London: Ashgate, 2006).

12. Maurice Halbwachs, *La classe ouvrière et les niveaux de vie* (Paris: Alcan, 1912). Halbwachs's concept of *genre de vie* is discussed in Victoria De Grazia and Ellen Furlough, eds., *The Sex of Things: Gender and Consumption in Historical Perspective* (Berkeley: University of California Press, 1996), 153.

13. Simone Cinotto, "'Sunday Dinner? You Had To Be There!' Food, Family, and Community among Italian Immigrants of New York," in *Italian Folk: Vernacular Culture in Italian-American Lives*, ed. Joseph Sciorra (New York: Fordham University Press, 2010), 11–44.

14. Scott Lash and John Urry, *Economies of Signs and Space* (Thousand Oaks, Calif.: Sage, 1994); Anthony Giddens, *Modernity and Self-Identity: Self and Society in the Late Modern Age* (Stanford; Calif.: Stanford University Press, 1991); Ulrich Beck, *Risk Society: Towards a New Modernity* (Thousand Oaks, Calif.: Sage, 1992).

15. Werner Sollors, ed., *The Invention of Ethnicity* (New York: Oxford University Press, 1991); Homi K. Bhabha, *The Location of Culture* (New York: Routledge, 1994).

16. Dick Hebdige, *Subculture: The Meaning of Style* (New York: Routledge, 1981); Arjun Appadurai, *Modernity at Large: Cultural Dimensions of Globalization* (Minneapolis: University of Minnesota Press, 1996).

17. Stuart Ewen, *All Consuming Images: The Politics of Style in Contemporary Culture* (New York: Basic Books, 1990).

18. William Boelhower, "Pushcart Economics: The Italians in New York," in *Public Space, Private Lives: Race, Gender, Class, and Citizenship in New York, 1890–1929*, ed. William Boelhower and Anna Scacchi (Amsterdam: VU University Press, 2004), 97–110; Pasquale Verdicchio, "Imaging America: The Photography of Lewis Hine and Jacob Riis," in ibid., 333–340; Joseph P. Cosco, *Imagining Italians: The Clash of Romance and Race in American Perceptions, 1880–1910* (Albany: State University of New York Press, 2003).

19. Jean-Christophe Agnew, "Coming Up for Air: Consumer Culture in Historical Perspective," in *Consumption and the World of Goods*, ed. John Brewer and Roy Porter (New York: Routledge, 1994), 27. On the development of a modern urban consumer culture in early twentieth-century United States, Jackson Lears, *Fables of Abundance: A Cultural History of Advertising in America* (New York: Basic Books, 1995); Roland Marchand, *Advertising the American Dream: Making Way for Modernity, 1920–1940* (Berkeley: University of California Press, 1986).

20. Michael La Sorte, *La Merica: Images of Italian Greenhorn Experience* (Philadelphia: Temple University Press, 1985), 147.

21. Charlotte Kimball, "An Outline of Amusements Among Italians in New York," *Charities* 5, no. 12 (August 1900): 1–8; Lillian W. Betts, "Italian Peasants in a New Law Tenement," *Harper's Bazaar* 38 (1904): 802–805; Lillian W. Betts, "The Italian in New York," *University Settlement Studies Quarterly* (October 1905–January 1906): 90–104; Louise C. Odencrantz, *Italian Women in Industry: A Study of Conditions in New York City* (New York: Russell Sage Foundation, 1919); Marjorie Roberts, "Italian Girls on American Soil," *Mental Hygiene* 13 (October 1929): 757–68; Eloise Griffith, "A Social Worker Looks at Italians," *Journal of Educational Sociology* 5 (1931): 172–177.

22. Elizabeth Ewen, *Immigrant Women in the Land of Dollars: Life and Culture on the Lower East Side, 1890–1925* (New York: Monthly Review Press, 1985); Kathy Peiss, *Cheap Amusements: Working Women and Leisure in Turn-of-the-Century New York* (Philadelphia: Temple University Press, 1986); Josephine Roche, "The Italian Girl," in *The Neglected Girl*, ed. Ruth Smiley True (New York: Survey Associates,

1914), 95–118; Dorothy Reed, *Leisure Time of Girls in a "Little Italy"* (New York: Columbia University Press, 1932).

23. Amerigo Ruggiero, *Italiani in America* (Milan: Fratelii Treves, 1937), 148.

24. Piero Bevilacqua, "Emigrazione transoceanica e mutamenti dell'alimentazione calabrese tra Ottocento e Novecento," *Quaderni Storici* 47, no. 2 (1981): 520–555.

25. Mike Featherstone, *Consumer Culture and Postmodernism* (Thousand Oaks, Calif.: Sage, 2007).

26. Robert Park and Herbert Miller, *Old World Traits Transplanted* (New York: Henry Holt, 1921), 147.

27. David Roediger, *Working Toward Whiteness: How America's Immigrants Became White* (New York: Basic Books, 2005), 188.

28. Gino Massullo, "L'economia delle rimesse," in *Storia dell'emigrazione italiana. Vol. 1. Partenze*, eds. Piero Bevilacqua, Andreina De Clementi, and Emilio Franzina (Rome: Donzelli, 2001), 161–183.

29. Donna Gabaccia, *From Sicily to Elizabeth Street: Housing and Social Change Among Italian Immigrants, 1880–1930* (Albany: State University of New York Press, 1984).

30. U.S. Bureau of the Census, *Fifteenth Census of the United States, 1930: Population. Special Report on Foreign Born White Families by Country of Birth of Head* (Washington, D.C.: Government Printing Office, 1933).

31. Lizabeth Cohen, "Embellishing a Life of Labor: An Interpretation of the Material Culture of American Working-Class Homes," *Journal of American Culture* 3, no. 4 (Winter 1980): 752–775; Jennifer Lucchino, "Deciphering Italian American Kitchen Design," in *A Tavola: Food, Tradition, and Community Among Italian Americans*, ed. Edvige Giunta and Sam Patti (New York: AIHA, 1998); Lara Pascali, "Two Stoves, Two Refrigerators, Due Cucine: The Italian Immigrant Home with Two Kitchens," *Gender, Place, and Culture* 13, no. 6 (2006): 685–695.

32. Lizabeth Cohen, *Making a New Deal: Industrial Workers in Chicago, 1919–1939* (New York: Cambridge University Press, 1990).

33. Cinotto, "Sunday Dinner."

34. Marie J. Concistré, "A Study of a Decade in the Life and Education of the Adult Immigrant Community in East Harlem," Ph.D. dissertation, New York University, 1943, 341.

35. Leonard Covello, *The Social Background of the Italo-American School Child: A Study of the Southern Italian Family Mores and Their Effect on the School Situation in Italy and America* (Totowa, N.J.: Rowman and Littlefield, 1972); Thomas Kessner, *The Golden Door: Italian and Jewish Immigrant Mobility in New York City, 1880–1915* (New York: Oxford University Press, 1977); Miriam Cohen, *Workshop to Office: Two Generations of Italian Women in New York City, 1900–1950* (Ithaca, N.Y.: Cornell University Press, 1993).

36. Robert A. Orsi, *The Madonna of 115th Street: Faith and Community in Italian Harlem, 1880–1950* (New Haven: Yale University Press, 1985).

37. Simone Cinotto, *The Italian American Table: Food, Family, and Community in New York City* (Urbana: University of Illinois Press, 2013), 72–101.

38. Benedict Anderson, *Imagined Communities: Reflections on the Origin and Spread of Nationalism* (London: Verso, 1991).

39. On earlier Italian immigrant spectatorship in the age of mass migration, see Giorgio Bertellini, "Shipwrecked Spectators: Italy's Immigrant at the Movies in New York, 1906–1916," *The Velvet Light Trap: A Critical Journal of Film and Television* 44 (Fall 1999): 39–53.

40. Maxine Seller, "The Education of the Immigrant Woman," *Journal of Urban History* 4, no. 3 (May 1978): 307–330; Alan Kraut, "The Mal'Occhio Versus Modern Medicine: The Challenge of Italian Health Traditions to Public Health in New York City a Century Ago, *Italian American Review* 6, no. 1 (Spring–Summer 1994): 56–79; Angela Danzi, *From Home to Hospital: Jewish and Italian American Women and Childbirth, 1920–1940* (Lanham, Md.: University Press of America, 1997).

41. Michel Foucault, *The History of Sexuality, Vol. 1: An Introduction* (New York: Vintage, 1990); Michel Foucault, *Discipline and Punish: The Birth of the Prison* (New York: Vintage, 1995).

42. Donna Gabaccia, "Inventing Little Italy," *Journal of the Gilded Age and Progressive Era* 6, no. 1 (2007): 7–41; Giorgio Bertellini, "Black Hands and White Hearts: Italian Immigrants as 'Urban Racial Types' in Early American Film Culture," *Urban History* 31, no. 3 (2004): 374–398; Mario Maffi, *Gateway to the Promised Land: Ethnic Cultures on New York's Lower East Side* (Amsterdam: Rodopi, 1994).

43. Mikhail Mikhailovich Bakhtin, *The Dialogical Imagination* (Austin: University of Texas Press, 1981 [1935]).

44. Theodore Dreiser, *The Color of a Great City* (New York: Boni and Liveright, 1923), 269–270. Emphasis mine.

45. Walter Benjamin, *Illuminations: Essays and Reflections*, ed. Hannah Arendt (New York: Schocken Books, 1968).

46. Featherstone, *Consumer Culture and Postmodernism*, 23; Norbert Elias, *The Civilizing Process: Sociogenetic and Psychogenetic Investigations* (Malden, Mass.: Blackwell, 2000 [1939]).

47. Matthew F. Jacobson, *Whiteness of a Different Color: European Immigrants and the Alchemy of Race* (Cambridge, Mass.: Harvard University Press, 1999); Angela M. Blake, *How New York Became American, 1890–1924* (Baltimore: Johns Hopkins University Press, 2006); Sabine Haenni, *The Immigrant Scene: Ethnic Amusements in New York, 1880–1920* (Minneapolis: University of Minnesota Press, 2008); Chad C. Heap, *Slumming: Sexual and Racial Encounters in American Nightlife, 1885–1940* (Chicago: University of Chicago Press, 2009); Miriam Hansen, "Pleasure, Ambivalence, Identification: Valentino and Female Spectatorship," *Cinema Journal* 25, no. 4 (Summer 1986): 6–32.

48. Caroline F. Ware, *Greenwich Village, 1920–1930: A Comment on American Civilization in the Post-War Years* (New York: Houghton-Mifflin, 1935); George Chauncey, *Gay New York: Gender, Urban Culture, and the Making of the Gay Male World, 1890–1940* (New York: Basic Books, 1995).

49. Fasanella's *Family Supper* (1972) is now on permanent display in the Great Hall at Ellis Island Immigration Museum. Pietro di Donato, *Christ in Concrete: A Novel* (New York: Bobbs-Merrill, 1939).

50. Cohen, *Making a New Deal*.

51. David A. J. Richards, *Italian American: The Racializing of an Ethnic Identity* (New York: New York University Press, 1999).

52. Meg Jacobs, *Pocketbook Politics: Economic Citizenship in Twentieth-Century America* (Princeton: Princeton University Press, 2007); Dana Frank, "Housewives, Socialists, and the Politics of Food: The 1917 New York Cost-of-Living Protests," *Feminist Studies* 11, no. 2 (Summer 1985): 355–385; Annelise Orleck, "'We Are That Mythical Thing Called the Public': Militant Housewives during the Great Depression," *Feminist Studies* 19, no. 1 (Spring 1993): 147–172; Sylvie Murray, *The Progressive Housewife: Community Activism in Suburban Queens, 1945–1965* (Philadelphia: University of Pennsylvania Press, 2003).

53. Simone Cinotto, "Italian Americans and Public Housing in New York, 1937–1941: Cultural Pluralism, Ethnic Maternalism and the Welfare State," in *Democracy and Social Rights in the Two Wests*, ed. Alice Kessler-Harris and Maurizio Vaudagna (Turin: Otto, 2009), 281–307.

54. Nathan Glazer and Daniel Moynihan, *Beyond the Melting Pot: The Negroes, Puerto Ricans, Jews, Italians and Irish of New York City* (Cambridge, Mass.: MIT Press, 1968), 17.

55. Jonathan Rieder, *Canarsie: The Jews and Italians of Brooklyn against Liberalism* (Cambridge, Mass.: Harvard University Press, 1985); Chris McNickle, *To Be Mayor of New York: Ethnic Politics in the City* (New York: Columbia University Press, 1993); Maria C. Lizzi, "'My Heart Is as Black as Yours': White Backlash, Racial Identity, and Italian American Stereotypes in New York City's 1969 Mayoral Campaign," *Journal of American Ethnic History* 27, no. 3 (Spring 2008): 43–80.

56. Gerald D. Suttles, *The Social Order of the Slum: Ethnicity and Territory in the Inner City* (Chicago: University Of Chicago Press, 1970), 17.

57. Herbert J. Gans, *The Urban Villagers: Group and Class in the Life of Italian-Americans* (New York: Free Press, 1962), 181–196.

58. Ibid., 194–195.

59. Eric Schneider, *Vampires, Dragons, and Egyptian Kings: Youth Gangs in Postwar New York* (Princeton: Princeton University Press, 2001), 78–105.

60. Thomas J. Ferraro, *Feeling Italian: The Art of Ethnicity in America* (New York: New York University Press, 2004).

61. Robert Warshow, "Film Chronicle: The Gangster as Tragic Hero," *Partisan Review* 15, no. 2 (1948): 243.

62. Giorgio Bertellini, "Duce/Divo: Masculinity, Racial Identity, and Politics among Italian Americans in 1920s New York City," *Journal of Urban History* 31, no. 5 (2005): 685–726.

63. Warshow, "The Gangster as Tragic Hero," 244.

64. Donald Yu, "How Tiger Woods Lost His Stripes: Post-Nationalist American Studies as a History of Race, Migration, and the Commodification of Culture," in *Post-Nationalist American Studies*, ed. John Carlos Rowe (Berkeley: University of California Press, 2000), 223–248.

65. Stephen Gundle, "Sophia Loren, Italian Icon," *Historical Journal of Film, Radio and Television* 15, no. 3 (August 1995): 380.

66. Francesca Canadé Sautman, "Women of the Shadows: Italian American Women, Ethnicity, and Racism in American Cinema," *Differentia* 6–7 (1994): 219–246.

67. George Lipsitz, *Time Passages: Collective Memory and American Popular Culture* (Minneapolis: University of Minnesota Press, 2001); Stephanie Coontz, *The Way We Never Were: American Families and the Nostalgia Trap* (New York: Basic Books, 2000).

68. Jacobson, *Roots Too*, 96–108.

69. Bourdieu, *Distinction*.

70. Giddens, *Modernity and Self-Identity*.

71. Robert Viscusi, "The Situation," *I-Taly* (January 25, 2010), http://www.i-italy.org/12693/situation.

72. S. E. Cupp, "Italians, Blame the 'Guidos' on MTV's *Jersey Shore*—Not the Network," *Daily News* (December 30, 2009).

73. Lizabeth Cohen, *A Consumer's Republic: The Politics of Mass Consumption in Postwar America* (New York: Knopf, 2003); Gary Cross, *An All-Consuming Century: Why Commercialism Won in Modern America* (New York: Columbia University Press, 2000); David Harvey, *The Condition of Postmodernity: An Enquiry into the Origins of Cultural Change* (Cambridge, Mass.: Blackwell, 1990); Fredric Jameson, *Postmodernism, or the Cultural Logic of Late Capitalism* (Durham, N.C.: Duke University Press, 1991); Mark Gottdiener, *The Theming of America: Dreams, Visions, and Commercial Spaces* (Boulder, Colo.: Westview Press, 1997); Sharon Zukin, *Landscapes of Power: From Detroit to Disney World* (Berkeley: University of California Press, 1993).

74. Jeffrey Louis Decker, "Beyond White Ethnicity," *American Quarterly* 58, no. 4 (December 2006): 1239–1247.

75. Thomas Guglielmo, *Italians, Race, Color, and Power in Chicago, 1890–1945* (New York: Oxford University Press, 2004).

76. Marcus Lee Hansen, *The Problem of the Third Generation Immigrant* (Rock Island, Ill.: Augustana Historical Society, 1938).

77. Jefferson R. Cowie, *Stayin' Alive: The 1970s and the Last Days of the Working Class* (New York: New Press, 2012).

78. David Lowenthal, *The Past Is a Foreign Country* (Cambridge: Cambridge University Press, 1985).

79. George J. Sanchez, "Race, Nation, and Culture in Recent Immigration Studies," *Journal of American Ethnic History* 18, no. 4 (Summer 1999): 66–84.

80. Marilyn Halter, *Shopping for Identity: The Marketing of Ethnicity* (New York: Schocken Books, 2000).

81. Warren J. Belasco, "Ethnic Fast Foods: The Corporate Melting Pot," *Food and Foodways* 1, no. 2 (1987): 1–30.

82. Mary Waters, *Ethnic Options: Choosing Identities in America* (Berkeley: University of California Press, 1990).

83. Donald Tricarico, "The 'New' Italian American Ethnicity," *Journal of Ethnic Studies* 12, no. 3 (Fall 1984): 75–93.

84. Nick Gillespie, "The Census and The Sopranos: Adventures in a Post-Racial America," *Reason* (May 2001), http://reason.com/archives/2001/05/01/the-census-and-the-sopranos. On *The Sopranos* as representation of Italian American life, see Regina Barreca, ed., *A Sitdown with the Sopranos: Watching Italian American Culture on T.V.'s Most Talked About Series* (New York: Palgrave, 2002).

85. Tricarico, "The New Italian American Ethnicity."

86. See for example, "Religion of Lucky Pieces, Witches, and the Evil Eye," *World Outlook* (October 1917): 24–28.

87. Simone Cinotto, " 'Buy Italiano!' Italian American Food Importers and Ethnic Consumption in 1930s New York," in *Italian Americans: A Retrospective on the Twentieth Century*, ed. Paola Sensi-Isolani and Anthony Tamburri (New York: AIHA, 2001), 167–178.

88. Paul Gilroy, *The Black Atlantic: Modernity and Double-Consciousness* (Cambridge, Mass.: Harvard University Press, 1993).

89. Dario Gaggio, *In Gold We Trust: Social Capital and Economic Change in the Italian Jewelry Towns* (Princeton: Princeton University Press, 2007).

90. I borrow the definition from Inderpal Grewal, *Transnational America: Feminisms, Diasporas, Neoliberalisms* (Durham, N.C.: Duke University Press, 2005).

91. Simone Cinotto, "Consuming the European Other: Italian Cookbooks, The End of Labor, and the Transnational Formation of Taste in the United States," in *Beyond the Nation: Pushing the Boundaries of U.S. History from a Transatlantic Perspective*, ed. Ferdinando Fasce, Maurizio Vaudagna, and Raffaella Baritono (Turin: Otto, 2013).

92. Carlo Levi, *Christ Stopped at Eboli: The Story of a Year* (New York: Farrar, Straus and Co., 1947), 131.

93. Sean Nixon, "Exhibiting Masculinity," in *Representation: Cultural Representations and Signifying Practices*, ed. Stuart Hall (London: Sage, 1997), 291–336.

94. Harvey Levenstein, "The American Response to Italian Food, 1890–1930," *Food and Foodways* 1, no. 1 (1985): 1–30.

95. Jonathan Morris, "Making Italian Espresso, Making Espresso Italian," *Food and History* 8, no. 2 (2010): 155–183.

1. Visibly Fashionable: The Changing Role of Clothes in the Everyday Life of Italian American Immigrant Women   VITTORIA CATERINA CARATOZZOLO

1. Alain Corbin, *The Lure of the Sea: Discovery of the Seaside in Western World 1750–1840* (Berkeley: University of California Press, 1994), vii.

2. Ernesto De Martino, *Sud e Magia* (Milan: Feltrinelli, 2008).

3. Anne Hollander, *Sex and Suits* (New York: Kodansha International, 1994), 19.

4. Elizabeth Wilson, *Adorned in Dreams: Fashion and Modernity* (London: Virago Press, 1987), 2–3.

5. Simona Segre Reinach, *Un mondo di mode: Il vestire globalizzato* (Rome: Laterza, 2011).

6. Alex Balasescu, *Fashion Design and Orientalism*, http:/inhouse.lau.edu.lb/bima/papers/Alex_Balasescu .pdf, p. 4.

7. Georg Simmel, "Fashion," *American Journal of Sociology* 62, no. 6 (May 1957): 541–558.

8. Alberto Abruzzese "Essere moda: Appunti sui modi di affermarsi nel mondo ovvero sul mercato delle identità," in *Communifashion*, ed. Alberto Abruzzese and Nello Barile (Rome: Sossella, 2001), 7–8.

9. Valerie Steele, "Retro Fashion," *Artforum* (December 1990): 24.

10. Manuela Fraire, "No Frills, No-Body, Nobody," in *Accessorizing the Body: Habits of Being*, ed. Cristina Giorcelli and Paula Rabinowitz (Minneapolis: University of Minnesota Press, 2011), 8.

11. Ibid.

12. Andrea Temple and June F. Tyler, *Ellis Island*, http://www.americansall.com/PDFs/02-americans-all/ 12.9.pdf, p. 16.

13. Ibid.

14. Susan Sontag, *On Photography* (New York: Penguin Books, 1979), 63.

15. Nicolas Bourriaud, *The Radicant* (New York: Lukas & Sternberg, 2009).

16. Colin Campbell, *The Romantic Ethic and the Spirit of Modern Consumerism* (Oxford: Basil Blackwell, 1987).

17. Barbara A. Schreier, *Becoming American Women: Clothing and the Jewish Immigrant Experience, 1880–1920* (Chicago: Chicago Historical Society, 1994), 97.

18. Susan Sontag, "One Hundred Years of Italian Photography," in *Where the Stress Falls* (New York: Vintage, 2003), 220.

19. Marshall McLuhan, "Myth and Mass Media," in *Media Research: Technology, Art, Communication*, ed. Michel A. Moos (Amsterdam: G+B Arts International, 1997), 6.

20. Sontag, *On Photography*, 55.

21. William Boelhower, "Pushcart Economics: The Italians in New York," in *Public Space, Private Lives: Race, Gender, Class and Citizenship in New York, 1890–1929*, ed. William Boelhower and Anna Scacchi (Amsterdam: VU University Press, 2004), 101.

22. Roland Barthes, *Camera Lucida: Reflections on Photography* (New York: Hill and Wang, 1982), 57–58.

23. Edna Woolman Chase and Ilka Chase, *Always in Vogue* (London: Victor Gollancz Ltd., 1954), 42.

24. Miriam Cohen, *Workshop to Office: Two Generations of Italian Women in New York City 1900–1950* (Ithaca, N.Y.: Cornell University Press, 1993), 51–53. For a discussion on the social and political implications of these figures, see Nancy C. Carnevale, "Culture of Work: Italian Immigrant Women Homeworkers in the New York City Garment Industry 1890–1914," in *A Coat of Many Colors: Immigration, Globalization, and Reform in New York City's Garment Industry*, ed. Daniel Soyer (New York: Fordham University Press, 2005), 141–167.

25. Josephine Roche, "The Italian Girl," in *The Neglected Girl*, ed. Ruth S. True (New York: Survey Associates, 1914), 110.

26. Elizabeth Ewen, *Immigrant Women in the Land of Dollars: Life and Culture on The Lower East Side, 1890–1925* (New York: Monthly Review Press, 1985), 243.

27. Ibid., 15.

28. Michel de Certeau, *The Practice of Everyday Life* (Berkeley: University of California Press, 1984), xii.

29. Cohen, *Workshop to Office*, 69.

30. Kathy L. Peiss, *Cheap Amusements: Working Woman and Leisure in Turn-of-the-Century New York* (Philadelphia: Temple University Press, 1986), 64.

31. Roche, "The Italian Girl," 116–117.

32. Ibid., 106, 101–102, 118.

33. Louise C. Odencrantz, *Italian Women in Industry: A Study of Conditions in New York City* (New York: Russell Sage Foundation, 1919), 290, 41.

34. Siegfried Kracauer, *The Mass Ornament: Weimar Essays* (Cambridge, Mass.: Harvard University Press, 1995), 76–79.

35. Odencrantz, *Italian Women in Industry*, 266.

36. Ibid., 44.

37. Elizabeth Ewen, *Immigrant Women in the Land of Dollars*, 251.

38. Ibid., 247.

39. Chase and Chase, *Always in Vogue*, 42.

40. Elizabeth Ewen, *Immigrant Women in the Land of Dollars*, 246.

41. Carnevale, "Culture of Work," 141.

42. Ibid., 146.

43. Ibid., 161–162.

44. Jennifer Guglielmo, "Italian Women Proletarian Feminism in the New York City Garment Trades, 1890s–1940s," in *Women, Gender and Transnational Lives. Italian Workers of the World*, (Toronto: University of Toronto Press, 2002), 255.

45. Ibid., 255, 257.

46. Ibid., 255.

47. Ibid., 264.

48. Ibid.

49. Elizabeth Ewen, *Immigrant Women in the Land of Dollars*, 260.

50. Simmel, "Fashion," 548.

51. Roland Barthes, "Le dandysme et la mode," in *The Language of Fashion* (New York: Berg, 2006), 69.

52. Matilde Serao, "È stata vinta?" *Il Progresso Italo-Americano* (February 12, 1911).

53. Helen Barolini, *Umbertina* (New York: Feminist Press, 1999), 96.

54. Schreier, *Becoming American Women*, 5.

55. Roche, "The Italian Girl," 118.

56. Susan Porter Benson, "Living on the Margin," in *The Sex of Things: Gender and Consumption in Historical Perspective*, ed. Victoria de Grazia and Ellen Furlough (Berkeley: University of California Press, 1996), 214–215.

57. Ibid., 228.

58. Cohen, *Workshop to Office*, 71.

59. William Leach, *Land of Desire: Merchants, Power, and the Rise of a New American Culture* (New York: Vintage, 1993), 95.

60. Georg Simmel, "The Berlin Trade Exhibition," cited in Christoph Grunenberg, "Wonderland: Spectacles of Display from the Bon Marché to Prada," in *Shopping: A Century of Art and Consumer Culture*, ed. Christoph Grunenberg and Max Hollein (Ostfildern-Ruit, Germany: Hatje Cantz Publishers, 2002), 19.

61. Barolini, *Umbertina*, 135.

62. Joanne Entwistle, "Fashion and the Fleshy Body: Dress as Embodied Practice," *Fashion Theory* 4, no. 3 (2000): 337.

63. Richard Martin, "Introduction," *American Ingenuity: Sportswear 1930s–1970s* (New York: 1998), 17.

64. Charles McGovern, "Consumption and Citizenship," in *Getting and Spending: European and American Consumer Societies in the Twentieth Century*, ed. Susan Strasser, Charles McGovern, and Matthias Judt (New York: Cambridge University Press, 1998), 55.

2. Making Space for Domesticity: Household Goods in Working-Class Italian American Homes, 1900–1940 MADDALENA TIRABASSI

1. Maddalena Tirabassi, "The American Pie: L'americanizzazione degli immigrati e la nascita della società dei consumi," *Movimento Operaio e Socialista* 8, no. 2 (1985): 201–218.

2. Carla Bianco, *The Two Rosetos* (Bloomington: Indiana University Press, 1974), 143.

3. Joseph Sciorra, ed., *Italian Folk: Vernacular Culture in Italian-American Lives* (New York: Fordham University Press, 2010); Joseph Sciorra, "Miracles in a Land of Promise: Transmigratory Experiences and Italian American Ex-Votos," in *Graces Received: Painted and Metal Ex-Votos from Italy*, ed. Rosangela Briscese and Joseph Sciorra (New York: Calandra Italian American Institute, 2012); Jerome Krase, "Little Italies in New York City: A Semiotic Approach," *Italian American Review* 5, no. 1 (Spring 1996): 103–116; Donna Gabaccia, *From Sicily to Elisabeth Street: Housing and Social Change Among Italian Immigrants, 1880–1930* (Albany: State University of New York Press, 1984); Simone Cinotto, "All Things Italian: Italian American Consumers and the Commodification of Difference," *VIA: Voices in Italian Americana* 21, no. 1 (2010): 3–44.

4. Sciorra, *Italian Folk*, dustjacket.

5. Maddalena Tirabassi, ed., *Itinera: Paradigmi delle migrazioni italiane* (Turin: Edizioni della Fondazione Giovanni Agnelli, 2005).

6. Social reformers dedicated to the subject a vast literature, published and unpublished, which is impossible to list entirely. See Sophonisba Breckinridge, *New Homes for Old* (New York: Harper, 1921); Phyllis H. Williams, *South Italian Folkways in Europe and America: A Handbook for Social Workers, Visiting Nurses, School Teachers and Physicians* (New York: Russell & Russell, 1938); Margaret Hobbie, *Italian American Material Culture: A Directory of Collections, Sites, and Festivals in the United States and Canada* (New York: Greenwood Press, 1992).

7. Between 1880 and 1914, migrants from the southern regions of Italy were 3,273,299 (79.9 percent) out of a total of 4,097,700.

8. *Atti della Giunta per l'Inchiesta sulle condizioni della classe agraria: Vol. 13* (Rome: Forzani, 1885), 56–57; Maddalena Tirabassi, "Trends of Continuity and Signs of Change among Italian Immigrant Women," in *Le stelle e le strisce: Studi americani e militari in onore di Raimondo Luraghi*, ed. Valeria Gennaro Lerda (Milan: Bompiani, 1998), 287.

9. *Atti della Giunta per l'Inchiesta sulle condizioni della classe agraria: Vol. 7* (Rome: Forzani, 1883), 194.

10. *Atti della Giunta per l'Inchiesta sulle condizioni della classe agraria: Vol. 9* (Rome: Forzani, 1883), 63.

11. *Atti della Giunta per l'Inchiesta sulle condizioni della classe agraria: Vol. 12* (Rome: Forzani, 1884), 469–471.

12. Williams, *South Italian Folkways*, 42–44.

13. *Atti della Giunta per l'Inchiesta sulle condizioni della classe agraria*, 12:158–159.

14. Maddalena Tirabassi, "Bourgeois Men, Peasant Women: Rethinking Domestic Work and Morality in Italy," in *Women, Gender and Transnational Lives: Italian Workers of the World*, ed. Donna Gabaccia and Franca Iacovetta (Toronto: University of Toronto Press, 2002), 106–129.

15. In some areas outside around the northern town of Verona, one of the writers of the Inchiesta described houses made with cane walls covered with reeds and straw. Houses in the nearby mountains, he noted, were sturdier but dirtier. Indeed, all investigators for the Inchiesta Jacini emphasized how dirty rural homes were in Veneto, explaining that women's work in the fields left them with little time for housework. Again, such poor houses were not equipped nor designed for living, but to protect peasants from the hardships of weather and provide them with some space for sleeping. *Atti della Giunta per l'Inchiesta sulle condizioni della classe agraria: Vol. 5* (Rome: Forzani, 1882), 278–279; *Atti della Giunta per l'Inchiesta sulle condizioni della classe agraria: Vol. 4* (Rome: Forzani, 1882), 7.

16. Linda Reeder, "When Men Left Sutera: Sicilian Women and Mass Migration, 1880–1920," in Gabaccia and Iacovetta, *Women, Gender and Transnational Lives*, 45–75.

17. *Giunta Parlamentare d'inchiesta sulle condizioni dei contadini nelle province meridionali e nella Sicilia: Vol. 3* (Rome: Tip. Naz. G. Bertero, 1909–1910), 498–500; *Giunta Parlamentare d'inchiesta sulle condizioni dei contadini nelle province meridionali e nella Sicilia: Vol. 5*, 57.

18. *Giunta Parlamentare d'inchiesta sulle condizioni dei contadini nelle province meridionali e nella Sicilia*: Vol. 6, 832.

19. *Atti della Giunta per l'Inchiesta sulle condizioni della classe agraria:* Vol. 5, 504.

20. *Atti della Giunta per l'Inchiesta sulle condizioni della classe agraria: Vol. 2* (Rome: Forzani, 1881), 186–187.

21. The Museum of Italian Ethnography opened in Florence in 1907, but ethnography as a discipline developed only in the 1930s. Stefano Cavazza, "La folkloristica italiana e il fascismo: Il Comitato Nazionale per le Arti Popolari," *La Ricerca Folklorica* 15 (1987): 109–122; Michael E. Harkin, "Ethnohistory's Ethnohistory: Creating a Discipline from the Ground Up," *Social Science History* 34, no. 2 (Summer 2010): 113–128; Maddalena Tirabassi, "Amy Bernardy e il Primo congresso di etnografia," *Archivio Storico dell'Emigrazione Italiana* (2011): 18–24.

22. Luca De Risi, "L'etnografia italiana all'estero," *La Ricerca Folklorica* 39 (1999): 135. On exhibitions, see Emilio Franzina, "La tentazione del museo: Piccola storia di mostre ed esposizioni sull'emigrazione italiana negli ultimi cent'anni," *Archivio storico dell'emigrazione italiana* 1 (2005): 165–182; Patrizia Audenino, "La mostra degli italiani all'estero: prove di nazionalismo," *Storia in Lombardia* 28, no. 1 (2008): 211–224.

23. Amy A. Bernardy, "L'etnografia delle 'piccole italie,'" in *Atti del Primo Congresso di Etnografia italiana: Roma, 19–24 ottobre 1911*, ed. Società di Etnografia Italiana (Perugia: Unione tipografica cooperativa, 1912), 173–182; Amy A. Bernardy, *Passione italiana sotto i cieli stranieri* (Florence: Le Monnier, 1931).

24. Bernardy, "L'etnografia delle piccole italie," 174.

25. Charlotte Gower Chapman, *Milocca: A Sicilian Village* (Cambridge, Mass.: Schenkman, 1971), 35.

26. At the beginning of the 1900s, each immigrant was allowed a little over two hundred pounds of luggage. Casimiro Marro, *Manuale pratico dell'emigrante all'Argentina, Uruguay e Brasile* (Turin: S.G.S., 1889), 23–24.

27. B. Amore, *An Italian American Odyssey: Life Line/Filo della Vita: Through Ellis Island and Beyond*, (New York: Fordham University Press, 2007), 23–27, 185.

28. Judith Ann Trolander, *Settlement Houses and the Great Depression* (Detroit: Wayne State University Press, 1975), 121–133.

29. Gould, "The Housing Problem," 64.

30. Elizabeth Ewen, *Immigrant Women in the Land of Dollars: Life and Culture on the Lower East Side* (New York: Monthly Review Press, 1985), 148–161; Amy A. Bernardy, "L'emigrazione delle donne e dei fanciulli nella North Atlantic Division, Stati Uniti d'America," *Bollettino dell'emigrazione* 1 (1909): 1–139: Amy A. Bernardy, "L'emigrazione delle donne e dei fanciulli negli Stati del Centro e dell'Ovest della Confederazione Americana," *Bollettino dell'emigrazione* 1 (1911).

31. Bernardy, "L'emigrazione delle donne e dei fanciulli negli stati del Centro e dell'Ovest," 53, 64.

32. Mary Sherman, "Manufacturing Foods in the Tenements," *Charities and the Commons* 16 (1906): 669.

33. Bernardy, "L'emigrazione delle donne e dei fanciulli negli stati del Centro e dell'Ovest," 80–81.

34. Williams, *South Italian Folkways*, 45–46.

35. Bernardy, "L'emigrazione delle donne e dei fanciulli negli stati del Centro e dell'Ovest," 56.

36. Gabaccia, *From Sicily to Elizabeth Street*, 80–83.

37. Bernardy, "L'emigrazione delle donne e dei fanciulli negli stati del Centro e dell'Ovest," 57.

38. Gladys Spicer Fraser, "The Value and Technique of Foreign Handicraft Exhibits," box 13, folder 145, International Institute of Boston (hereafter IIB), Immigration History Research Center, University of Minnesota.

39. Bianco, *The Two Rosetos*, 22, 24.

40. Marc Fasanella, "The Utopian Vision of an Immigrant's Son: The Oil on Canvas Legacy of Ralph Fasanella," *Italian Americana* 27, no. 2 (Summer 2010): 125–136.

41. Lizabeth Cohen, "Embellishing a Life of Labor: An Interpretation of the Material Culture of American Working-Class Homes, 1885–1915," *Journal of American Culture* 3, no. 4 (Winter 1980): 752, 754.

42. Asa Briggs, *Victorian Things* (London: Penguin, 1988), 226–228.

43. Sarah Abigail Leavitt, *From Catherine Beecher to Martha Stewart: A Cultural History of Domestic Advice* (Chapel Hill, N.C.: Duke University Press, 2002), 114.

44. Lewis E. Palmer, "The Day's Work of a 'New Law' Tenement Inspector," *Charities and the Commons* 17 (1906–1907): 80–90.

45. Mabel Kittredge, *Housekeeping Notes: How to Furnish and Keep House in a Tenement Flat* (New York: Century, 1918), 93.

46. Ibid. See also Stuart Ewen and Elizabeth Ewen, *Channel of Desire: Mass Images and the Shaping of American Consciousness* (New York: McGraw-Hill, 1982), 37.

47. Leavitt, *From Catherine Beecher to Martha Stewart*, 94.

48. Cohen, "Embellishing a Life of Labor," 756.

49. Tirabassi, "The American Pie," 201.

50. Cohen, "Embellishing a Life of Labor," 761.

51. Ibid., 770.

52. Jean-Christophe Agnew, "Coming Up for Air: Consumer Culture in Historical Perspective," *Consumption and the World of Goods*, ed. John Brewer and Roy Porter (New York: Routledge, 1993), 27.

53. Maddalena Tirabassi, *Il Faro di Beacon Street: Social workers e immigrate negli Stati Uniti, 1910–1939* (Milan: Angeli, 1990).

54. Nationality workers were trained in immigration history and law, methods of teaching English as a second language, case-work methods applied to foreign communities, geography, history and politics of immigrant countries, and the cultural background of immigrants, including their material culture, moral codes, and family structure.

55. Tirabassi, *Il Faro di Beacon Street*; Bernardy, "L'emigrazione delle donne e dei fanciulli negli stati del Centro e dell'Ovest," 57.

56. Gianfausto Rosoli, "Religione e immigrazione negli USA: Riflessioni sulla storiografia," *Studi Emigrazione* 28, no. 103 (1991): 291–304; see also Robert A. Orsi, *The Madonna of 115th Street: Faith and Community in Italian Harlem* (New Haven: Yale University Press, 1985). Leonard Covello, *The Social Background of the Italian-American School Child: A Study of Southern Italian Family Mores and Their Effect on the School Situation in Italy and in America* (Leiden: E. J. Brill, 1967), 144.

57. *Atti della Giunta per l'Inchiesta sulle condizioni della classe agraria*, 10:511.

58. Bernardy, "L'emigrazione delle donne e dei fanciulli negli stati del Centro e dell'Ovest," 178.

59. Sciorra, "Miracles in a Land of Promise," 40.

60. Alice Sickels Lillaquist, "The Upper Levee Neighborhood" (M.A. thesis, University of Minnesota, 1938), 54–55.

61. Clara Corica Grillo, "On Study of Survivals of Customs of Italians and How They Conflict with Attitudes in America," Clara Corica Grillo Papers, 1928–1977, IIB.

62. Bianco, *The Two Rosetos*, 84–89.

63. Cohen, "Embellishing a Life of Labor," 761.

64. Fraser, "The Value and Technique of Foreign Handicraft Exhibits."

65. Sickels, "The Upper Levee Neighborhood," p. 108.

66. "Sezione emigrazione," in *Atti del Primo Congresso Nazionale delle Donne Italiane* (Rome: Stabilimento Tipografico della Società Editrice Laziale, 1912), 515–577.

67. George E. Pozzetta, "Immigrants and Craft Arts: Scuola d'Industrie Italiane," in *The Italian Immigrant Woman in North America*, ed. Betty Boyd Caroli, Robert F. Harney, and Lydio F. Tomasi (Toronto: AIHA, 1978), 141.

68. Sickels, "The Upper Levee Neighborhood."

69. "Report of the Italian Secretary, April, May June 1931," box 18, IIB.

70. Maddalena Tirabassi, "L'Italia piccola delle emigrate," in *L'Italia alla prova dell'Unità*, ed. Simonetta Soldani (Turin: Franco Angeli, 2011), 131–150.

71. Maddalena Tirabassi, *Italian Signs in America* (Turin: OAT, 2010), Video.

72. Maddalena Tirabassi, "Migrazioni e segni italiani nel mondo," *TAO* 4 (Turin: OAT, 2010): 30–33; Krase, "Little Italies in New York City"; Rem Koolhaas, *Delirious New York: A Retroactive Manifesto for Manhattan* (New York: Monacelli Press, 1994); James Monroe Hewlett, *The Nation's Metropolis* (New York: Brentano's, 1921). Regina Soria has evidenced the Italian contribution to U.S. artistic and architectural life, listing 350 immigrant painters, sculptors, stonecutters, plasterers, and carvers who actively "shaped" America. Regina Soria, *American Artists of Italian Heritage, 1776–1945: A Biographical Dictionary* (Rutherford, N.J.: Fairleigh Dickinson University Press, 1993).

73. Maureen Meister, *Architecture and the Arts and Crafts Movement in Boston: Harvard's H. Longfellow Warren* (Hanover, N.H.: University Press of New England, 2003), 2.

74. The Luna Park in Coney Island, opened in 1903, was inspired in the mind of its creator Frederick Thompson by Renaissance models, and included views of the Vesuvius, the fall of Pompei, the Canal Grande and Palazzo Ducale in Venice. Tony Judt noted that "in early-twentieth-century America, were carefully modeled on Rome: the dimensions of Penn Station in New York were calibrated to those of the Baths of Caracalla (AD 217), while the barrel vault ceiling in Washington's Union Station borrowed directly from the transept vaults in the Baths of Diocletian (AD 306)." Tony Judt, "The Glory of the Rails," *New York Times Review of Books* 57, no. 20 (December 23, 2010): 61.

75. Gloria Nardini, "Fare Bella Figura con Sprezzatura," in *Reconstructing Italians in Chicago: Thirty Authors in Search of Roots and Branches*, ed. Dominic Candeloro and Fred L. Gardaphé (Chicago: Italian Cultural Center at Casa Italia, 2011), 291; Lara Pascali, "Two Stoves, Two Refrigerators, Due Cucine: The Italian Immigrant Home with Two Kitchens," *Gender, Place and Culture* 13, no. 6 (2006): 685–695.

Notes to pages 71–73 267

3. In Italy Everyone Enjoys It—Why Not in America? Italian Americans and Consumption in Transnational Perspective During the Early Twentieth Century ELIZABETH ZANONI

1. This chapter is a reprint, with slight modifications, of my article "Returning Home in the Imaginary: Advertisements and Consumption in the Italian-American Press," in the special issue "Italian American History and Consumer Culture," ed. Simone Cinotto, of *VIA: Voices in Italian Americana* 21, no. 1 (Spring 2011): 45–61. I would like to thank Simone Cinotto and Donna Gabaccia for their helpful comments on multiple drafts of this essay.

2. Ad for Martini & Rossi, *Il Progresso Italo-Americano* (September 10, 1939): 4.

3. Arjun Appadurai, "Disjuncture and Difference in the Global Cultural Economy," in *Theorizing Diaspora: A Reader*, ed. Jana Evans Braziel and Anita Mannur (Malden, Mass.: Blackwell, 2003), 25–47.

4. David Gerber, *Authors of Their Lives: The Personal Correspondence of British Immigrants to North America in the Nineteenth Century* (New York: New York University Press, 2006); Bruce Elliott, David Gerber, and Suzanne Sinke, eds., *Letters Across Borders: The Epistolary Practices of International Migrants* (New York: Palgrave, 2006); Sonia Cancian, *Families, Lovers, and their Letters: Italian Postwar Migration to Canada* (Winnipeg: University of Manitoba Press, 2010); Yves Frenette, Marcel Martel, and John Willis, eds., *Envoyer et recevoir: Lettres et correspondances dans les diasporas francophones* (Québec: Presses de l'Université Laval, 2006).

5. Rudolph Vecoli, "The Italian Immigrant Press and the Construction of Social Reality, 1850–1920," in *Print Culture in a Diverse America*, ed. James P. Danky and Wayne A. Wiegand (Urbana: University of Illinois Press, 1998), 17–33. For an early study of the immigrant press, see Robert E. Park, *The Immigrant Press and Its Control* (New York: Harper & Brothers, 1922).

6. Robert Goldman, *Reading Ads Socially* (New York: Routledge, 1992); Jean Baudrillard, *The Consumer Society: Myths and Structures* (London: Sage, 1998); Grant McCracken, *Culture and Consumption: New Approaches to the Symbolic Character of Consumer Goods and Activities* (Bloomington: Indiana University Press, 1988). On the history of advertising in the United States, see especially Jackson Lears, *Fables of Abundance: A Cultural History of Advertising in America* (New York: Basic Books, 1995); Roland Marchand, *Advertising the American Dream: Making Way for Modernity, 1920–1940* (Berkeley: University of California Press, 1986).

7. Simone Cinotto, "All Things Italian: Italian American Consumers and the Commodification of Difference," *VIA: Voices in Italian Americana* 21, no. 1 (Spring 2011): 3–44.

8. Denise Brennan, *What's Love Got to Do with It? Transnational Desires and Sex Tourism in the Dominican Republic* (Durham, N.C.: Duke University Press, 2004), 18.

9. Nan Enstad, *Ladies of Labor, Girls of Adventure: Working Women, Popular Culture, and Labor Politics at the Turn of the Twentieth Century* (New York: Columbia University Press, 1999); Kathy Peiss, *Cheap Amusements: Working Women and Leisure in Turn-of-the-Century New York* (Philadelphia: Temple University Press, 1986); Elizabeth Ewen, *Immigrant Women in the Land of Dollars: Life and Culture on the Lower East Side* (New York: Monthly Review Press, 1985); Andrew R. Heinze, *Adapting to Abundance: Jewish Immigrants, Mass Consumption, and the Search for American Identity* (New York: Columbia University Press, 1990); George Sanchez, *Becoming Mexican American: Ethnicity, Culture, and Identity in Chicano Los Angeles, 1900–1945* (New York: Oxford University Press, 1993); Barbara Schreier, *Becoming American Women: Clothing and the Jewish American Experience, 1880–1920* (Chicago: Chicago Historical Society, 1995).

10. Simone Cinotto, *The Italian American Table: Food, Family, and Community in New York City* (Urbana: University of Illinois Press, 2013); Hasia Diner, *Hungering For America: Italian, Irish, and Jewish Foodways in the Age of Migration* (Cambridge, Mass.: Harvard University Press, 2001); Donna R. Gabaccia, *We Are What We Eat: Ethnic Food and the Making of Americans* (Cambridge, Mass.: Harvard University Press, 1998); Donna R. Gabaccia, "Ethnicity in the Business World: Italians in American Food Industries," *Italian American Review* 6, no. 2 (1997–98): 1–19; Simone Cinotto, "'Buy Italiano!': Italian American Food Importers and Ethnic Consumption in 1930s New York," in *Italian Americans: A Retrospective on the Twentieth Century*, ed. Paola Sensi-Isolani and Anthony Tamburri (New York: AIHA, 2001), 167–178.

11. Lizabeth Cohen, *Making a New Deal: Industrial Workers in Chicago, 1919–1939* (New York: Cambridge University Press, 1990); Meg Jacobs, *Pocketbook Politics: Economic Citizenship in Twentieth-Century America* (Princeton: Princeton University Press, 2005).

12. Donna R. Gabaccia, *Italy's Many Diasporas* (Seattle: University of Washington Press, 2000); Carl Levy, ed., *Italian Regionalism: History, Identity and Politics* (Oxford: Berg, 1996); Robert Lumley and Jonathan Morris, eds., *The New History of the Italian South: The Mezzogiorno Revisited* (Exeter: University of

Exeter Press, 1997); John E. Zucchi, "Paesani or Italiani? Local and National Loyalties in an Italian Immigrant Community," in *The Family and Community Life of Italian Americans*, ed. Richard Juliani (New York: Center for Migration Studies, 1983), 147–160.

13. Ad for Florio Marsala, *Il Progresso Italo-Americano* (October 20, 1935): 11. See also ad for Florio Marsala, *Il Progresso Italo-Americano* (November 19, 1939): 9.

14. Ad for Pastene, *Il Progresso Italo-Americano* (November 17, 1935), illustrated section. For other examples of export advertisements that included a regional emphasis, see the ad for G. P. Papadopoulos, *Il Progresso Italo-Americano* (January 10, 1915); ad for Buitoni, *Il Progresso Italo-Americano* (December 3, 1926); ad for Cirio, *Il Progresso Italo-Americano* (September 10, 1939): 4; ad for Medaglia D'Oro, *Il Progresso Italo-Americano* (September 3, 1939), illustrated section.

15. Ad for Pastene, *Il Progresso Italo-Americano* (November 17, 1935), illustrated section.

16. Publicity ad, *Il Progresso Italo-Americano* (October 31, 1926): 7-S.

17. Mark Choate, *Emigrant Nation: The Making of Italy Abroad* (Cambridge, Mass.: Harvard University Press, 2008); R. J. B. Bosworth, *Italy and the Wider World, 1860–1960* (London: Routledge, 1996). Italian economist and future president Luigi Einaudi was one of the first advocates for capitalizing commercially on Italian immigrants in the Americas. See Luigi Einaudi, *Un principe mercante: Studio sulla espansione coloniale italiana* (Turin: Fratelli Bocca Editori, 1900).

18. Choate, *Emigrant Nation*, 14. On Italian Chambers of Commerce abroad, see especially Giovanni Luigi Fontana and Emilio Franzina, eds., *Profili di Camera di Commercio Italiane all'estero* (Cantanzaro: Rubbettino Editore, 2001); Emilio Franzina, "Le comunità imprenditoriali italiane e le Camere di commercio all'estero (1870–1945)," in *Tra identità culturale e sviluppo di reti: Storia delle Camere di commercio italiane all'estero*, ed. Giulio Sapelli (Cantanzaro: Rubbettino Editore, 2000), 15–102.

19. Matteo Pretelli, "Italia e Stati Uniti: 'Diplomazia culturale' e relazioni commerciali dal fascismo al dopoguerra," *Italia Contemporanea* 241 (2005): 523–534; Stefano Luconi and Guido Tintori, *L'ombra lunga del fascio: Canali di propaganda fascista per gli italiani d'America* (Milan: M & B Publishing, 2004); Stefano Luconi, "Etnia e patriottismo nella pubblicità per gli italo-americani durante la Guerra d'Etiopia," *Italia Contemporanea* 241 (2005): 514–522; Cinotto, "Buy Italiano."

20. William E. Simeone, "Fascists and Folklorists in Italy," *Journal of American Folklore* 91, no. 359 (1978): 543–557; Piero Meldini, "L'emergere delle cucine regionali: L'Italia," in *Storia dell'alimentazione*, ed. Jean-Louis Flandrin and Massimo Montanari (Rome: Laterza, 1997), 658–664.

21. On antifascist activities of Italians in the United States, see Fraser M. Ottanelli, "'If Fascism Comes to America We Will Push It Back into the Ocean': Italian American Antifascism in the 1920s and 1930s," in *Italian Workers of the World: Labor Migrations and the Formation of Multiethnic States*, eds. Donna R. Gabaccia and Fraser M. Ottanelli (Urbana: University of Illinois Press, 2001), 178–195.

22. Philip V. Cannistraro, "The Duce and the Prominenti: Fascism and the Crisis of Italian American Leadership," *Altreitalie* (July–December 2005): 77–78; Philip V. Cannistraro, *Blackshirts in Little Italy: Italian Americans and Fascism, 1921–1929* (West Lafayette, Ind.: Bordighera Press, 1999); Stefano Luconi, *La "Diplomazia Parallela": Il regime fascista e la mobilitazione politica degli Italo-Americani* (Milan: Angeli, 2000); Stefano Luconi, "The Italian-Language Press, Italian American Voters, and Political Intermediation in Pennsylvania in the Interwar Years," *International Migration Review* 33, no. 4 (Winter 1999): 1031–1061; Matteo Pretelli, "Tra estremismo e moderazione: Il ruolo dei circoli fascisti italo-americani nella politica estera Italiana degli anni Trenta," *Studi Emigrazione* 40, no. 150 (2003): 315–323; Matteo Pretelli, "Culture or Propaganda? Fascism and Italian Culture in the United States," *Studi Emigrazione* 43, no. 161 (2006): 171–192.

23. See for example, ad for Cesare Conti, *Il Progresso Italo-Americano* (April 8, 1900): 4; ad for J. Personeni, *Il Progresso Italo-Americano* (June 29, 1900): 3; ad for Luigi Peirano, *Il Progresso Italo-Americano* (June 29, 1900): 4; ad for Meridional Cheese & Oil Co., *Il Progresso Italo-Americano* (October 7, 1905): 8.

24. Cinotto, *The Italian American Table*, 105–154; Gabaccia, *We Are What We Eat*, 149–174; Cinotto, "Buy Italiano."

25. See for example, ad for United States Macaroni Factory, *Il Progresso Italo-Americano* (January 13, 1900): 1; ads for Ernesto Petrucci, Luigi Peirano, and P. Gargiulo & Bro, *Il Progresso Italo-Americano* (August 23, 1900): 4; ads for Castruccio & Sons, and B. Piccardo, *Il Progresso Italo-Americano* (April 1, 1905): 6; ads for Sigari Tommaso Cassese, A. Cassese & Co, and Fabbrica di Sigari dei Fratelli Razzetti, *Il Progresso Italo-Americano* (April 1, 1905): 4; ad for Italian Cigar & Tobacco Co. Scanga Bros, New York, *Il Progresso Italo-Americano* (June 29, 1900): 3.

26. Cinotto, "Buy Italiano."

27. See, for example, ad for the Italo-American Cigars Tobacco Co., *Il Progresso Italo-Americano* (June 29, 1900): 3; ads for Ernesto Petrucci, Luigi Peirano and P. Gargiulo & Bros., *Il Progresso Italo-Americano* (August 23, 1900): 4; ad for the Italian Grocery Store, *Il Progresso Italo-Americano* (October 6, 1917): 3; ad for the Spinosa Wine Co., *Il Progresso Italo-Americano* (September 10, 1917): 2.

28. The Italian Chamber of Commerce San Francisco, *Hidden Treasures of San Francisco* (San Francisco: Italian Chamber of Commerce of San Francisco, 1927).

29. Ad for Elvea, Vitelli & Company, *Il Progresso Italo-Americano* (March 3, 1935): 3.

30. See for example Gary Gereffi and Miguel Korzeniewicz, *Commodity Chains and Global Capitalism* (Westport, Conn.: Greenwood Press, 1994); Gary Gereffi, John Humphrey, and Timothy Sturgeon, "The Governance of Global Value Chains," *Review of International Political Economy* (2005): 78–104. For a good review of the development of changing trends in commodity chain literature see Jennifer Bair, "Global Capitalism and Commodity Chains: Looking Back, Going Forward," *Competition and Change* 9, no. 2 (2005): 153–180.

31. A short list of innovative scholarship that explores how cultural dimensions and social relations influenced and continue to influence the operation of global markets and consumer identities would include, Michel Callon, ed., *The Laws of the Markets* (Oxford: Blackwell, 1998); Arjun Appadurai, "Global Ethnoscapes: Notes and Queries for a Transnational Anthropology," in *Recapturing Anthropology: Working in the Present*, ed. Richard Fox (Santa Fe: SAR Press, 1991), 191–210; Arjun Appadurai, *The Social Life of Things: Commodities in Cultural Perspectives* (Cambridge: Cambridge University Press, 1986); Daniel Miller, *Material Culture and Mass Consumption* (Oxford: Blackwell, 1987); Richard Wilk, ed., *Fast Food/Slow Food: The Cultural Economy of the Global Food System* (Lanham, Md.: Altamira Press, 2006); Rachel Schurman and William Munro, "Targeting Capital: A Cultural Economy Approach to Understanding the Efficacy of Two Anti-Genetic Engineering Movements," *American Journal of Sociology* 115, no. 1 (2009): 155–202.

32. Ad for Florio Marsala, *Il Progresso Italo-Americano* (November 21, 1937): 9.

33. Ad for L. Gandolfi & Co., Inc., *Il Progresso Italo-Americano* (December 5, 1926): 9.

34. Ad for Elvea, Vitelli & Company.

35. Donna R. Gabaccia and Fraser M. Ottanelli, eds., *Italian Workers of the World: Labor Migrations and the Formation of Multiethnic States* (Urbana: University of Illinois Press, 2001); Donna Gabaccia and Franca Iacovetta, eds., *Women, Gender, and Transnational Lives: Italian Workers of the World* (Toronto: University of Toronto Press, 2002). On the radical immigrant press in the United States, see Marcella Bencivenni, *Italian Immigrant Radical Culture: The Idealism of the Sovversivi in the United States, 1890–1940* (New York: New York University Press, 2011).

36. Ad for Motta Panettone, *Il Progresso Italo-Americano* (November 23, 1939): 7; ad for Motta Panettone, *Il Progresso Italo-Americano* (November 28, 1937): 8; ad for Motta Panettone, *Il Progresso Italo-Americano* (December 5, 1937): 4.

37. Victoria de Grazia, with Ellen Furlough, eds., *The Sex of Things: Gender and Consumption in Historical Perspective* (Berkeley: University of California Press, 1996); Leonore Davidoff and Catherine Hall, *Family Fortunes: Men and Women of the English Middle Class* (London: Longman, 1999); Erika D. Rappaport, *Shopping for Pleasure: Women in the Making of London's West End* (Princeton: Princeton University Press, 2000); Lisa Tiersten, *Marianne in the Market: Envisioning Consumer Society in Fin-de-Siècle France* (Berkeley: University of California Press, 2001).

38. Donna R. Gabaccia, "Women of the Mass Migrations: From Minority to Majority, 1820–1930," in *European Migrants: Global and Local Perspectives*, ed. Dirk Hoerder and Leslie Page Moch (Evanston, Ill.: Northwestern University Press, 1996), 90–111.

39. Steven Ruggles et al., *Integrated Public Use Microdata Series: Version 5.0 [Machine-readable database]* (Minneapolis: University of Minnesota, 2010).

40. Sarah J. Mahler and Patricia R. Pessar, "Gendered Geographies of Power: Analyzing Gender Across Transnational Spaces," *Identities* 7, no. 4 (2001): 442–459.

41. De Grazia, *The Sex of Things*; Susan Porter Benson, *Counter Cultures: Saleswomen, Managers, and Customers in American Department Stores, 1890–1940* (Urbana: University of Illinois Press, 1986); Peiss, *Cheap Amusements*; Enstad, *Ladies of Labor, Girls of Adventure*.

42. Ad for Bertolli, *L'Italia* (November 27, 1932).

43. Ad for Bertolli, *L'Italia* (August 14, 1932).

44. Ad for Caffe Pastene, *Il Progresso Italo-Americano* (November 17, 1935), illustrated section.

45. Linda Reeder, *Widows in White: Migration and the Transformation of Rural Italian Women, Sicily, 1880–1920* (Toronto: University of Toronto Press, 2003); Gabaccia, *Italy's Many Diasporas*, 94–99.

46. On gendered media images of food and domesticity intended for white, middle-class, female readers in the United States, see Jennifer Scanlon, *Inarticulate Longings: The Ladies' Home Journal, Gender, and the Promises of Consumer Culture* (New York: Routledge, 1995), 133–134; Jessamyn Newhaus, "Is Meatloaf for Men? Gender and Meatloaf Recipes, 1920–1960," in *Cooking Lessons: The Politics of Gender and Food*, ed. Sherrie A. Inness (Lanham, Md.: Rowman & Littlefield, 2001), 87–109; Amy Bentley, "Inventing Baby Food: Gerber and the Discourse of Infancy in the United States," in *Food Nations: Selling Taste in Consumer Societies*, ed. Warren Belasco and Philip Scranton (New York: London: Routledge, 2002), 92–112; Laura Shapiro, *Perfection Salad: Women and Cooking at the Turn of the Century* (New York: Farrar, Straus, and Giroux, 1986); Sherrie A. Inness, ed., *Kitchen Culture in America: Popular Representations of Food, Gender, and Race* (Philadelphia: University of Pennsylvania Press, 2001).

47. Ad for Florio, *Il Progresso Italo-Americano* (October 1, 1939): 5-S.

48. Ad for Locatelli, *Il Progresso Italo-Americano* (October 20, 1935): 10.

49. Ad for Bertolli, *L'Italia* (August 14, 1932).

50. Micaela di Leonardo, "The Female World of Cards and Holidays: Women, Families, and the Work of Kinship," *Signs* 12, no. 3 (Spring 1987): 450–453.

51. Luigi De Rosa, *Emigranti, capitali, banche 1896–1906* (Naples: Banco di Napoli, 1980); Francesco Balletta, *Il Banco di Napoli e le rimesse degli emigrati, 1914–1925* (Naples: Arte tipografica, 1972); Luigi Mittone, "Le rimesse degli emigrati fino al 1914," *Affari sociali internazionali* no. 4 (1984): 125–160; Gino Massullo, "Economia delle rimesse," *Storia dell'emigrazione italiana: Partenze*, eds. Piero Bevilacqua, Andreina De Clementi, and Emilio Franzina (Rome: Donzelli, 2001), 161–183.

52. Dino Cinel, *National Integration of Italian Return Migration, 1870–1929* (Cambridge: Cambridge University Press, 1991); Mark Wyman, *Round-Trip to America: The Immigrants Return to Europe, 1880–1930* (Ithaca, N.Y.: Cornell University Press, 1993); Betty Boyd Caroli, *Italian Repatriation from the United States, 1900–1914* (New York: Center for Migration Studies, 1973).

4. Sovereign Consumption: Italian Americans' Transnational Film Culture in 1920s New York City   GIORGIO BERTELLINI

I dedicate this essay to Donna Gabaccia, *maestra* of historical research and critical rigor, with admiration.

1. *Il Progresso Italo-Americano* (hereafter *PIA*) (August 22, 1923): 14.

2. Founded in 1921 as Compagnia Italiana dei cavi Telegrafici Sottomarini (Italcable), the company's initial plan was to lay underwater cables only between Italy and Argentina. After a second contract with the Italian government, signed by Mussolini on February 5, 1923, Italcable expanded its goal to include connections between Italy and North America. See Bruno Bottiglieri, *Italcable: un'impresa italiana nello sviluppo internazionale delle telecomunicazioni* (Milan: Angeli, 1995), 31–50.

3. *La "Italcable" ed i suoi cavi per le Americhe: nell'inaugurazione del cavo Anzio-Buenos Aires XII Ottobre 1925* (Milan: Modiano, 1925), 10.

4. Overlooking the Union Telegraph Co.'s actual ownership and management of the New York–Azores route, the advertisement promoted the entire Rome–New York segment as a single, Italian connection— *cavo italiano*—whose unprecedented realization required "Italians in America" to contribute "morally and financially."

5. On the political relevance of technologies of communication across the Atlantic, see Frederik Nebeker, *Dawn of the Electronic Age: Electrical Technologies in the Shaping of the Modern World, 1914 to 1945* (Hoboken, N.J.: Wiley Institute of Electrical and Electronics Engineers, 2009).

6. On Eduardo Migliaccio, "Farfariello," see Esther Romeyn, *Street Scenes: Staging the Self in Immigrant New York, 1880–1924* (Minneapolis: University of Minnesota Press, 2008), 101–122; and Giorgio Bertellini, *Italy in Early American Cinema: Race, Landscape and the Picturesque* (Bloomington: Indiana University Press, 2010), 265–268.

7. For a critique of past debates and the formulation of a possible alternative, see Bertellini, *Italy in Early American Cinema*, 238–244, and passim.

8. A more recent example of resilient conflation of race with color and problematic disengagement with whiteness studies is Alice Maurice, *The Cinema and Its Shadow: Race and Technology in Early Cinema* (Minneapolis: University of Minnesota Press, 2013). I sought to address the importance of whiteness studies in the study of early cinema in Bertellini, *Italy in Early American Cinema*, 164–204. As for the relevance of immigrants' own popular culture, American studies scholars have done a better job at that: Sabine Haenni's *The Immigrant Scene: Ethnic Amusements in New York, 1880–1920* (Minneapolis: University of Minnesota

Press, 2008), and Romeyn's *Street Scenes* have bridged linguistic and disciplinary territories by showing that the same ocean liners that transported hundreds of thousands of immigrants also brought to America a lively tradition of performers, plays, songs, and films.

9. On movie palaces, see Maggie Valentine, *The Show Starts on the Sidewalk: An Architectural History of the Movie Theatre* (New Haven, Conn.: Yale University Press, 1994).

10. The expression "temples of classness" is from Peter Stead, *Film and the Working Class: The Feature Film in British and American Society* (London: Routledge, 1989), 18. The other quotes are drawn from Jeffrey F. Klenotic, "'Four Hours of Hootin' and Hollerin'': Moviegoing and Everyday Life Outside the Movie Palace," in *Going to the Movies: Hollywood and the Social Experience of Cinema*, ed. Richard Maltby, Melvyn Stokes, and Robert C. Allen (Exeter: University of Exeter Press, 2007), 154.

11. Richard Butsch, *The Making of American Audiences: From Stage to Television, 1750–1990* (New York: Cambridge University Press, 2000), 162, 165.

12. See Jeffrey F. Klenotic, "Class Markers in the Mass Movie Audience: A Case Study in the Cultural Geography of Moviegoing, 1926–1932," *Communication Review* 2, no. 4 (1998): 461–495. On nonurban contexts, see Kathryn H. Fuller, *At the Picture Show: Small Town Audiences and the Creation of Movie Fan Culture* (Washington, D.C.: Smithsonian Institution Press, 1996).

13. Randolph Bourne, "Trans-National America," *Atlantic Monthly* 118 (July 1916): 86–97.

14. Max Watson, "Making Americans by Movies," *Photoplay* 19, no. 6 (May 1921): 42.

15. "The Melting Pot," *Photoplay* 14, no. 6 (November 1918): 21.

16. Horace M. Kallen, "Democracy vs. the Melting Pot," *The Nation* (February 25, 1915): 219; Bourne, "Trans-National America," 96.

17. "The Hollywood Boulevardier Chats," *Motion Picture Classic* 17, no. 6 (June 1923): 74.

18. See Caroline F. Ware, *Greenwich Village, 1920–1930: A Comment on American Civilization in the Postwar Years* (Berkeley: University of California Press, 1994 [1935]); and George Chauncey, *Gay New York: Gender, Urban Culture, and the Making of the Gay Male World, 1890–1940* (New York: Basic Books, 1995).

19. In *Santa Lucia Luntana* (1931), for instance, a group of immigrants seemingly behave according to a familiarly nostalgic notion of Neapolitanness, but their new understanding of what it means to return to Italy reveals instead a rearticulation of Italian identity according to such American ideals as work ethics and exertion toward success. Bertellini, "You Can Go Home Again (and Again): *Santa Lucia Luntana* (1931), the Film," in *Neapolitan Postcards: The Canzone Napoletana as Transnational Subject*, ed. Goffredo Plastino and Joseph Sciorra (Lanham, Md.: Scarecrow Press, forthcoming).

20. Established in the 1826 as the New York Theatre (but soon renamed Bowery Theatre), it was the theatrical center for New York's Lower East Side, catering to Irish, German, Jewish, Italian, and eventually Chinese immigrants. Beginning in 1879 it was also known as Thalia Theater. It burned down on June 5, 1929 and was never rebuilt. The Teatro Italiano was also known as Tony Pastor's New Fourteenth Street Theatre, from the name of the American stage impresario and theatre owner who was instrumental to the success of American vaudeville. The theatre closed in 1928.

21. *PIA* (November 27, 1920): 4; *PIA* (April 22, 1924): 5; *PIA* (March 12, 1921): 4; *PIA* (August 21, 1921): 4. Throughout this study I have adopted the following procedure to identify English-language translations of Italian film titles. If a film was distributed with an English title, I give it: for instance, *La caduta di Troia* (The Fall of Troy, Itala Film, 1912), unless the Italian and English titles coincide, as in the case of *Cabiria* (Itala Film, 1914). When no English title is available, either because the film was never distributed in the United States or the United Kingdom or because no English title is currently known, I have included a literal translation in square brackets: *Amore tragico* [Tragic Love, Cines, 1912]. All translations into English are mine.

22. Despite the poet's defeat under the combined pressure of the American and Italian governments to abandon his claims of annexing Fiume (or turn it into sovereign Italian territory within Yugoslavia), *Il Progresso* had appreciated D'Annunzio's actions including his decision to hand over the city and not escalate violent tensions. See "La voce del Paese rassegnato al sacrificio trova la via del cuore in D'Annunzio," *PIA* (December 8, 1920): 1. The paper kept covering him positively by giving space to adaptations of his theatrical work, his son's films, and even his 1925 meeting with Mussolini.

23. The original *Maciste* (1915) was still advertised in the early and mid-1920s. *PIA* (July 22, 1922): 4; *PIA* (November 7, 1925): 5. For a recent critical analysis of Maciste films, see Jacqueline Reich, "Slave to Fashion: Masculinity, Suits, and the Maciste Films of Italian Silent Cinema," in *Fashion in Film*, ed. Adrienne Munich (Bloomington: Indiana University Press, 2011), 236–259.

24. *PIA* (July 2, 1921): 4.

25. *PIA* (October 9, 1921): 16; *PIA* (October 14, 1921): 4.

26. "La cinematografia italiana: Conversando con Gabriellino d'Annunzio," *PIA* (October 9, 1921): 13.

27. Ibid. *La nave* was eventually distributed in the United States in 1924 and was exhibited, with its Italian title, at the Teatro Italiano on West Fourteenth Street and Sixth Avenue. *PIA* (June 22, 1924): 2.

28. *PIA* (September 7, 1924): 5; *PIA* (September 21, 1924): 4.

29. *PIA* (April 8, 1924): 5. Identical pleas had accompanied the reissue of *Dante's Inferno* (Milano Films, 1911). Cf. *PIA* (October 14, 1921): 4.

30. In 1921, *Assunta Spina* was at Acierno's Thalia Theatre, and in 1925 at the Fifth Avenue Theatre (Fifth Avenue and Fourth Street) in Brooklyn, while in June 1922 the Teatro Olympic was screening *Capitan Blanco* (1914). *PIA* (October 27, 1921): 4; *PIA* (September 28, 1925): 5; *PIA* (June 18, 1922): 4.

31. *PIA* (June 17, 1921): 4; *PIA* (August 16, 1921): 4.

32. "The artistic career of Enrico Caruso is as well-known as that of any great general of statesman," wrote James Gibbons Huneker in 1919. "He is a national figure. . . . He is a great artist and he is something rarer, a genuine man. The combination is unusual in the ranks of singers, musicians, and other modest folk." "Most Idolized Singer," *New York Times* (March 23, 1919).

33. "Le gravissime Condizioni di Enrico Caruso," *PIA* (February 17, 1921): 1.

34. Ibid.

35. "Su e giú per il Greater New York: Gli Italiani e Caruso," *PIA* (February 18, 1921): 3.

36. *PIA* (September 27, 1924): 5.

37. *PIA* (November 2, 1924): S-4.

38. "*Gli ultimi giorni di Pompei*: I miracoli della Cinematografia Italiana," *PIA* (December 13, 1925): S-1. The film was apparently screened in Italy only in 1926.

39. "Un ente per il cinematografo in Italia," *PIA* (October 8, 1926): 13.

40. "Arte ed Artisti: *Nerone* al Lyric Theatre," *PIA* (May 24, 1922): 4.

41. *PIA* (January 24, 1926): 5. On the film's production and reception history, see Kevin Brownlow, *The Parade's Gone By . . .* (New York: Bonanza Books, 1968), 386–414.

42. *PIA* (February 16, 1926): 11.

43. *PIA* (January 26, 1922): 5. The promotion was for a remake of *The Sign of the Rose* (1922). A few years later, *Il Progresso* commented that no other American stage or film actor deserved more gratitude from Italian immigrants. "Una nuova film di George Beban," *PIA* (November 22, 1925): 11. On Beban's career, see Giorgio Bertellini, "George Beban: Character of the Picturesque," in *Star Decades: The 1910s*, ed. Jennifer Bean (New Brunswick, N.J.: Rutgers University Press, 2011): 155–173.

44. "D. Fairbanks e M. Pickford festeggiati a Firenze," *PIA* (April 27, 1926): 2.

45. "Mussolini to Receive Fairbanks," *New York Times* (May 9, 1926).

46. "Film Stars See Mussolini," *New York Times* (May 11, 1926).

47. Returning from Rome, Arthur T. Kelly, vice president of United Artists Corp., reported that Mussolini remained happily impressed by the recent Douglas Fairbanks film, *The Black Pirate*. "Omaggi a Fairbanks," *PIA* (October 23, 1926): 11.

48. John P. Diggins, *Mussolini and Fascism: The View from America* (Princeton: Princeton University Press, 1972).

49. By including a translation of an article appeared in the *New York Sun*, *Il Progresso*, for instance, commented on the regime's cooptation of Luigi Pirandello ("*fascista riconosciuto*") and its use of theater ("*per diffondere le dottrine fasciste*"). "Mussolini adopera le arti," *PIA* (April 18, 1926): 2.

50. *PIA* (April 11, 1924): 1.

51. William Harrison "Jack" Dempsey held the World Heavyweight Championship from 1919 to 1926. He was known for his aggressive style and exceptional punching power. These quotations are from "Un entusiasta di Mussolini: Ciò che narra del Duce il celebre D.W. Griffith," *PIA* (May 10, 1924): 3.

52. For a broader discussion of Valentino and Mussolini in both Italy and America, see Giorgio Bertellini, "Duce/Divo: Masculinity, Racial Identity, and Politics among Italian Americans in 1920s New York City," *Journal of Urban History* 31, no. 5 (2005): 685–726.

53. On his trip to Europe, his wife, and their divorce, see "Greater New York: Rodolfo Valentino a Parigi," *PIA* (August 16, 1923): 2; "Il sorriso dello Sceicco," *PIA* (August 21, 1924): 6; "La moglie di Valentino a New York," *PIA* (August 19, 1925): 4; "Rodolfo Valentino divorzia? L'idolo del sesso gentile romperà la catena coniugale?" *PIA* (August 1, 1925): 3, 7.

54. "Rodolfo Valentino e la sua gara di bellezza," *PIA* (May 2, 1923): 5. One of the two judges was Howard Chandler Christy as a jury member of the "Fame and Fortune" beauty contest promoted by *Motion Picture Classic* magazine. Its 1921–22 edition had awarded its top recognition to Clara Bow.

55. On his new contract with First National Pictures and the end of his contractual obligations with Famous Players, see "Valentino riacquista la sua libertà artistica," *PIA* (July 20, 1923): 3. For a discussion of comparable Italian debates, see Bertellini, "The Atlantic Valentino: the 'Inimitable Lover' as Racialized and Gendered Italian," in *Intimacy and Italian Migration: Gender and Domestic Lives in a Mobile World*, ed. Loretta Baldassar and Donna Gabaccia (New York: Fordham University Press, 2011), 37–48.

56. "La nostra gara fra le singorine italiane degli Stati Uniti," *PIA* (April 17, 1924): 3.

57. "Chi è l'Italiano più popolare negli Stati Uniti," *PIA* (April 17, 1924): 3.

58. *PIA* (July 30, 1924): 10. Maidina Pictures (987 Eight Avenue at West Fifty-Third Street) boasted a special relation with Filoteo Alberini, founder of Cines. *PIA* (January 25, 1925): 8. Similar companies included Flying Arrow Pictures Inc. (1658 Broadway, between West Fifty-First Street and West Fifty-Second Street) and Sacania Film Inc. (174 Second Avenue at East Eleventh Street). *PIA* (January 1, 1926): 10.

59. "Il boicottaggio contro Rodolfo Valentino impedito dalla polizia," *PIA* (December 15, 1925): 2; "Il Fromboliere," *Il Popolo d'Italia* (January 30, 1926), reported in Silvio Alovisio and Giulia Carluccio, eds., *Intorno a Rodolfo Valentino: Materiali italiani, 1923–1933* (Turin: Kaplan, 2009), 107.

60. Several sources indicate that Valentino's letter was first published in the Italian American newspaper *Corriere d'America* (New York) on February 15, 1926, and reprinted in Italy in *L'Impero* (Rome) on March 12, 1926. Falbo's *Il Progresso* article, however, appeared months earlier, on the last day of 1925. See Alovisio and Carluccio, *Intorno a Rodolfo Valentino*, 108–109 (for a copy of the letter) and, for a discussion, see Emily W. Leider, *Dark Lover: The Life and Death of Rudolph Valentino* (New York: Farrar, Straus and Giroux, 2003), 352–353; Bertellini, "Duce/Divo," 688.

61. I. C. Falbo, "Valentino scrive," *PIA* (December 31, 1925): 1. The same argument was put forward in "Rendiamo giustizia a Rodolfo Valentino," *L'Italia—The Italian Daily News* (San Francisco) (April 11, 1926), now in Alovisio and Carluccio, *Intorno a Rodolfo Valentino*, 110–111.

62. Falbo, "Valentino scrive," 1.

63. Consider how distant Italy was to Italian film consumers in late 1950s Boston as described in Herbert J. Gans's *The Urban Villagers: Group and Class in the Life of Italian Americans* (New York: Free Press, 1982 [1962]), 181.

64. More research is needed on the distribution of Italian newsreels and fiction films in 1930s America. As of this writing, University of Michigan doctoral students Pierluigi Erbaggio and Roberto Vezzani, respectively, are at work on these topics.

5. Consuming *La Bella Figura*: Charles Atlas and American Masculinity, 1910–1940   DOMINIQUE PADURANO

1. My gratitude extends to many who helped with this essay: to Pauline Cowle and June Coffee for sending me written pieces; to Joe Merrette for speaking with me about his experiences as a DT student; to students in my 2011–12 AP U.S. History class for reading and commenting on a draft version of this piece; and to Simone Cinotto, who deftly edited it. All errors, of course, are my own. My statement here is basely on purely anecdotal evidence. Of the half-dozen men who had used *Dynamic Tension* that I interviewed, only one—the sole Italian American—knew of Atlas's Italian heritage. My father, Dominick Padurano, and uncle, Albert Albano, also both Italian American (but neither of whom had used *Dynamic Tension*), knew that Atlas was an Italian immigrant.

2. I will refer to my subject as "Angelo Siciliano" when the narrative focuses on the period before 1920 and "Charles Atlas" for the period after 1925; for the years in between I will refer to him by both names since he employed both. Interview with Charles Atlas Jr., December 1, 2005 (hereafter CAJR1).

3. On the topic of consumption in the making of ethnicity, see Marilyn Halter, *Shopping For Identity: The Marketing of Ethnicity* (New York: Schocken, 2000).

4. Giorgio Bertellini, "DUCE/DIVO: Masculinity, Racial Politics and Identity among Italian Americans in 1920s New York City," *Journal of Urban History* 31, no. 5 (July 2005): 685–726; Ernesto Chavez, "'Ramon Is Not One of These': Race, Class, and Sexuality in the Construction of Silent Actor Ramón Novarro's Star Image," *Journal of the History of Sexuality* 20, no. 3 (September 2011): 520–544.

5. George Chauncey discusses the exclusion of homosexuality from the public sphere in the 1930s in *Gay New York: Gender, Urban Culture, and the Making of the Gay Male World, 1890–1940* (New York: Basic Books, 1994), 331–354. "He-man," a term frequently invoked by Atlas's ads of the 1930s, entered the lexicon in the mid-1920s. *Oxford English Dictionary* (New York: Oxford University Press, 2009).

6. Virginia Yans-McLaughlin, *Family and Community: Italian Immigrants in Buffalo, 1880–1930* (Ithaca, N.Y.: Cornell University Press, 1977).

7. CAJR1. On Angelo's work in a leather factory, Maurice Zolotow, "You, Too, Can Be a New Man," *Saturday Evening Post* (February 7, 1942): 59, and CAJR1.

8. Angelo Siciliano (Chas. Atlas), "Building the Physique of a 'Greek God,' " *Physical Culture* (November 1921): 37.

9. Ibid., 37.

10. Ibid., 38–39.

11. While some version of this incident might have occurred, I doubt its authenticity as written, not only because Atlas contradicted this story twenty years later, citing a youthful brawl in Brooklyn as the catalyst for his adoption of strength training, but also because bodybuilders since at least Eugen Sandow, whom Atlas claimed to have idolized as a teen, had typically situated their conversion to physical culture within a gallery of Greco-Roman art. Zolotow, "You, Too, Can Be a New Man," 59; David L. Chapman, *Sandow the Magnificent: Eugen Sandow and the Beginnings of Bodybuilding* (Urbana, Ill.: University of Illinois Press, 2006), 5; G. Mercer Adam, ed., *Sandow on Physical Training* (New York: J. Selwin Tait & Sons, 1894), 24–25.

12. Jackson Lears, *Fables of Abundance: A Cultural History of Advertising in America* (New York: Basic Books, 1995). It is likely that referring to antiquity, as well as posing as ancient statuary, shielded early bodybuilders from claims of obscenity by such "vice fighters" as Anthony Comstock as their photographs were circulated through the mail.

13. Kathy Peiss, *Cheap Amusements: Working Women and Leisure in Turn-of-the-Century New York* (Philadelphia: Temple University Press, 1986). I have benefited from Sarah Chinn's analysis of bottom-up changes wrought by immigrant adolescents in *The Invention of Modern Adolescence: Children of Immigrants in Turn-of-the-Century America* (New Brunswick, N.J.: Rutgers University Press, 2008).

14. Gloria Nardini, *Che Bella Figura! The Power of Performance in an Italian Ladies' Club in Chicago* (Albany: State University of New York Press, 1999), 7, 9, 15.

15. Record Group 122, Docket 2542, Box 1778, NARA.

16. *Physical Culture* (British edition) (November 1914), front cover.

17. Zolotow, "You, Too, Can Be a New Man," 59; CAJR1; George Butler, Charles Gaines, and Charles P. Roman, *Yours In Perfect Manhood, Charles Atlas: The Most Effective Fitness Program Ever Devised* (New York: Simon & Schuster, 1982); Earle Liederman to Ottley Coulter, November 14, 1917, H. J. Lutcher Stark Center for Physical Culture and Sports at the University of Texas at Austin.

18. For the visual nature of one particularly powerful turn-of-the-century "cheap amusement," see Miriam Hansen, *Babel and Babylon: Spectatorship in American Silent Film* (Cambridge, Mass.: Harvard University Press, 1994). For the prevalence of images of people within the realm of early photographic arts, see Walter Benjamin, "The Work of Art in the Age of Its Technological Reproducibility," in *Walter Benjamin: Selected Writings, Volume 4: 1938–1940* (Cambridge, Mass.: Harvard University Press, 2003), 251–283; Freud quote from "Three Essays on the Theory of Sexuality," in *The Freud Reader*, ed. Peter Gay (New York: Norton, 1989), 251.

19. For the confluence of Italian immigrants and bohemian artists in Greenwich Village around the 1910s and 20s, see Chauncey, *Gay New York*, 227–270. Quote from Charles P. Roman, recollecting Atlas's words, in Butler, Gaines, and Roman, *Yours In Perfect Manhood*, 49; quotes from Whitney and list of works for which Atlas had posed in Robert Lewis Taylor, "I was Once a 97-Pound Weakling," *New Yorker* (January 3, 1942): 24. Other artists' quotes from artists' folder, Charles Atlas Collection, Smithsonian Institution, National Museum of American History (hereafter NMAH/CAC).

20. *Physical Culture* (July 1922): 22–23; *Physical Culture* (September 1922): 19. My connection of Atlas and Townsend during these years is based not only on the artist's reputation as a photographer of dancers and physical culturists, but also on the look of the Spear Bearer portrait and the fact that other portraits of Atlas during the 1920s bear Townsend's distinctive signature. However, the *Physical Culture* portrait published after Atlas's victory does not contain this visible signature, despite its resemblance to other Townsend works. For more on Townsend's oeuvre, David S. Shields, "Broadway Photographs: Art Photography and the American Stage, 1900–1930," http://rcc.psc.sc.edu, accessed February 8, 2012.

21. Jerry Cowle, "As I Did It," *Sports Illustrated* (June 11, 1979): 93; Photographs of Atlas and teenaged girls dancing and young children exercising outdoors, ca. 1925–29, Unprocessed boxes 9–11, NMAH/CAC; "Gardener and poultry man," *New York Times* (June 5, 1925): 34.

22. Box 1, Folder 8, Lesson 1; Folder 10, Lesson 1; Folder 12, Lesson 1; all NMAH/CAC.

23. "Atlas System of Health, Strength and Physique Building," Box 1, Folders 8, 12 and 24, NMAH/CAC; Earle Liederman, Leighton Collection, ca. 1925 and Antone Matysek, "Instructions in Muscle Control," 1920, Stark Center; Charles Atlas, Ltd., "Dynamic Tension," ca. 1931, Record Group 122, Docket 1951, Box 1317, NARA; WMAC [sic] radio transcript, May 15, 1936, Unprocessed boxes 9–11, NMAH/CAC.

24. State of New York Certificate and Record of Marriage, 1918, Number 684, Municipal Archives of the City of New York. For children's birthdates and son's nickname, see CAJR1 and "Modern Hercules and Adonis Says Sleep and Fresh Air Made Him the Handsomest Man," *New York Evening Telegram* (January 26, 1922): 18; 1920 U.S. Census, 1925 New York City and 1933 Brooklyn Telephone Directories; Simone Cinotto, "All Things Italian: Italian American Consumers and the Commodification of Difference," *VIA: Voices in Italian Americana* 21, no. 1 (2010): 9.

25. For Atlas in white- or ivory suits, see Siciliano, "Building the Physique of a Greek God": 36; "Coney's Mardi Gras Ends in Blaze of Glory," *Daily News* (September 21, 1936), and in press photos of the same event; Atlas and Boy Scout photographs, ca. 1936; "Atlas Giving Awards to Others" folder; and Atlas posing in front of an automobile, ca. 1936, all in in Unprocessed boxes 9–11, NMAH/CAC. Less than ten months after opening the Physical Culture Institute in midtown Manhattan a New York County bankruptcy judge ruled that Charles Atlas, Ltd. and its owner owed more than $2,000 to the Paige Detroit Company. "Business Records," *New York Times* (October 15, 1926): 40.

26. On Italian American men's love of cars, Cinotto, "All Things Italian."

27. In an interview on July 14, 2004, Roger P. Roman said that he believed that Atlas had donated a good deal of money after his wife's death and his own retirement to the Catholic Church. On Atlas's religious devotion, see "St. Bernadette Picnic Tomorrow at Ulmer Park," *Brooklyn Spectator* (July 31, 1936); Marian Leifsen, "Charles Atlas Legend Started in Bay Ridge," *Home Reporter and Sunset News* (n.d., 1971): 16; Leland Southerland, "Charles Atlas," *The Floridian* (n.d., 1972): 19–23.

28. On southern Italians' experience with food scarcity, Hasia R. Diner, *Hungering for America: Italian, Irish, and Jewish Foodways in the Age of Migration* (Cambridge, Mass.: Harvard University Press, 2001), 24–45.

29. "New Incorporations," *New York Times* (February 19, 1929): 54.

30. Mirra Komarovsky, *The Unemployed Man and His Family: The Effect of Unemployment Upon the Status of the Man in Fifty-Nine Families* (New York: Dryden Press, 1940), 27, 23, 132, 45, 47.

31. John Berger, *Ways of Seeing* (London: Penguin Books, 1972), 47, 54.

32. Italian futurist Filippo Marinetti, quoted in Benjamin, "The Work of Art."

33. Bertellini, "DUCE/DIVO." For Mussolini's gendered, embodied use of spectacle, Simonetta Falasca-Zamponi, *Fascist Spectacle: The Aesthetics of Power in Mussolini's Italy* (Berkeley: University of California Press, 2000) and Sergio Luzzatto, *The Body of Il Duce: Mussolini's Corpse and the Fortunes of Italy* (New York: Metropolitan Books, 2005). For the importance of impenetrability in the male fascist mindset, see Klaus Theweleit, *Male Fantasies: Volume 2, Male Bodies, Psychoanalyzing the White Terror* (Minneapolis: University of Minnesota Press, 1989). For a discussion of the distinction between the heroic and erotic male, especially as it pertains to classical art, see Kenneth R. Dutton, *The Perfectible Body: The Western Ideal of Male Physical Development* (New York: Continuum, 1995).

34. Roland Marchand, *Advertising the American Dream: Making Way for Modernity, 1920–1940* (Berkeley: University of California Press, 1986), 328.

35. Photographs of Charles Atlas, Jack Dempsey and others in front of WMCA microphone, 1936, Unprocessed boxes 9–11; WMAC (sic) radio transcript, May 15, 1936, Unprocessed boxes 9–11; "Baer Still Trains On and One and On for Battle with Lou Nova," Springfield, Mass. *Republican* (May 26, 1939), Box 4, Folder 13; "Atlas' Muscles Amaze Champion Joe Louis," Williamsport, Pa., *Grit* (September 4, 1938), Unprocessed boxes 9–11; Sam Leff, "Joe Jinks," Tulare, Calif. *Advance Register* (November 7, 1945), Box 4, Folder 20; all in NMAH/CAC.

36. In the October 1933 issue of *Physical Culture,* for instance, Atlas's is the only full-page advertisement for a fitness course. By May 1938, *Physical Culture* published only four ads for fitness products: editor Macfadden's own course; a one-third page ad for Tommy Loughran; a one-sixth page ad for Hercules Exercisers (all on back pages); and Atlas's own full-page ad on page three.

37. "Muscle Makers," *Time* (February 22, 1937): 75; "Muscle Business," *Fortune* (January 1938): 10. These figures must be taken with a grain of salt, though, since this later article cites the number of Atlas's clients over the same fifteen-year period as 350,000: William Allen, "Charles Atlas Sells $10,000,000 Self-Improvement By Mail," *Mail Order Journal* (1939), Charles Atlas, Ltd., Harrington Park, N.J. (hereafter CAL).

38. "Striking Likeness," Binghamton, N.Y., *Sun*, 27 January 1936, Unprocessed boxes 9–11, NMAH/CAC. An interesting detail corroborating the extent of Atlas's celebrity in 1936 is that the caption only instructed viewers, by including the indication "right," on how to find the president's photograph, not Atlas's.

39. "Finding as to the Facts and Conclusion," July 10, 1937, Record Group 122, Docket 2542, Box 1778, NARA; Joe Weider and Ben Weider, with Mike Steere, *Brothers of Iron: Building the Weider Empire* (New York: Sports Publishing, 2006).

40. Beautiful Baby Contest," Yorkville, N.Y., *Advance* (n.d., 1936); "Disappointed Mothers Mob Judges After Baby Parade at Coney Island," *Brooklyn Daily Eagle* (n.d., 1936); "Pony Stampede Fells 12 at Coney Babies' Parade," *New York Herald Tribune* (n.d., 1936), all at CAL. WMCA Broadcast transcript, "Most Healthy and Perfectly Developed Boy' Contest," Unprocessed boxes 9–11, NMAH/CAC. "Children Boost Fair to Record Week-Day Mark," *New York Herald Tribune* (July 4, 1940): 7; Milton Bracker, "Turnstiles at Fair Click Record Tune," *New York Times* (July 4, 1940): 13.

41. Lisa Jacobson, "Manly Boys and Enterprising Dreamers: Business Ideology and the Construction of the Boy Consumer, 1910–1930," *Enterprise and Society* 2 (June 2001): 225–258; Record Group 122, Docket 3308, Box 2496, 84–87, NARA.

42. Charles Atlas, Ltd., "The Insult That Made a Man Out of 'Mac,'" *Physical Culture* (August 1932): 11; R. B. to Charles Atlas, CAL. Business figures from Record Group 122, Docket 3308, Box 2496, 121, NARA.

43. List of magazines that Charles Atlas, Ltd. advertised in during 1931 from Record Group 122, Docket 1952, File 1952-3-2, 4, NARA.

44. Lears, *Fables of Abundance*; Nardini, *Che Bella Figura!* 19–20.

6. Radical Visions and Consumption: Culture and Leisure among the Early Twentieth-Century Italian American Left   MARCELLA BENCIVENNI

1. "Pic-Nic Libertario," *La Questione Sociale* (July 7, 1906): 3.

2. Maurice Halbwachs, *La classe ouvriere et les niveaux de vie* (Paris: Alcan, 1912).

3. See, for example, Tom Goyens, *Beer and Revolution: The German Anarchist Movement in New York City, 1880–1914* (Urbana: University of Illinois Press, 2007), 177–182; Hartmut Keil and John B. Jentz, eds., *Germans Workers in Chicago: A Documentary History of Working-Class Culture from 1850 to World War I* (Urbana: University of Illinois Press, 1998), 203–210; Bruce C. Nelson, *Beyond the Martyrs: A Social History of Chicago's Anarchists, 1870–1900* (New Brunswick, N.J.: Rutgers University Press, 1988), 137–139; and Roy Rosenzweig, *Eight Hours for What We Will: Workers and Leisure in an Industrial City, 1870–1920* (Cambridge: Cambridge University Press, 1983), 65–90.

4. See for example Stuart Ewen, *Captains of Consciousness: Advertising and the Social Roots of Consumer Culture* (New York: McGraw Hill, 1976); Richard Wightman Fox and T. J. Jackson Lears, eds., *The Culture of Consumption: Critical Essays in American History, 1880–1980* (New York: Pantheon Books, 1983); Daniel Bell, *The End of Ideology* (New York: Free Press, 1962); Andrew Heinze, *Adapting to Abundance: Jewish Immigrants, Mass Consumption, and the Search for American Identity* (New York: Columbia University Press, 1990); Herbert J. Gans, "Symbolic Ethnicity: The Future of Ethnic Groups and Cultures in America," *Ethnic and Racial Studies* 1, no. 1 (January 1979): 1–20; and for the Italian experience, Richard Alba, *Italian Americans: Into the Twilight of Ethnicity* (Englewood Cliffs, N.J.: Prentice Hall, 1985).

5. Rosanne Currarino, "The Politics of 'More': The Labor Question and the Idea of Economic Liberty in Industrial America," *Journal of American History* 93, no. 1 (June 2006): 19.

6. Lizabeth Cohen, *Making a New Deal: Industrial Workers in Chicago, 1919–1939* (Cambridge: Cambridge University Press, 1990; and "Encountering Mass Culture at the Grassroots: The Experience of Chicago Workers in the 1920s," *American Quarterly* 41, no. 1 (March 1989): 6–33; James R. Barrett, "Americanization from the Bottom Up: Immigration and the Remaking of the Working Class in the United States, 1880–1930," *Journal of American History* 79, no. 3 (December 1992): 996–1019.

7. Lizabeth Cohen, *A Consumers' Republic: The Politics of Mass Consumption in Postwar America* (New York: Vintage Books, 2003), 8.

8. See the pioneering work of Rudolph Vecoli: "The Italian Immigrants in the United States: Labor Movement from 1880 to 1929," in *Gli italiani fuori d'Italia*, ed. Bruno Bezza (Milan: Angeli, 1983), 257–306; "Italian American Workers, 1880–1920: Padrone Slaves or Primitive Rebels?" in *Perspectives in Italian Immigration and Ethnicity*, ed. Silvano M. Tomasi (New York: Center for Migration Studies, 1977), 25–49; "Primo Maggio: May Day Observances among Italian Immigrant Workers, 1890–1920," *Labor's Heritage* 7 (Spring 1996), 28–4; and "Free Country: The American Republic Viewed by the American Left, 1880–1920,"

in *In The Shadow of the Statues of Liberty*, ed. Marianne Debouzy (Urbana: University of Illinois Press, 1992), 35–56. Among the most recent monographs devoted to the study of Italian immigrant radicalism see: Donna Gabaccia, *Militants and Migrants: Rural Sicilians Become American Workers* (New Brunswick, N.J.: Rutgers University Press, 1988); Gerald Meyer, *Vito Marcantonio: Radical Politician, 1902–1954* (Albany: State University of New York, 1989); Elisabetta Vezzosi, *Il socialismo indifferente: Immigrati italiani e il partito socialista negli Stati Uniti* (Rome: Edizioni Lavoro, 1991); Michael Topp, *Those Without a Country: The Political Culture of Italian American Syndicalists* (Minneapolis: University of Minnesota Press, 2001); Donna Gabaccia and Fraser Ottanelli, eds., *Italian Workers of the World: Labor Migration and the Formation of Multiethnic States* (Urbana: University of Illinois Press, 2001); Donna Gabaccia and Franca Iacovetta, eds., *Women, Gender and Transnational Lives: Italian Workers of the World* (Toronto: University of Toronto Press, 2002); Philip V. Cannistraro and Gerald Meyer, eds., *The Lost World of Italian American Radicalism: Politics, Labor and Culture* (Westport, Conn.: Praeger, 2003); Nunzio Pernicone, *Carlo Tresca: Portrait of a Rebel* (New York: Palgrave, 2003); Jennifer Guglielmo, *Living the Revolution: Italian Women's Resistance and Radicalism in New York City, 1880–1945* (Chapel Hill: The University of North Carolina Press, 2010); and Marcella Bencivenni, *Italian Immigrant Radical Culture: The Idealism of the Sovversivi in the United States, 1890–1940* (New York: New York University Press, 2011).

9. "Ai compagni d'Italia," *L'Anarchico* (February 1, 1888). *L'Anarchico* was published monthly until June 1888.

10. For the early history of the Italian American radical movement see Mario De Ciampis, "Storia del Movimento socialista rivoluzionario italiano," *La Parola del Popolo* 9, no. 37 (December 1958–January 1959): 136–163.

11. See Dirk Hoerder, *The Immigrant Labor Press in America*, 3 vols. (New York: Greenwood Press, 1987).

12. On Ybor City, see Gary R. Mormino, "The Radical World of Ybor City"; on San Francisco, see Paola Sensi Isolani, "Italian Radicals and Union Activists in San Francisco," both in Cannistraro and Meyer, *The Lost World of Italian American Radicalism*; on Barre, see Mari Tomasi, "The Italian Story in Vermont," *Vermont History* 28, no. 1 (January 1960): 73–87; on Paterson, see George W. Carey, "The Vessel, the Deed, and the Idea: Anarchists in Paterson, 1895–1908," *Antipode* 10–11 (1979): 46–58; on New York, see Nunzio Pernicone, "Italian Immigrant Radicalism in New York," in *The Italians of New York*, ed. Philip Cannistraro (New York: New York Historical Society, 1999), 77–90.

13. For a historical interpretation of the May Events, see Louise Tilly, "I Fatti di Maggio: The Working Class of Milan and the Rebellion of 1898," in *Modern European Social History*, ed. R. J. Bezucha (Lexington, Mass.: D. C. Heath, 1972), 124–158.

14. Michael Topp, "The Italian American Left: Transnationalism and the Quest for Unity," in *The Immigrant Left in the United States*, ed. Paul Buhle and Dan Georgakas (Albany: State University of New York, 1996), 121.

15. Bencivenni, *Italian Immigrant Radical Culture*, 43–46.

16. "Riflessioni sull'umanitarismo' del capitalismo americano," *Alba Nuova* (September 22, 1923): 2.

17. Vincenzo Vacirca, "La fabbrica dei cittadini," *Il Solco* (July 1927): 22.

18. "La vergogna dell'America," *Il Proletario* (October 28, 1911): 1.

19. "A proposito del massacro del New Jersey," *Il Fuoco* (February 15, 1915): 1.

20. "Mario Rapisardi Literary Society," *Alba Nuova* (September 1921): 3.

21. "Ciò che non vive non arde," *Il Fuoco* (October 15, 1914): 1.

22. "Pel giornale quotidiano," *Il Proletario* (December 6, 1902): 1.

23. See "Alfabeto igienico del lavoratore," *Lotta di Classe* (June 30, 1916): 2.

24. The paper was published until 1919. See Hoerder, *The Immigrant Labor Press*, 3:97–98.

25. Paul Avrich, *Sacco and Vanzetti: The Anarchist Background* (Princeton: Princeton University Press, 1991), 56.

26. See in particular the anticlerical newspaper *L'Asino* (1892–1925) and Pernicone, *Carlo Tresca*, 45.

27. Cited in Pernicone, *Carlo Tresca*, 45.

28. Francisco Ferrer (1859–1909) was executed in 1909, but the idea of the Modern School had a lasting influence among anarchists and socialists in both Europe and the United States. See Emma Goldman, *Living My Life* (New York: Dover, 1970), 456–458, 475.

29. Bellalma Forzato-Spezia, *Per le nuove generazioni* (New York: Nicoletti Bros. Press, 1911), 12, 22, 27, 29. All translations from Italian are mine. For a discussion of Forzato-Spezia, see Marcella Bencivenni, "Les formes d'expression des immigrées italiennes d'extrême gauche aux États-Unis, 1890–1930," *Politique et*

administration du genre en migration, ed. Philippe Rygiel (Paris: Publibook, 2011), 189–208; and Bencivenni, *Immigrant Radical Culture*, 144–146.

30. Avrich, *Sacco and Vanzetti*, 55–56; Vecoli, "The Italian Immigrants in the United States Labor Movement," 277.

31. See Maria Grazia Rosada, *Le Universitá Popolari in Italia, 1900–1918* (Rome: Editori Riuniti, 1975).

32. Bartolomeo Vanzetti, *The Story of a Proletarian Life* (Boston: Sacco-Vanzetti Defense Committee, 1923).

33. Colette Hyman, *Staging Strikes: Workers' Theatre and the American Labor Movement* (Philadelphia: Temple University Press, 1997), 2. See also Robert Leach, *Revolutionary Theatre* (London: Routledge, 1994); and Malcolm Goldstein, *Political Stage* (Oxford: Oxford University Press, 1974).

34. "Teatro del Popolo," *Il Lavoro* (January 12, 1918): 4.

35. Vincenzo Vacirca, "Il Teatro del Popolo," *Il Lavoro* (January 19, 1918): 5.

36. "Il Teatro del Popolo: Prima rappresentazione," *Il Lavoro* (January 26, 1918): 6.

37. See for example Michele Agulhon, "La sociabilità come categoria storica," *Dimensioni e problemi della ricerca storica* no. 1 (1992); M. Ridolfi, *Il circolo virtuoso: Sociabilità democratiche, associazionismo e rappresentanza politica nell'Ottocento* (Florence: Centro Editoriale Toscano, 1990); *Movimento operaio e socialista*, Special Issue: "Proletari in osteria" no. 1 (1985); William Sewell, *Work and Revolution in France* (Cambridge: Cambridge University Press, 1980); and E. P. Thompson, *The Making of the English Working Class* (New York: Vintage, 1966).

38. Rosenzweig, *Eight Hours for What We Will*, 53.

39. Goyens, *Beer and Revolution*.

40. Franco Ramella, *Terra e telai: Sistema di parentela e manifattura nel biellese dell'800* (Turin: Einaudi, 1983); Renato Monteleone "Socialisti o 'ciucialiter'? Il PSI e il destino delle osterie tra socialità e alcolismo," *Movimento operaio e socialista* 1 (1985): 12. The translation from the Italian is mine.

41. *Il Proletario* (October 28, 1911): 2. For other examples of anarchist cafes see also Kenyon Zimmer's doctoral dissertation, "The Whole World is Our Country: Immigration and Anarchism in the United States, 1885–1940" (University of Pittsburgh, 2010), 154–155.

42. Cited in Paul Avrich, *Anarchist Voices: An Oral History of Anarchism in America* (Edinburgh: AK Press, 2005), 154.

43. Cited in Zimmer, "The Whole World Is Our Country," 156.

44. For a study of music among workers and immigrants see: Victor Greene, *A Singing Ambivalence: American Immigrants between Old World and New, 1830–1930* (Kent, Ohio: Kent State University Press, 2004); Ferdinando Fasce, "Singing in the Shop: Fabbrica, migranti e musica negli Stati Uniti della Grande guerra," in *L'oceano dei suoni: Migrazioni, musica e razze nella formazione delle società euroatlantiche*, ed. Pierangelo Castagneto (Turin: Otto, 2007), 121–144; Fasce, "Singing at Work: Italian Immigrants and Music during the Epoch of World War I," *Italian Americana* 27 (2009): 133–148.

45. Richard Brazier, "The Story of the I.W.W.'s Little Red Songbook," in *The Big Red Songbook*, ed. Archie Green, David Roediger, Franklin Rosemont, and Salvatore Salerno (Chicago: Charles H. Kerr, 2007), 375.

46. Avrich, *Anarchist Voices*, 155.

47. *Il Grido degli Oppressi* (November 30, 1894; September 29, 1894). See also *La Questione Sociale* (February 11, 1899; August 15, 1895).

48. Rosenzweig, *Eight Hours for What We Will*, 4.

49. Richard J. Oestreicher, *Solidarity and Fragmentation: Working People and Class Consciousness in Detroit, 1875–1900* (Urbana: University of Illinois Press, 1989).

50. Nelson, *Beyond the Martyrs*; Goyens, *Beer and Revolution*.

51. "Currarino, "The Politics of More": 18. See also Kathy Peiss, *Cheap Amusements: Working Women and Leisure in Turn-of-the-Century New York* (Philadelphia: Temple University Press, 1986); and Lawrence B. Glickman, *A Living Wage: American Workers and the Making of Consumer Society* (Ithaca, N.Y.: Cornell University Press, 1997).

52. Currarino, "The Politics of More," 17.

53. Lawrence Glickman, "Workers of the World, Consume: Ira Steward and the Origins of Labor Consumerism," *International Labor and Working-Class History* 52 (Fall 1997): 72–86.

54. Victoria De Grazia, with Ellen Furlough, eds., *The Sex of Things: Gender and Consumption in Historical Perspectives* (Berkeley: University of California Press, 1996), 153.

55. Avrich, *Anarchist Voices*, 180.

56. "To the American People," *La Questione Sociale* (November 17, 1900); *La Questione Sociale* (December 8, 1900; February 14, 1901).

57. Guglielmo, *Living the Revolution,* 172–173.

58. Cohen, Making a New Deal, 101–120.

59. Pernicone, "Italian Immigrant Radicalism in New York," 89.

60. Benedict Anderson, *Imagined Communities: Reflections on the Origin and Spread of Nationalism* (London: Verso, 1991).

7. Italian Americans, the New Deal State, and the Making of Citizen Consumers   STEFANO LUCONI

1. For case studies, see John M. Allswang, *A House for All Peoples: Ethnic Politics in Chicago, 1890–1936* (Lexington: University Press of Kentucky, 1971); Gerald H. Gamm, *The Making of New Deal Democrats: Voting Behavior and Realignment in Boston, 1920–1940* (Chicago: University of Chicago Press, 1989).

2. Richard J. Jensen, "The Cities Reelect Roosevelt: Ethnicity, Religion, and Class in 1940," *Ethnicity* 8 (1981): 189–195.

3. Stefano Luconi, "La partecipazione politica in America del Nord," in *Storia dell'emigrazione italiana: Arrivi,* ed. Piero Bevilacqua, Andreina De Clementi, and Emilio Franzina (Rome: Donzelli, 2002), 492–495.

4. Matteo Pretelli, *L'emigrazione italiana negli Stati Uniti* (Bologna: il Mulino, 2011), 76, 78, 120–21; Elizabeth Zanoni, "'Per Voi, Signore': Gendered Representations of Fashion, Food, and Fascism in *Il Progresso Italo-Americano* during the 1930s," *Journal of American Ethnic History* 31, no. 3 (Spring 2012): 33–71.

5. Elizabeth Ewen, *Immigrants in the Land of Dollars: Life and Culture on the Lower East Side, 1890–1925* (New York: Monthly Review Press, 1985).

6. Virginia Yans-McLaughlin, *Family and Community: Italian Immigrants in Buffalo, 1880–1930* (Ithaca, N.Y.: Cornell University Press, 1977), 129.

7. Joseph W. Sullivan, *Marxists, Militants & Macaroni: The I.W.W. in Providence's Little Italy* (Kingston: Rhode Island Labor History Society, 2000).

8. Gary R. Mormino and George E. Pozzetta, *The Immigrant World of Ybor City: Italians and Their Latin Neighbors in Tampa, 1885–1985* (Urbana: University of Illinois Press, 1987), 127.

9. Kevin Mumford, *Newark: A History of Race, Rights, and Riots in America* (New York: New York University Press, 2007), 27.

10. Martin Halpern, "Labor," in *A Companion to Franklin D. Roosevelt,* ed. William D. Pederson (Malden, Mass.: Wiley-Blackwell, 2011), 174–175; Lisa McGirr, "The Interwar Years," in *American History Now,* ed. Eric Foner and Lisa McGirr (Philadelphia: Temple University Press, 2011), 140–141.

11. David M. Kennedy, *Freedom from Fear: The American People in Depression and War, 1929–1945* (New York: Oxford University Press, 1999), 122–123; Lizabeth Cohen, "The New Deal State and the Making of Citizen Consumers," in *Getting and Spending: European and American Consumer Societies in the Twentieth Century,* ed. Susan Strasser, Charles McGovern, and Mathias Judt (New York: Cambridge University Press, 1998), 111–125.

12. Lizabeth Cohen, *A Consumer's Republic: The Politics of Mass Consumption in Postwar America* (New York: Random House, 2003), 18–31; Meg Jacobs, *Pocketbook Politics: Economic Citizenship in Twentieth-Century America* (Princeton: Princeton University Press, 2005), 93–175.

13. Alan Brinkley, *The End of Reform: New Deal Liberalism in Recession and War* (New York: Knopf, 1995), 70–72.

14. Kennedy, *Freedom from Fear,* 151–152.

15. "L''Industry' e il 'Bank Bill' ieri approvati," *Il Progresso Italo-Americano* (June 14, 1933): 1, 10.

16. Serafino Romualdi, "Il salario minimo che diventa massimo," *La Stampa Libera* (April 21, 1933): 4; Nix, "Passare all'offensiva," *La Stampa Libera* (April 25, 1933): 4.

17. Serafino Romualdi, "Nuove direttive al Dipartimento del lavoro," *La Stampa Libera* (April 27, 1933): 4.

18. "Il generale Johnson spiega il fine e la portata del 'Recovery Act,'" *La Stampa Libera* (June 27, 1933): 1.

19. "Fall Seasonal Upturn," *Il Messaggero* (October 1, 1936): 4.

20. "F. D. Roosevelt e il suo 'record,'" *Il Progresso Italo-Americano* (October 25, 1936): sect. 2, 1.

21. "... Per non morire ..." *Il Progresso Italo-Americano* (July 1, 1936): 5.

22. Raimondo Fazio, "Ricostruzione e controllo," *La Stampa Libera* (June 22, 1933): 4.

23. Romualdi, "Nuove direttive al Dipartimento del lavoro."

24. "La solita fraseologia," *La Stampa Libera* (April 21, 1933): 2.

25. Dominick Sorrenti, "Per la settimana di trenta ore," *La Stampa Libera* (April 11, 1933): 4.

26. Josephine DeCredico as quoted in Jessan Dunn DeCredico, "Josephine DeCredico," *Mirror* 3 (1977): 33.

27. Transcript of an interview with Antonetta Filippone by Michael Jenusonis, Providence, August n.d., 1994, p. 7, Subject Vertical File, "Outlet Company," Rhode Island Historical Society, Providence.

28. Katherine Marcello as quoted in Naida D. Weisberg, *Diamond Are Forever, but Rhinestones Are for Everyone: An Oral History of the Costume Jewelry Industry of Rhode Island* (Providence: Providence Jewelry Museum, 1999), 114.

29. "Il discorso del Dr. Caso alla stazione WOV," *Il Progresso Italo-Americano* (October 22, 1936): 2.

30. Jane Addams, *Forty Years at Hull-House: Vol. 2* (New York: Macmillan, 1935), 231–232; Thomas Kessner, *The Golden Door: Italian and Jewish Immigrant Mobility in New York City, 1880–1915* (New York: Oxford University Press, 1977), 151–152; Donna R. Gabaccia, *From Sicily to Elizabeth Street: Housing and Social Change among Italian Immigrants, 1880–1930* (Albany: State University of New York Press, 1984), 102; Yans-McLaughlin, *Family and Community*, 177.

31. Robert A. Orsi, *The Madonna of 115th Street: Faith and Community in Italian Harlem, 1880–1950* (New Haven, Conn.: Yale University Press, 1985), 42.

32. Ibid., 43; V. Aquino, "Mania di sequestri ipotecari in Canarsie," *La Stampa Libera* (July 19, 1933): 4.

33. As quoted in Salvatore J. LaGumina, *The Immigrants Speak: Italian Americans Tell Their Stories* (New York: Center for Migration Studies, 1979), 196.

34. As quoted in Jonathan Rieder, *Canarsie: The Jews and Italians in Brooklyn against Liberalism* (Cambridge, Mass.: Harvard University Press, 1985), 32.

35. Nina Pietrantonio, "Maria DiManna," *Mirror* 3 (1977): 4.

36. "Lorena Hickok to Harry Hopkins, Washington, D.C., August 6, 1933," Lorena Hickok Papers, Box 11, Folder "Aug. through Oct. 1933," Franklin D. Roosevelt Library, Hyde Park, N.Y.

37. John F. Bauman, "Public Housing in the Depression: Slum Reform in Philadelphia Neighborhoods in the 1930s," in *The Divided Metropolis: Social and Spatial Dimension of Philadelphia*, ed. William W. Cutler III and Howard Gillette Jr. (Westport, Conn.: Greenwood Press, 1980), 242.

38. For the Home Owners' Loan Corporation, see C. Lowell Harriss, *History and Policies of the Home Owners' Loan Corporation* (New York: National Bureau of Economic Research, 1951).

39. Amy E. Hillier, "Who Received Loans? Home Owners' Loan Corporation Lending and Discrimination in Philadelphia in the 1930s," *Journal of Planning History* 2 (2003): 13.

40. "Il vero trionfo di una nuova idea," *La Libera Parola* (July 4, 1936): 1; Beniamino Arena, "Lettere e adesioni pervenute alla divisione dem. italiana," *Il Progresso Italo-Americano* (October 9, 1936): 2.

41. Henry Sollo, "Per chi voteremo," *Il Progresso Italo-Americano* (October 30, 1936): 6.

42. "Ida Y. M. Antonelli to James Farley, Providence, September 7, 1936," Papers of the Women's Division of the Democratic National Committee, Box 145, Folder "Correspondence, Rhode Island, A–Z, 1935–1936," Roosevelt Library.

43. Thomas A. Guglielmo, *White on Arrival: Italians, Race, Color, and Power in Chicago* (New York: Oxford University Press, 2003), 148.

44. John Bodnar, Roger Simon, and Michael P. Weber, *Lives of Their Own: Blacks, Italians, and Poles in Pittsburgh, 1900–1960* (Urbana: University of Illinois Press, 1982), 256.

45. *The Public Papers and Addresses of Franklin D. Roosevelt, 1937: The Constitution Prevails* (New York: Macmillan, 1941), 1–6; *The Public Papers and Addresses of Franklin D. Roosevelt, 1944–45: Victory and the Threshold of Peace* (New York: Harper, 1950), 32–42.

46. Italo C. Falbo, "Avanti sulla stessa via," *Il Progresso Italo-Americano* (January 21, 1937): 6; "Il discorso del Presidente al Congresso degli S. U.," *La Tribuna Italiana d'America* (January 14, 1944): 1.

47. "Our Choice," *Unione* (November 1, 1940): 1.

48. "Molti democratici difendono il New Deal," *Gazzetta del Massachusetts* (October 7, 1944): 8; "Roosevelt e l'Italia," *Unione* (November 2, 1944): 6.

49. "Looking Ahead," *La Voce Coloniale* (October 28, 1944): 1.

50. Cohen, "The New Deal State," 125.

51. "Industria disonesta," *Italian Echo* (June 29, 1934): 1; "La nostra crociata," *Il Progresso Italo-Americano* (October 22, 1936): 5; "Contro i mistificatori del falso olio d'oliva," *Gazzetta del Massachusetts* (October 31, 1936): 3.

52. Simone Cinotto, *The Italian American Table: Food, Family, and Community in New York City* (Urbana: University of Illinois Press, 2013).

53. "Lionel E. Opie to Franklin D. Roosevelt, Pawtucket, R.I., December 10, 1932," Papers of the National Democratic Committee, Box 704, Folder "Rhode Island, After Election, N–P," Roosevelt Library.

54. "Il problema degli sfratti," *La Stampa Libera* (June 16, 1933): 4.

55. "La legge per salvare le abitazioni ipotecate e in pericolo di esproprio," *Gazzetta del Massachusetts* (June 24, 1933): 1, 8.

56. "Gli inquilini di Williamsburg contro il caro-fitto," *La Stampa Libera* (March 26, 1938): 4.

57. For the Wagner-Steagall Act, see Timothy L. McDonnell, *The Wagner Housing Act* (Chicago: Loyola University Press, 1957).

58. Norma Lasalle Daoust, "Housing the Poor: The Early Years of Public Housing in Providence," *Rhode Island History* 51 (1993): 24–25.

59. "Paraders Demand East Side Housing," *New York Times* (January 9, 1938): 25; "Harlem Reforms Urged," *New York Times* (January 23, 1938): 19; Mark Naison, *Communists in Harlem during the Depression* (Urbana: University of Illinois Press, 1983), 228, 271; Leonard Covello, "A High School and Its Immigrant Community: A Challenge and an Opportunity," *Journal of Educational Sociology* 9, no. 2 (February 1936): 345; "I residenti della East Harlem ad una grande adunata," *La Stampa Libera* (March 22, 1938): 3; Leonard Covello, *The Heart Is the Teacher* (New York: McGraw-Hill, 1958), 220; Robert Whitney Peebles, *Leonard Covello: A Study of an Immigrant's Contribution to New York City* (New York: Arno Press, 1978), 223–228; Michael C. Johanek and John L. Puckett, *Leonard Covello and the Making of Benjamin Franklin High School: Education as if Citizenship Mattered* (Philadelphia: Temple University Press, 2007), 184–86; Simone Cinotto, "A Place Called Home: Italian Americans and Public Housing in New York, 1937–1941," in *Small Towns, Big Cities: The Urban Experience of Italian Americans*, ed. Dennis Barone and Stefano Luconi (New York: Italian American Historical Association, 2010), 59–66.

60. "Due ragazzi feriti e altri tre gravemente ustionati in un incendio a Harlem," *Il Progresso Italo-Americano* (March 22, 1939): 3; "Child Death Toll in Fire Now 4," *New York Times* (March 22, 1939): 23.

61. Jennifer Guglielmo, *Living the Revolution: Italian Women's Resistance and Radicalism in New York City, 1880–1945* (Chapel Hill: University of North Carolina Press, 2010), 258–263; Cinotto, "A Place Called Home," 66–68. Both quotations are from "Harlem Parade for Better Housing, March 25, 1939," Leonard Covello Papers, Box 43, Folder 10, Balch Institute Collection, Historical Society of Pennsylvania, Philadelphia.

62. Landon R. Y. Storrs, *Civilizing Capitalism: The National Consumers' League, Women's Activism, and Labor Standards in the New Deal Era* (Chapel Hill: University of North Carolina Press, 2000).

63. Nicholas Dagen Bloom, *Public Housing That Worked: New York in the Twentieth Century* (Philadelphia: University of Pennsylvania Press, 2008), 100.

64. Cohen, *A Consumers' Republic*, 31–41. For the gendered social programs of the New Deal, see Suzanne Mettler, *Dividing Citizens: Gender and Federalism in New Deal Public Policy* (Ithaca, N.Y.: Cornell University Press, 1998).

65. Lizabeth Cohen, "Citizens and Consumers in the Century of Mass Consumption," in *Perspectives on Modern America: Making Sense of the Twentieth Century*, ed. Harvard Sitkoff (New York: Oxford University Press, 2001), 150.

66. Gerald Meyer, *Vito Marcantonio: Radical Politician, 1902–1954* (Albany: State University of New York Press, 1989), 70–72.

67. Vito Marcantonio, *I Vote My Conscience: Debates, Speeches and Writings of Vito Marcantonio*, ed. Annette T. Rubinstein (New York: Vito Marcantonio Memorial, 1956), 109.

68. Alan Shaffer, *Vito Marcantonio: Radical in Congress* (Syracuse, N.Y.: Syracuse University Press, 1966), 70.

69. "$7,690,390 Housing for East Harlem," *New York Times* (September 17, 1939): 9; "Per l'erezione de le case popolari in East Harlem," *Il Progresso Italo-Americano*, September 20, 1939, 5. For the failure in Providence, see Daoust, "Housing the Poor," 30.

70. "Housing Project in 1st Ave. Started," *New York Times* (March 3, 1940): 14; "Il Sindaco La Guardia rompe il terreno nell'East Harlem pei nuovi alloggi economici," *Il Progresso Italo-Americano* (March 3, 1940): 3.

71. "East River Houses Gets First Tenants," *New York Times* (April 2, 1941): 25.

72. Annelise Orleck, "'What Are That Mythical Thing Called the Public': Militant Housewives during the Great Depression," *Feminist Studies* 19 (1993): 158–159.

73. Maria Darri, "Il costo dei viveri," *Il Progresso Italo-Americano* (June 22, 1935): 6.

74. Libero Del Vecchio, "Le tariffe della luce elettrica," *Il Progresso Italo-Americano* (May 29, 1935): 6.

75. Guglielmo, *Living the Revolution*, 263.

76. Beth S. Wenger, *New York Jews and the Great Depression: Uncertain Promise* (Syracuse, N.Y.: Syracuse University Press, 1999), 125–126; Naison, *Communists in Harlem*, 149–150.

77. Lizabeth Cohen, *Making a New Deal: Industrial Workers in Chicago, 1919–1939* (New York: Cambridge University Press, 1990).

78. "Continua il programma alla radio della Camera di Commercio Italiana di New York per la difesa, la diffusione, il consumo dei prodotti italiani negli Stati Uniti," *La Rivista Commerciale Italo Americana* (November 16, 1935): 14–17; "Consumare prodotti italiani è un dovere patriottico," *Eco del Rhode Island* (January 24, 1936): 8; "I problemi e le possibilità del Commercio Italiano negli S.U.," *Il Progresso Italo-Americano* (May 24, 1936): 11, 14.

79. "Discorso del Dott. Pietro P. Carbonelli pronunziato alla stazione radio WOV," *Il Grido della Stirpe* (January 25, 1936): 1.

80. "La parola d'ordine per gl'Italiani nel mondo," *Gazzetta del Massachusetts* (May 30, 1936): 2.

81. Nadia Venturini, *Neri e italiani a Harlem: Gli anni Trenta e la guerra d'Etiopia* (Rome: Edizioni Lavoro, 1990), 137–138.

82. Mariangela Paradisi, "Il commercio estero e la struttura industriale," in *L'economia italiana nel periodo fascista,* ed. Pierluigi Ciocca and Gianni Toniolo (Bologna: il Mulino, 1976), 300; Renzo De Felice, *Mussolini, il Duce: Gli anni del consenso, 1929–1936* (Turin: Einaudi, 1974), 705.

83. Cohen, *Making a New Deal,* 108–109, 112–113, 116–120, 152–154, 235–238, 325; Michael E. Parrish, *Anxious Decades: America in Prosperity and Depression, 1920–1941* (New York: Norton, 1992), 74–78.

84. For a case study, see Stefano Luconi, "From the Construction of Ethnic Identity to Assimilation: Italian Americans and Consumerism in Providence, Rhode Island, 1900–1960," *VIA: Voices in Italian Americana* 21, no. 1 (2010): 62–81.

85. Francesco Macaluso, "La legittima difesa e solidarietà di razza," *La Rassegna Italiana* (September 1, 1938): 1; "Microbe Warfare," *Il Popolo Italiano* (September 25, 1938): 1.

86. Giuseppe Genovese, "Un passo falso degli ebrei," *Corriere Siciliano* (October 20, 1938): 8. For Genovese's Fascist connections, see Gaetano Salvemini, *Italian Fascist Activities in the United States,* ed. Philip V. Cannistraro (New York: Center for Migration Studies, 1977), 178–179.

87. "Boycott," *Fair Play* (September 15, 1938): 4.

88. "A. Ferrero to the Ministry of the Interior, New York City, September 6, 1938," Records of the Ministry of the Interior, Casellario Politico Centrale, Box 160, Folder 2113, Archivio Centrale dello Stato, Rome, Italy. For Antonini, see Guido Tintori, "Amministrazione Roosevelt e '*Labor* etnico': Un caso italiano: Luigi Antonini," Ph.D. dissertation, University of Milan, 2005.

89. George E. Pozzetta, "'My Children Are My Jewels': Italian American Generations during World War II," in *The Home-Front War: World War II and American Society,* eds. Kenneth Paul O' Brien and Lynn Hudson Parsons (Westport, Conn.: Greenwood Press, 1995), 73; Salvatore J. LaGumina, *The Humble and the Heroic: Wartime Italian Americans* (Youngstown, N.Y.: Cambria Press, 2006), 108–109.

90. Testimony of Angelo Gualdaroni as quoted in *Boundless Lives: Italian Americans of Western Pennsylvania,* ed. Mary Brignano (Pittsburgh: Historical Society of Western Pennsylvania, 1999), 81.

91. Bodnar, Simon, and Weber, *Lives of Their Own,* 256.

92. Testimony of Samuel R. Sciullo as quoted in *Boundless Lives,* 177.

93. Richard D. Alba, *Italian Americans: Into the Twilight of Ethnicity* (Englewood Cliffs, N.J.: Prentice Hall, 1985), 82.

94. Micaela di Leonardo, *The Varieties of Ethnic Experience: Kinship, Class, and Gender among California Italian Americans* (Ithaca, N.Y.: Cornell University Press, 1984), 239–240.

95. LaGumina, *The Humble and the Heroic,* 89–90.

96. As quoted in Stephen Puleo, *The Boston Italians: A Story of Pride, Perseverance, and Paesani, from the Years of the Great Immigration to the Present Day* (Boston: Beacon Press, 2007), 89–90.

97. Gary R. Mormino and George E. Pozzetta, "Ethnics at War: Italian Americans in California during World War II," in *The Way We Really Were: The Golden State in the Second Great War,* ed. Roger W. Lotchin (Urbana: University of Illinois Press, 2000), 156–157.

98. Salvatore J. LaGumina, *From Steerage to Suburb: Long Island Italians* (New York: Center for Migration Studies 1988), 201–202, 208–209; Gary R. Mormino and George E. Pozzetta, "Italian Americans and the 1940s," in *The Italians of New York: Five Centuries of Struggle and Achievement,* ed. Philip V. Cannistraro (New York: New York Historical Society and John D. Calandra Italian American Institute, 1999), 150–151; Joshua M. Zeit, *White Ethnic New York: Jews, Catholics, and the Shaping of Postwar Politics* (Chapel Hill: University of North Carolina Press, 2007), 15.

99. Frank J. Cavaioli, "Corona's Little Italy," in *Through the Looking Glass: Italian & Italian/American Images in the Media,* ed. Mary Jo Bona and Anthony Julian Tamburri (New York: American Italian Historical Association, 1996), 201.

100. Mormino and Pozzetta, *The Immigrant World of Ybor City,* 299–300.

101. Paul Pisicano as quoted in Studs Terkel, *"The Good War": An Oral History of World War II* (New York: Pantheon, 1984), 142.

102. Guglielmo, *Living the Revolution*, 263–264.

103. Guglielmo, *White on Arrival*, 146–171.

104. Schaffer, *Vito Marcantonio*, 196–97; Meyer, *Vito Marcantonio*, 164–167; Robert Orsi, "The Religious Boundaries of an Inbetween People: Street *Feste* and the Problem of the Dark-Skinned Other in Italian Harlem, 1920–1990," *American Quarterly* 44, no. 3 (1992): 328–329.

105. Samuel Lubell, *The Future of American Politics* (New York: Harper & Row, 1965), 216; Vincent Tortora, "Italian Americans Vote Republican," in *A Documentary History of the Italian Americans*, ed. Wayne Moquin and Charles Van Doren (New York: Praeger, 1974), 401–404.

8. Italian Americans, Consumerism, and the Cold War in Transnational

Perspective   DANIELLE BATTISTI

1. Wendy Wall, *Inventing the American Way: The Politics of Consensus from the New Deal to the Civil Rights Movement* (New York: Cambridge University Press, 2009); Lizabeth Cohen, *A Consumer's Republic: The Politics of Mass Consumption in Postwar America* (New York: Knopf, 2003).

2. John Diggins, *Mussolini and Fascism: The View from America* (Princeton: Princeton University Press, 1972).

3. "Immigration and Nationality Act of 1952," 66 Stat. 163, 8 U.S.C., 1101 (1952). While most scholars continue to view this legislation as exclusionary, it did provide for token immigration from countries with nonwhite populations that had previously been fully excluded from immigrating to the United States.

4. Wall, *Inventing the American Way*.

5. Victoria De Grazia, *Irresistible Empire: America's Advance through Twentieth Century Europe* (Cambridge, Mass.: Harvard University Press, 2005).

6. Elaine Tyler May, *Homeward Bound: American Families in the Cold War Era* (New York: Basic Books, 1999), 10–29; 143–162; Lizabeth Cohen, *A Consumer's Republic*.

7. For the white ethnic movement to the suburbs, see Cohen, *A Consumer's Republic*. For a case study of Italian American movement to the suburbs, see Salvatore LaGumina, *From Steerage to Suburbs: Long Island Italians* (New York: Center for Migration Studies, 1998). See also Richard Alba, *Italian Americans: Into the Twilight of Ethnicity* (Englewood Cliffs, N.J.: Prentice Hall, 1985). For a study of Italian Americans who resisted movement out of ethnic neighborhoods into the suburbs, see Jordan Stanger-Ross, *Staying Italian: Urban Change and Ethnic Life in Postwar Toronto and Philadelphia* (Chicago: University of Chicago Press, 2009).

8. James Edward Miller, *The United States and Italy, 1940–1950: The Politics of Diplomacy and Stabilization* (Chapel Hill: University of North Carolina Press, 1986); John Lamberton Harper, *America and the Reconstruction of Italy, 1945–1948* (New York: Cambridge University Press, 1986).

9. "National War Fund to Open Its Last Drive This Month," *New York Times* (August 4, 1945). For 1946 figures, see "Taylor Urges Self Rule for Italian People," *New York Herald Tribune* (January 2, 1947).

10. *Il Progresso Italo-Americano* (January 1946–December 1947).

11. "Analysis of Material Contributed to American Relief for Italy, Inc.," Juvenal Marchisio Collection, Center for Migration Studies, Staten Island, Box 6, Folder "Miscellaneous Documents"; "Notes of Meeting with Juvenal Marchisio, re: American Relief for Italy Inc.," George Quilici Collection, Immigration History Research Center, University of Minnesota, Box 1, Folder 17, "Antifascism, Italian American Victory Council, 1942–45."

12. Franca Iacovetta, *Gatekeepers: Reshaping Immigrant Lives in Cold War Canada* (Toronto: Between the Lines, 2006), 147–150.

13. Ibid.

14. For an overview of American foreign policy concerns during the early Cold War, see Walter LaFeber, *America, Russia, and the Cold War, 1945–2006* (New York: McGraw Hill, 2006), 1–80.

15. Miller, *The United States and Italy*, 154–271; Paul Ginsborg, *A History of Contemporary Italy: Society and Politics, 1943–1988* (New York: Palgrave, 2003), 72–120.

16. Ginsborg, *A History of Contemporary Italy*; Robert A. Ventresca, *From Fascism to Democracy: Culture and Politics in the Italian Election of 1948* (Toronto: University of Toronto Press, 2004).

17. Ventresca, *From Fascism to Democracy*, 61–99; Miller, *The United States and Italy*, 154–271.

18. There was a very small minority of active Italian American socialists and communists in the postwar United States that did not support the aims of the Letters to Italy Campaign. See *L'Unità Del Popolo* of New York City and *Il Popolo* of Philadelphia.

19. Wendy I. Wall, "America's 'Best Propagandists': Italian Americans and the 1948 'Letters to Italy' Campaign," in *Cold War Constructions: The Political Culture of United States Imperialism, 1945–1966*, ed. Christian G. Appy (Amherst: University of Massachusetts Press, 2000), 89–109.

20. Ibid., 101–104.

21. "Pleas to Italy Ask Vote Against Reds," *New York Times* (April 4, 1948).

22. Wall, "America's Best Propagandists," 101.

23. Ibid.

24. For an excellent discussion of how American remittances and returnees remade turn of the century rural Italian lifestyles, including altering land and home ownership, household consumption, diets, and education levels, see Linda Reeder, *Widows in White: Migration and the Transformation of Rural Women, Sicily, 1880–1928* (Toronto: University of Toronto Press, 2003). See also Mark Wyman, *Round-Trip to America: The Immigrants Return to Europe, 1880–1930* (Ithaca, N.Y.: Cornell University Press, 1996) and Dino Cinel, *The National Integration of Italian Return Migration* (New York: Cambridge University Press, 2002). Likewise, Italian cultural patterns influenced Italian American consumption as well. See Elizabeth Zanoni, " 'Per Voi, Signore': Gendered Representations of Fashion, Food, and Fascism in *Il Progresso Italo-Americano* during the 1930s," *Journal of American Ethnic History* 31, no. 3 (Spring 2012): 33–71.

25. Ventresca, *From Fascism to Democracy*, 240–241.

26. For arguments about the role of American tourism in shaping Cold War Europe, see Christopher Endy, *Cold War Holidays: American Tourism in France* (Chapel Hill: University of North Carolina Press, 2004).

27. For recent work examining postwar Italian immigrant correspondences with family members in Italy, see Sonia Cancian, *Families, Lovers, and Their Letters: Italian Postwar Migration to Canada* (Winnipeg: University of Manitoba Press, 2010).

28. For a general discussion of transatlantic consumption patterns, see Kristin Hoganson, *Consumers' Imperium: The Global Production of American Domesticity, 1865–1920* (Chapel Hill: University of North Carolina Press, 2007).

29. Robert Ventresca argues that aid from the United States and the Vatican's mobilization of anticommunist voters were far more influential than Italian American propaganda in determining the outcome of the 1948 elections. Ventresca, *From Fascism to Democracy*, 4–14, 240–241.

30. For a full discussion of this complex transformation, see De Grazia, *Irresistible Empire*, 337–457.

31. Wall, "America's Best Propagandists," 104–106.

32. "Uticans and Italy Vote," *Utica Observer Dispatch* (April 24, 1948).

33. Wall, "America's Best Propagandists," 105.

34. Marina Maccari Clayton, "Communists of the Stomach: Italian Migration and International Relations in the Cold War Era," *Studi Emigrazione* 41, no. 155 (2004): 327–336.

35. George Spatuzza, "An Appeal to All Americans of Italian Origin, November 1947," George Spatuzza Collection, Immigration History Research Center, Box 1, Folder 1. The appeal was circulated among Order of the Sons of Italy in America chapters, the press, and was entered into the Congressional Record on November 20, 1947 by Wayland Brooks.

36. Wall, "America's Best Propagandists," 101.

37. "Italian Asks Help of U.S. Catholics," *New York Times* (March 22, 1948).

38. For changes in the postwar Italian economy and the growing culture of mass consumption in postwar Italy, see DeGrazia, *Irresistible Empire*, 336–457.

39. Wall, *Inventing the American Way*. See also Robert L. Fleegler, " 'Forget All Differences until the Forces of Freedom Are Triumphant': The World War II–Era Quest for Ethnic and Religious Tolerance," *Journal of American Ethnic History* 27, no. 2 (Winter 2008): 59–84; Kevin Schultz, *Tri-Faith America: How Catholics and Jews Held Postwar American to its Protestant Promise* (New York: Oxford University Press, 2011).

40. Wall, *Inventing the American Way*; Cohen, *A Consumer's Republic*.

41. May, *Homeward Bound*.

42. For the argument that Italians and others were considered "less desirable" but nonetheless white from an earlier date, see Thomas Guglielmo, *White on Arrival: Italians, Race, Color, and Power in Chicago, 1890–1945* (New York: Oxford University Press, 2003). For the argument that Eastern and Southern Europeans underwent a process of racialization and became increasingly white in the United States, see Matthew F. Jacobson, *Whiteness of a Different Color: European Immigrants and the Alchemy of Race* (Cambridge, Mass.: Harvard University Press, 1998) and David Roediger, *Working Toward Whiteness: How*

America's Immigrants Became White, the Strange Journey from Ellis Island to the Suburbs (New York: Basic Books, 2005). There is a general consensus that by World War II, Ellis Island immigrants had laid full claims to whiteness in the United States.

43. For the integration of white ethnic groups into American suburbs and the exclusion of African Americans, see Cohen, *A Consumer's Republic*; Thomas Sugrue, *The Origins of the Urban Crisis: Race and Inequality in Postwar Detroit* (Princeton: Princeton University Press, 2005). For Italian American suburbanization, see Alba, *Italian Americans*; LaGumina, *From Steerage to Suburbs*; Richard Alba, "Social Assimilation Among American Catholic National Origin Groups," *American Sociological Review* 41, no. 6 (December 1976): 1030–1046.

44. Mae Ngai, *Impossible Subjects: Illegal Aliens and the Making of Modern America* (Princeton: Princeton University Press, 2005), 227–264.

45. "ACIM Introductory Letter, April 1953," ACIM-National, Center for Migration Studies, Box A2, "Chapter Correspondence," Folder "Chicago Chapter."

46. Daniel Tichenor, *Dividing Lines: The Politics of Immigration Reform in America* (Princeton: Princeton University Press, 2002), 197–201.

47. For evidence of ACIM lobbying activity, see ACIM-National, Center for Migration Studies, Box E4, Folders "Campaign for HR 7376 Celler Bill," "Celler Bill HR 2076," "Bill S 1917 Watkins Bill," and "Bill HR 6827, S 2585 by Celler and Lehman"; ACIM-National, Center for Migration Studies, Box E11, Folder "Legislative Background 1952"; ACIM-National, Center for Migration Studies, "Juvenal Marchisio testimony before House Subcommittee, June 10, 1953," Box E9, Folder "House Subcommittee Hearings"; "ACIM-National Memo to Chapters, August 5, 1953," Carolyn Sinelli Burns Papers, Bentley Historical Library, University of Michigan, Ann Arbor, Box 1, Folder "ACIM 1953 Legislation."

48. For an excellent discussion of the formation of American refugee and displaced persons policy during the Cold War and the construction of both terms, see Carl Bon Tempo, *Americans at the Gates: The United States and Refugees During the Cold War* (Princeton: Princeton University Press, 2008).

49. Ibid., 34–59.

50. For a discussion of postwar nativism among American policymakers, see Daniel Tichenor, *Dividing Lines: The Politics of Immigration Control in America* (Princeton: Princeton University Press, 2002), 176–218.

51. Hungarian refugees after 1957 encountered similar stigmas; see Bon Tempo, *Americans at the Gates*, 60–85.

52. Danielle Battisti, "Relatives, Refugees, and Reform: Italian Americans, Italian Immigrants, and Immigration Reform during the Cold War, 1945–1965," Ph.D. dissertation, State University of New York at Buffalo, 2010.

53. ACIM-National, Center for Migration Studies, Boxes E30, E31, E39, E 47, "Immigration Case Files, A–Z"; Boxes F1–F5, "Refugee Case Files."

54. May, *Homeward Bound.*

55. War Relief Services, National Catholic Welfare Conference Records, Center for Migration Studies, Staten Island, Box 1, Folder "Hickey-Freeman"; "List of Italian Refugees, Tailors and Dressmakers," ACIM-Chicago Chapter, Immigration History Research Center, Box 1, Folder 2; "Hart Schaffner & Marx n.d. letter to ACIM Chicago," ACIM-Chicago Chapter, Immigration History Research Center, Box 1, Folder 3, "Correspondence 1955." See also, "Luigi Antonini letter to ACIM-New York City, 1.22.57–2.28.57," ACIM-National, Center for Migration Studies, Box E51, Folder "Oxford Clothes"; ACIM-National, Center for Migration Studies, Box F1, Folder "Re: Shoemakers Project."

56. For representative cases of resettlement assistance from ACIM and partner organizations, see "Detroit Chapter Report 1952–1957," ACIM-National, Center for Migration Studies, Box A20, "Chapters and Committees," Folder "Detroit Chapter."

57. Carolyn Burns, "Suggested Recommendations for the Sub-committee on Immigration and Citizenship to the Detroit Area Conference of Catholic Women," Carolyn Burns Papers, Bentley Historical Library, University of Michigan, Box 4, Folder "National Conference of Catholic Women, 1964"; "Detroit Chapter Report 1952–1957," ACIM-National, Center for Migration Studies, Box A20, "Chapters and Committees," Folder "Detroit Chapter."

58. Quote from "A New Standard of Living, ACIM Dispatch, March 1959," ACIM-National, Center for Migration Studies, Box D.

59. Quote from "A New Standard of Living, ACIM Dispatch, March 1959," ACIM-National, Center for Migration Studies, Box D.

60. Mark Wyman estimates that upwards of 50 percent of Italian immigrants from 1880 to 1930 were migratory workers who returned to Italy after temporary migration to the United States. The vast majority were men. Wyman, *Round-Trip to America*; Cinel, *The National Integration of Italian Return Migration*. For a case study of migrant men who immigrated to the Americas in this period while maintaining transnational households in Italy, see Reeder, *Widows in White*.

61. "Immigrant Vasari Extolls America," *Fra Noi* (July 1961).

62. "From Italy to Chicago: The Dramatic Success Story of Our Italian Americans, Part 3," *Chicago Tribune Magazine* (August 19, 1962).

63. *Chicago Sun Times* (May 30, 1956; June 18, 1956; June 21, 1956); *New World Chicago* (October 18, 1955; October 21, 1955).

64. "Giuseppe Merola Report, Detroit Chapter Report 1952–1957," ACIM-National, Center for Migration Studies, Box A20, "Chapters and Committees," Folder "Detroit Chapter."

65. "Italians in Chicago," Oral History Project Records, Immigration History Research Center. Data collected circa 1980 by the University of Illinois at Chicago Oral History Department; the collection includes 113 interviews from Italian Americans in the greater Chicago area.

66. Sam Ori, "Italians in Chicago," Oral History Project Records, Immigration History Research Center.

9. Italian Doo-Wop: Sense of Place, Politics of Style, and Racial Crossovers in Postwar New York City   SIMONE CINOTTO

1. Jay-Z featuring Alicia Keys, "Empire State of Mind," in *The Blueprint 3*, Roc Nation, 2009, MP3.

2. Hip-hop has recently been a popular language for articulating such affinities, beginning with the tendency of black male rap performers to model their dress and imagery after Hollywood-style Italian Mafioso and 1950s Italian crooners. Before Jay-Z, rapper Snoop Doggy Dogg named one of his CDs *The Dogg Father* (1996) in obvious homage to *The Godfather* movies ("I'm Lucky Luciano, 'bout to sing soprano," Snoop raps in the album), while Nas filled his *Can't Forget About You* (2007) with references to the Rat Pack (Frank Sinatra, Dean Martin, and Sammy Davis Jr.). John Gennari, "Passing for Italian," *Transition* 72 (1996): 36–48.

3. Simona Frasca, *Birds of Passage: I musicisti napoletani a New York (1895–1940)* (Lucca: Libreria Musicale Italiana, 2010).

4. Lolis Eric Elie, "Exploring Black, Italian Connections," *Times-Picayune* (August 23, 1999): B1; Will Friedwald, "Keeping in Touch With Their Roots," *New York Sun* (May 16, 2006): 15; Joseph Sciorra, "Hip Hop from Italy and the Diaspora: A Report from the 41st Parallel," *Altreitalie* no. 24 (January–June 2002): 86–104; Joseph Sciorra, "The Mediascape of Hip-Wop: Alterity and Authenticity in Italian North American Hip-Hop," in *Global Media, Culture, and Identity: Theory, Case, and Approaches*, ed. Rohit Chopra and Radhika Gajjala (New York: Routledge, 2011), 33–51.

5. Jennifer Guglielmo and Salvatore Salerno, eds., *Are Italians White? How Race Is Made in America* (New York: Routledge, 2003).

6. Stuart L. Goosman, *Group Harmony: The Black Urban Roots of Rhythm and Blues* (Philadelphia: University of Pennsylvania Press, 2005); Anthony Gribin and Matthew M. Schiff, *The Complete Book of Doo-Wop* (Iola, Wis.: Krause, 2000); Philip Groia, *They All Sang on the Corner: A Second Look at New York City's Rhythm and Blues Vocal Groups* (Port Jefferson, N.Y.: Phillie Dee Enterprises, 1983).

7. Gribin and Schiff, *The Complete Book of Doo-Wop*; Ed Ward, "Italo-American Rock," in *The Rolling Stone Illustrated History of Rock & Roll*, ed. Jim Miller (New York: Random House/Rolling Stone Press, 1980), 132–135. Earlier scholarly discussions of Italian doo-wop include John Michael Runowicz, *Forever Doo-Wop: Race, Nostalgia, and Vocal Harmony* (Amherst: University of Massachusetts Press, 2010), 63–68; Joseph Sciorra, "Who Put the Wop in Doo-Wop? Some Thoughts on Italian Americans and Early Rock and Roll," *Voices in Italian Americana* 13, no. 1 (2002): 16–22; Alessandro Buffa, "'On the Street Where you Live': Italian American Doo-Wop in Postwar New York," *Anglistica* 13, no. 1 (2009): 51–59.

8. Thomas Kessner, *The Golden Door: Italian and Jewish Immigrant Mobility in New York City, 1880–1915* (New York: Oxford University Press, 1977), 33.

9. Robert Connolly and Pellegrino D'Acierno, "Italian American Musical Culture and Its Contribution to American Music," in *The Italian American Heritage: A Companion to Literature and Arts*, ed. Pellegrino D'Acierno (New York: Garland, 1999), 387–490; Ferdinando Fasce, "Singing at Work: Italian Immigrants and Music during the Epoch of World War I," *Italian Americana* no. 27 (2009): 133–148; Sabine Haenni, *The Immigrant Scene: Ethnic Amusements in New York, 1880–1920* (Minneapolis: University of Minnesota Press, 2008), 95–142; Giovanni De Luna, "Canzoni per raccontare la storia: La radio e gli Italoamericani," in *L'occhio*

e l'orecchio dello storico: Le fonti audiovisive nella ricerca e nella didattica della storia (Florence: La Nuova Italia, 1993), 171–200; Stanislao G. Pugliese, ed., *Frank Sinatra: History, Identity, and Italian American Culture* (New York: Macmillan, 2004).

10. George Lipsitz, *Footsteps in the Dark: The Hidden Histories of Popular Music* (Minneapolis, University of Minnesota Press, 2007), xx–xxi.

11. Herbert J. Gans, *The Urban Villagers: Group and Class in the Life of Italian-Americans* (New York: Free Press, 1962), 83.

12. Donna Gabaccia, "Inventing Little Italy," *Journal of the Gilded Age and Progressive Era* 6, no. 1 (January 2007): 7–41.

13. Donna Gabaccia, "Little Italy's Decline: Immigrant Renters and Investors in a Changing City," in *The Landscape of Modernity: New York City, 1900–1940*, ed. David Ward and Olivier Zunz (Baltimore: Johns Hopkins University Press, 1992), 235–251.

14. According to the U.S. Immigration Commission, in 1908 only 1.3 percent of families with a foreign-born Southern Italian head in New York City lived in homes they owned (sample blocks from "Elizabeth Street, Spring to Houston, East Side," and "East One Hundred and Fourteenth Street, Second to First Avenue, North Side"). United States Senate, *Reports of the Immigration Commission. Vol. 26. Immigrants in Cities: Study of Selected Districts in New York, Chicago, Philadelphia, Boston, Buffalo, Cleveland, and Milwaukee, with Statistics and Tables. Vol. 1.* (Washington, D.C.: Government Printing Office, 1911), 209. By 1930, a total of 53,849 families whose head of family was Italian-born lived in their own homes; 144,835 rented. Few Italian homeowners lived in Manhattan: only 1,213 families as compared to 31,196 in Brooklyn, 11,012 in Queens, 7,371 in the Bronx, and 3,057 in Staten Island (Richmond). Bureau of the Census, *Fifteenth Census of the United States, 1930: Population. Special Report on Foreign Born White Families by Country of Birth of Head* (Washington, D.C.: Government Printing Office, 1933), 162–164.

15. Richard Reeves, "Bronx Aides Meet on Racial Fights: Continued Violence Feared in the Belmont Section," *New York Times* (April 5, 1967): 37.

16. Joshua B. Freeman, *Working-Class New York: Life and Labor since World War II* (New York: New Press, 2000), 196–199; Jim Sleeper, *Closest Of Strangers: Liberalism and the Politics of Race in New York* (New York: Norton, 1991), 116–132; Joshua Zeitz, *White Ethnic New York: Jews, Catholics, and the Shaping of Postwar Politics* (Chapel Hill: University of North Carolina Press, 2007), 11–38.

17. Eric Schneider, *Vampires, Dragons, and Egyptian Kings: Youth Gangs in Postwar New York* (Princeton: Princeton University Press, 2001), 78–105.

18. David Hinckley, "Fred Milano, Singer with Dion and the Belmonts, Dead at 72; Started Out on Bronx Street Corners," *Daily News* (January 2, 2012).

19. Dion DiMucci with Davin Seay, *The Wanderer: Dion's Story* (New York: Beech Tree Books, 1988), 92.

20. Buffa, "On the Street Where You Live," 55.

21. Jerome Krase, "The Present/Future of Little Italies," *Brooklyn Journal of Social Semiotics Research* 1, no. 1 (Spring 1999): 1–22.

22. DiMucci, *The Wanderer*, 76.

23. Sam Howe Verhovek, "A Wanderer, Dion Returns to His Roots: Dion Wanders Back to Bronx Roots," *New York Times* (June 19, 1987): B4.

24. DiMucci, *The Wanderer*, 73.

25. Herbert Gutman, *Work, Culture, and Society in Industrializing America: Essays in American Working-Class and Social History* (New York: Vintage, 1976), 16.

26. Arjun Appadurai, "The Production of Locality," in *Counterworks: Managing the Diversity of Knowledge*, ed. Richard Fardon (London: Routledge, 1995), 204–225. On music and the production of place, see Keith Negus, *Popular Music in Theory* (Hanover, N.H.: University Press of New England, 1996), 164–189; Sara Cohen, "Sounding Out the City: Music and the Sensuous Production of Place," *Transactions of the Institute of British Geographers* 20, No. 4 (1995): 434–446.

27. Keith Negus invites "to consider some of the ways that popular music is mediated by a series of technological, cultural, historical, geographical factors." *Popular Music in Theory*, 65. For how this group of factors worked at once to shape rock and roll into an immensely popular form of culture see, Keir Keightley, "Reconsidering Rock," in *The Cambridge Companion to Pop and Rock*, ed. Simon Frith, Will Straw, and John Street (New York: Cambridge University Press, 2001), 109–142.

28. Tony Fletcher, *All Hopped Up and Ready To Go: Music from the Streets of New York* (New York: Norton, 2009), 96–122; Steven F. Lawson, "Race, Rock and Roll, and the Rigged Society: The Payola Scandal

and the Political Culture of the 1950s," in *The Achievement of American Liberalism: The New Deal and Its Legacies*, ed. William F. Chafe (New York: Columbia University Press, 2003), 205–242.

29. Groia, *They All Sang on the Corner*, 8.

30. Charlie Horner and Todd Baptista, "The Johnny Maestro Story," *Echoes of the Past* 92 (2010).

31. For a contemporary account of what Freed's rock and roll concerts were like and the reactions they provoked see, Gertrude Samuels, "Why They Rock and Roll—And Should They?" *New York Times Magazine* (January 12, 1958): SM16.

32. Lawson, "Race, Rock and Roll, and the Rigged Society"; Glenn C. Altschuler, *All Shook Up: How Rock 'n' Roll Changed America* (New York: Oxford University Press, 2004), 142–160; John Jackson, *American Bandstand: Dick Clark and the Making of a Rock 'n' Roll Empire* (New York: Oxford University Press, 1999).

33. Horner and Baptista, "The Johnny Maestro Story."

34. The proliferation of independent local record labels promoting rock and roll was for a good part a consequence of the battle between performance-rights organizations ASCAP and BMI for the control of songwriting revenues, and the choice of the latter to invest on rock and roll to free itself from ASCAP's hegemony. Lawson, "Race, Rock and Roll, and the Rigged Society," 214–216.

35. Edward R. Engel, *White & Still All Right!* (Scarsdale, N.Y.: Crackerjack Press, 1977), 65–78.

36. DiMucci, *The Wanderer*, 89.

37. Fletcher, *All Hopped Up*, 107.

38. Freeman, *Working-Class New York*, 35.

39. Horner and Baptista, "The Johnny Maestro Story"; Engel, *White & Still All Right!*, 27.

40. Bill Yousman, "Blackophilia and Blackophobia: White Youth, the Consumption of Rap Music, and White Supremacy," *Communication Theory* 13, no. 4 (2003): 369, 387. Yousman's paper is based on bell hooks' classic essay, "Eating the Other: Desire and Resistance," in *Black Looks: Race and Representation* (Boston: South End Press, 1992), 21–39.

41. Horner and Baptista, "The Johnny Maestro Story."

42. Ibid.

43. The role of consumerism in empowering the civil rights movement is explored in Robert E. Weems, *Desegregating the Dollar: African American Consumerism in the Twentieth Century* (New York: New York University Press, 1998); Lizabeth Cohen, *A Consumers' Republic: The Politics of Mass Consumption in Postwar America* (New York: Vintage, 2003); Jason Chambers, *Madison Avenue and the Color Line: African Americans in the Advertising Industry* (Philadelphia: University of Pennsylvania Press, 2008).

44. DiMucci, *The Wanderer*, 81.

45. David Gonzales, "Acts of Hate From the Past: Bias Crimes in New York City Are Nothing New," *New York Times* (February 1, 1992): 25.

46. Transcript of Nick Santamaria's talk at the "Italian American and Early Rock and Roll" symposium at the John D. Calandra Italian American Institute, Queens College, CUNY, Flushing, NY, May 10, 2003, cited in Runowicz, *Forever Doo-Wop*, 67.

47. DiMucci, *The Wanderer*, 75.

48. George Lipsitz, *Dangerous Crossroads: Popular Music, Postmodernism and the Focus of Place* (New York: Verso, 1997), 17.

49. John Gennari, "Giancarlo Giuseppe Alessandro Esposito: Life in the Borderlands," in Guglielmo and Salero *Are Italians White?*, 241–242.

50. Keightley, "Reconsidering Rock," 115.

51. Rick Lyman, "Still in Love, and the Love Still Grows," *New York Times* (July 31, 1997): C11–C12.

10. Consuming Italian Americans: Invoking Ethnicity in the Buying and Selling of Guido   DONALD TRICARICO

1. Herbert Gans, "Symbolic Ethnicity: The Future of Ethnic Groups and Culture in America," *Ethnic and Racial Studies* 2, no. 1 (1979): 1–20.

2. Donald Tricarico "The 'New' Italian American Ethnicity," *Journal of Ethnic Studies* 12, no. 3 (Fall 1984): 75–94.

3. Eugene E. Roosens, *Creating Ethnicity: The Power of Ethnogenesis* (Newbury Park, Calif.: Sage, 1989).

4. Pierre Bourdieu, *Distinction: A Social Critique of the Judgment of Taste* (Cambridge, Mass.: Harvard University Press, 1984).

5. Simon Frith, *Sound Effects: Youth, Leisure and the Politics of Rock 'n' Roll* (New York: Pantheon, 1981).

6. George Lipsitz, *Dangerous Crossings: Popular Music, Postmodernism and the Focus of Place* (New York: Verso, 1994), 26.

7. Greg Dimitriadis, *Performing Identity/Performing Culture: Hip Hop as Text, Pedagogy, and Lived Practice* (New York: Peter Lang, 2009).

8. Murray Milner, *Freaks, Geeks, and Cool Kids: American Teenagers, Schools, and the Culture of Consumption* (New York: Routledge: 2004).

9. Leonard Covello, *The Social Background of the Italo American Schoolchild* (Amsterdam: E. J. Brill: 1967).

10. Herbert Gans, *The Urban Villagers: Group and Class in the Life of Italian-Americans* (Glencoe, Ill.: Free Press, 1984), 64–70.

11. Donald Tricarico, *The Italians of Greenwich Village* (New York: Center for Migration Studies, 1984).

12. William Foote Whyte, *Street Corner Society: The Social Structure of an Italian Slum* (Chicago: University of Chicago Press, 1943).

13. Gerald Suttles, *The Social Order of the Slum: Ethnicity and Territory in the Inner City* (Chicago: University of Chicago Press, 1968), 65.

14. Howard Pinderhughes, *Race in the Hood: Conflict and Violence Among Urban Youth* (Minneapolis: University of Minnesota Press, 1997). Urban danger is a dominant motif, specifically gangs and the Mafia, in the mainstream media, e.g., Martin Scorsese's *Mean Streets*.

15. Joe A. Austin, "Knowing Their Place," in *Generations of Youth: Youth Cultures and History in Twentieth-Century America*, ed. Joe A. Austin and Michael N. Willard (New York: New York University Press, 1998), 240–252.

16. Working-class, greaser consumption was thrown into relief as a marginal and inferior taste culture in the mainstream media imaginary. The 1970s TV sitcom *Happy Days* and Hollywood movie *Grease* signified an Italian American greaser style by relying on a few core elements such as black leather jackets and customized cars. In both narratives, Italian American greaser youth culture was meaningfully constructed on the periphery of more formidable leisure-based consumption: the "preppie" or campus styles of suburban middle-class and upper-middle-class whites signaled by button-down collars, pressed chinos, and penny loafers. These styles and the blue-collar and lower-class communities in which they were embedded were in eclipse and thus were the basis of nostalgia rather than moral panic. This can account for ambivalence toward Italian greasers. For a fuller discussion, see Donald Tricarico, "Dressing Italian Americans for the Spectacle: What Difference Does Guido Perform?" in *The Men's Fashion Reader*, ed. Andrew Reilly and Sarah Cosbey (New York: Fairchild, 2008), 265–278.

17. Tricarico, "The 'New' Italian American Ethnicity."

18. School culture may have actually inhibited youth consumption styles. Paula Fass describes a "student culture" for Italian American teenagers in the middle-class area of Bay Ridge in the 1930s and 1940s. She discerns a structural dynamic whereby "youth society shaped ethnicity" into "new American identities" in "a strategic interaction between inherited traditions" and "patterns of adaptation" within the larger society, including peer pressure ("forces of imitation"). However, she does not even hint at a pattern of consumption. Paula Fass, *Outside In: Minorities and the Transformation of American Education* (New York: Oxford University Press, 1998), 114.

19. Donald Tricarico "Guido: Fashioning an Italian American Youth Identity," *Journal of Ethnic Studies* 19, no. 1 (Spring 1991): 41–66.

20. The gathering noise of Italian American youth as producers of disco not just consumers has not received the careful historical investigation it deserves. Tim Lawrence, *Love Saves the Day: A History of American Dance Music Culture, 1970–1979* (Durham, N.C.: Duke University Press, 2003): 190.

21. Echols makes the case that an anti-disco film may have entered into the public enmity. It is possible that it fueled antagonism for Guido in rock-based youth culture. *Saturday Night Fever* also takes an anti–Italian American position, especially with strong images of family dysfunction. Tony Manero became a youth culture icon and the prototype of Guido in southern Brooklyn because he personifies the appropriation of stylish consumption within street culture—he even fought like them. And it situated an emerging consumption style in Italian American culture. See Alice Echols, *Hot Stuff: Disco and the Remaking of American Culture* (New York: Norton, 2009): 151–155.

22. Luis Alvarez, *The Power of the Zoot: Youth Culture and Resistance during World War II* (Berkeley: University of California Press, 2005), 86.

23. Echols, *Hot Stuff*, 179.

24. Lawrence, *Love Saves the Day*, 3.

25. Echols, *Hot Stuff*, 179.

26. Lawrence, *Love Saves the Day*, 305.

27. Echols, *Hot Stuff*, 179.

28. John Storey, *Cultural Consumption and Everyday Life* (New York: Bloomsbury USA, 1999): 168.

29. For a description of 1980s Guido style, see Tricarico, "Guido."

30. Holly Alford, "The Zoot Suit: Its History and Influence," *Fashion Theory* 8, no. 2 (2004): 225–236.

31. Kai Fikentscher, *You Better Work! Underground Dance Music in New York City* (Hanover, N.H.: University Press of New England, 2000).

32. Tricarico, "Dressing Italian Americans for the Spectacle."

33. Lawrence, *Love Saves the Day*.

34. Walter Hughes maintains that *Saturday Night Fever* provided a narrative that "heterosexualized disco." I would argue that a Guido narrative legitimated disco for other working-class "bridge and tunnel" youth. Urban street culture traditions like Guido and hip-hop have injected homophobia into a club pose. See Walter Hughes, "In the Empire of the Beat: Disciples and Disco," in *Microphone Fiends: Youth Music and Youth Culture*, ed. Andrew Ross and Tricia Rose (New York: Routledge, 1994), 147–157.

35. While bodybuilding is work, it is predicated on consumption, very much like dancing. Fikentscher, *You Better Work!*

36. Robert J. C. Ross, "The Teddy Boy as Scapegoat," *Doshisha Studies in Language and Culture* 1, no. 2 (1998): 263–291.

37. Tricarico, "Dressing Italian Americans for the Spectacle."

38. Nicholas Confessore, "Hip Hop Is Spoken Here, But With a Queens Accent," *New York Times* (May 21, 2006).

39. Local Mafia ownership of gay dance clubs into the late 1960s furnished protection against laws regulating the morality of same-sex dancing, which helped nurture the disco scene that flowered in the early 1970s.

40. Paul Willis, *Common Culture: Symbolic Work at Play in the Everyday Cultures of the Young* (Boulder, Colo.: Westview, 1990).

41. Paul Chatterton and Robert Hollands, *Urban Nightscapes: Youth Cultures, Pleasure Spaces and Corporate Power* (New York: Routledge, 2003), 11.

42. Mike Brake, *Comparative Youth Culture: The Sociology of Youth Cultures and Youth Subcultures in America, Britain and Canada* (New York: Routledge, 1985).

43. Penelope Eckert, *Jocks and Burnouts: Social Categories and Identity in the High School* (New York: Teachers College Press, 1989): 20.

44. Dimitriadis, *Performing Identity/Performing Culture*, 13.

45. Milner, *Freaks, Geeks, and Cool Kids*, 9–12.

46. Alvarez, *The Power of the Zoot*, 89.

47. Donald Tricarico, "Narrating Guido: Contested Meanings of an Italian American Youth Subculture" in *Anti-Italianism: Essays on Prejudice*, ed. William J. Connell and Fred Gardaphé (New York: Palgrave Macmillan), 177–178.

48. Donald Tricarico, "Bellas and Fellas in Cyberspace: Mobilizing Italian Ethnicity for Online Youth Culture," *Italian American Review* 1, no. 1 (Winter 2011): 1–34.

49. Donald Tricarico, "In a New Light: Italian American Ethnicity in the Mainstream," in *The Ethnic Enigma: The Salience of Ethnicity for European-Origin Groups*, ed. Peter Kivisto (Philadelphia: Balch Institute for Ethnic Studies, 1989).

50. Roosens, *Creating Ethnicity*, 141.

51. Stephen E. Cornell and Douglas Hartmann, *Ethnicity and Race: Making Identities in a Changing World* (Thousand Oaks, Calif.: Pine Forge, 2007), 87.

52. Tricarico, "Bellas and Fellas in Cyberspace," 9. A cognitive orientation to consumption is illustrated in the home page profile of a nineteen-year-old female who adapted an American Express Card television advertisement for a cyber self:

Price List
Versace Top $379
Prada Thong $95
Moschino Pants $95
Dolce and Gabbana Bra $119
Gucci Purse $320

Cabrio GLX $27,000

The Look When I Step Out of My Car

Priceless

53. WKTU also acknowledged a Latino market in a business model that ignored a predominantly black hip-hop audience loyal to Hot 97, which happened to replace WKTU.

54. *NJGuido* was founded by a self-identified Guido in his early twenties whose ancestry was only half-Italian and was nostalgic about summers spent at the Jersey Shore with his family. See Libby Copeland, "Strutting Season," *Washington Post* (July 6, 2003): DO5.

55. Why has MTV produced a reality show that showcases an Italian American youth subculture? Guido was not on the radar of the national media culture. MTV was able to merchandise it as something new and amenable to branding. Guido is a readymade symbol that identifies the brand; Italian ethnicity makes the brand more salient. Guido style tradition has street culture roots—the element of urban authenticity that sells Black youth culture in the suburbs. Guido began selectively poaching hip-hop before it diffused to mainstream youth. MTV exploited a connection to gangsta when it casted Guido as "the hottest pimps." As such, Guido can appeal to a suburban youth market that crosses over to hip-hop, but not blackness. Reality TV specializes in the depiction of cultures that invites the disdain of tasteful constituencies. *Jersey Shore* is about the widest possible commercial recognition for Guido, not respect or "cool" as a style. *Jersey Shore* was undoubtedly produced with full knowledge of the expressive depreciation of Guido style in youth culture circles. This suggests that MTV may be selling Guido as uncool to cool kids everywhere. It may also be selling the opportunity to disparage Guido by tapping into ethnic prejudice. Merchandising Guido allows MTV to access a market that is marginal to youth cultures based on rock and hip-hop. This is a position inhabited by diverse European-ancestry youth in metropolitan New York City including Greeks, Russian Jews, and Albanians. Their consumption styles negotiate aspirations to whiteness in relation to blacks and Latinos, on one hand, and class mobility in relation to Manhattan elites and hipsters gentrifying their own outer borough neighborhoods, on the other. Guido is the precedent followed by these more recently arrived immigrant groups as suggested in the name "Greedo" used for Greeks in Queens. As the first season *Jersey Shore* ended, MTV began testing for a new reality show focusing on a "Russian" youth scene in Brighton Beach nightclubs.

56. Whereas *American Bandstand* sanitized greaser in the 1960s to fit into mainstream youth culture, hooking up is central to the current script. Risky sex may be a late capitalist counterpart to risky financial investments by institutions too big to fail. Italian audiences for the 2011 *Jersey Shore* season filmed in Florence perhaps related this motif to the sexual narratives in the sensational murder trial of the American exchange student Amanda Knox that was then taking place in Perugia, although they certainly could relate to the bombastic sexual exploits of Prime Minister Silvio Berlusconi.

57. References to unacceptable ethnic differences may help explain a failed attempt to merchandise Guido by a startup designer brand, Guido New York. In one promotional image, the elevated B train tracks that run along New Utrecht Avenue and 86th Street unmistakably marks the historic Guido turf of southern Brooklyn. Other images portray tough posing males in tracksuits; one is leaning against a cool car while holding a baseball bat, a signifier of street culture, not sport. Designs reflected a "tough-guy sex appeal" in "marked contrast to the metro sexual ambiguity that has dominated the marketplace in recent years." Mafia masculinity was referenced when one of John Gotti's celebrity grandsons was used as a runway model for the company's 2004 line. However, in marked contrast to FUBU, the advertising campaign distanced itself from the subculture it was merchandising. Guido New York conceded that "the name 'Guido'" is an "image" or "stereotype" that "may be perceived as negative," in particular "something that is less desirable" and "less than classy." Its design signature "re-contextualized and appropriated the word not the stereotype." Tricarico, "Dressing Italian Americans for the Spectacle."

58. On the social psychology of new classes, see Joseph Vidich and Arthur J. Vidich, *The New American Society: The Revolution of the Middle Class* (Chicago: Quadrangle, 1971), 121.

59. Neil Genzlinger, "Surf, Skin and Jersey: What's Not to Love?" *New York Times* (January 4, 2010).

60. Virginia Heffernan, "Speech Therapy," *New York Times Magazine* (January 24, 2010): 20–21.

61. Nancy Franklin, "Jersey Jetsam," *New Yorker* (January 18, 2010).

62. Tricarico, "Narrating Guido," 171–172.

63. Robert A. Orsi, *The Madonna of 115th Street: Faith and Community in Italian Harlem 1880–1950* (New Haven: Yale University Press, 1985). Orsi frames consumption within the family as a sacred ritual involving food prepared in the kitchen.

64. This does not preclude new consumption styles as a more encompassing ethnic route. Moreover, this goes beyond an arriviste status culture. It is also imprinted by traditional ethnic values which can explain

disproportionate and visible expenditure for the family home (i.e., house pride involving disproportionate spending on the "domus" as a definitive symbol of the family's status) and youth "spoiled" by consumption: "Daddy, can you buy me a brand new BMW? Sure, princess, anything you want?" (an informant's characterization of "Howard Beach girls").

65. Tricarico, "Narrating Guido," 179–184.

66. The contested politics of Guido on both sides of the ethnic boundary were noteworthy because it became part of the media spectacle. MTV mined the public controversy, which included an alleged death threat to publicize the first season, even proposing to interview antidefamation officials for its "news" program. Concessions were won from MTV to mute references to Italian American ethnicity, and specifically the words "Guido" and "Guidette," for the following season. Since the MTV brand was firmly entrenched by then, these signifiers were no longer necessary. In any case, the antidefamation position was flawed by the failure to recognize that Guido is both an ethnic slur and an ethnic consumption culture. For a consideration of the strident internal conversation within the Italian American community, see the Internet portal i-Italy, which streamed the colloquium organized by the John D. Calandra Institute in New York City on January 21, 2010, at www.i-Italy.org, accessed October 2, 2010.

67. The low-brow, mass culture character of Guido was openly displayed when the fourth season of *Jersey Shore* transplanted consumption routines honed in Seaside Heights to Florence, with the Uffizi Gallery and the Duomo replacing the boardwalk as a place marker. It is noteworthy that the Italian press translated Guido as *tamarro*, a term that mocks a boorish, lower-taste culture.

68. The ability of ethnic traditions to insulate against urban youth culture and specifically hip-hop is recognized by "segmented assimilation theory," see the theoretical discussion in Natasha Warikoo, *Balancing Acts: Youth Culture in the Global City* (Berkeley: University of California Press, 2010), 3–5. I interpret this more widely in reference to all types of crossing including cultures that are not "oppositional." See Tricarico, "Narrating Guido" and Tricarico "Bellas and Fellas in Cyberspace."

69. Willis, *Common Culture*, 3–6.

70. Amy L. Best, *Prom Night: Youth, Schools, and Popular Culture* (New York: Routledge, 2000), 167. Guido cannot be said to be a "radical intervention," since it struggles to reconcile a traditional ethnic identity with core American beliefs about consumption.

71. Gans, "Symbolic Ethnicity."

72. Richard D. Alba, *Italian Americans: Into the Twilight of Ethnicity* (Englewood Cliffs, N.J.: Prentice-Hall, 1984), 173.

73. Carl Bankston and Jacques Henry, "Endogamy among Louisiana Cajuns: A Social Class Explanation," *Social Forces* 77, no. 4 (1999): 1317–1338.

74. Tricarico, "In a New Light."

11. The Double Life of the Italian Suit: Italian Americans and the "Made in Italy" Label COURTNEY RITTER

1. Marilyn Halter, *Shopping for Identity: The Marketing of Ethnicity* (New York: Schocken, 2000).

2. Interview with Lucio Caputo, Head, Italian Trade Commission in New York, 1975–1982, November 26, 2008.

3. Yuppies, "young urban professionals" or "young upwardly mobile professionals," benefited financially from the economic policies of the Reagan era and expressed their social standing through luxury consumption. See Gary Cross, *An All-Consuming Century: Why Commercialism Won in Modern America* (New York: Columbia University Press, 2000), for a more detailed explanation.

4. Richard H. Brodhead, "Strangers on a Train: The Double Dream of Italy in the American Gilded Age," *Modernism/Modernity* 1, no. 2 (1994): 1–19.

5. Maria Laurino, "Discovering a Voice of One's Own," in *Adjusting Sites: New Essays in Italian American Studies*, ed. William Boelhower and Rocco Pallone (Stony Brook, N.Y.: Filibrary, 1999), 292.

6. The major texts on Third Italy and Italian industrial development, include Arnaldo Bagnasco and Charles Sabel, eds., *Small and Medium-Size Enterprises: Social Change in Western Europe* (London: Pinter, 1995); Arnaldo Bagnasco, *Tre Italie: la problematica territoriale dello sviluppo italiano* (Bologna: il Mulino, 1977); Michael H. Best, *The New Competition: Institutions of Industrial Restructuring* (Cambridge, Mass.: Harvard University Press, 1990); Michael L. Blim, *Made in Italy: Small-Scale Industrialization and Its Consequences* (New York: Praeger, 1990); Aldo Bonomi, *Il Capitalismo Molecolare: la società al lavoro nel Nord Italia* (Turin: Einaudi, 1997); Anna Bull and Paul Corner, *From Peasant to Entrepreneur: The Survival of*

the *Family Economy in Italy* (Oxford: Berg, 1993); Dario Gaggio, *In Gold We Trust: Social Capital and Economic Change in the Italian Jewelry Towns* (Princeton: Princeton University Press, 2007); Michael J. Piore and Charles F. Sabel, *The Second Industrial Divide* (New York: Basic, 1984); Sylvia Junko Yanaisako, *Producing Culture and Capital: Family Firms in Italy* (Princeton: Princeton University Press, 2002).

7. Gaggio, *In Gold We Trust*, 3.

8. Yanaisako, *Producing Culture and Capital*.

9. Melissa Aronczyk, "Branding the Nation: Mediating Space, Value, and Identity in the Context of Global Culture," Ph.D. dissertation, New York University, 2008.

10. David Harvey, *The Conditions of Postmodernity: An Inquiry into the Origins of Cultural Change* (Hoboken, N.J.: Wiley-Blackwell, 1991).

11. Nicola White, *Reconstructing Italian Fashion: America and the Development of the Italian Fashion Industry* (Oxford: Berg, 2000), 12.

12. Philip Mattera, *Off the Books: The Rise of the Underground Economy* (New York: Palgrave, 1986), 93; Victoria De Grazia, "Changing Consumption Regimes in Europe, 1930–1970: Comparative Perspectives on the Distribution Problem," in *Getting and Spending: European and American Consumer Societies in the Twentieth Century*, ed. Susan Strasser, Charles McGovern, and Matthias Judt (Cambridge: Cambridge University Press, 1998), 80; Gaggio, *In Gold We Trust*, 252; Valerie Steele, *Fashion, Italian Style* (New Haven: Yale University Press, 2003), 117; Gabriele Morello, "International Product Competitiveness and the 'Made in' Concept," in *Product-Country Images: Impact and Role in International Marketing*, ed. Nicolas Papadopoulos and Louise A. Heslop (New York: International Business, 1993), 286; "A 'Data Bank' for the Italian Clothing Sector: An Initiative of the Italian Fashion Corporation," *Italy Exports* (April 1974): 50; Enrico Gennaro, *Stati Uniti: Mercati e opportunità per le piccole e medie imprese italiane* (Milan: 24 Ore, 1987), 179.

13. Gennaro, *Stati Uniti*, 179.

14. Fiorella Padoa Schioppa Kostoris, *The Sheltered Economy: Structural Problems in the Italian Economy* (Oxford: Clarendon, 1993), 122; Ministero del bilancio e della programmazione economica, *Programma Economico Nazionale: 1971–1975* (Rome: Istituto Poligrafico dello Stato, 1972), 159; 231–32.

15. Salvatore Pappalardo, "How Should Promotion Activities Be Planned?" *Italy Exports* (March 1975): 22.

16. Caputo interview.

17. John Fairchild, *Chic Savages: Inside the Glamorous, Fashionable World of the Super-Rich* (New York: Pocket, 1989), 29; Caputo interview.

18. White, *Reconstructing Italian Fashion*, 162.

19. Ibid.

20. Morello, "International Product Competitiveness," 286.

21. Naomi Klein, *No Logo: No Space, No Choice, No Jobs* (New York: Picador, 2000), 14.

22. Ibid., 21.

23. Chiara Giannelli Buss, "Lo stilismo nella moda maschile," in *La Moda Italiana: Dall'antimoda allo stilismo*, ed. Grazietta Butazzi and Alessandra Mottola Molfino (Milan: Electa, 1987), 232.

24. David Livingstone, "Italian Fetes All the Rage," *Globe and Mail* (November 22, 1983): F8.

25. Genevieve Buck, "Italian Fashion, Spy Light Up ACLU Benefit," *Chicago Tribune* (April 12, 1989): 18.

26. Teri Agins, "Who Loves Armani? Actors, Car Washers, and Senior V.P.s," *Wall Street Journal* (October 31, 1990): A1.

27. Adam Arvidsson, *Marketing Modernity: Italian Advertising from Fascism to Post-Modernity* (London: Routledge, 2003), 127.

28. Stephen Gundle, "Hollywood Glamour and Mass Consumption in Postwar Italy," *Journal of Cold War Studies* 4, no. 3 (Summer 2002): 97.

29. Deborah Silverman, *Selling Culture: Bloomingdale's, Diana Vreeland, and the New Aristocracy of Taste in Reagan's America* (New York: Pantheon, 1986).

30. Interview with Stan Schmidt, buyer of Italian textiles, New York, March 12, 2009.

31. Caputo interview.

32. William Leach, *Land of Desire: Merchants, Power and the Rise of a New American Culture* (New York: Vintage, 1993), 62–63.

33. Silverman, *Selling Culture*.

34. Woody Hochswender, "Images of Man, Labeled Armani," *New York Times* (December 21, 1990): C36.

35. Caputo interview.

36. Amy Alson, "Big Brands, Small Print," *Marketing and Media Decision* (October 1988): 54; Lisa Anderson, "Ciao, Milano," *Chicago Tribune* (May 2, 1984): C3.

37. Philip H. Dougherty, "Italian Trade Panel Announces Print Drive," *New York Times* (December 30, 1980): D18.

38. Kennon Breazeale, "In Spite of Women: *Esquire* Magazine and the Construction of the Male Consumer," *Signs* 20, no. 1 (Autumn 1994): 6; Cross, *All-Consuming Century*, 169.

39. Anderson, "Ciao, Milano": C3.

40. Dick Hebdige, *Hiding in the Light: On Images and Things* (London: Routledge, 1988), 106.

41. Victoria De Grazia, *Irresistible Empire: America's Advance through Twentieth-Century Europe* (Cambridge, Mass.: Harvard University Press, 2006), 198.

42. Alberto Denzler Von Botha, "Alitalia: The Cultured Airline: le sponsorizazzioni nella strategia di comunicazione Alitalia," *Comunicazioni sociali* 2, no. 3–4 (1980): 347–56.

43. Harvey Levenstein, "The American Response to Italian Food, 1890–1930," *Food and Foodways* 1, no. 1 (1985): 1–24.

44. Claudia Brush Kidwell, *Suiting Everyone: The Democratization of Clothing in America* (Washington, D.C.: Smithsonian Institution Press, 1974), 115.

45. Fred L. Gardaphé, "A Class Act: Understanding the Italian/American Gangster," in *Screening Ethnicity: Cinematographic Representations of Italian Americans in the United States*, ed. Anthony J. Tamburri and Anna Camaiti Hostert (Boca Raton, Fla.: Bordighera, 2002); Aaron Baker, and Juliann Vitullo, "Screening the Italian-American Male," in *Masculinity: Bodies, Movies, Culture*, ed. Peter Lehman (New York: Routledge, 2001).

46. David E. Ruth, *Inventing the Public Enemy: The Gangster in American Culture, 1918–1934* (Chicago: University of Chicago Press, 1996), 75.

47. Giorgio Bertellini, *Italy in Early American Cinema: Race, Landscape and the Picturesque* (Bloomington: Indiana University Press, 2009), 228.

48. Lee Bernstein, *The Greatest Menace: Organized Crime in Cold War America* (Amherst: University of Massachusetts Press, 2002), 108.

49. Herbert Gans, *Urban Villagers: Group and Class in the Life of Italian-Americans* (Glencoe, Ill.: Free Press, 1962),185.

50. John Gennari, "Passing for Italian: Crooners and Gangsters in Crossover Culture," *Transition* 72 (Fall 1997): 36–48.

51. Dominic J. Capeci, "Al Capone: Symbol of a Ballyhoo Society," *Journal of Ethnic Studies* 2, no. 4 (Winter 1975): 33.

52. Nicholas Antongiavanni, *The Suit: A Machiavellian Approach to Men's Style* (New York: Collins, 2006), 189.

53. Hochswender, "Images of Man, Labeled Armani."

54. Ruth, *Inventing the Public Enemy*, 75.

55. Buss, "Lo stilismo nella moda maschile," 237–243.

56. Rob Kroes, *If You've Seen One, You've Seen the Mall: Europeans and American Mass Culture* (Urbana: University of Illinois Press, 1996).

57. Gardaphé, "A Class Act"; Ruth, *Inventing the Public Enemy*, 67; Cross, *All-Consuming Century*, 169; T. J. Jackson Lears, *No Place of Grace: Anti-Modernism and the Transformation of American Culture, 1880–1920* (Chicago: University of Chicago Press, 1994).

58. Donald Tricarico, "The 'New' Italian-American Ethnicity," *Journal of Ethnic Studies* 12, no. 3 (Fall 1984): 86.

59. Maria Laurino, *Were You Always an Italian? Ancestors and Other Icons of Italian America* (New York: Norton, 2000), 61.

60. Tricarico, "The 'New' Italian-American Ethnicity."

61. Agins, "Who Loves Armani?"

62. Jon Kraszewski, "Coming to a Beach Near You! Examinations of Ethnic and State Identity in *Jersey Shore*," *FlowTV*, University of Texas at Austin, entry posted February 19, 2010, http://flowtv.org/2010/02/coming-to-a-beach-near-you-examinations-of-ethnic-and-state-identity-in-jersey-shore-jon-kraszewski-seton-hall-university.

63. For histories regarding the revitalization of New York City for upper class elites, see Sharon Zurkin, *Loft Living: Culture and Capital in Urban Change* (New Brunswick, N.J.: Rutgers University Press, 1989), and Miriam Greenberg, *Branding New York: How a City in Crisis was Sold to the World* (New York: Routledge, 2008). For examples of how *Jersey Shore* cast members are described, see Elisa Lipsky-Karasz, "Charm School," *Harper's Bazaar* (May 2010): 162; Rob Sheffield, "America's Inner Guido," *Rolling Stone* (January 21, 2010): 26.

64. Emma Rosenblum, "The Situation With the Situation: Mike 'The Situation' Sorrentino Talks about Everything That's Come from His Appearance on *Jersey Shore*," *New York Magazine* (June 28, 2010).

12. Sideline Shtick: The Italian American Basketball Coach and Consumable Images of Racial and Ethnic Masculinity   JOHN GENNARI

1. Frank Deford, "Geno Auriemma + Diana Taurasi = Love, Italian Style," *Sports Illustrated* 99, n. 20 (November 24, 2003): 124–133. See also Geno Auriemma with Jackie MacMullan, *Geno: In Pursuit of Perfection* (New York: Warner Books, 2006).

2. *Hoop Dreams*, dir. Steve James (Kartemquin Films, 1994).

3. I was introduced to D'Acierno's term *dagotude* at the symposium "For a Dangerous Pedagogy: A Manifesto for Italian and Italian American Studies," Hofstra University, April 15, 2010. A good introduction to D'Acierno's powerful and provocative scholarship is his essay "The Making of the Italian American Cultural Identity: From *La Cultura Negata* to Strong Ethnicity," which serves as the introduction to his edited volume *The Italian American Heritage: A Companion to Literature and Arts* (New York: Garland Publishing, 1999), xxiii–liv.

4. The relevant portion of Vitale's appearance in *Hoop Dreams* is conveniently accessible on YouTube at http://www.youtube.com/watch?v=LWd50dFHW2A (accessed April 2, 2013).

5. Among the voluminous writings about Vaccaro, I especially recommend Ric Bucher, "The Last Don," *espnmag.com*, available at http://espn.go.com/magazine/vol5no23vaccaro.html (accessed 2 August 2011); and Jason Zengerle, "The Pivot," *The New Republic* 238, no. 4839 (July 9, 2008): 24–26, 31–32.

6. Bucher, "The Last Don."

7. For a smart discussion of the racial and gender politics of Bobby Knight's approach, see Jeffrey Lane, *Under the Boards: The Cultural Revolution in Basketball* (Lincoln: University of Nebraska Press, 2007), 147–196.

8. Curry Kirkpatrick, "A New Mr. Bones Has a Winner," *Sports Illustrated* 30, no. 4 (January 27, 1969): 48–49.

9. Rick Reilly, "I've Gotta Be Me," *Sports Illustrated* 80, no. 9 (March 7, 1994): 72–82.

10. The phrase "Hoya Paranoia"—Hoya being the Georgetown mascot—was introduced in 1980 by Mark Asher of the *Washington Post*. Asher was referring to the insecurity of Georgetown fans, their sense that local media were slighting the Hoyas in favor of the University of Maryland. This original meaning was soon lost, however, as the term came to refer—not quite logically—to the fear Georgetown would induce in its opponents. *Sports Illustrated* reporter Curry Kirkpatrick put a different spin on the term when he used it to voice his grievance as a victim of coach John Thompson's adversarial stance toward the media and tight control over access to his players. See Kirkpatrick, "Hang on to Your Hats . . . and Heads," *Sports Illustrated* 6, no. 12 (March 19, 1984): 20–25.

11. James T. Fisher, "Clearing the Streets of the Catholic Lost Generation," in *Catholic Lives, Contemporary America*, ed. Thomas Ferraro (Durham, N.C.: Duke University Press, 1997), 76–103. The citation is on page 95.

12. Writing about Catholic high school basketball in the 1990s in his book *The Last Shot: City Streets, Basketball Dreams* (New York: Simon & Schuster, 1996), Darcy Frey observed that in New York and many other cities the Catholic leagues "siphon off the best public school players by offering a safer environment, better academic preparation, and travel budgets for out-of-town tournaments" (40–41). In a project similar to *Hoop Dreams*, Frey tracked the lives of African American high school players in the Coney Island section of Brooklyn.

13. Quoted in Kirkpatrick, "Hang on to Your Hats."

14. Rick Pitino and Bill Reynolds, *Born to Coach: A Season with the New York Knicks* (New York: NAL, 1988), 191.

15. Kirkpatrick, "Hang on to Your Hats."

16. Tim Layden, "The Upset," *Sports Illustrated* 100, no. 13 (March 29, 2004): 70–80.

17. *Perfect Upset: The 1985 Villanova vs. Georgetown NCAA Championship*, written by Brian Hyland (HBO, 2005).

18. Ed Pinckney with Bob Gordon, *Ed Pinckney's Tales from the Villanova Hardwood* (Champaign, Ill.: Sports Publishing), 142.

19. Layden, "The Upset."

20. Pinckney and Gordon, *Ed Pinckney's Tales*, 16.

21. Ibid., 146. The Villanova athletic department person was Jim Delorenzo.

22. Ibid., 91.

23. *Perfect Upset.*

24. I have in mind here Matthew Jacobson's discussion of how the ethnic and racial tensions of the *Rocky* films relate to the white backlash against the civil rights movement; see Matthew F. Jacobson, *Roots Too: White Ethnic Revival in Post-Civil Rights America* (Cambridge, Mass.: Harvard University Press, 2006), 98–110. But I don't mean to suggest that Massimino was in any way an adherent of white ethnic backlash ideology; indeed, I know nothing about Massimino's politics. Like other basketball coaches of his time, he worked on the front lines of the new world that was created by the civil rights revolution, interacting with African Americans much more than other leaders at his own university. Such coaches are among the occupational groups that deserve much more study for their roles in shaping America's post–civil rights social order.

25. Gary McLain (as told to Jeffrey Marx), "A Bad Trip: The Downfall of a Champion," *Sports Illustrated* 66, no. 11 (March 16, 1987): cover, 42–64.

26. Pinckney and Gordon, *Ed Pinckney's Tales*, 186.

27. *Perfect Upset.*

28. John Feinstein chronicles Valvano's rise and fall in *A March to Madness* (New York: Little Brown & Company, 1998), 50–55. Valvano's downfall was precipitated by the publication of a book that framed itself as an exposé: Peter Golenbock's *Personal Fouls: The Broken Promises and Shattered Dreams of Big Money Basketball at Jim Valvano's North Carolina State* (New York: Simon & Schuster, 1989).

29. Two superb accounts of Valvano's shtick on which I have relied heavily are Curry Kirkpatrick, "How King Rat Became the Big Cheese," *Sports Illustrated* 59, no. 24 (December 5, 1983): 76–90, and Gary Smith, "As Time Runs Out," *Sports Illustrated* 78, no. 1 (January 11, 1993): 10–25.

30. Michael Freeman, *ESPN: The Uncensored History* (Lanham, Md.: Rowman & Littlefield, 2000), 167.

31. On Italian Americans and sports talk radio, see Alan Eisenstock, *Sports Talk: A Journey Inside the World of Sports Talk Radio* (New York: Pocket Books, 2001), 109–166; and Nick Paumgarten, "The Boys," *New Yorker* (August 30, 2004), 75–83.

32. Reilly, "I've Gotta Be Me," 76.

33. Steve Rushin, "Your Choice, Babeee!" *Sports Illustrated* 84, no. 13 (April 1, 1996): 120.

34. Kirkpatrick, "How King Rat Became the Big Cheese."

35. Marty Dobrow, *Going Bigtime: The Spectacular Rise of UMass Basketball* (Northampton, Mass.: Summerset Press, 1996), 42–43.

36. Quoted in Harvey Araton, "Calipari a Good Fit to Coach Kentucky," *New York Times* (April 1, 2009), B11–12.

37. For a discussion of the NBA dress code, see Lane, *Under the Boards*, 27–68.

38. Press reports in the summer of 2009 revealed that Pitino had paid hush money to a woman with whom he had had consensual sex in a Louisville restaurant earlier in the decade. The woman later was convicted of extortion.

39. Three times Calipari has led his teams to the Final Four. The first two times (UMass in 1996 and Memphis in 2008) his teams were disqualified retroactively when their star players were discovered to be in violation of NCAA eligibility rules.

40. Lane, *Under the Boards*, xvi.

13. The Immigrant Enclave as Theme Park: Culture, Capital, and Urban Change in New York's Little Italies   ERVIN KOSTA

1. Beverly Solochek, "In Little Italy, the Word Is Risorgimento," *New York Times* (May 1, 1977).

2. Sam Roberts, "Little Italy, Littler by the Year," *New York Times* (February 22, 2011).

3. Donna Gabaccia has traced the invention of the term "Little Italy," replacing "Italian colony" or "Italian quarter," in New York during the 1880s, denoting specific places where Italian immigrants and their children lived. In this chapter, I will use the term in a more contemporary sense, to denote those Little Italies that have declined residentially but flourished commercially. See Gabaccia, "Inventing Little Italy," *Journal of the Gilded Age and Progressive Era* 6, no. 1 (January 2007): 7–41.

4. Greg Gittrich, "Mangia! An Italian Fete," *New York Times* (August 14, 1997).

5. Some ethnic enclaves did mount successful resistance against "encroachment." For a discussion of Queens' Forest Hills, Brooklyn's Canarsie, and four Chicago neighborhoods, see, respectively, Richard

Sennett, *The Fall of Public Man* (New York: Knopf, 1976); Jonathan Rieder, *Canarsie: The Jews and Italians of Brooklyn Against Liberalism*, (Cambridge, Mass.: Harvard University Press, 1982); and William Julius Wilson and Richard P. Taub, *There Goes the Neighborhood: Racial, Ethnic, and Class Tensions in Four Chicago Neighborhoods and Their Meaning for America* (New York: Knopf, 2007).

6. Two watershed studies of ethnic identity that appeared in 1990 were largely based on residents of nonurban areas. See Mary Waters, *Ethnic Options: Choosing Identities in America* (Berkeley: University of California Press, 1990) and Richard Alba, *Ethnic Identity: The Transformation of White America* (New Haven: Yale University Press, 1990).

7. Jerome Krase, "The Present/Future of Little Italies," *Brooklyn Journal of Social Semiotics Research* 1, no. 1 (Spring 1999): 1–22.

8. Jan Lin, *The Power of Urban Ethnic Places: Cultural Heritage and Community Life* (New York: Routledge, 2011), 14–16.

9. Mark Gottdiener, *The Theming of America: Dreams, Visions, and Commercial Spaces* (Boulder, Colo.: Westview Press, 1997).

10. Sharon Zukin, *Loft Living: Culture and Capital in Urban Change* (Baltimore: Johns Hopkins University Press, 1982), and *Cultures of Cities* (Malden, Mass.: Blackwell, 1995).

11. See Jason Hackworth and Josephine Rekers, "Ethnic Packaging and Gentrification: The Case of Four Neighborhoods in Toronto," *Urban Affairs Review* 41, no. 2 (November 2005): 211–236.

12. Marilyn Halter, *Shopping for Identity: The Marketing of Ethnicity* (New York: Schocken Books, 2000).

13. Mark Abrahamson, *Global Cities* (New York: Oxford University Press, 2004), 63–64.

14. Saskia Sassen, *The Global City: New York, London, Tokyo* (Princeton: Princeton University Press, 2001).

15. Lin, *The Power of Urban Ethnic Places*, 14; Krase, "The Present/Future of Little Italies."

16. David A. Badillo, "New Immigrants in the Bronx: Redefining a Cityscape," *Bronx County Historical Society Journal* 44, no. 1 (Spring–Fall 2007): 19–37.

17. The East Tremont debacle was documented in the seminal works of Robert Caro, *The Power Broker: Robert Moses and the Fall of New York* (New York: Knopf, 1974) and Marshal Berman, *All That is Solid Melts into Air: The Experience of Modernity* (New York: Penguin Books, 1988). For a contextualization of Moses's effect within the urban decline of the South Bronx, see Ray Bromley, "Not so Simple! Caro, Moses, and the Impact of the Cross-Bronx Expressway," *Bronx County Historical Society Journal* 35, no. 1 (Spring 1998): 5–29.

18. Jonathan Rieder, *Canarsie*.

19. For an analysis that includes a detailed outline of "white flight," jobs loss, deterioration of transportation links to Manhattan and general decline of Belmont and surrounding areas, see Bromley, "Not so Simple!" and Ray Bromley, "Globalization and the Inner-Periphery: A Mid-Bronx View," *Annals of the American Academy of Political and Social Science* 551 (May 1997): 191–207.

20. Sharon Zukin and Ervin Kosta, "Bourdieu Off-Broadway: Managing Distinction on a Shopping Block in the East Village," *City and Community* 3, no. 2 (2004): 101.

21. For an explanation of the revitalization of the urban core through cycles of capital, see Neil Smith, *The New Urban Frontier: Gentrification and the Revanchist City* (New York: Routledge, 1996). For a review of the emerging consensus on the intertwined role of culture and economics in urban renewal, see Sharon Zukin, "Gentrification: Culture and Capital in the Urban Core," *Annual Review of Sociology* 13 (1987): 129–147.

22. Donna Gabaccia, "Little Italy's Decline: Immigrant Renters and Investors in a Changing City," in *The Landscape of Modernity: Essays on New York City, 1900–1940*, ed. David Ward and Olivier Zunz (New York: Russell Sage Foundation), 235–251.

23. Francis X. Clines, "About New York: Miracle on Spring Street," *New York Times* (March 28, 1978).

24. Alfred E. Clark, "Chinatown Stretching Borders Into Little Italy," *New York Times* (August 1, 1969).

25. Clines, "About New York."

26. Ibid.

27. Frank J. Prial, "Little Italy Is Restive as Chinatown Expands," *New York Times* (April 26, 1974).

28. Ada Louise Huxtable, "A Recession-Proof Plan to Rescue Little Italy," *New York Times* (May 4, 1975); Glenn Fowler, "City to Revive and Refurbish Little Italy," *New York Times* (September 20, 1974); Solochek, "In Little Italy, the Word Is Risorgimento."

29. Judith Cummings, "'Little Italy Is Love' and Mulberry Street Becomes a Mall for the Weekend," *New York Times* (December 1, 1974); "A Pedestrian Mall Along Mulberry Street Is Opening Today," *New York Times* (November 30, 1974).

30. Glenn Fowler, "Preservation of Little Italy Urged: Some Ethnic Tension," *New York Times* (September 3, 1976); Solochek, "In Little Italy, the Word Is Risorgimento."

31. Fred Ferretti, "Spring Guide to Boulevard of Pasta," *New York Times* (March 11, 1977); Mimi Sheraton, "Some New Eating Places in Little Italy," *New York Times* (March 26, 1976); Solochek, "In Little Italy, the Word Is Risorgimento."

32. To outline the changes in the commercial scene of both neighborhoods, I consulted the Cole Reverse Business Directories, which provide lists of all the registered businesses by address starting in 1971. I limited the sample to the core commercial strips of both areas, excluding surrounding blocks that tend to be commercially less dense. On Mulberry Street, I included the businesses on the section between Canal and East Houston Streets, but excluded businesses south of Canal Street because of their association with Chinatown. I also left out of the sample the businesses on Elizabeth Street, because unlike Mulberry's concentration of restaurants, Elizabeth Street has developed a concentration on boutique clothing stores. "Mulberry Street" will heretofore refer to the section between Canal and East Houston Streets. On Belmont, the spatial business sample required the inclusion of blocks on two streets. Arthur Avenue is the main commercial center of the area, from East Houston Street to the north until its intersection with Crescent and East 184th Streets to the south. The intersecting East 187th Street is also a major commercial corridor, particularly around the Arthur Avenue intersection. I therefore included the businesses on East 187th Street between Lorillard Place and Beaumont Avenue. The resulting sample is between one-half and twice as large as the Mulberry Street sample in terms of blocks included and overall number of businesses. "Arthur Avenue" will heretofore refer to both sections described earlier.

33. Cole data allows tracing the emergence of non-Italian businesses over the decades. In both areas, an analysis of business names reveals the increasing commercial presence of the new residential groups, such as Asian businesses on Mulberry Street and Hispanic businesses in Belmont. In contrast to the residential ethnic succession, the commercial penetration of these non-Italian stores remains modest on Arthur Avenue and moderate on Mulberry Street. Because both areas successfully maintain the Little Italy designation of their commercial strips, the commercial presence of non-Italian businesses will not be discussed here.

34. Gabaccia, "Inventing Little Italy": 7.

35. Seth Kugel, "The D Train to Cannoli Heaven," *New York Times* (September 3, 2006).

36. Clines, "About New York."

37. Ferretti, "Spring Guide to Boulevard of Pasta"; Sheraton, "Some New Eating Places in Little Italy."

38. The first category singles out restaurants, given their proliferation and centrality to areas designated as Little Italy. The general rule was to include businesses that provide full service for their prepared food including establishments that go by the less formal names of *trattoria, luncheonette,* or *bistro*. The second category singles out cafés and pizzerias. It includes businesses that serve light food or fast food, usually lack full waiting service, provide at least some tables for customers, and usually serve as venues for socializing. In addition to cafés and pizza parlors, typical businesses that fall under this category include pastry shops that often serve as cafés and deli stores that prepare (gourmet) sandwiches. This category also includes establishments typical of an earlier era, such as candy and ice cream stores. Social clubs that were a staple of immigrant neighborhoods in earlier decades also fall under this category, where socializing took place and coffee was served. Similarly, bars have been included, but not community centers or the occasional benevolent society. Chinese restaurants were also included, unless the researcher has been able to ascertain that they provide full table service. The third category includes the variety of (specialty) food stores, such as cheese and pork stores, bakery and homemade pasta/ravioli stores, fruit and vegetable stands (inside the Arthur Avenue Retail Market), fish and poultry stores, and wine and liquor stores. Minimarkets and supermarkets will be included in this category. Similar to pastry stores, bakeries often also carry pastries and on occasion may have a few tables inside the establishment. But since their staple product is bread, they have been included in this category. Likewise grocery stores often have deli counters where customers can order sandwiches, but because this is not a significant part of their business activity, they are counted as food stores.

39. Quoted in Steve Kurutz, "Partying Like It's 1999," *New York Times* (September 28, 2003).

40. Bruce Lambert, "Neighborhood Report: Lower Manhattan; A Little Italy Festival Marco Polo Would Love," *New York Times* (September 19, 1993).

41. Quoted in Roberts, "Little Italy, Littler by the Year."

42. For an ethnographic account on the continued centrality of street *feste* in Italian Harlem, see Robert Orsi, "The Religious Boundaries of an Inbetween People: Street *Feste* and the Problem of the Dark-Skinned Other in Italian-Harlem, 1920–1990," *American Quarterly* 44, no. 3 (September 1992): 322.

43. Rocky D'Erasmo, *Fordham Was a Town: A Nostalgic Look into Fordham's Little Italy During the Twenties and Thirties* (San Diego: D'Erasmo, 1978), 91.

44. Stephen M. Samtur and Paula de Marta Mastroianni, *Little Italy of the Bronx: Belmont & Arthur Avenue* (Scarsdale, N.Y.: Back in the Bronx Publishing, 2003); Anthony LaRuffa, *Monte Carmelo: An Italian American Community in the Bronx* (New York: Gordon and Breach Science Publishers, 1988).

45. D'Erasmo, *Fordham Was a Town*, 85. An observer talks about the statue of Our Lady of Monteverde being paraded through the streets of Throgs Neck. The celebration might have been a parallel one, or may have followed Belmonters subsequently moving to Throgs Neck. Bill Twomey, *The Bronx: In Bits and Pieces* (Bloomington, Ind.: Rooftop Publishing, 2007), 140.

46. LaRuffa, *Monte Carmelo*, 114.

47. Ibid., 115.

48. He often asks the band at hand to perform or plays the record of what he calls "the official song of the neighborhood," Cool Change's "On the Streets of the Bronx Is Where I Want to Be." The song appeared during the opening and closing credits of *A Bronx Tale*, a 1993 movie directed by Robert De Niro that takes place in the Italian Belmont of the 1960s and is popular with the crowd in front of the makeshift stage.

49. San Gennaro's coverage in the New York Times in this section refers to the following articles, unless noted otherwise: Craig Claiborne, "Food, Festivo Napolitano," *New York Times* (September 13, 1960); McCandlish Phillips, "'Little Italy' Begins San Gennaro Fete," *New York Times* (September 15, 1962); Alfred E. Clark, "San Gennaro Fete Opens 9-Day Run," *New York Times* (September 13, 1964); Lesley Oelsner, "Bravura and Bitterness Mix At Festival of San Gennaro," *New York Times* (September 19, 1969); Murray Schumach, "46th San Gennaro Festival Sings to a New Tune," *New York Times* (September 16, 1972); Fred Ferretti, "And on Mulberry St., a Midday With a Neapolitan Flavor," *New York Times* (September 17, 1976); "San Gennaro Festival Feast Day Proves a Delight for Gastronomes," *New York Times* (September 20, 1976); Ari L. Goldman, "Grand Old Festa of Mulberry St. Is On," *New York Times* (September 12, 1980).

50. See www.sangennaro.org.

51. Roberts, "Little Italy, Littler by the Year."

52. "The Socks, the Sausage and the Snub," *New York Times* (April 15, 2007).

53. Seth Mydans, "San Gennaro Festival Adding New Flavors," *New York Times* (September 9, 1983).

54. "The Socks, the Sausage and the Snub."

55. See note 50. The remainder of the section refers to the feast's official webpage.

56. Cummings, "Little Italy Is Love."

14. We Are Family: Ethnic Food Marketing and the Consumption of Authenticity in Italian-Themed Chain Restaurants   FABIO PARASECOLI

I thank Stefani Bardin and Amy Orr for their help and their observations on this project.

1. http://www.youtube.com/watch?v=6WERx6BKFmA.

2. Barbara Kirshenblatt-Gimblett, "Theorizing Heritage." *Ethnomusicology* 39, no. 3 (1995): 369.

3. John Mariani and Galina Mariani, *The Italian American Cookbook: A Feast of Food from a Great American Cooking Tradition* (Boston: Harvard Common Press, 2000); Joan Tucci and Gianni Scappin, *Cucina & Famiglia: Two Italian Families Share Their Stories, Recipes, and Traditions* (New York: Morrow, 1999); Nancy Verde Barr, *We Called It Macaroni: An American Heritage of Southern Italian Cooking* (New York: Knopf, 1996).

4. Simone Cinotto, *The Italian American Table: Food, Family, and Community in New York City* (Urbana: University of Illinois Press, 2013); Joel Denker, *The World on the Place: A Tour through the History of America's Ethnic Cuisine* (Boulder: Westview Press, 2003), 5–26; Hasia Diner, *Hungering for America: Italian, Irish, and Jewish Foodways in the Age of Migration* (Cambridge, Mass.: Harvard University Press, 2001), 21–83; Donna Gabaccia, *We Are What We Eat: Ethnic Food and the Making of Americans* (Cambridge, Mass.: Harvard University Press, 1998); Louise DeSalvo and Edvige Giunta, *The Milk of Almonds: Italian American Women Writers on Food and Culture* (New York: Feminist Press, 2002); Harvey Levenstein, *Paradox of Plenty: A Social History of Eating in Modern America* (Berkeley: University of California Press, 2003); Harvey Levenstein, *Revolution at the Table: The Transformation of the American Diet* (Berkeley: University of California Press, 2003); Jane Ziegelman, *97 Orchard: An Edible History of Five Immigrant Families in One New York Tenement* (New York: HarperCollins, 2010), 183–227.

5. Simone Cinotto, *Soft Soil, Black Grapes: The Birth of Italian Winemaking in California* (New York: New York University Press, 2012); Simone Cinotto, "Sunday Dinner? You Had to Be There! The Social Significance

of Food in Italian Harlem, 1920–1940," in *Italian Folk: Vernacular Culture in Italian American Lives*, ed. Joseph Sciorra (New York: Fordham University Press, 2011), 11–29; John Allan Cicala, "Cuscuzu in Detroit, July 18, 1993: Memory, Conflict, and Bella Figura during a Sicilian American Meal," in *Italian Folk: Vernacular Culture in Italian American Lives*, ed. Joseph Sciorra (New York: Fordham University Press, 2011), 31–48; Michael A. Di Giovine, "La Vigilia Italo Americana: Revitalizing the Italian American Family Through the Christmas Eve 'Feast of the Seven Fishes,'" *Food and Foodways* 18, no. 4 (2010): 181–208; Judith Goode, Karen Curtis, and Janet Theophano, "Menu Negotiation in the Maintenance of an Italian American Community," in *Food in the Social Order: Studies of Food and Festivities in Three American Communities*, ed. Mary Douglas (New York: Routledge, 2003), 143–218; John Mariani, *How Italian Food Conquered The World* (New York: Palgrave McMillan, 2011); Francesca Muccini, "From Italian 'Cibo' to American Food: The Construction of the Italian American Identity through Food," Ph.D. dissertation, Arkansas State University, 2006; Lara Pascali, "The Italian Immigrant Basement Kitchen in North America," in Sciorra, *Italian Folk*, 49–61; Dick Rosano, *Wine Heritage: The Story of Italian American Vintners* (San Francisco: Wine Appreciation Guild, 2000); Julia Flynn Siler, *The House of Mondavi: The Rise and Fall of an American Wine Dynasty* (New York: Gotham Books, 2007).

6. Marguerite DiMino Buonopane, *The North End Italian Cookbook* (Guilford, Conn.: Globe Pequot Press, 2004); Frank Pellegrino, *Rao's Cookbook: Over 100 Years of Italian Home Cooking* (New York: Random House, 1998); Gerard Renny, *The Men of the Pacific Street Social Club Cook Italian: Home-Style Recipes and Unforgettable Stories* (New York: HarperCollins, 1999); Michael Ronis, *Carmine's Family-Style Cookbook: More Than 100 Classic Italian Dishes to Make at Home* (New York: St. Martin's Press, 2008); Nancy Tregre Wilson, *Louisiana's Italians: Food, Recipes, and Folkways* (Gretna, La.: Pelican, 2005); Ann Volkwein, *The Arthur Avenue Cookbook: Recipes and Memories from the Real Little Italy* (New York: HarperCollins, 2004).

7. Henry Hill and Priscilla Davis, *The Wise Guy Cookbook: My Favorite Recipes From My Life as a Goodfella to Cooking on the Run* (New York: New American Library, 2002); Joseph Iannuzzi, *The Mafia Cookbook: Revised and Expanded* (New York: Simon & Schuster, 2001); Allen Rucker and Michele Scicolone, *The Sopranos Family Cookbook: As Compiled by Artie Bucco* (New York: Warner Books, 2002).

8. Pieter Desmet and Hendrik Schifferstein, "Sources of Positive and Negative Emotions in Food Experience," *Appetite* 50, no. 2–3 (2008): 290–301; John Edwards and Inga-Britt Gustafsson, "The Five Aspects Meal Model," *Journal of Foodservice* 19, no. 1 (2008): 4–12; John Edwards and Inga-Britt Gustafsson, "The Room and Atmosphere as Aspects of the Meal: A Review," *Journal of Foodservice* 19, no. 1 (2008): 22–34; Sunghyup Sean Hyun, "Predictors of Relationship Quality and Loyalty in the Chain Restaurant Industry," *Cornell Hospitality Quarterly* 51, no. 2 (2010): 251–267; Howard G. Schutz, "Eating Situations, Food Appropriateness, and Consumption," in *Not Eating Enough: Overcoming Underconsumption of Military Operational Rations*, ed. Bernadette M. Marriott (Washington, D.C.: National Academy Press, 1995), 341–359.

9. Amy Gregory, Youcheng Wang, and Robin DiPietro, "Towards a Functional Model of Website Evaluation: A Case Study of Casual Dining Restaurants," *Worldwide Hospitality and Tourism Themes* 2, no. 1 (2010): 68–85.

10. Noushi Rahman, "Toward a Theory of Restaurant Décor: An Empirical Examination of Italian Restaurants in Manhattan," *Journal of Hospitality & Tourism Research* 34, no. 3 (2010): 330–340.

11. Joan Teller, "The Treatment of Foreign Terms in Chicago Restaurant Menus," *American Speech* 44, no. 2 (1969): 91–105; Naomi Trolster and Liora Gvion, "Trends in Restaurant Menus: 1950–2000," *Nutrition Today* 42, no. 6 (2007): 255–62; Ann Zwicky and Arnold Zwicky, "America's National Dish: The Style of Restaurant Menus," *American Speech* 55, no. 2 (1980): 83–92.

12. Alan Beardsworth and Alan Bryman, "Late Modernity and the Dynamics of Quasification: The Case of the Themed Restaurant," *Sociological Review* 47, no. 2 (1999): 228–257.

13. Claus Ebster and Irene Guist, "The Role of Authenticity in Ethnic Theme Restaurants," *Journal of Foodservice Business Research* 7, no. 2 (2005): 41–52.

14. Lucy M. Long, ed., *Culinary Tourism* (Lexington: University Press of Kentucky, 2003).

15. Jennifer DeJesus and Robert Guang Tian, "Understanding Cultural Factors in Food Consumption: An Experiential Case Study of Consumers at an Ethnic Restaurant," *High Plains Applied Anthropologist* 1, no. 24 (2004): 27–40.

16. David Beriss and David Sutton, *The Restaurants Book: Ethnographies of Where We Eat* (Oxford: Berg, 2007).

17. Roland Barthes, "Rhetoric of the Image," in *Classic Essays on Photography*, ed. Alan Trachtenberger (New Haven: Leete's Island Books, 1980), 269–285; 273.

18. David Girardelli, "Commodified Identities: The Myth of Italian Food in the United States," *Journal of Communication Inquiry* 28, no. 4 (2004): 307–324.

19. Anna Camaiti Hostert, "Big Night, Small Days," in *Screening Ethnicities: Cinematographic Representations of Italian Americans in the United States*, ed. Anna Camaiti Hostert and Anthony Julian Tamburri (New York: Bordighera Press, 2008), 249–258; Margaret Coyle, "Il Timpano—To Eat Good Food Is to Be Close to God: The Italian American Reconciliation of Stanley Tucci and Campbell Scott's Big Night," in *Reel Food: Essays on Food and Film*, ed. Anne Bower (New York: Routledge, 2004), 41–60; Fred L. Gardaphé, "Linguine and Lust: Notes on Food and Sex in Italian American Culture," in *Leaving Little Italy: Essaying Italian American Culture* (Albany: SUNY Press, 2003), 137–150; Marlisa Santos, "Leave the Gun, Take the Cannoli: Food and Family in the Modern American Mafia Film," in *Reel Food: Essays on Food and Film*, ed. Anne Bower (New York: Routledge, 2004): 209–218.

20. *Brinker Fact Sheet*, http://brinker.mediaroom.com/index.php?s=12569.

21. www.maggianos.com, accessed September 9, 2011.

22. Ann McBride, "Food Porn," *Gastronomica* 10, no. 1 (2010): 38–46.

23. http://www.bertuccis.com/about-us/: http://investing.businessweek.com/research/stocks/private/snapshot.asp?privcapId=317916; http://www.referenceforbusiness.com/history2/56/Bertucci-s-Corporation.html, accessed February 2, 2012.

24. http://www.bertuccis.com, accessed September 27, 2011.

25. http://www.bertuccis.com/about-us, accessed September 27, 2011.

26. Josée Johnston and Shyon Baumann, *Foodies: Democracy and Distinction in the Gourmet Foodscape* (New York: Routledge, 2010).

27. http://www.darden.com/restaurants/olivegarden.

28. http://www.olivegarden.com/My-Olive-Garden, accessed October 4, 2011.

29. http://www.olivegarden.com/About-Us/News-and-Media/Articles/Italian-Family-Reunions, accessed October 4, 2011.

30. http://www.olivegarden.com/Connections-to-Italy/Culinary-Institute-of-Tuscany.

31. The *Time Magazine* newsfeed quoted the posts of an anonymous manager that denies that the chains owns a school and that actually managers are taken to a hotel during the off-season where they are offered sparse information about Italian food, while spending most of their time sightseeing. http://newsfeed.time.com/2011/04/15/what-actually-goes-on-at-olive-gardens-culinary-institute-in-tuscany, accessed October 4, 2011.

32. http://www.huffingtonpost.com/2011/09/15/michelle-obama-olive-garden_n_963740.html.

Contributors

Danielle Battisti is assistant professor of history at the University of Nebraska–Omaha. She is writing a study of Italian Americans and the politics of immigration reform in the post–World War II era. She is the author of "The American Committee on Italian Migration, Anti-Communism, and Immigration Reform," *Journal of American Ethnic History* (Winter 2012).

Marcella Bencivenni is associate professor of history at Hostos Community College of the City University of New York. She is the author of *Italian Immigrant Radical Culture: The Idealism of the Sovversivi in the United States* (New York University Press, 2011) and coeditor with Ron Hayduk of "Radical Perspectives in Immigration," a special issue of *Socialism and Democracy* (November 2008).

Giorgio Bertellini is associate professor in the Department of Screen Arts and Cultures and the Department of Romance Languages and Literatures at the University of Michigan. His most recent publications include the award-winning *Italy in Early American Cinema: Race, Landscape, and the Picturesque* (Indiana University Press, 2010), Italian and English editions of *Emir Kusturica* (Editrice Il Castoro, 2011; University of Illinois Press, 2014), and the anthology *Italian Silent Cinema: A Reader* (John Libbey/Indiana University Press, 2013).

Vittoria Caterina Caratozzolo teaches courses in fashion theory at the "Sapienza" University of Rome. Her article "A Safety Pin for Elizabeth: Hard-Edge Accessorizing from Punk Subculture to High Fashion" appears in *Exchanging Clothes: Habits of Being 2*, edited by Cristina Giorcelli and Paula Rabinowitz (University of Minnesota Press, 2012). She is a contributor to the exhibit catalogue *The Glamour of Italian Fashion 1945–2014* (Victoria and Albert Museum, 2014) with her essay "Reorienting Fashion: Italy's Wayfinding after World War II."

Simone Cinotto teaches history at the University of Gastronomic Sciences, Pollenzo, Italy, where he is the director of the master's program in Food Culture and Communications: Food, Place, and Identities. He is the author of *The Italian American Table: Food, Family, and Community in New York City* (University of Illinois Press, 2013) and *Soft Soil, Black Grapes: The Birth of Italian Winemaking in California* (New York University Press, 2012).

John Gennari is associate professor of English and U.S. Ethnic Studies at the University of Vermont. He is the author of *Blowin' Hot and Cool: Jazz and Its Critics* (University of Chicago Press, 1996) and is completing a book manuscript on Italian American and African American intersections in music, film, sports, food, and other forms of expressive culture.

Ervin Kosta is assistant professor of sociology at Hobart and William Smith Colleges. He conducts research on the remapping of the neighborhood structure of American urban areas as gentrification, immigration, and new labor relations replace Fordist dynamics of city building. He is currently working on a book manuscript on ethnic identity in Arthur Avenue in the Bronx.

Stefano Luconi teaches U.S. history at the University of Padua. His publications include *From Paesani to White Ethnics: The Italian Experience in Philadelphia* (SUNY Press, 2001) and *The Italian-American Vote in Providence, Rhode Island, 1916–1948* (Fairleigh Dickinson University Press, 2004).

Dominique Padurano is an independent scholar and the author of several articles on gender and ethnic identity, including, "'Dear Friend': Charles Atlas, American Masculinity, and the Bodybuilding Testimonial, 1894–1944," in *Testimonial Advertising in the American Marketplace: Emulation, Identity, Community*, edited by Marlis Schweitzer and Marina Moskowitz (Palgrave Macmillan, 2009). Dr. Padurano is currently working on a cultural biography of Charles Atlas.

Fabio Parasecoli is associate professor and coordinator of food studies at the New School in New York City. Recent publications include *Food Culture in Italy* (Greenwood, 2004) and *Bite Me! Food in Popular Culture* (Berg, 2008). He is general editor with Peter Scholliers of the six-volume *Cultural History of Food* (Berg, 2012).

Courtney Ritter is a doctoral candidate in the Department of Screen Arts and Cultures at the University of Michigan. Her dissertation links the emergence of a distinct style of early Italian television programming to the postwar project to democratize that nation.

Maddalena Tirabassi is the director of the Centro Altreitalie on Italian Migration and the editor of *Altreitalie*. She is vice president of AEMI (European Migration Institutions). Her publications include *I motori della memoria: Le donne piemontesi in Argentina* (Rosenberg & Sellier, 2010) and *Itinera: Paradigmi delle migrazioni italiane* (Edizioni della Fondazione Giovanni Agnelli, 2005).

Donald Tricarico is professor of sociology at CUNY/Queensborough. His work has focused on changing forms of urban ethnic culture in New York, commencing with the 1984 publication of *The Italians of Greenwich Village*. His interest in urban Italian American culture centers on the youth subculture known as Guido.

Elizabeth Zanoni is assistant professor in the Department of History at Old Dominion University. She is the author of "'Per Voi, Signore': Gendered Representations of Fashion, Food, and Fascism in Il Progresso Italo-Americano during the 1930s," *Journal of American Ethnic History* (Spring 2012) and "Transitions in Gender Ratios among International Migrants, 1820–1930" with Donna Gabaccia in *Social Science History* (Summer 2012).

Index